# HOME RENOVATION

# HOME RENOVATION

## FRANCIS D.K. CHING
## DALE E. MILLER

A VNR BOOK
JOHN WILEY & SONS, INC.
NEW YORK   CHICHESTER   WEINHEIM   BRISBANE   SINGAPORE   TORONTO

Copyright © 1983 by John Wiley & Sons, Inc. All rights reserved.

Published simultaneously in Canada.

Library of Congress Cataloging-in-Publication Data:

Ching, Francis D.K., 1943-
    Home Renovation
    Bibliography: p. 334
    Includes index
    1. Dwellings—Remodeling.    I. Miller, Dale E.
II. Title.
TH4816.C45    1983    643'.7    83-5896
ISBN 0-471-28869-1

Printed in the United States of America

 23  22  21  20  19  18  17  16

*for Emily*

# CONTENTS

# INTRODUCTION

The renovation of your home – altering, enlarging, or renewing it to accommodate changes in your family needs or lifestyle – can be a challenging yet rewarding undertaking. A remodeling project requires the homeowner to muster and coordinate the necessary resources of time, labor and materials. Repairing and improving a house also requires patience, endurance, and the commitment to follow through once construction has started.

Despite the challenges, the rewards of a carefully planned and successfully completed project can be significant. Within the familiar surroundings of your home, you can personalize your living environment. You can tailor your rooms into functional, comfortable and aesthetically-pleasing settings that fit your lifestyle and taste. Once completed, the improvements can add economic and aesthetic value to your home.

Remodeling may also be a more economically viable alternative to moving or building a new home. An existing house, if structurally sound, can generally be expanded or updated at a lower cost than that of building a new house. Remodeling projects can often be divided into manageable do-it-yourself projects which can save money and provide an added sense of personalization in your home.

The opportunity to renovate can be the persuasive factor in deciding to purchase an older home. The home may be attractive for its charm and style, its spatial feeling, or its historical significance. You may like its established landscaping or its neighborhood. Its potential value may be well worth the effort required to renovate it.

A renovation project can be the relatively simple conversion of a room to another use or the consolidation of two rooms into a larger space. It can involve the opening up of a room to a new outdoor courtyard, or it can be the more complicated task of planning, designing, and building an entire addition from the foundation up to a new roof. While some projects will require only a day's work, others will take more time. These can be planned and accomplished over a period of time so that your home evolves and grows with you. A renovation project, therefore, can be tailored to your specific needs and situation.

The purpose of this book is to help you in this endeavor. The first chapter discusses the planning and preparation that must precede any decision to remodel, and outlines those factors which will affect the nature and scope of the project. It also outlines possible design solutions for you to explore. Succeeding chapters then describe these basic types of remodeling projects, the factors that govern their design, and the elements that go into their construction.

Every remodeling project is unique. Houses are products of the times when they were built. Style and construction techniques have changed over the years, and your individual needs and wants are unique. It would be difficult, therefore, for this book to discuss the entire range of materials and techniques, or provide hard-and-fast rules for every situation you may encounter in your remodeling project. An understanding of the principles and systems involved should be more useful to you in the planning and construction of your project than specific details which may not apply to your situation.

Emphasis is placed on basic principles, common building materials and proven techniques. Allowances, however, should be made for regional variations and preferences that exist for materials, standards, and building code requirements. The homeowner, designer or builder, must be flexible and be able to make substitutions where necessary.

Although this book is intended primarily for the homeowner who is contemplating a renovation project, it can also be helpful to the designer or builder who may be assisting the homeowner in the endeavor. Whether you work alone or with professional assistance, the ultimate goal of this book is to help you renew - revitalize - your home and make it a more comfortable, practical, and attractive living environment.

# 1 PLANNING & DESIGN

As you prepare to repair, update or remodel your home, it is useful to review your long-range plans, evaluate what you already have, and clarify what you want to achieve with the improvement. This first chapter discusses a planning and design process that can help you with this review, and guide you in determining the nature, scope and feasibility of your renovation project.

There are three parts to this chapter. The first outlines a method to help you better understand your present home, and evaluate its strengths and weaknesses. The second section suggests a procedure for consolidating your wants and needs, and assessing the resources and limitations that will affect the practicality of your goals. The last section describes a range of possible solutions for your consideration, and refers you to the pertinent chapters that follow for information about their construction.

## PLANNING & DESIGN

Your renovation project can be both a challenging and rewarding experience. If properly planned and successfully completed, it can make your home more livable and also add to its value. But before you begin any repairs or improvements, take time to review your long-range plans for your home.

- How long do you plan to live in your present home?
- How do you use your home, and how might this change in the coming years?
- What sort of appearance do you wish your home to have?
- What, ultimately, do you envision your house to be?

Your answers to these questions will affect the nature and scope of your home improvements, how much you do, and how much time, effort and money you invest in the work.

If you plan to sell your house within a few years, you should carefully consider how much added value the house will have for the expense incurred by the repairs or alterations. If you plan on living in your present home for as long as you can predict, however, you may consider meeting your living needs more important than the economic return on the investment. In this latter case, you may also have the freedom of scheduling and undertaking a series of projects that could be accomplished over a period of time.

Consider whether there will be changes in how you use your home in the coming years. If you intend for your family to grow, your planning should allow for expanding your house. Any improvements you make now should not interfere with this expansion. If you are a couple whose children will be leaving home soon, you may want to

## A PLANNING PROCESS

### 1. REVIEW LONG-RANGE PLANS FOR YOUR HOUSE

   A. Do you plan to sell or keep your home for as long as you can predict?
   B. How will you be using your home in the coming years?
   C. What image or appearance do you want your home to have?

### 2. DOCUMENT EXISTING CONDITIONS

   A. Measure and draw floor plans.
   B. Study house structure, and the mechanical and electrical systems.
   C. Study site and exterior conditions.

### 3. DETERMINE WANTS AND NEEDS

   A. Functional Considerations:
   - Efficient use of space.
   - Effective circulation patterns.
   - Zoning of activities for desired privacy or socializing.
   B. Technical Considerations:
   - Correcting structural defects.
   - Repairing material deterioration.
   - Proper functioning of mechanical systems.
   - Energy conservation.
   - Safety considerations.
   - Correcting code violations.
   C. Aesthetic Considerations:
   - Desired appearance, image and style of exterior, and interior rooms.

### 4. ASSESS RESOURCES AND LIMITATIONS

   A. Available funds and equity.
   B. Available time, skills and materials.
   C. Zoning, building code and deed requirements or restrictions.
   D. Professional assistance required: architect, engineer, builder.

consider changing the pattern of living spaces in your home, or dividing your house into separate living units, one of which can be rented or used by a single member of the family.

These choices should be based not only on what you can afford, or what is available, but also on what you envision your house to be. How does the image and appearance of your home reflect the personality of those who live there? How does the shape and pattern of its rooms fit your lifestyle?

Do you envision your home as a private retreat, sheltered from your neighbors and the street? Is it an exuberant showplace to entertain friends? Do you want your home to be a place to relax, study, raise a family, or run a business? Do you want your house to center itself around a specific interest or hobby? Or do you want it simply to provide a warm place that doesn't leak?

Writing down these objectives and concerns will help you clarify your plans, and will serve as a useful reference as you begin to explore specific ways to renovate and improve your home.

## 5. EXPLORE POSSIBLE DESIGN SOLUTIONS

A. Make repairs and correct defects.
B. Enhance existing space:
  • Design with light, color and furnishings.
C. Re-arrange existing space:
  • Add or remove walls.
  • Add or remove windows and doors.
D. Convert unused space:
  • Convert an attic, basement or garage into livable space.
E. Add new space:
  • Add a new room,
  • Add another story or floor.
  • Add dormers or bay windows.

## 6. MAKE DECISIONS

A. Make preliminary design decisions.
B. Re-check against (1), (2), (3), (4).
C. Make revisions as necessary.

## 7. PREPARE FOR CONSTRUCTION

A. Prepare final plans.
B. Estimate costs, and do cost/benefit study.
C. Arrange necessary financing.
D. Acquire required permits.
E. Schedule construction:
  • Purchase materials.
  • Arrange for contracting or sub-contracting services.
  • Arrange for building department inspections.

## 8. BEGIN CONSTRUCTION

A. Site preparation.
B. Foundation work.
C. Framing floors, walls and roof.
D. Closing in: windows, exterior doors and finishes.
E. Special construction, such as stairs.
F. Heating, plumbing, electrical work.
G. Interior finish work.

## DOCUMENTING WHAT YOU HAVE

If you have lived in your house for several years, you already know much of what you like or dislike about it. You are also probably well aware of its idiosyncrasies. Before proceeding from your long-range plans to more specific problems and solutions, however, you should re-acquaint yourself with your house - its structure, its mechanical systems, the pattern and quality of its spaces.

Gathering information in a methodical manner will help you understand what you have to work with, and facilitate organizing and clarifying problem areas. This information is usually needed as the first step in finding effective solutions to the problem areas. While long-range plans may influence what you wish to achieve with your renovation project, the existing conditions of your home can either limit what you can do, or suggest opportunities for development. You may find that the sunroom you want would be shaded most of the time by a neighboring house. However, enlarging windows in another area may bring in the desired light, and may work well with an outdoor courtyard.

To begin learning about what you have, first document your home's layout with floor plans. Having these floor plans is important in planning your repairs or remodeling. They provide you with the means to study how the rooms in your house are laid out, oriented to their surroundings, and how they are used. On these drawings, you can record the layout of your house's structural and mechanical systems. These drawings also provide a convenient place for you to note items of concern, jot down ideas, and explore possible solutions. Finally, for any extensive remodeling work, plans will have to be submitted to your building department for approval and to ensure that health and safety requirements of your local building code are met.

If you wish to save yourself the time and effort of measuring your house and drawing its floor plans, check with the architect who designed it, or the builder who built it. They may be able to supply you with a set of construction drawings which would contain a wealth of useful information about your house. If you do not know who designed or built your house, your local building department may still have your house plans on file. State or local historic offices, or university libraries, sometimes have this information on older historic houses.

Do not be concerned if you cannot obtain a set of construction drawings for your house. Measuring its rooms and drawing a plan of their layout is not a complicated task. And in the process of doing so, you may gain insights into your house you may otherwise not have had.

The materials you need to measure and draw your floor plans are:

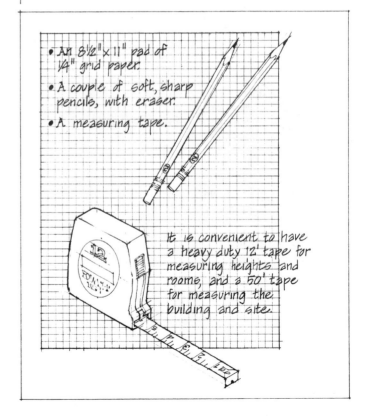

- An 8½" x 11" pad of ¼" grid paper.

- A couple of soft, sharp pencils, with eraser.

- A measuring tape.

It is convenient to have a heavy duty 12' tape for measuring heights and rooms, and a 50' tape for measuring the building and site.

# MEASURING YOUR HOUSE

In drawing your floor plans, first measure and draw the individual rooms of your house. Begin in any room by measuring the overall dimensions of the room and drawing its outline on the ¼" grid paper. Draw the room so that each ¼" in the drawing equals approximately one-foot of the actual room dimension (a scale of ¼" = 1'-0"). Next measure and indicate key points along each wall (edges of windows and doors, projections, alcoves, etc.). The accuracy of the drawings is not important at this step. These measurements, however, should be accurately taken and indicated.

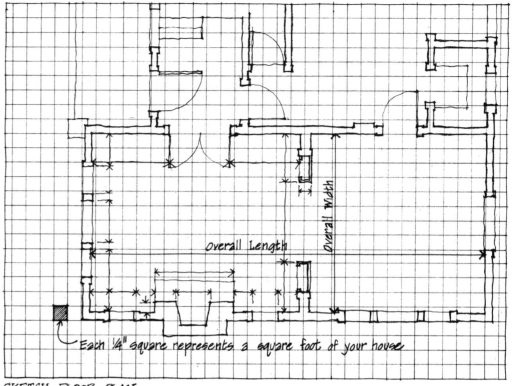

Each ¼" square represents a square foot of your house

SKETCH FLOOR PLAN
Always start with a room's overall dimensions. For most purposes, accuracy beyond a ½" is not necessary.

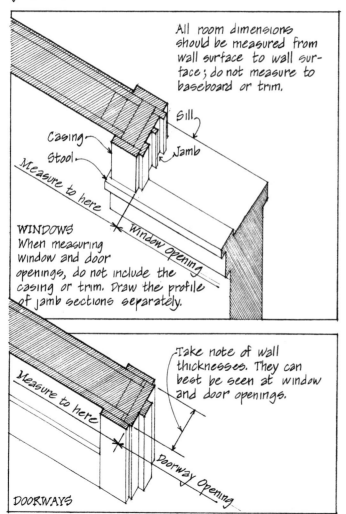

All room dimensions should be measured from wall surface to wall surface; do not measure to baseboard or trim.

Sill
Casing
Stool
Jamb
Measure to here
Window Opening

## WINDOWS
When measuring window and door openings, do not include the casing or trim. Draw the profile of jamb sections separately.

Take note of wall thicknesses. They can best be seen at window and door openings.

Measure to here
Doorway Opening

## DOORWAYS

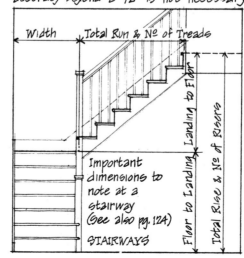

Width · Total Run & Nº of Treads

Floor to Landing · Landing to Floor

Total Rise & Nº of Risers

Important dimensions to note at a stairway (See also pg. 12A)

## STAIRWAYS

Remember to measure a room's ceiling, window and door heights.

Floor to Top of Opening
Floor to Sill · Opening Height
Floor to Top of Opening

## HEIGHTS

# DRAWING FLOOR PLANS

When you have all of the rooms on one floor roughly drawn and accurately measured, you are ready to re-draw them to scale on a single sheet and combine them into a floor plan. Use a consistent scale throughout. A scale of 1/4" = 1'-0" (1/4" of your drawing equals one-foot of your house) is convenient to use, and is the scale most often used in house plans.

**NOTES:**

1. Draw sections of walls between window and door openings heavily to distinguish them from other parts of the drawing.
2. Draw doors and indicate the direction in which they swing; note the sizes of windows and doors.
3. Draw the outline of significant features, such as countertops, bathroom fixtures, and fireplaces.
4. Note direction of stairs.
5. Any significant overhead elements, such as exposed beams or dropped ceilings, can be dashed in.
6. Label rooms and note their overall dimensions.
7. Note the heights of ceilings and window sills above the floor.

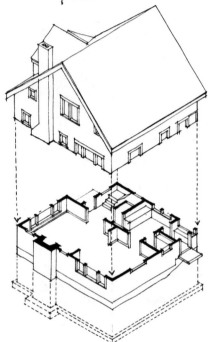

FLOOR PLANS

A floor plan is a view looking straight down after a horizontal cut is made through the house walls, a few feet above the floor, and the top portion of the house is removed.

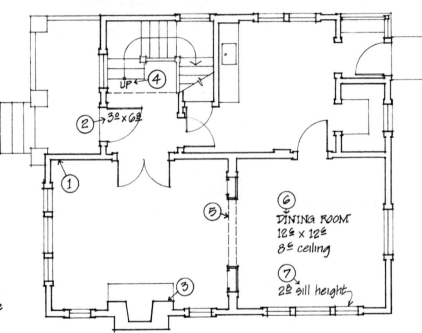

FIRST FLOOR PLAN

The plans of individual rooms can be properly related by aligning the doorways they share in common. At this point, it would be useful to check the accuracy of your plan by comparing its dimensions with the exterior dimensions of your house.

When you have completed the floor plan drawings, you can have them photocopied fairly inexpensively. These copies can then be used as base drawings for studying the pattern of rooms in your house, the layout of its systems, and ideas for repairs or improvements. Even if you decide to hire an architect, designer, or builder to help you with your renovation project, these studies can make you a better-informed partner in the design process.

Supplement these drawings with photographs of the interior walls of rooms, and drawings or photographs of the exterior elevations of your house.

## DRAWING THE SITE PLAN

The legal description of your property and a plot map that shows its dimensions and configuration can generally be obtained from your local real estate assessor's office. Your property lines may be indicated by surveyor's stakes, or you may be able to get, from the local public works department, the dimension of your property line from a public improvement (curb, sidewalk, or centerline of street).

Measure the dimensions of your lot and draw its outline to scale (usually 1/8" or 1/16" = 1'-0"). Assuming you already know the exterior dimensions of your house, locate it by measuring the distance from the exterior walls to the front, side and rear lot lines.

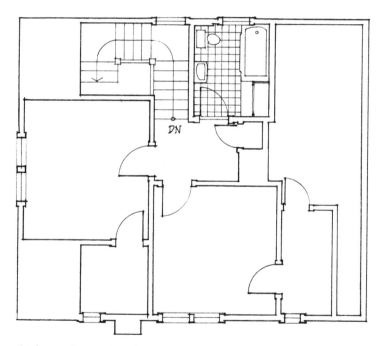

SECOND FLOOR PLAN

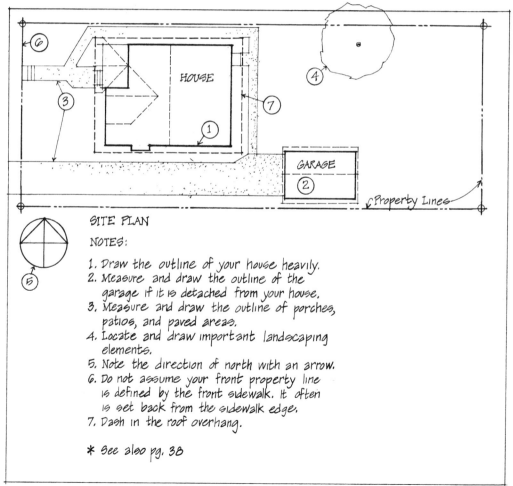

SITE PLAN

NOTES:

1. Draw the outline of your house heavily.
2. Measure and draw the outline of the garage if it is detached from your house.
3. Measure and draw the outline of porches, patios, and paved areas.
4. Locate and draw important landscaping elements.
5. Note the direction of north with an arrow.
6. Do not assume your front property line is defined by the front sidewalk. It often is set back from the sidewalk edge.
7. Dash in the roof overhang.

* See also pg. 38

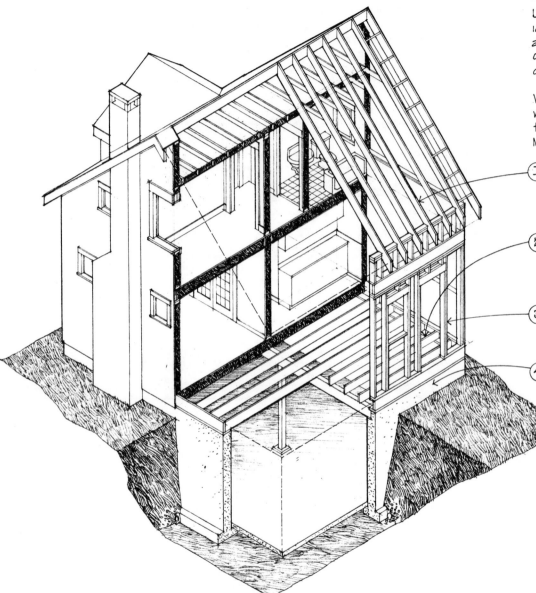

## YOUR HOUSE STRUCTURE

Understanding the structural system of your house –
identifying its major components, the direction of floor
and roof spans, and the location of vertical supports –
can help you determine the relative feasibility of altering
or adding on to any of its structural members.

Visualize the structural components of your house as
working together, like the skeletal frames of our bodies,
to transfer their loads downward to the supporting earth.
Most houses consist of four major parts:

1. The roof, protecting the interior from the weather,
   carries its own weight plus the load of snow, rain and
   wind, and transfers this load to vertical supports
   through sheathing, decking, rafter or beams.

2. Floors support their own weight and the weight of
   people and furnishings, and transfer this load to
   vertical elements through sheathing, floor joists and
   beams.

3. The vertical supports, load-bearing walls and columns,
   carry roof and floor loads through studs or posts, and
   transfer the loads to the foundation.

4. The foundation transfers all of the house loads to
   the supporting earth, and secures the structure to
   the ground.

## DESIGN LOADS

Design loads are assumed to act in a vertical or horizontal manner. Diagonal forces can be divided into vertical and horizontal elements.

Vertical forces consist of dead loads and live loads:
1. Dead loads are static forces, and consist generally of the weight of materials and permanently-attached equipment, about 10 lbs./s.f.
2. Live loads are moving or transient forces, and consist of the weight of people and furniture on each floor, about 40 lbs./s.f. Roof live loads consist of the weight of accumulated snow, up to 30 lbs./s.f., depending on local conditions.

Horizontal forces on a house include wind and earthquake loads. These will, of course, vary according to local conditions. They are resisted primarily by the vertical planes of walls made rigid by their sheathing or diagonal bracing.

The sizes of structural members are determined by their strength and the loads they must carry. More specific information about the sizing of structural members is given in succeeding chapters.

## DIAGRAMMING THE HOUSE STRUCTURE

Wood-frame houses usually use joists to frame their floors, and rafters or trusses to frame their roofs. Since these structural members span between, and in a direction perpendicular to their supports, you can identify load-bearing walls and beams by the direction of joist/rafter spans and by the location of joist/rafter ends, including interior joints.

Mark the location of walls on your floor plans, indicate the direction of the joist and rafter spans, and note where joists or rafters end over interior walls. This diagram will be useful if you intend to remove any walls in your remodeling.

Floor joists may span in different directions in different sections of your house. If you have a basement, it is a good place to start inspecting your structural system since the first floor joists and their supports are often exposed.

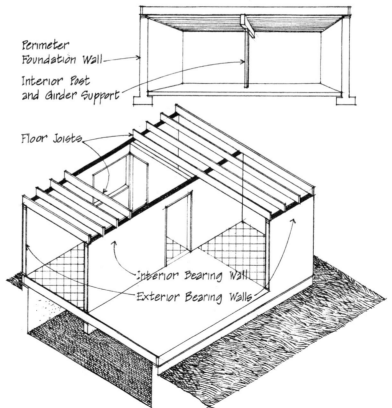

Perimeter Foundation Wall

Interior Post and Girder Support

Floor Joists

Interior Bearing Wall

Exterior Bearing Walls

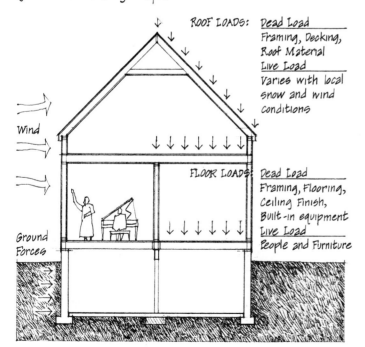

ROOF LOADS:
Dead Load
Framing, Decking, Roof Material
Live Load
Varies with local snow and wind conditions

Wind

FLOOR LOADS:
Dead Load
Framing, Flooring, Ceiling Finish, Built-in equipment
Live Load
People and Furniture

Ground Forces

**1**

Entrance Head

Line Drop

Conduit

Electric Meter

House Circuits

Service Panel

ELECTRICAL SYSTEM

Since slim electrical cable is easily routed through wall, floor and ceiling framing, simply note the location of the main service panel, outlets, light fixtures, and switches. Mapping each circuit can best be done by turning off one circuit breaker (or unscrewing one fuse) at a time, and testing each outlet or light fixture for power.

# MECHANICAL & ELECTRICAL SYSTEMS

Any alteration or addition to your house may require an adjustment to, or an extension of, your mechanical (heating and plumbing) and electrical systems. The location of the existing service lines will affect the location of new service lines and outlets. The more distant these new outlets, the longer the new service runs, and the more expensive they are to install. Even if functional considerations require long extensions of your present utility lines, you should know at what points the new connections can be made.

Since most utility lines are distributed within the framing spaces of your house, and are thus hidden from view, knowing their path is an important consideration when altering or removing walls and portions of floors. Removing a wall that contains a plumbing ventilation pipe, for example, will require re-routing the pipe, and may be complicated and expensive.

Your basement or utility room is the best place to begin examining your mechanical and electrical systems. Indicate on a copy of your floor plans, for each of the systems, the point of service entry, meter and panel locations, your furnace, hot water heater, and the main lines of distribution. Pay particular attention to those lines that rise vertically through your house. Also note on your floor plans the locations of fixtures, switches, outlets and registers.

You should also know where any underground water, sewer, power, and fuel (gas or oil) lines are placed. If you have an underground fuel tank or a septic tank and drain field, locate their positions since you will not be able to build over them.

ELECTRICAL PLAN SYMBOLS

| | | |
|---|---|---|
| Service Panel | Fluorescent Fixture | Convenience Outlet (Duplex Receptacle) |
| Wall Fixture Outlet | S Single-pole Switch | Convenience Outlet with Switch |
| Ceiling Fixture Outlet | S₃ Three-way Switch | Waterproof Convenience Outlet |
| Pull Switch Fixture | Floor Outlet | Range Outlet |

20

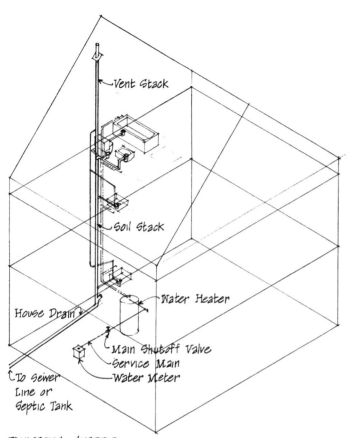

## PLUMBING SYSTEM

In mapping your plumbing system, it is important to locate the main 3" or 4" soil stack that carries waste matter to the house drain line. Plumbing fixtures are usually grouped around the soil stack as it rises through the house to become the vent stack. From the basement, you can usually see where the soil stack begins to rise. From the outside, you can usually see where the vent stack penetrates the roof.

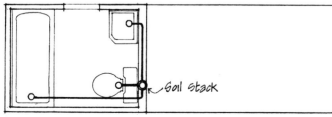

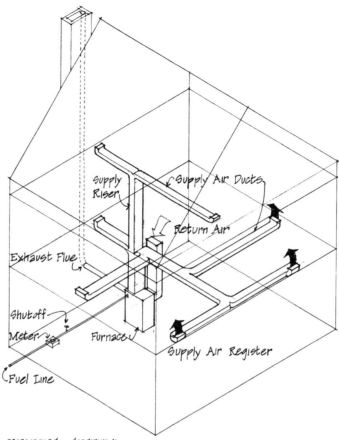

## HEATING SYSTEM

Trace the ductwork back from the registers (or the hot water pipes back from the radiators) to the furnace (or boiler unit). Again, it is important to note where the main supply runs are located, and especially where they rise through the house. Also note the location of any return air grills and ductwork.

PLAN SYMBOLS

| | |
|---|---|
| Wall Register | Radiator |
| Floor Register | |
| Supply Air Duct | |
| Return Air Duct | |

## EVALUATING WHAT YOU HAVE

In measuring your house, drawing its floor plans, and diagramming its systems, you have already begun to discover what condition your house is in. Indications of potential problems, such as water stains, leaking pipes and settlement cracks, are easily noticed. Functional deficiencies, such as conflicting doorswings, and aesthetic ones, like dark spaces or faded colors, may also have become more evident.

The following section is a guide for evaluating the technical, functional and aesthetic aspects of your house. With this working knowledge, you will be better prepared to plan improvements in an efficient manner.

While you will be concentrating on looking for deficiencies, areas that need repairs or improvement, do not neglect the strengths or assets of your home. Keep in mind what you like about its present condition. You would not want to improve one part of your house and, in the process, sacrifice other parts that you enjoy and work well for you.

## TECHNICAL CONSIDERATIONS

The following is a checklist to guide you in inspecting the technical aspects of your house. This outline is organized according to major elements of a house structure and its systems. Since houses vary with age, style and geographic location, it is not feasible to cover all possible conditions. You may discover items that do not appear on the outline. Add them to the list. Some items may not apply to your house. Ignore them. The important thing is to be as thorough as possible in your inspection.

For additional help with this inspection, consult your local agencies. The building department may offer assistance in checking for compliance with health and safety requirements of the building code. The fire department can inspect for fire hazards, and suggest improvements for fire prevention and safety. Your public utility company may provide useful information on the maintenance of appliances and energy conservation. Be sure to understand, before you arrange for an inspection by a local governmental agency, whether the inspection results are advisory, or whether you must correct all items found to be deficient within a limited amount of time.

Architects, engineers, and home-inspection consultants also conduct inspections for a fee. Particularly when there are questions of structural problems for which the cause cannot be determined, professional assistance is recommended.

# A HOME INSPECTION CHECKLIST

## 1. GENERAL OVERVIEW

Stand back and take a look at the exterior of your house.

☐ Are there signs of settling?
☐ Does house sit level on its foundation?
☐ Does roof ridge appear to sag?
☐ Does chimney lean or tilt?
☐ Are there obvious signs of decay?
☐ Does ground water collect around the foundation after a rain?
☐ Is yard free of trash and overgrowth, particularly around the foundation?

## 2. EXTERIOR FOUNDATION AND BASEMENT WALLS

An unstable foundation is a severe problem for which professional help is needed.

☐ Is the foundation wall cracked? Small, hairline cracks may be okay. Large, open cracks may get worse. Active cracks can be determined only by observation over several months.
☐ Does the foundation tilt or lean?
☐ Does any masonry have loose or crumbling mortar?
☐ Is there proper drainage? Is ground sloped away from the foundation? Do downspouts channel water away from the house, to a drywell or drainwell?
☐ Do basement window-wells collect water?
See also (8) Basements.

## 3. EXTERIOR WALLS

Most problems are caused by moisture and insect damage.

☐ Is wood siding or trim warped or swollen?
☐ Are there any open joints in siding?
☐ Is aluminum siding warped or dented?
☐ Are there signs of decay under window sills?
☐ Are there signs of insect damage along the lower edge of siding?
☐ Is any paint chipped, peeling, or blistered?
☐ Does masonry have cracks or loose mortar?

## 4. ROOFS

Roofs can be checked when dry, preferably within a day or two after a rain.

☐ Are there signs of wear indicating a need for replacement?
☐ Are composition shingles curled or losing their surface granules?
☐ Are wood shingles ragged, rotting, or broken?
☐ Is built-up roofing blistered, brittle, or soft in spots?
☐ Are joints around chimneys, dormers, plumbing vents, and along valleys cracked? Are there signs of leaking?
☐ Is roof flashing rusty, decayed, or loose-fitting?
☐ Is roof structure sound? Does it feel springy or spongy when walked on?
☐ Are soffit boards loose?
☐ Are there adequate vents along eave, ridge or gable ends?
☐ Are gutters loose, corroded, or sagging?
☐ Are gutters clean and free of debris?
☐ Do gutters slope properly to downspouts?
See also (14) Attics.

## A HOME INSPECTION CHECKLIST

**5.** EXTERIOR DOORS

Doors should operate smoothly, and be weathertight and secure.

☐ Are doors warped? Can you see daylight around or under them when closed?

☐ Are doors weatherstripped? Are joints around door frames caulked?

☐ Are any thresholds worn, weathered, or decayed?

☐ Is hardware secure and operating well?

☐ Do doors have deadbolt locksets for security?

**6.** WINDOWS

Windows should be weathertight.

☐ Are windows drafty when closed? Are they weatherstripped?

☐ Is caulking around window frames cracked?

☐ Does glass fit securely in sashes?

☐ Are there gaps in the glazing putty? Is putty brittle?

☐ Are wood frames decayed?

☐ Do windows have security locks?

☐ Is at least one window in each bedroom operable and large enough to serve as an emergency fire exit? (See Building Codes: Fire Safety, pg. 41)

**7.** PORCHES

Porches are exposed to weather and vulnerable to decay and insect damage.

☐ Is porch pulling away from house? Are stairs and railings secure?

☐ Do wood members and supports show signs of decay? Wood should not be in contact with the ground.

☐ Is there a porch-light for safety?

**8.** BASEMENTS AND CRAWL SPACES

Basements are good areas to check for settlement cracks, ground water leakage, the condition of floor joists, and the mechanical and electrical systems.

☐ Are there signs of settling? Are there large, open, unaligned cracks in walls?

☐ Do basement walls bow inward?

☐ Do basement walls have damp spots or show scaling?

☐ Is any untreated wood in direct contact with soil?

☐ Has concrete been poured around untreated wood?

☐ Are there signs of decay or insect damage on wood posts, sill plates, beams, or joists?

☐ Is crawl space well-ventilated? Does it have an effective soil vapor barrier?

**9.** INTERIOR ROOMS

Interior surfaces deteriorate due to wear, structural distortion, and the presence of moisture.

☐ Are there signs of settling? Are there cracks in walls or ceilings? Cracks that increase in size or number may indicate settling in the house structure.

☐ Do floors feel springy, or appear wavy or tilted? A marble placed on a floor will help indicate a sloping floor surface.

☐ Are concrete slabs badly cracked?

☐ Are there signs of moisture? Do walls or ceilings bulge or have water-stains, especially below bathrooms or along exterior walls?

☐ Do hard-surface floors feel spongy?

**10.** KITCHENS

Check for watertightness around the sink, and for fire safety.

☐ Are joints along the countertop and splashboard buckled or separated?

☐ Is sealer around sink loose or cracked?

☐ Is exhaust fan and filter clean and free of grease?

☐ Is a fire extinguisher, rated B/C to handle grease, flammable liquid, and electrical fires, handy?
See also (16) Plumbing.

**11.** BATHROOMS

Check for water leaks, dampness and mildew.

☐ Are there open joints where water can seep through in wall coverings or along the floor?

☐ Is caulking loose or missing around the tub, shower or lavatory sink?

☐ Is any ceramic tile cracked or broken? Is any grout loose or crumbling?

☐ Is bathroom adequately ventilated?
See also (15) Electrical, and (16) Plumbing systems.

**12.** STAIRWAYS

Stairs should be structurally sound and safe to traverse.

☐ Do stairs, railings and supports feel sturdy?

☐ Does the framing around the stair opening show evidence of sagging?

☐ Do wood members show signs of decay?

☐ Are stairways safe? Are they too steep or narrow?

☐ Is there adequate headroom clearance?

☐ Are there sturdy handrail supports?

☐ Is there a light and light switch at both the top and bottom of stairs?

☐ Are there smoke detectors properly located in the hall leading to bedrooms?

**13.** FIREPLACES

Check for proper operation, condition of masonry, and fire safety.

☐ Does fireplace draw properly? Chimney should draw smoke from a lit newspaper at least within a minute.

☐ Is there a damper? Does it close tightly?

☐ Is any masonry cracked or loose? Is any mortar crumbling or missing?

☐ Is flue lined? Is there a heavy coat of soot or creosote in flue?

☐ Does chimney have a rain cap?

**14.** ATTIC SPACES

The attic is a good place to check for roof leakage and weakening of the roof structure.

☐ Are any rafters or sheathing sagging or loose?

☐ Are there signs of moisture leaking around the chimney, plumbing vents, skylights, or along walls and valleys?

☐ Are there signs of dampness along the eaveline or in the insulation?

☐ Is the attic space properly ventilated?

☐ Is there sufficient thermal insulation?

# A HOME INSPECTION CHECKLIST

## 15. ELECTRICAL SYSTEM

Is the electrical system wired to meet your demands? Are there any safety hazards?

☐ Is the main electrical service panel large enough to handle house loads? A 100 Amp minimum service is recommended for a 3 BR house; a 200 Amp service if there is electric heating.

☐ Are any circuits overloaded? Do any fuses blow or do circuit breakers trip regularly? Do any lights dim or flicker when an appliance is turned on?

☐ Are there enough outlets in each room? Are they conveniently located? Rooms should have at least one outlet on each wall.

☐ Bathroom outlet should be protected by a Ground-Fault Interruptor (GFI).

☐ Is any insulation on wiring, cords or plugs worn, cracked, brittle or split?

☐ Do all switches and outlets have protective plates?

☐ Are extension cords for appliances heavy-duty rated?

☐ Are any extension cords used unsafely - eg., run under carpets, punctured by tacks?

☐ Is the electrical system properly grounded?

## 16. PLUMBING SYSTEM

Check for leaks, and for proper flow and drainage.

☐ Are there any signs of leaking? Are there signs of rust or crusting along pipes and fittings?

☐ Do any faucets leak?

☐ Do drains empty rapidly without bubbling?

☐ Is water flow adequate? Can two or three fixtures be turned on without noticeable loss of flow.

☐ Is there a hammering sound when a faucet is turned on and off rapidly?

☐ Does hot water heater operate properly? Is temperature setting too high? A setting of 120°F is usually sufficient (140°F if you have a dishwasher). Noise in hot water pipes when hot water tap is turned on may indicate setting too high.

☐ Is there sediment at the bottom of the hot water tank?

☐ Is there a pressure-relief valve installed on the hot water tank?

☐ Do all fixtures have individual shut-off valves and functioning traps?

## 17. HEATING SYSTEM

Check for safety and efficiency.

☐ Has the heating system's fuel or energy consumption increased over the last several years?

☐ Can you smell fumes from the furnace?

☐ Is heat distributed evenly through the house?

☐ Is the thermostat centrally located out of the way of drafts?

☐ Do supply register dampers operate properly?

☐ Are there dust coatings in the filters, air duct system or outlets?

☐ Are flammable materials stored close to furnace?

After completing the inspection, note the problem areas on a copy of your floor plans and list the repair and maintenance work the house needs. Organize the list according to the severity of the problem. Before repairing cosmetic defects, you should take care of the following:

1. Structural deficiencies, conditions that endanger the structure of your house, such as a leaking roof, decaying structural supports, or termite infestation.

2. Fire hazards, such as faulty electrical wiring, worn insulation and overloaded circuits;

3. Hazardous conditions that can cause accidents, such as loose floor boards, weak railings, or decaying stair treads;

Care should be taken to solve the cause of a problem and not simply treat the symptom. A crack can be patched, but it will reappear if the crack is caused by a foundation settling because of poor drainage around the house.

The solutions to most structural and mechanical problems are obvious. A structural post may have to be replaced. Additional electrical circuits may be required. A furnace may need servicing or be replaced. Although you may be able to do some of this work yourself, professional assistance may be required to comply with building code requirements and to deal with technical details.

| CRITICAL ITEM | PROJECT WORKSHEET | | ASSISTANCE REQUIRED | COST ESTIMATE | JOB COMPLETED |
|---|---|---|---|---|---|
| | Problem Area | Action Required | | | |
| | | | | | |
| | | | | | |
| | | | | | |
| | | | | | |
| | | | | | |
| | | | | | |
| | | | | | |
| | | | | | |
| | | | | | |
| | | | | | |
| | | | | | |
| | | | | | |
| | | | | | |
| | | | | | |
| | | | | | |
| | | | | | |

# FUNCTIONAL CONSIDERATIONS

This section is a guide for evaluating how your home accommodates your activities and satisfies your living needs. Functional inadequacies, such as lack of space or poorly-planned layouts, are often the stimuli that lead to the decision to remodel or renovate.

Your floor plans are again a useful place to record and study how you use your house, and to identify possible areas for improvement. First, study each room or area of your house and list the following:

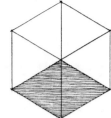

| ROOM: <br><br><br> Size: | ACTIVITY: |
|---|---|
| Who uses the room? | |
| How often ? | |
| Should be close to... | |
| Privacy ? | |
| Furnishings ? | |
| Natural light ? | |
| Special Requirements ? | |
| | COMPATIBLE ACTIVITIES: <br><br> POSSIBLE IMPROVEMENTS: |

## 1. HOW IS THE ROOM USED ?

☐ For what type(s) of activity ? Reading, conversation, cooking, eating, bathing, sleeping, making music, growing plants, etc. ?

☐ Are these quiet activities ? Noisy activities ?

☐ What other activities are compatible and can share the same space ?

☐ Are there conflicting uses now occurring in the room at the same time (eg. watching TV and listening to music) ?

## 2. WHO USES THE ROOM ?

☐ Which members of the family ?

☐ Is the room used primarily by groups or individuals ?

☐ Is there enough privacy for the user(s) ?

## 3. WHEN IS THE ROOM USED ?

☐ How often is the room used ? Daily, twice a week, rarely?

☐ During what times of the day ? Mornings, afternoons, evenings, all day ?

☐ Can the room be used for different activities at different times of the day or week ?

## 4. WHAT GOES IN THE ROOM ?

☐ What type of furnishings ? How many pieces ?

☐ What type and how much seating is needed ?

☐ Is there a need for special equipment, fixtures, or appliances ? Is there sufficient storage space ?

☐ How are the furnishings arranged ? Is there enough room ?

## 5. WHAT IS THE ROOM LIKE ?

☐ Is the room large enough and shaped well for its intended use(s) ?

☐ Does it have sufficient light ? What type of daylight ?

☐ Does the room lack warmth, color or character ?

☐ Are there exterior views available ?

Include in your list entrance areas and space used for circulation, getting from one room to the next, and one part of the house to another. Color this space in on your floor plans and indicate points of entry with arrows.

In addition to studying the individual rooms of your house, evaluate their overall pattern and how they relate to one another and the site. Indicate the following, using colors or tones to differentiate between types of rooms and activities, arrows to signify relationships, and x's to indicate incompatible uses or undesirable relationships.

## 6. WHAT SPACES ARE USED FOR CIRCULATION?

☐ Trace typical, often-used paths through your house on your floor plans. Does any path interfere with the use of a space or how it is furnished?

☐ Are there any rooms that are difficult to reach?

☐ How much space is used for movement through the house? Does the amount seem excessive?

☐ Can any part of the circulation space be used for other purposes as well, such as a gallery for art-work or an alcove for reading.

☐ Are the house entrances protected from the weather? Do they provide a buffer between the outside and the inside? Do they unnecessarily intrude into a space?

☐ Is there adequate storage space at the entranceways?

## 7. HOW ARE THE ROOMS LAID OUT AND RELATED?

☐ Which rooms are group or communal spaces?

☐ Which rooms are used primarily by individuals?

☐ Which spaces require isolation and privacy?

☐ Which rooms have noise-generating activities?

☐ Is the house generally well-zoned for privacy, types of activities, and compatibility of uses?

☐ Which rooms or activities should be located close to each other for convenience?

☐ Are there adjacent rooms with incompatible uses?

☐ Which rooms can be used for different activities at different times?

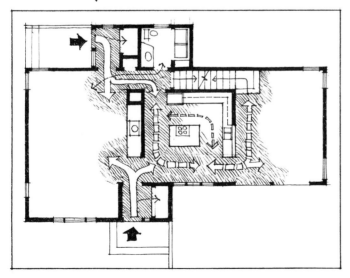

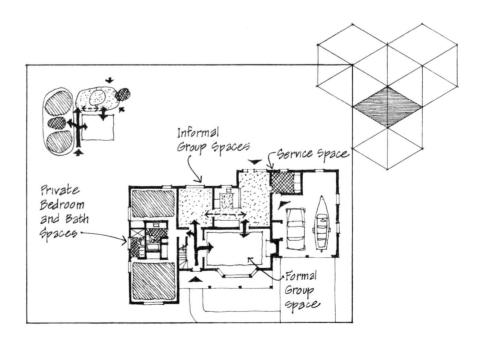

Informal Group Spaces

Service Space

Private Bedroom and Bath Spaces

Formal Group Space

# AESTHETIC CONSIDERATIONS

The aesthetic features and qualities of your house should also be evaluated. Your home should feel secure, comfortable, and provide an aesthetically-pleasing environment for your living needs. Its spaces should not only be large enough, but also be well-proportioned, comfortably furnished, and lit well for their intended use.

Although these considerations may be less critical to your health and safety than the structural soundness of your house, they often determine how pleasant your home is to live in. Even if your roof does not leak, and your heating system keeps you warm in the coldest weather, what do they matter if the quality of your rooms and spaces are bland or unpleasant to the eye to the point where you avoid their use?

Fortunately, many aesthetic problems can be solved with good interior design. And these solutions do not necessarily increase the cost of a remodeling project. The important issue is that the materials you would ordinarily require for a renovation should be carefully selected and coordinated with what already exists.

If a new entry door is needed to replace an older, warped one, selection of an appropriate design and color is just as important as choosing to install a door with good insulation value and weather-stripping. If a room is to be repainted, selecting the right color for the scale and intended use of the space is just as important as the quality of the paint itself.

Review each of the rooms in your house and evaluate its aesthetic strengths and weaknesses.

## 1. SHAPE AND FORM

☐ How do the proportions of the room affect the use of the space and how it is furnished?
☐ Does the room seem to be too long or narrow?
☐ Does the ceiling appear to be too low for the size of the room?
☐ Are there awkward corners or tight spots?

## 2. LIGHT

☐ Does the room have daylight? Does it illuminate the entire space or only part of it?
☐ Does the room receive sunlight? During what part of the day?
☐ Is the room too dimly lit? Is the room too bright?
☐ Are there problems with glare?
☐ Is there appropriate lighting for the intended use(s) of the room?

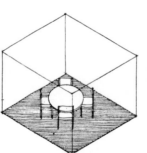
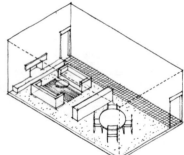

PROPORTION: Square rooms have a static, formal quality; elongated rooms encourage movement along their length, but can be sub-divided into functional areas with furnishings.

LIGHT

SCALE: Two rooms with different spatial qualities.

### 3. FURNISHINGS

☐ Are the furnishings appropriate for the use of the space?
☐ Are the furnishings in scale with one another and the size of the space?
☐ Are the various pieces visually in harmony with one another?

### 4. COLORS, TEXTURES, PATTERNS

☐ Are the room's colors too dark, too bright, or too bland?
☐ Are the room's colors, textures and patterns in harmony with one another? Is there a dominant color or pattern?
☐ Are there too many colors, textures or patterns?
☐ Are there conflicting colors or patterns?

### 5. DETAILS

☐ Is there a consistent style or use of trim?
☐ Have changes been made to the original trim work?
☐ Is there a mismatch between new and original trim?
☐ Are the various trim pieces in proportion with one another?

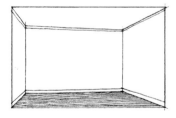
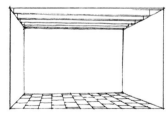
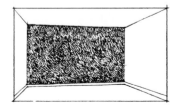
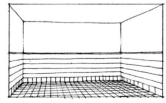

COLOR, PATTERN & TEXTURE: These qualities of a room's surfaces greatly affects a room's character.

### 6. OVERALL DESIGN

☐ How do the individual design elements work together within the room?
☐ Is the arrangement of elements, shapes, colors and patterns visually balanced?
☐ Is the room visually busy?
☐ Does the room have an organizing focus or center of interest such as a fireplace, a collection of memorabilia, or a loom?
☐ Does the room have an outlook or pleasant view?
☐ What overall mood or feeling does the room convey?
☐ Open spaciousness, or intimate coziness?
☐ Does the room seem formal or casual? Stimulating or restful? Warm or cool?

SYMMETRICAL BALANCE    ASSYMMETRICAL BALANCE

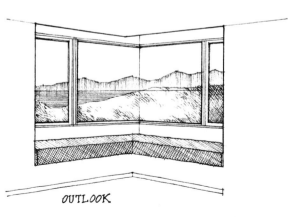

OUTLOOK

## EXTERIOR APPEARANCE

Most remodeling work proceeds from the inside out. Interior concerns are usually thought of and dealt with first. These interior modifications can, however, affect the exterior of a house. A window enlarged or moved for better daylight within a room could adversely affect the exterior composition of your house. A room-sized addition can be well-planned in terms of your interior layout but ruin what is now a pleasant outdoor space.

When remodeling or altering the exterior appearance of your house, allow the original style or character of the house to serve as a guide in selecting roofing and siding materials, proportioning and placing windows, and deciding on details and trim. After the remodeling or addition has been completed, the new and old portions should look as if they belong together.

While a house should be true to itself, it also contributes to the character of a street and neighborhood, and owes something to the environment to which it belongs. If you are situated in a rural setting, or in an area where houses are quite distant from each other, then perhaps it is more important to relate your house to the landscape. But in urban and suburban settings, it is important to note how your house, and any alterations or additions to it, relates to its neighbors.

Relating your house (and any alterations to it) to its surroundings does not mean that you have to sacrifice your need for self-expression or originality. Nor does it mean that all houses on a street must be identical or be of the same style. There is room for individuality and variety. A neighborly house can be harmonious with other houses by sharing a common trait, such as scale, proportion, or use of certain materials. It can, at the same time, differ from them in its window treatments, details, or landscaping.

Study the exterior appearance of your house, particularly if you are considering altering it during the remodeling or adding on to it in some manner. If drawings of the exterior are not available, take photographs of each side of your house and enlarge the prints to an appropriate scale. You can then use photocopies of these prints to trace or draw over.

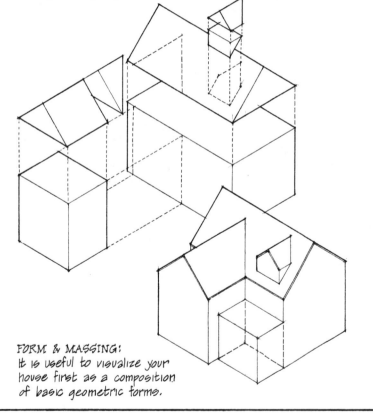

FORM & MASSING:
It is useful to visualize your house first as a composition of basic geometric forms.

## 1. NOTE COSMETIC PROBLEMS THAT MAY EXIST

- ☐ Roof defects.
- ☐ Warped or deteriorated siding.
- ☐ Peeling or blistered paint.
- ☐ Deteriorating or distorted window frames.
- ☐ Warped or broken trim.
- ☐ Loose gutters.
  See also pg. 23

## 2. NOTE THE STYLE OF YOUR HOUSE

- ☐ Overall form and massing of your house.
- ☐ Silhouette of the roofline.
- ☐ Texture and pattern of the siding material.
- ☐ Proportion of the windows and doors.
- ☐ Proportion and use of trim.
- ☐ Have any alterations or additions been made that seem out of place?

## 3. NOTE WHERE POSSIBLE CHANGES CAN BE MADE

- ☐ Possible location(s) for an addition.
- ☐ Possible use of roof dormers.
- ☐ Possible location of new entrances.

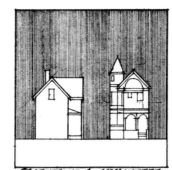
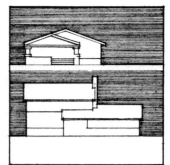

PROPORTION & SILHOUETTE

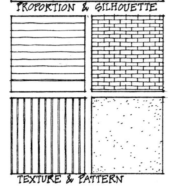
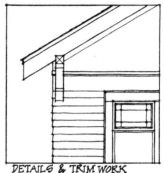

TEXTURE & PATTERN    DETAILS & TRIM WORK

# YOUR SITE

How your house is situated on its site, and how its rooms are oriented to the path of the sun, prevailing winds, outdoor spaces and the landscape, constitute another area of study. Although the orientation of your site is already determined and there may be conditions beyond your control, such as the height of the trees in your neighbor's yard, there may be modifications you can reasonably make to your own house to take advantage of or control these conditions.

Review the orientation of the rooms in your house to the conditions of its site, keeping in mind how the rooms are used. To supplement your own observations, detailed information on the sun, wind, temperature and rain or snow in your community can be obtained from your local weather bureau.

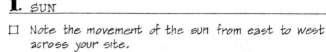

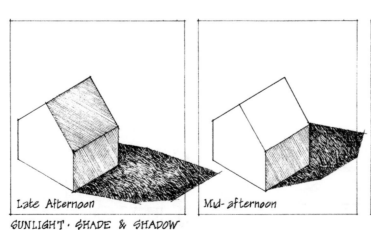

## 1. SUN

☐ Note the movement of the sun from east to west across your site.

☐ How high does the sun rise in the summer?

☐ How low is the sun at midday during the winter?

☐ Which rooms receive morning sun? Which activities would benefit from this morning sunlight?

☐ Which rooms face south and receive sunlight during most of the day? Do these rooms take advantage of the solar heat gain during the winter? How is this sunlight controlled in the summer?

☐ Which rooms face west and receive low, late-afternoon sun or sunset views? Is there a problem with too much heat or glare?

☐ Which rooms face north and have pleasant, even daylight, but little sunlight?

☐ Are there trees or adjacent structures that block out desirable sunlight? Can they be removed?

Summer Sunset
Winter Sunset
N
W
S
E
Summer Sunrise
Winter Sunrise

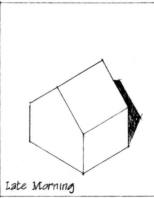
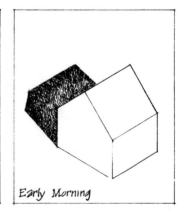

Late Afternoon    Mid-afternoon    Late Morning    Early Morning

SUNLIGHT · SHADE & SHADOW

## 2. WIND

☐ From what direction does the prevailing wind blow?
☐ How does this change with the seasons?
☐ Are windows located to take advantage of natural ventilation during warm, summer months?
☐ From what direction does severe weather, high winds, heavy rains or snow come?
☐ Are entrances, porches and patios buffered from these conditions? Are the windows, siding and roof facing these conditions protected and maintained properly?

## 3. VIEW

☐ Are there attractive views from your site? From which rooms?
☐ Are windows placed to take advantage of these views?
☐ Can pleasant views be created within your site?
☐ Are there undesirable views from any of your rooms? Can these be screened by landscaping, fencing, or window treatments?

## 4. NOISE

☐ Are there any noise sources that detract from the use of any of your rooms?
☐ Can the noise be dampened by window shutters or landscaping? Can you change the use of the room?

## 5. OUTDOOR SPACES

☐ Are there areas of your yard that can be developed into outdoor rooms, courtyards or decks?
☐ Do these areas receive sunlight? Are they protected from strong winds and rain? Do they have a reasonable degree of privacy?
☐ Which rooms are adjacent to these outdoor areas?
☐ Can these rooms be opened out, as with french doors, to relate directly to a patio or deck space?

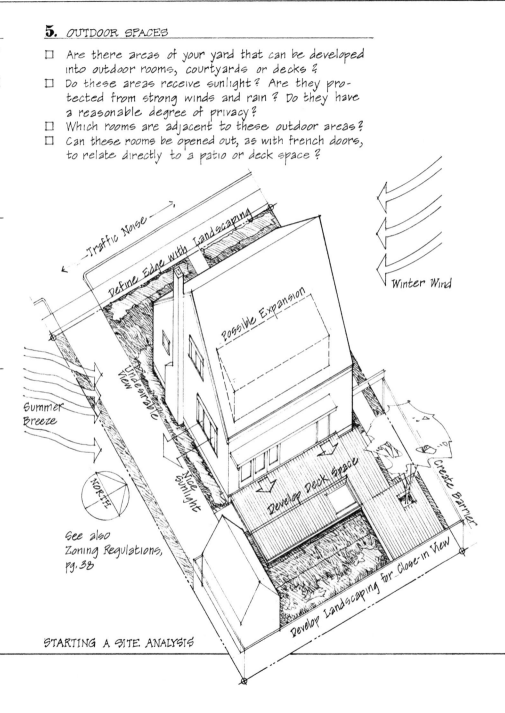

See also Zoning Regulations, pg. 38

STARTING A SITE ANALYSIS

## ASSESSING LIMITATIONS & RESOURCES

Before proceeding from the evaluation of your house and its site to exploring solutions to problems that exist, you should assess those factors that might limit what you can do in your renovation project.

Building and zoning codes might limit the size and height of the addition you are planning. The cost of the addition might be more than you can afford at this time, and you may therefore have to concentrate on the highest priority items. How long you are willing to live in a house disrupted by construction work may determine how you schedule the project.

MONEY

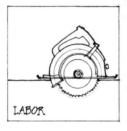

LABOR

TIME

REGULATIONS

## BUILDING COSTS & FINANCING

The amount of money available establishes a general limit to the work you will be able to do on your home. This limit is defined by:

- The amount of cash you have,
- The monthly amount you can or are willing to spend in repaying a loan,
- The potential value of your home, less the amount you now owe on it, and
- Your psychological spending limits.

Direct available cash, for most people, is a workable limit only for restricted, do-it-yourself projects. For larger projects, home equity and home improvement loans are generally available if you have:

1. A good credit record.
2. A stable employment history.
3. Significant equity in your home (present value less the amount owed.)
4. An ability to meet the new loan payments in addition to your present living costs.
5. A detailed home improvement plan where the work will enhance the value of the house. The plan must usually include architectural plans, a construction bid or detailed cost estimate, and a construction schedule.

These loans are available from various sources, including credit unions, savings and loan associations, commercial banks, and finance companies. For lower income homeowners, community-sponsored housing rehabilitation loans or neighborhood revitalization programs may also be available. The loan fees, repayment terms, interest rates, and loan restrictions vary substantially on available loans. Careful review and comparison, therefore, is required to find a loan that provides the best match with your needs and financial capabilities.

The other side of the money question is, "How much will it cost?" Remodeling cost estimates are difficult to predict accurately. It is not always possible to predict what complications can arise when walls, floors and ceilings are opened up to determine how a house was built and what deterioration has occurred. To get a quick, rough estimate of how much a major remodeling job will cost, you can use the cost per square foot method. To build an uncomplicated, standard house or full addition in 1982, the cost can vary from $35 to $50 a square foot of completed floor area. For a contractor-completed major improvement within an existing house, the cost may be 15% to 20% less.

The elements in these costs, and the proportion they represent of the total costs, are:
- Foundations................................ 8% - 12%
- Floor systems................................ 8% - 10%
- Walls........................................ 28% - 32%
- Roof........................................ 8% - 10%
- Finishes.................................... 15% - 20%
- Heating, plumbing, and electrical systems. 18% - 22%
- Cabinets and fixed equipment.......... 8% - 12%
- Site preparation, utility, landscaping, and financing costs are not included in the cost figures.

Your construction costs will be greater if your project involves complex construction, uses custom and expensive finishes, or is an addition to be built on a steep site or over poor soil. Kitchen and bathroom remodeling work is often more expensive. Your construction costs can also increase if your project is poorly organized and built with incomplete plans.

Your construction costs can be reduced in the following ways. You can manage the construction work, and purchase the required materials and work directly from suppliers and trade contractors. You must perform all the work normally done by the general contractor. In addition to scheduling and coordinating the work, you must obtain the necessary permits and arrange for inspections. For an extensive project, you may have to register as an employer and be responsible for withholding taxes, social security and unemployment costs, and disability insurance. Being your own general contractor can save you up to 20% of the full project costs, depending on how well your organize and manage the job.

Completing all of the finish work yourself can save you 10% to 40% of the project costs. This requires careful coordination with the contractor who is doing the rest of the work. Your responsibilities, and the liability for your work, should be clearly stated in the contract.

Finally, if you have the skill, experience and confidence, you may decide to build your remodeling project yourself. This can save you 30% to 60% of the project costs.

To assist you in figuring out the probable cost of your specific project, several resources are available. Cost estimating books are published each year with updated costs for completing thousands of construction tasks. Several specialty estimating guides are published on remodeling and renovating costs. In addition, professionals (architects, designers, contractors) experienced in remodeling work can provide valuable advice on the probable construction cost of your project and the cost of various alternatives.

# ZONING REGULATIONS

Zoning regulations, as enacted by local ordinance, establish boundaries for certain land uses, and regulate the size, location, and occupancy of buildings within each land use area. If you are considering adding on to your house in any manner, or changing its occupancy or use, check your local zoning code that applies to your neighborhood for the following:

## 1. MAXIMUM OR MINIMUM AREA AND DENSITY

☐ The residential land use zone may require a minimum lot size and restrict the type of occupancy (ie. the number of living units allowed.)

☐ Some zoning regulations may require a certain minimum floor area, while others will restrict the total allowable floor area.

## 2. REQUIRED SETBACKS

☐ Front setback is the minimum allowable distance from the front wall of the house to the front property line. On a corner lot, you may have the option of calling either of the sides facing the street the front.

☐ Side setback is the minimum allowable distance from the side walls of the house to the side property lines. This is sometimes expressed as the allowable sum of both side yards with a certain minimum for each.

☐ Rear setback is the minimum allowable distance from the rear of the house to the rear property line.

☐ Detached garages may be exempt from side and rear setback requirements.

☐ Porches, low-lying decks, roof overhangs, and architectural projections, such as bay windows, may be exempt from setback requirements, and also not count as part of the lot coverage.

## 3. LOT COVERAGE

☐ Lot coverage is the maximum allowable percentage of your lot area that can be covered by the house, garage, and other structures. An addition to your house will increase your lot coverage.

☐ The maximum allowable lot coverage may be less than the area bounded by the required setback lines.

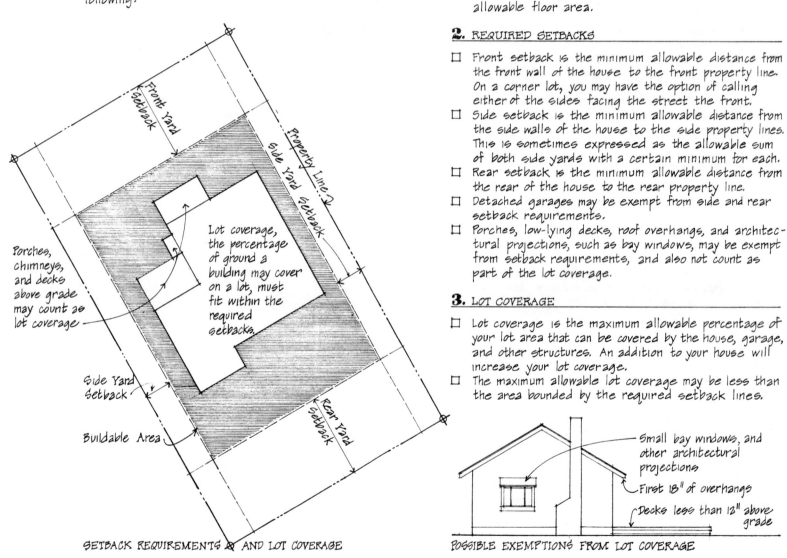

SETBACK REQUIREMENTS & AND LOT COVERAGE

POSSIBLE EXEMPTIONS FROM LOT COVERAGE

## 4. MAXIMUM ALLOWABLE HEIGHT

- ☐ The maximum allowable height of a building is usually restricted and generally measured from the existing grade to the top of the roof.
- ☐ On sloping lots, this height may be measured from the average of the high and low points where the house meets the ground. Or the maximum allowable height may be limited by a line parallel to the slope of the site.
- ☐ Extensions above the allowable height may be permissable for certain pitched roofs, dormers and chimneys.
- ☐ Fences higher than 6' may not be permitted without a variance.

## 5. EASEMENTS AND RIGHT-OF-WAYS

- ☐ Check with your local land use or zoning office, and review your property deed, to see if other parties, such as a utility company or your neighbor, may have the right of access across a part of your lot. This may further restrict your buildable area.

## 6. PARKING REQUIREMENTS

- ☐ Parking requirements are important factors if you are considering converting your garage into living space, or increasing the occupancy of your house.
- ☐ The code may require additional, covered or enclosed parking spaces.

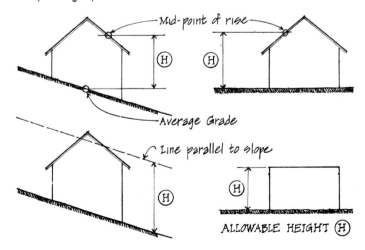

ALLOWABLE HEIGHT (H)

## 7. DESIGN REQUIREMENTS

- ☐ Certain design features or amenities, such as roof pitch, exterior siding material, or porches, may be regulated by the zoning code or by protective covenants contained in your property deed.
- ☐ Some communities have design review boards that must approve any new construction.

## 8. VARIANCES

- ☐ Variances to code requirements may be allowed if you can prove undue hardship or practical difficulties, and also demonstrate your plans will not adversely affect your neighbors, adjacent properties, or the public welfare. Check with your local land use office or building department regarding the procedure for requesting a variance.

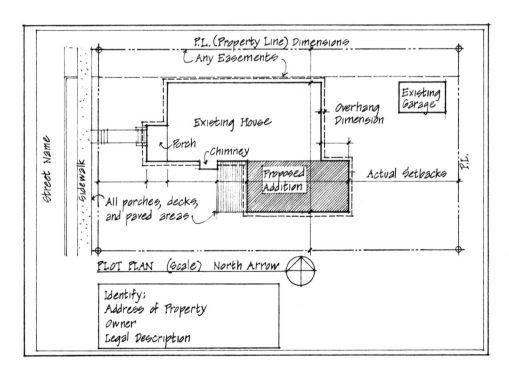

TYPICAL PLOT PLAN & INFORMATION GENERALLY REQUIRED

# BUILDING CODES

While zoning regulations control the size, location and occupancy or use of buildings, building codes are concerned primarily with how buildings are built. They establish minimum standards for the quality and size of materials used, provide construction guidelines for structural and fire safety, and set criteria for the installation of mechanical, plumbing and electrical systems.

Many communities have adopted the Uniform Building, Mechanical, and Plumbing Codes, and the National Electrical Code, with amendments for local concerns or conditions. In all cases, consult your local building department to find out which codes are in force in your area. You should become familiar with their requirements and how they will affect what you build and how you build it.

During the initial planning and design stages, and before you finalize your plans, review them with the building department to avoid having to alter them at a later date due to a regulation you may have overlooked. Be sure to check with the appropriate departments if the mechanical, plumbing or electrical codes are administered by different departments.

The following is a brief outline of some key areas of your building code to check when planning your renovation project.

## 1. ROOMS

☐ Minimum dimensions and areas for certain rooms such as bedrooms: For habitable rooms other than kitchens, 7' is usually the minimum width.

☐ Minimum height of ceilings is usually 7'-6". For halls, bathrooms and kitchenettes, a 7' ceiling may be allowed.

☐ For rooms with sloping or furred ceilings, the minimum ceiling height may be required only over a portion of their floor area.

☐ Requirements for windows in habitable rooms: For natural light, the required glass area is usually 1/10th of a room's floor area, with a minimum of 10 s.f. For natural ventilation, the required operable opening is usually 1/20th of the floor area, with a minimum of 5 s.f.

☐ Windowless kitchens and bathrooms may be allowed if mechanically ventilated.

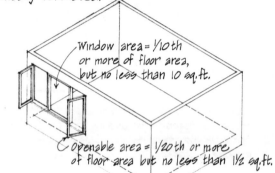

Window area = 1/10th or more of floor area, but no less than 10 sq.ft.

Openable area = 1/20th or more of floor area but no less than 1½ sq.ft.

LIGHT AND VENTILATION

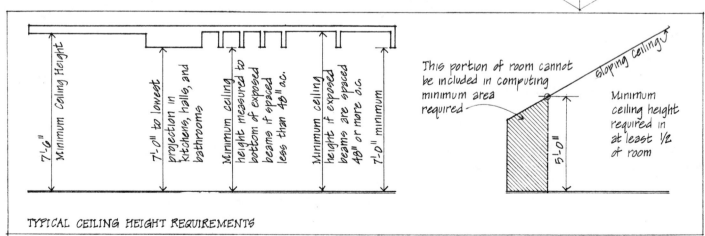

TYPICAL CEILING HEIGHT REQUIREMENTS

7'-6" Minimum Ceiling Height

7'-0" to lowest projection in kitchens, halls, and bathrooms

Minimum ceiling height measured to bottom of exposed beams if spaced less than 48" o.c.

Minimum ceiling height if exposed beams are spaced 48" or more o.c.

7'-0" minimum

This portion of room cannot be included in computing minimum area required

5'-0"

sloping ceiling

Minimum ceiling height required in at least ½ of room

### 2. STRUCTURE

☐ For floors of residences, the structural design live load is usually 40 lbs./s.f.; for garages, 50 lbs./s.f.
☐ Check the requirements for:
☐ The foundation system.
☐ Maximum spans for the size and strength of beams, joists and rafters.
☐ Floor and roof sheathing requirements.
☐ Wall framing and sheathing requirements.

### 3. CONSTRUCTION

☐ Check the requirements for:
☐ The minimum width and steepness of stairs.
☐ The placement and height of handrails.
☐ The use of safety glass for sliding glass doors and skylights.

### 4. FIRE SAFETY

☐ Check the requirements for:
☐ Emergency fire exits, especially from second story bedrooms, and the minimum size of window openings used as fire exits (typically, a minimum net opening of 5 to 6 s.f., a minimum opening width of 20" and opening height of 24", and a maximum sill height of 44".)
☐ The separation of adjacent structures and roofs.
☐ The prevention of fire spread by the use of fire-resistant materials and construction in certain areas of the house, such as around heat-producing equipment and appliances.

### 5. HEATING, PLUMBING AND ELECTRICAL SYSTEMS

☐ Check the requirements for:
☐ The safe installation of heat-producing equipment, shut-off valves, heat regulators, and the enclosure around the equipment.
☐ The materials, minimum sizes, and layout of plumbing lines.
☐ The proper installation of traps and vents on sewage waste lines.
☐ The location of the main electrical service panel for emergency access.
☐ Proper grounding of the electrical system.
☐ Sizing of wiring for circuit and panel loads.
☐ The insulation and installation of wiring and fixtures.

### 6. ENERGY CONSERVATION

☐ Check the requirements for:
☐ The maximum heat loss and/or maximum glazed area of windows and skylights allowable.
☐ Thermal insulation of foundation, floor, wall and roof construction.
☐ Insulated glass, and weather-stripping of windows and exterior doors.

---

CODES AND SPONSORING ORGANIZATIONS:

UNIFORM BUILDING CODE
International Conference of Building Officials
5360 South Workman Mill Road
Whittier, California 90601

BASIC BUILDING CODE (BOCA)
Building Officials and Code Administrators International
17926 South Halstead Street
Homewood, Illinois 60430

STANDARD BUILDING CODE
Southern Building Code Congress (SBCC)
908 Montclair Road
Birmingham, Alabama 35213

UNIFORM PLUMBING CODE
International Association of Plumbing Officials
5032 Alhambra Avenue
Los Angeles, California 90032

NATIONAL ELECTRICAL CODE
National Fire Protection Agency (NFPA)
Batterymarch Park
Quincy, Massachusetts 02269

# BUILDING PERMITS

Building permits are generally required for any remodeling work you do, whether you erect, construct, enlarge, alter or convert any part of your house. In practice, however, small-scale projects may sometimes be allowed, if done by the homeowner, without a permit. On the other hand, a major renovation project may require separate building, plumbing, electrical and use permits. In some communities, each of these permits and the related codes are administered by different departments. If you hire contractors to build your project, their service usually includes obtaining the necessary permits. It is, however, ultimately your responsibility for having the required permits.

If you are doing the work yourself, applications for permits usually require the following information:

1. The project location: the street address and legal description of the property (tract, block, and lot numbers).
2. Occupancy and use of the structure.
3. A general description of the work.
4. Cost or valuation of the construction.
5. Two to four sets of construction drawings.

The fee for the required permits may be based on the cost of the work or the size of the construction.

At the time you obtain the necessary permits, be sure you understand what inspections are required and how to arrange for an inspection.

## EXPLORING SOLUTIONS

Any remodeling or renovation project you are considering will involve major choices (Do I really need a two-story addition?) and minor ones (What color should I paint this wall?). To begin exploring possible design solutions, consolidate your needs and wants from the previous studies you have made into a single list.

1. NECESSARY REPAIRS:
   • Structural defects.
   • Watertightness and control of moisture.
   • Material deterioration.
   • Functioning of mechanical and electrical systems.
   • Building code deficiencies.

2. FUNCTIONAL PROBLEMS:
   • Room relationships, layout and zoning.
   • The use of individual rooms.
   • Entrances, circulation spaces, and access to rooms.

3. AESTHETIC PROBLEMS:
   • Interior spaces.
   • Exterior appearance.

While solutions to structural and mechanical problems may be readily apparent, there is often more than one way to solve a functional or aesthetic problem. As you develop these possibilities, consider each in terms of relative cost, feasibility and appropriateness. Check each for compliance with applicable code requirements. Develop solutions that concentrate on specific areas or sections of your house. Avoid piecemeal solutions. Whichever solution you decide on, it should be:

A. AFFORDABLE:
   • It should fit within your budget or be able to be financed reasonably.

B. DOABLE:
   • It should fit into your time schedule.
   • Can you do part or all of the work yourself?
   • How much professional help will you need?

C. EFFICIENT:
   • Keep in mind the best solution is always the one that solves the most problems. Whenever possible, combine a technical repair with a functional and aesthetic improvement.

Of equal importance is the appropriateness of the solution for the style and character of your home. Unlike designing and building a new house, working with an older home requires that you work with what you already have. There already exists a framework for your design decisions. Any solution you choose should improve your house without sacrificing its good qualities. A good place to start developing a solution, therefore, is to note those features that should not or cannot be altered, moved or eliminated.

The following section outlines possible design solutions for you to explore. They are general in nature and are intended to provide with starting points from which you can develop your own specific solutions. Since the reason for considering a renovation project are usually functional or aesthetic in nature, these solution-types are categorized as follows:

1. ENHANCING EXISTING SPACE
2. RE-ARRANGING EXISTING SPACE
3. CONVERTING UNUSED SPACE
4. ADDING NEW SPACE

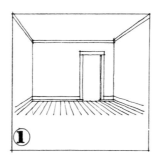
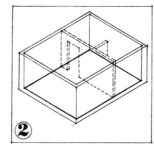
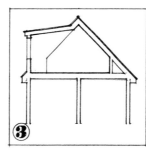
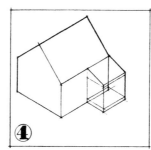

## ENHANCING EXISTING SPACE

If the major problem you have identified is a lack of space, first consider the most economical and least difficult ways there are of solving the problem.

Your present space may actually be adequate in area, but the furniture arrangement may make it appear cramped. Consider how new furniture groupings, centered around the activities in the space, can open the space up. Are there any unnecessary pieces that can be eliminated? Can some pieces serve more than one function? Perhaps purchasing new furniture whose scale is better suited to the size of the room can help make the room appear more spacious.

Lack of storage often creates cluttered rooms. If this is a problem, first consider what little-used items can be stored elsewhere. Then consider building efficient storage systems that make the most of vertical space and help organize other items while keeping them conveniently at hand.

If you are unhappy with the visual appearance of a room, consider the interior design of the space. A room can often be renewed with a fresh coat of paint. Improved lighting can brighten a space and enhance its function as well. The right selection of color, texture and pattern can make a room seem more spacious, warmer and more comfortable.

If a space problem cannot be solved by any of the preceding, consider how minor alterations can make a room work better for you.

The existing windows in a room may be hampering an efficient furniture layout with their size or spacing along a wall. Or the windows may not be positioned to take advantage of a pleasant view or the sunlight to which the room may be oriented. Consider how the existing windows in a room could be enlarged, moved, grouped, or be extended into a window seat.

The doors into a room may be creating a path through an activity area rather than around it. Consider whether any of the doorways could be moved to another, better location without adversely affecting any adjacent rooms. If visual or acoustical privacy is not an issue, could a doorway be enlarged to allow the room to open up into an adjacent space?

(SEE CHAPTER 2)

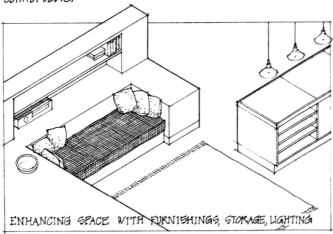

ENHANCING SPACE WITH FURNISHINGS, STORAGE, LIGHTING

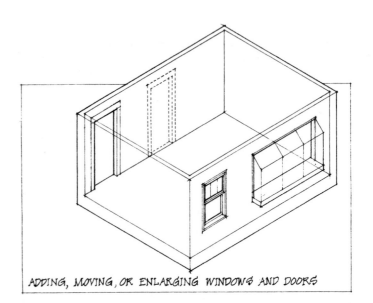

ADDING, MOVING, OR ENLARGING WINDOWS AND DOORS

## RE-ARRANGING SPACE

If enhancing an existing space or altering its use does not solve a space problem, consider extending the physical boundaries of the room. By moving or eliminating walls, you can improve the proportions of an awkwardly-shaped room or create a larger space from several smaller ones. Within the existing boundaries of your house, you can re-arrange walls and dramatically alter your room layout.

If you have a large room that you want to re-define into smaller, more usable spaces, you have several alternatives. You can build one or more new partitions, or you can define areas by raising or lowering portions of the floor or ceiling. You can also define areas within the room with furnishings, lighting or surface treatments. While the first approach may be desirable for visual and acoustical privacy, the last offers infinitely more flexibility in the future use of the room.

(SEE CHAPTER 2 - PG. 26)

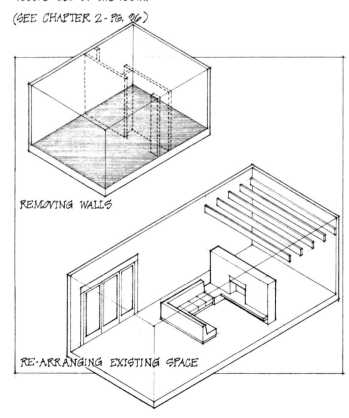

REMOVING WALLS

RE-ARRANGING EXISTING SPACE

## CONVERTING UNUSED SPACE

If enhancing or re-arranging your existing space is not needed, but you need more space, consider expanding into your attic or basement. Conversions of these spaces are usually less expensive than new additions since the need for a foundation and exterior framing is eliminated or greatly reduced. Attic and basement conversions may also be necessary if zoning regulations do not allow you to expand your house upward or outward.

Your attic may contain enough usable space with the required ceiling height. If not, the roof can be raised, or dormers added. These dormers can increase the usable floor area of the attic and accommodate windows for daylighting and ventilation.

Your basement, if not too damp, can be converted into a workshop or hobby room. If adequately daylit and ventilated, additional bedroom spaces can be created.

If you have a garage you are not using, it too can be converted into a living area.

(SEE CHAPTER 3)

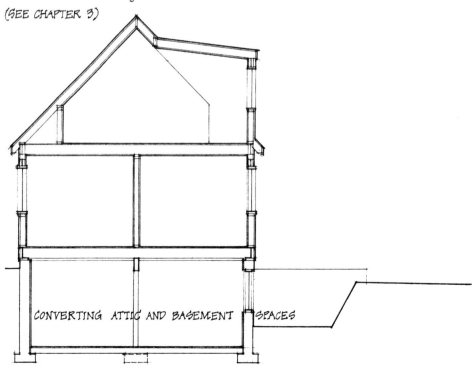

CONVERTING ATTIC AND BASEMENT SPACES

# ADDING NEW SPACE

If your home is in good condition and works well for you, and you simply need more space, then adding on may be the only answer to your space problems. Even here, however, you have choices, depending on how much space you need, where you need it, the size of your lot, and your financial resources. Additions can range in scale from bay windows and sunrooms to larger one-story and two-story extensions that require a new foundation, exterior walls, and roof structure.

An exterior wall of a room can be moved or extended outward a few feet to gain more space. Windows and skylights can further expand the space visually and enhance the daylighting of the room.

A full-scale addition requires careful study and integration with the existing house form and structure, but provides the most flexibility in the design and layout of the needed space. If your lot is large enough, an addition can expand your house horizontally. It can link your house with an existing garage. Or it can be a new second-story added to your single-story home or garage.

(SEE CHAPTER 4)

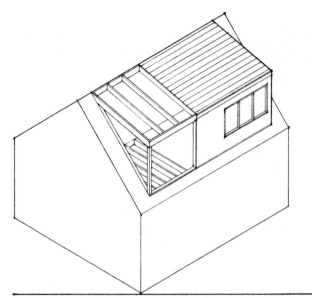

LARGE DORMER

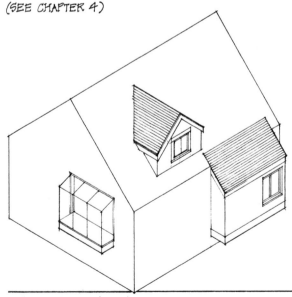

SMALL EXTENSIONS

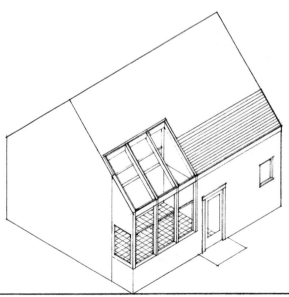

ADDING WIDTH

46

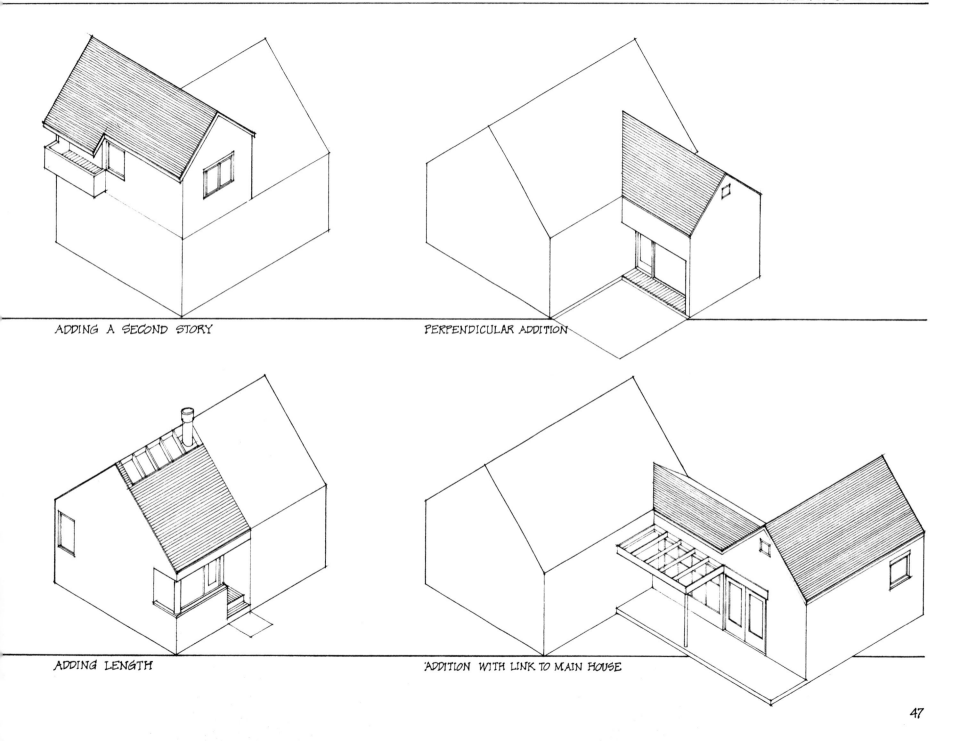

ADDING A SECOND STORY

PERPENDICULAR ADDITION

ADDING LENGTH

ADDITION WITH LINK TO MAIN HOUSE

# 2 IMPROVING EXISTING SPACE

If the major problem you face is a lack of space, or the inefficient use of what space you have, first consider the most economical and least difficult ways there are of solving the problem. This chapter discusses several alternatives – ways to enhance, modify and re-arrange space within the existing framework of your house. In each case, the emphasis is not simply on gaining more space, but rather on achieving quality space and more comfortable room settings for you and your family.

## ENHANCING EXISTING SPACE

The rooms in your house may be adequate in size and well-proportioned, but some may feel cramped, lack warmth, or be ill-suited to your aesthetic taste. Utilizing some principles of interior design, you may be able to renew these rooms without expensive structural alterations. This first section of the chapter discusses ways to enhance and improve existing space with light, color, and furnishings.

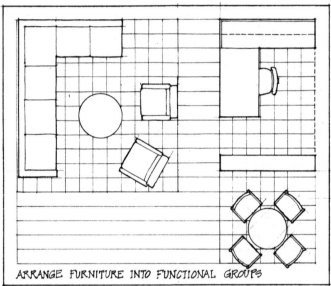

ARRANGE FURNITURE INTO FUNCTIONAL GROUPS

## FURNITURE

The arrangement of furniture in a room, or the size of the pieces, can make an adequately-sized room feel cramped and uncomfortable. Using scaled cut-outs of your furniture, try out new arrangements on a floor plan of the room.

- First eliminate any unnecessary pieces.
- Use furniture whose scale fits the size of the room.
- Arrange furniture into functional groupings, centered around the nature of the activities.
- Use furniture to direct traffic, and keep paths from disrupting a room's activities.
- If space is tight, consider using multi-functional pieces, ones that can be used for more than one purpose - a seat that contains storage, a vertical shelving unit with a desk.
- Also consider using foldable, easily movable furniture, or built-in furniture tailored to the size and shape of the room.

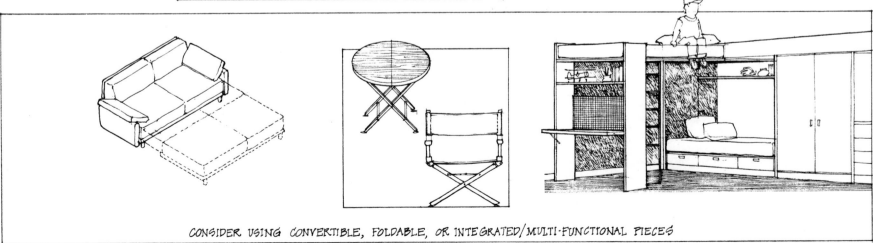

CONSIDER USING CONVERTIBLE, FOLDABLE, OR INTEGRATED/MULTI-FUNCTIONAL PIECES

## BUILT-IN FURNITURE

In really tight spaces, or awkardly shaped or proportioned rooms, consider using built-in furniture. While
built-ins lack the flexibility and mobility of freestanding
pieces, they can be tailored to fit the dimensions of
a room as well as your own dimensions.

Built-in furniture can make the most of the space
around or below windows, in small niches or alcoves,
in closets, or in between wall studs.

Built-in seating can double-function as table tops
and contain storage space as well. Shelving can be
built into recesses and blend into a wall's surface to
simplify its appearance. In converted attics, the
space beneath the roof along the eaves can be fitted
with built-in storage, desk space, or a day bed for
lounging.

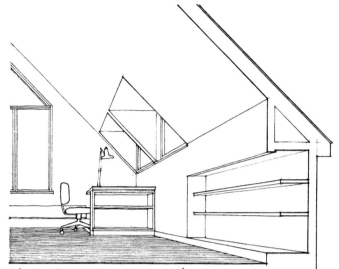

USING SPACE UNDER THE EAVES

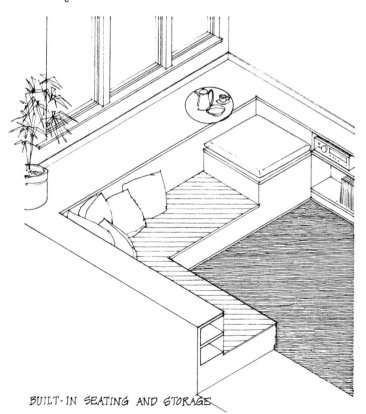

BUILT-IN SEATING AND STORAGE

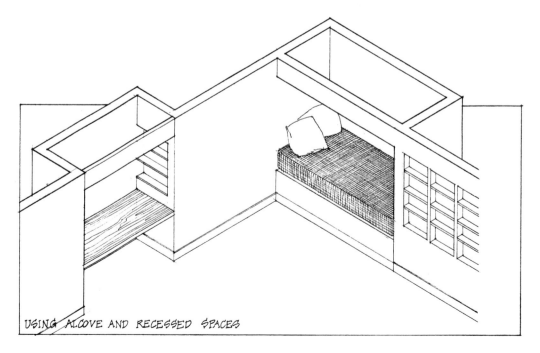

USING ALCOVE AND RECESSED SPACES

# PLANNING STORAGE

It is often easier to collect possessions than to find proper space to store them. Lack of storage space, or poorly planned storage areas, can result in cluttered rooms. Properly designed storage can help organize your belongings, make the most of what space a room has, and leave more room for activities and furnishings.

To begin planning the storage for your home, first eliminate any unnecessary items you have. Remove little-used items, such as seasonal decorations or equipment, to the attic, basement, or garage. Reserve articles that are used only about once a month for filling hard-to-reach storage spaces, backs of shelves, or awkward corners of cabinets.

Using a copy of your house floor plans, note which rooms need more or better storage space, and areas where storage can be added.

Within those rooms that need more or better storage, organize items according to how often they are used, who uses them, and where they are needed. To save time and steps, keep often-used items close at hand, not too low or too high or beyond your reach. Keep in mind the dimensional reach of those using the items.

Most importantly, use the volume of space within the room wisely. Using the vertical space above the height of work surfaces can free up additional floor area. Other, sometimes neglected, areas that can be used for storage include corners, wall areas between or below windows, behind or beneath furniture, space below stairs, and niches or stud spaces within walls.

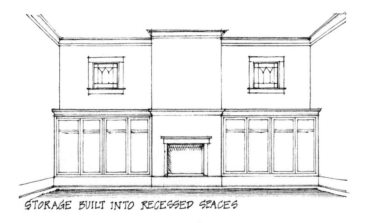

STORAGE BUILT INTO RECESSED SPACES

STORAGE BUILT AROUND A WINDOW

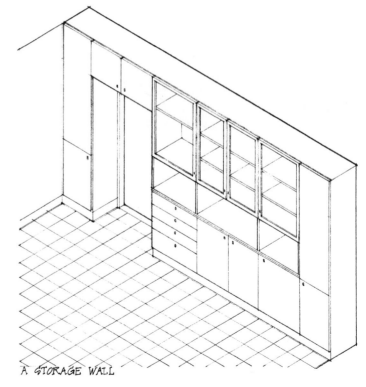

A STORAGE WALL

# TYPES OF STORAGE

Once you have an idea of how much storage you need, and where you need it, consider the type of storage required. Storage can be classified into two major categories: open and closed.

Open storage leaves items on display. Open shelving systems and wall units are ideal for displaying art objects, memorabilia, and collections. Concealed behind closet or cabinet doors, open shelving can be installed inexpensively to keep items easily accessible.

Closed storage - closets, cabinets and drawers - is useful for concealing items that tend to be cluttered or visually unattractive. Closed storage systems are also useful where dust is a problem, and cleaning is to be kept to a minimum. Where visibility as well as a dust-free space is desired, glass door fronts can be used.

Whether open or closed, a storage unit can be movable or built into a room. Movable units can be freestanding pieces of furniture, or modular units that stack or interlock to form various configurations. These are desirable if you anticipate changes in a room's use or your storage needs.

Built-in storage, on the other hand, can make use of a room's awkward spaces, blend in with a room's walls, or be custom-fitted for the size and proportion of the items to be stored.

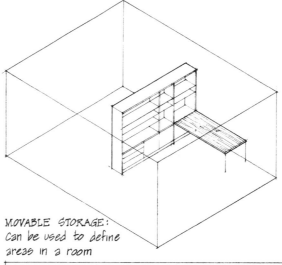

MOVABLE STORAGE:
Can be used to define areas in a room

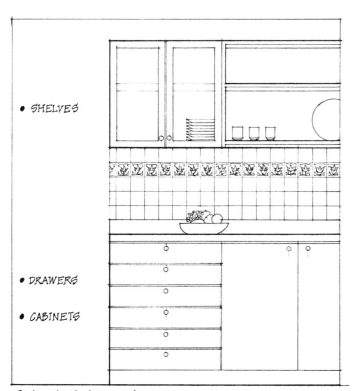

• SHELVES

• DRAWERS

• CABINETS

BASIC STORAGE TYPES

BUILT-IN STORAGE

## SHELVING

Shelves are any flat, horizontal projecting surfaces that can support the weight of the articles to be stored. They are relatively inexpensive to build and versatile enough to fit into almost any design situation. Shelves can be open or be concealed behind doors, glass fronts, or louvered shutters. They can be finely-detailed pieces of furniture, or be adjustable, demountable units of wood, metal or plastic. They can articulate a wall's surface, or form a freestanding wall that defines space.

Depending on the strength of its material and the spacing of its supports, shelving can be as narrow or wide and as short or long as you wish. Narrow shelves are ideal for small, slender items, such as bottles and glassware, while deeper shelves are required for books and bulky items. Avoid using shelves that are too deep for the items stored since it would be difficult to reach those articles that are furthest back.

For the shelving material, inexpensive particle board, plywood, solid 1"x or 2"x wood, even narrow hollow-core doors can be used. They can be painted or finished as desired. Their exposed edges can be finished with solid wood trim to the thickness desired.

For a lighter appearance, metal grating can be used. For both lightness and elegance, with emphasis on the articles displayed, acrylic and plate glass can be used. Their transparency can be enhanced with lighting from the sides, back, top, or below.

To help you select the proper spans for the shelving material you are using, the following table can be used. For heavy objects, reduce the span or use thicker material.

| MATERIAL: | SPAN: |
| --- | --- |
| 3/4" particle board | 24" - 28" |
| 3/4" plywood | 30" - 36" |
| 1" x 12" | 24" - 30" |
| 2" x 12" | 48" - 52" |
| 1/2" plate glass | 16" - 18" |

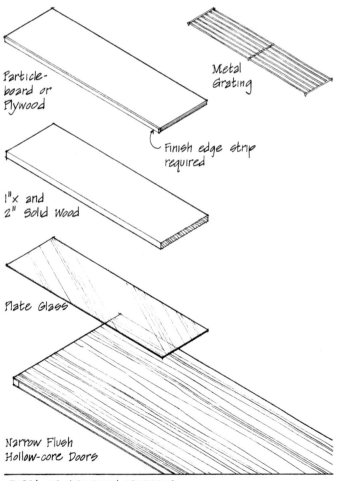

Particle-board or Plywood

Metal Grating

Finish edge strip required

1"x and 2" Solid Wood

Plate Glass

Narrow Flush Hollow-core Doors

TYPES OF SHELVING MATERIAL

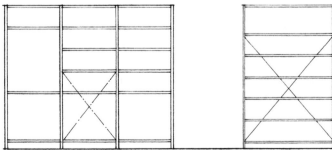

STOCK SHELVING UNITS · Many types of wood or metal systems are available.

## SHELVING SUPPORTS

Shelving can be supported in a number of ways. Temporary shelving can be supported on low tables, modular storage units, or file cabinets. They can span between vertical walls or ladders. They can be hung from walls or suspended from the ceiling.

The simplest and least expensive way to support a shelf is to use 1"x2" or 1"x3" cleats attached to end walls of cabinets or closets. Vertical ladder supports can also be fabricated from 1"x2"s to form a freestanding shelving unit.

To make the job of installing shelves easier, a variety of shelf hardware is available. If appearance is not a factor, steel angle brackets can be used to support medium loads.

Where endwall supports are not available or desired, and for adjustability and strength, shelving standards and brackets are ideal.

For a finished, built-in appearance, shelves can be supported by standards with end clips, or pins or dowels that fit into pre-drilled holes.

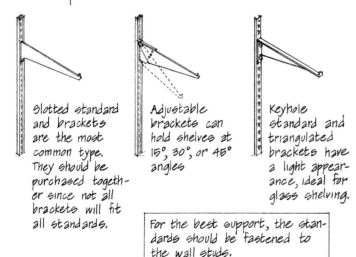

Slotted standard and brackets are the most common type. They should be purchased together since not all brackets will fit all standards.

Adjustable brackets can hold shelves at 15°, 30°, or 45° angles

Keyhole standard and triangulated brackets have a light appearance, ideal for glass shelving.

For the best support, the standards should be fastened to the wall studs.

SHELVING STANDARDS AND BRACKETS FOR WALL MOUNTING

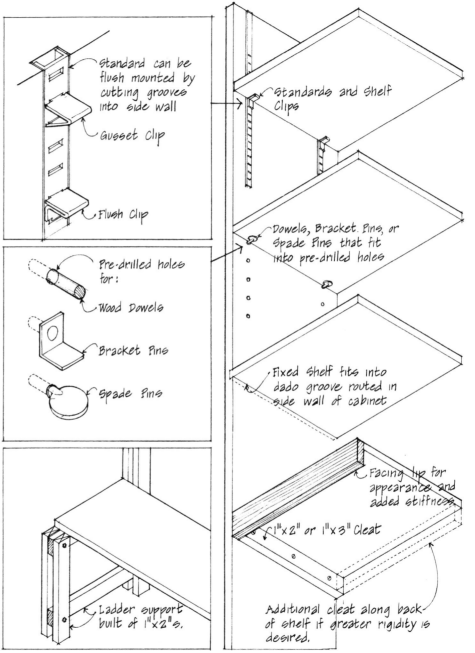

Standard can be flush mounted by cutting grooves into side wall

Gusset Clip

Flush Clip

Pre-drilled holes for:

Wood Dowels

Bracket Pins

Spade Pins

Ladder support built of 1"x2"s.

Standards and Shelf Clips

Dowels, Bracket Pins, or Spade Pins that fit into pre-drilled holes

Fixed shelf fits into dado groove routed in side wall of cabinet

Facing lip for appearance and added stiffness

1"x2" or 1"x3" Cleat

Additional cleat along back of shelf if greater rigidity is desired.

TYPES OF SUPPORTS FOR ENDS OF SHELVES

## CABINETS

Cabinets are upright storage units that can be subdivided into shelving, drawers, and open compartments. Although their contents can be open to view, cabinets generally have door fronts to conceal their interior. While the storage compartments can be sized according to what is stored, the visual appearance of cabinet work is due almost entirely to the design of their door fronts, hinges and hardware used.

There are many types of stock cabinets, of wood or metal, pre-finished or unfinished, that can be bought and installed by the homeowner. Familiar ones include:

## DRAWERS

Drawers provide concealed storage in containers that slide or roll toward you when opened. Because they provide access from above, they can have greater depth, from front to back, than shelves. They should be low enough to see into, and not so deep that things get lost in their depth. Drawers are best suited for storing small or flat items.

Drawers can be built into cabinets, or be hung from table, counter, or desk tops. Simple drawer guides can be used for drawers that contain lightweight items, but rolling mechanisms should be used for larger, heavier drawers.

For narrow drawers, a single handle or pull is sufficient. For wide drawers, two handles or pulls should be located closer to the ends, but be no more than 36" apart. Stops should be provided to keep large drawers from being pulled out of their casings.

Building your own drawers is not an easy task. Fortunately, a variety of stock drawer units can be found to suit your needs and budget.

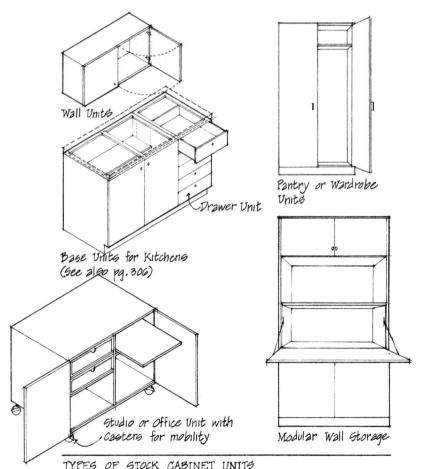

Wall Units

Drawer Unit

Base Units for Kitchens
(See also pg. 306)

Pantry or Wardrobe Units

Studio or Office Unit with Casters for mobility

Modular Wall Storage

TYPES OF STOCK CABINET UNITS

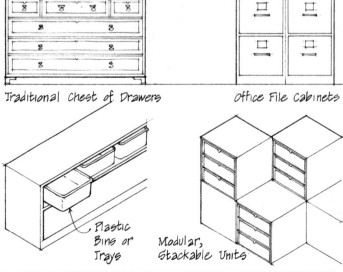

Traditional Chest of Drawers

Office File Cabinets

Plastic Bins or Trays

Modular, Stackable Units

TYPES OF DRAWER UNITS

# CLOSETS

Most closets in homes come minimally equipped with a single clothes pole and a top shelf. Linen closets may have several shelves. These closet spaces can usually be used more efficiently (ie. hold more of your belongings) if planned properly, re-organized, and fitted with additional shelves, drawers, or cabinets.

Inventory the things you need to store in each closet, and organize them by type and size. Plan the divisions or compartments that will best house your belongings. It is usually best to accommodate tall items first, and gradually work toward fitting in the smaller items. Place little-used items toward the top or bottom, reserving the middle area for things that should be easily reached.

If you have converted a bedroom into a study, workroom, or other use, its closet can likewise be converted into a library, desk/work area, or sewing center.

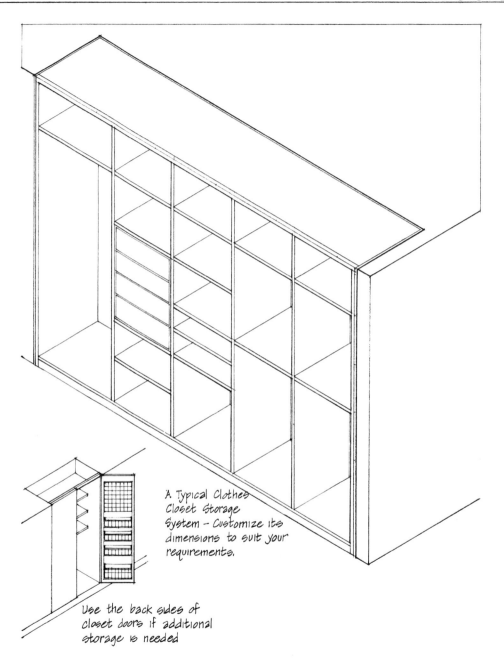

A Typical Clothes Closet Storage System – Customize its dimensions to suit your requirements.

Use the back sides of closet doors if additional storage is needed

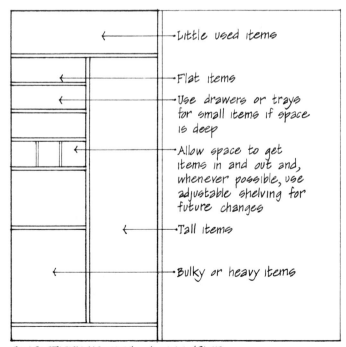

- Little used items
- Flat items
- Use drawers or trays for small items if space is deep
- Allow space to get items in and out and, whenever possible, use adjustable shelving for future changes
- Tall items
- Bulky or heavy items

COMPARTMENTALIZING CLOSET SPACE

# LIGHTING

The first purpose of lighting, of course, is to illuminate. Both natural daylighting and artificial lighting at night should be designed to provide a comfortable level of illumination for viewing without causing eyestrain or fatigue. Lighting design, however, involves not only determining the amount of light required within a space. It is also concerned with the location and pattern of the light sources (windows and light fixtures), the distribution and diffusion of the light, and the reflectance of this light off of the room's surfaces and objects within it.

This section on lighting discusses types of lighting, recommended levels of illumination, and functional and design criteria for improving the lighting within a room. For more information on daylighting with windows and skylights, see pgs. 68 and 120.

There are three types of lighting arrangements:

1. General or area lighting.
2. Task or local lighting.
3. Accent or decorative lighting.

Some rooms in your house, such as hallways and utility spaces, require only general lighting. Most rooms will require both general and task lighting. Important living areas should have all three.

Each type of lighting is created by the types of bulbs and fixtures used and, more importantly, by their location and arrangement in a room. The type of bulb used determines the amount and color of light emitted. The fixture determines the distribution and diffusion of the light. The location and arrangement of the fixtures determine the effect of the light on the space.

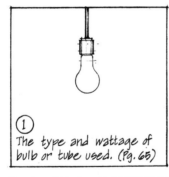

① The type and wattage of bulb or tube used. (Pg. 65)

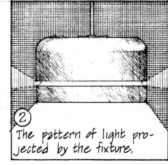

② The pattern of light projected by the fixture.

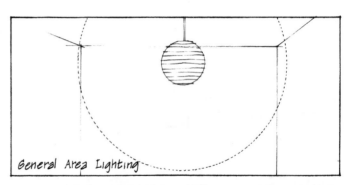

General Area Lighting

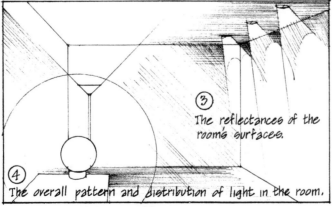

③ The reflectances of the room's surfaces.

④ The overall pattern and distribution of light in the room.

LIGHTING DESIGN FACTORS

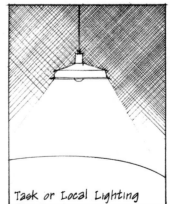

Task or Local Lighting

Accent or Decorative Light'g

TYPES OF LIGHTING

## GENERAL LIGHTING

General lighting is even, low-level illumination of an entire area, created either by ceiling fixtures or by wall-mounted valance or cove lighting. General or area lighting is used in most rooms for moving about, house-cleaning, and to reduce the contrast between local task lighting and a room's surfaces. It is also important for safe passage in entry spaces, along hallways and on stairways.

We see light only by its effect on, and its reflectance off of, surfaces and forms. And every surface will reflect some of the light it receives and absorb the rest. Light-colored and smooth surfaces will reflect more light than dark-hued or rough-textured surfaces. It therefore will require more light to brighten a room with dark-colored walls than to illuminate one with smooth, white walls.

Light also diminishes as it travels from its source. For the general illumination of a room, it is important that the light sources be placed close enough to ceiling or wall surfaces to wash them with light and thereby cause the surfaces to become light sources in themselves.

GENERAL LIGHTING GUIDELINES

| | | |
|---|---|---|
| SMALL ROOMS (150 s.f.) | Ceiling Fixture Recessed Floods Wall Valances | 150-200 Total Watts (4) R-20/50 W Units 8 to 12 Linear Feet |
| MEDIUM ROOMS (200 s.f.) | Ceiling Fixture Recessed Floods Wall Valances | 200-300 Total Watts (5 to 8) R-30/75 W Units 16 to 20 Linear Feet |
| LARGE ROOMS (250 s.f.) | Ceiling Fixture Recessed Floods Wall Valances | 1 Watt per sq. ft. 1.5 Watts per sq. ft. 1 Linear Foot per 15 sq. ft. |
| UTILITY ROOMS | Incandescent Fluorescent | 150 to 200 Total Watts 60 to 80 Total Watts |

RECOMMENDED REFLECTANCES FOR MAJOR SURFACES

| | | |
|---|---|---|
| CEILINGS | Pale Tints | 60% to 90% |
| WALLS | Medium Shades | 35% to 60% |
| FLOORS | Wood, Carpet, Tile | 15% to 35% |

Recessed or surface-mounted fluorescent fixtures.

Recessed floods with a wide spread beam.

Ceiling-mounted or suspended incandescent fixture with luminous diffuser.

CEILING SOURCES FOR GENERAL LIGHTING

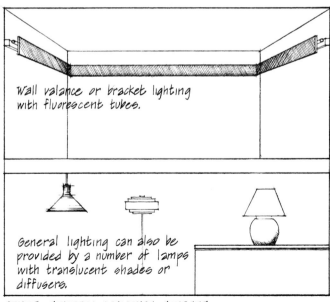

Wall valance or bracket lighting with fluorescent tubes.

General lighting can also be provided by a number of lamps with translucent shades or diffusers.

OTHER GENERAL LIGHTING SOURCES

## TASK LIGHTING

Task lighting provides localized illumination for what you're doing. It also contributes to the general illumination of a space.

For most visual tasks, 150 watts of incandescent or 40 watts of fluorescent lighting is sufficient. For working with fine details, 200-300 watts of incandescent or 60-80 watts of fluorescent lighting may be required.

To illuminate work surfaces and countertops, use 120 watts of incandescent or 20 watts of fluorescent lighting for every three feet of surface.

Since light diminishes as it travels from its source, it is important that the source for task lighting be close enough to the task area for the desired level of illumination without creating a glare problem. Although recessed ceiling fixtures can be used, suspended fixtures and portable lamps usually work more efficiently.

In all cases, the light source should be shielded from your direct line of sight, and positioned so as not to create shadows on the work area. The work surface itself should not be highly reflective, and should not be seen against too dark of a background.

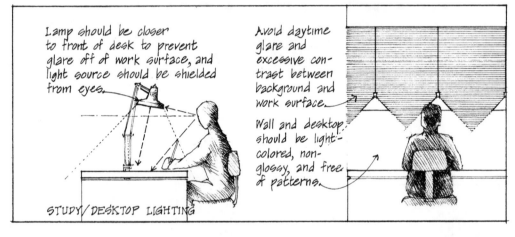

Lamp should be closer to front of desk to prevent glare off of work surface, and light source should be shielded from eyes.

Avoid daytime glare and excessive contrast between background and work surface.

Wall and desktop should be light-colored, non-glossy, and free of patterns.

STUDY/DESKTOP LIGHTING

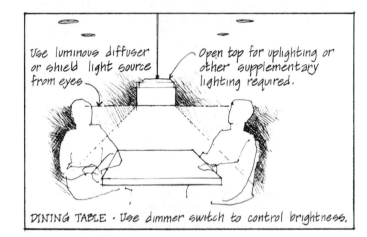

Use luminous diffuser or shield light source from eyes.

Open top for uplighting or other supplementary lighting required.

DINING TABLE · Use dimmer switch to control brightness.

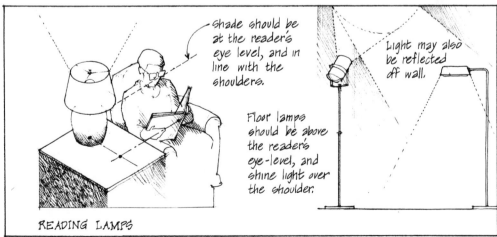

Shade should be at the reader's eye level, and in line with the shoulders.

Light may also be reflected off wall.

Floor lamps should be above the reader's eye-level, and shine light over the shoulder.

READING LAMPS

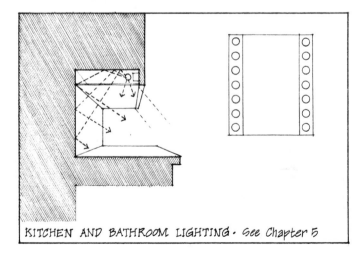

KITCHEN AND BATHROOM LIGHTING · See Chapter 5

## ACCENT LIGHTING

In addition to providing general and task illumination, lighting can be used as a purely visual design element to make a room more attractive.

Lighting can enliven a space with patterns of highlights and shadows. A fine line exists, however, between creating interest with a variety of lighting levels and causing glare with excessive contrast between bright and dim areas.

Lighting can accent desired features in a room, emphasize the texture of a wall surface, silhouette objects, illuminate artwork. It can also, by its absence, conceal undesirable features of a room.

Lighting can help define the limits of a space or articulate areas within a room. It can also soften the corners of a room, expand its boundaries, and make a small room seem more spacious.

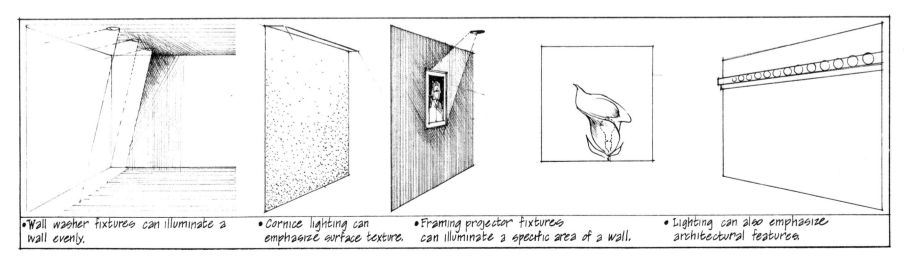

• Wall washer fixtures can illuminate a wall evenly.

• Cornice lighting can emphasize surface texture.

• Framing projector fixtures can illuminate a specific area of a wall.

• Lighting can also emphasize architectural features.

# LIGHT FIXTURES

There are many types of lighting fixtures and styles to choose from when designing general, task and accent lighting for a room. The following is an outline of the basic types of fixtures with recommendations for their use and location.

### SURFACE-MOUNTED FIXTURES

Surface fixtures can be mounted on walls or ceilings. Since they are highly visible, they should have diffusing glass or plastic shields, and their style should be compatible with that of the room. Clear or frosted glass can be used with low-wattage bulbs or when the light is controlled by a dimmer switch.

Surface-mounted fixtures are used primarily for general illumination, and usually will effectively wash or brighten the immediate surface area of the wall or ceiling on which they are mounted.

Since bulb type and wattage will vary with fixture design, consult the manufacturer's data for mounting and spacing recommendations.

### SUSPENDED FIXTURES

Fixtures suspended from the ceiling are used over dining tables, work surfaces, stairways, and in high-ceilinged spaces. Like surface-mounted fixtures, they are important design elements in any room.

Depending on their shield or diffuser, suspended fixtures can direct light upward, down, or both. They can also be glowing, luminescent forms.

If used for task lighting over a work surface, projecting light downward, a suspended fixture should be below your eye level. If at eye level, it should be dim. If bright, it should be kept above your eye level.

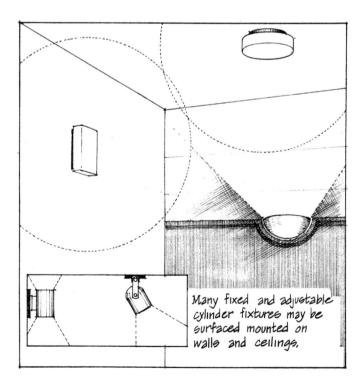

Many fixed and adjustable cylinder fixtures may be surfaced mounted on walls and ceilings.

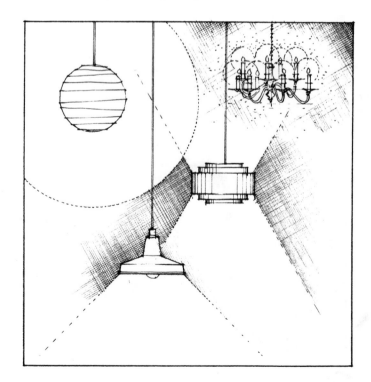

RECESSED FIXTURES

Recessed fixtures include fixed and adjustable down-lights, and incandescent bulbs or fluorescent tubes shielded by flush-mounted plastic diffusers.

Recessed downlights can light a traffic path, illuminate artwork, and wash a wall's surface. The actual spread of the beam from a downlight depends on its distance from the wall surface, the type of bulb used (spot or flood), and the type of reflector in the housing.

Recessed lighting panels are luminescent planes of light that are ideal for rooms with low ceilings. They provide soft, even light and, if large enough, can make a ceiling seem higher.

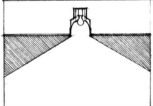

Wide spread beam provided by general service bulb and open reflector can be used for general lighting. More fixtures and wattage are required than with surface mounted or suspended fixtures.

Medium spread beam provided by reflector flood lamp can be used to illuminate table tops and work surfaces, or to light a specific area within a room.

Narrow spread beam provided by a reflector spot lamp in a deep reflector cone can be used for accent lighting. Avoid placing directly over a seating location.

TRACK LIGHTING

Track lighting consists of movable, adjustable incandescent spotlights or floodlights mounted on a track. Although usually mounted on the ceiling, track lights can also be mounted on a wall over a work counter or behind a bed.

The electrified track can be fed by a cord plugged into an existing receptacle, or be mounted to an existing ceiling outlet.

For illuminating walls up to 12' high with wall washer units, mount the track 2' to 4' away from the wall.

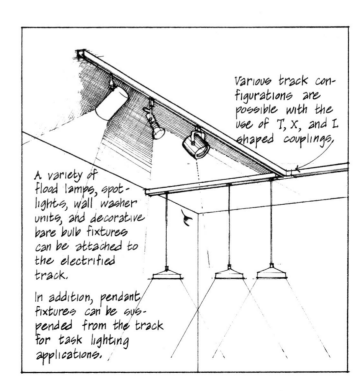

Various track configurations are possible with the use of T, X, and I shaped couplings.

A variety of flood lamps, spotlights, wall washer units, and decorative bare bulb fixtures can be attached to the electrified track.

In addition, pendant fixtures can be suspended from the track for task lighting applications.

# LIGHT FIXTURES

*(CONTINUED FROM PREVIOUS PAGE.)*

BUILT-IN LIGHT FIXTURES

Built-in fixtures - cove, cornice and valance lighting - are integrated into the walls and ceiling of a room and therefore require construction. They provide indirect, diffused light since the light sources (usually fluorescent tubes) are shielded from view and effectively wash adjacent wall or ceiling surfaces. Built-in fixtures are used for general illumination and to emphasize wall surfaces and treatments.

Cove lighting provides uplight, emphasizes the height of a ceiling, and can give a room a spacious feeling. Used at a lower height, behind built-in seating and in shelving units, it can illuminate walls and highlight displays.

Cornice lighting provides downlighting to illuminate walls and de-emphasize ceilings. It can also be used to balance the daylight from windows, highlight drapery and window treatments, and illuminate soffits. Small-scale versions of cornice lighting are especially useful for illuminating work surfaces and countertops that have shelves or cabinets above them.

Valance lighting provides both up and down lighting, washing wall or drapery surfaces as well as illuminating the ceiling surface. It can be used over windows and for general lighting in a room where ceiling fixtures are not practical or satisfactory.

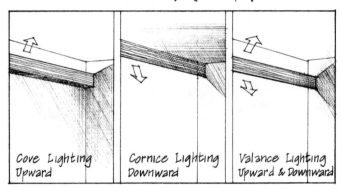

Cove Lighting
Upward

Cornice Lighting
Downward

Valance Lighting
Upward & Downward

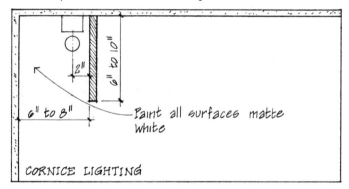

6" to 10"

2"

6" to 8"

Paint all surfaces matte white

CORNICE LIGHTING

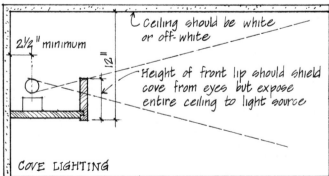

2½" minimum

12"

Ceiling should be white or off-white

Height of front lip should shield cove from eyes but expose entire ceiling to light source

COVE LIGHTING

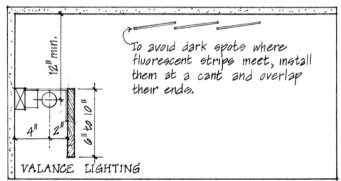

12" min.

6" to 10"

4"

2"

To avoid dark spots where fluorescent strips meet, install them at a cant and overlap their ends.

VALANCE LIGHTING

# LIGHT BULBS

Incandescent bulbs and fluorescent tubes remain the most common artificial light sources in the home. Incandescent bulbs are available in a variety of shapes, sizes and wattages. The bulbs may be frosted or have a milky-colored coating to enhance diffusion of the light and reduce glare. Some have silvered bowls to direct the light beam. Clear bulbs are used in fixtures with efficient reflectors, or as small, low-wattage decorative lamps.

Incandescent bulbs generate heat and are less efficient (ie. produce less light, measured in lumens, per watt) than fluorescent lamps. But they cost less, have an attractive, warm quality, and visually enhance forms and textures better than fluorescents.

Fluorescents provide three times as much light as incandescent bulbs for the same wattage, and since they operate at a cooler temperature, they can last up to 20 times longer. The linear form of the tubes also provides a greater light spread with less glare. This flat, diffused light quality, however, can be monotonous.

Many fluorescents have a bluish cast, while others will emphasize yellows and greens while killing pink tones. Many people therefore prefer deluxe warm white or natural white fluorescents for their warmer color rendition.

INCANDESCENT BULBS

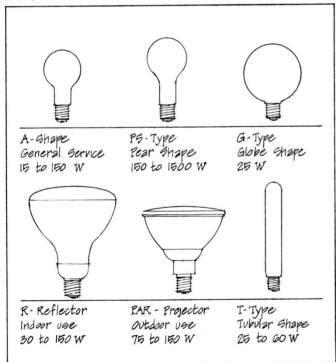

A-Shape
General Service
15 to 150 W

PS-Type
Pear Shape
150 to 1500 W

G-Type
Globe Shape
25 W

R- Reflector
Indoor use
30 to 150 W

PAR - Projector
Outdoor use
75 to 150 W

T-Type
Tubular Shape
25 to 60 W

FLUORESCENT TUBES

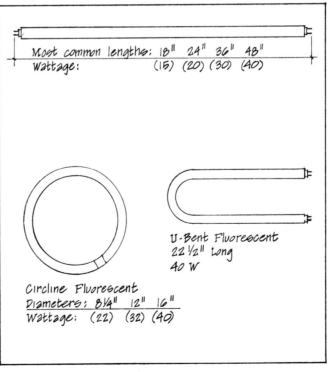

Most common lengths: 18" 24" 36" 48"
Wattage: (15) (20) (30) (40)

Circline Fluorescent
Diameters: 8¼" 12" 16"
Wattage: (22) (32) (40)

U-Bent Fluorescent
22 ½" Long
40 W

## COLOR · TEXTURE · PATTERN

The appearance of a room can be enhanced with color, texture and pattern. It can be renewed with a fresh coat of paint. It can be enlivened with patterns. Texture can soften and quiet a space. The following are a few basic considerations when treating a room's surfaces.

### IF A ROOM SEEMS SMALL

If a room seems small, limit your design palette. Select a dominant color or hue, and subordinate other design elements to it. Use light, neutral colors that recede to enhance a room's spaciousness. Avoid large patterns that visually crowd a space.

To visually raise a ceiling, paint it lighter than the walls, use low-scale furniture, and emphasize the verticals in the space.

To make a room seem wider, emphasize the horizontal elements of the short wall, and use a floor pattern whose stripes are parallel to the width. Also consider using mirrors along the long wall to create an illusion of greater width.

To enlarge the apparent floor area, paint or finish the baseboard in the same manner as the floor.

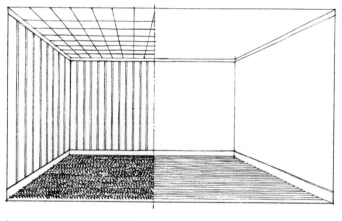

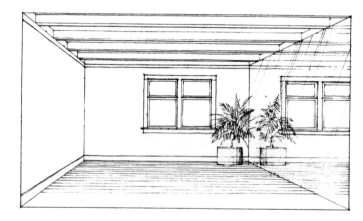

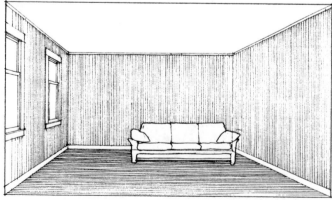

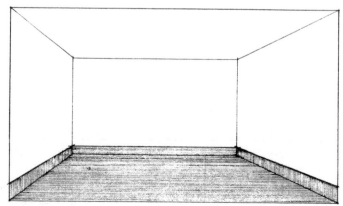

## IF A ROOM APPEARS CLUTTERED

If a room is cluttered or visually busy, simplify the color scheme, and eliminate distracting patterns and textures.

Emphasize the continuity of surfaces in the space. Paint details and distracting features the same color as the walls and ceiling. Stress the continuity of lines around the room with the height of furnishings and trimwork. Avoid too many jumps in height.

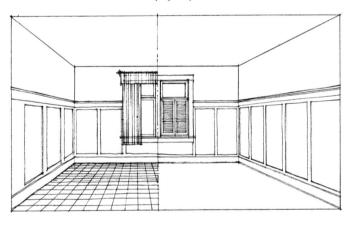

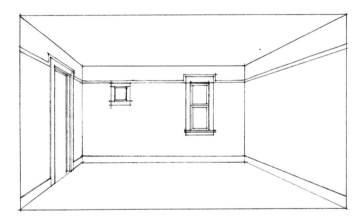

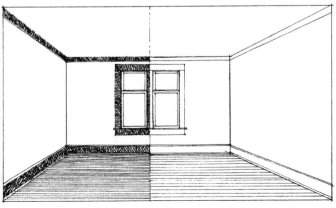

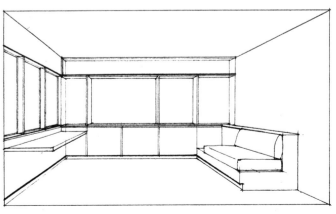

## MODIFYING SPACE

If you cannot make a room meet your needs by re-arranging its furnishings or renewing its surfaces and lighting, consider how alterations to its windows and doorways can make it work better for you. The following section discusses types of windows and doors, and basic considerations for their selection, installation or removal.

## ALTERING WINDOWS

Your desire to improve the daylighting of a room, or open it up further to a view or desirable breezes, may lead you to consider altering or adding windows in the room. Since these are not inexpensive tasks, first consider whether treatments or repairs of the existing windows can satisfy your needs.

Glare can be lessened by reducing the contrast between the window opening and the surrounding wall area, or by creating a deep, splayed opening with storage units on either side of the window. Glare from low, late afternoon sun can be controlled with awnings, shutters, or blinds.

Odd-shaped or mismatched windows can be unified with drapery treatments or integrated into a wall shelving system.

Deepening the window sill can create a display shelf, window seat, or small desk area.

Drafty windows can be repaired and weather-stripped, and their frames caulked.

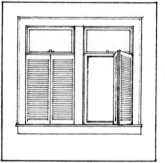
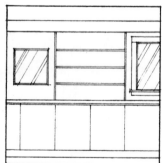

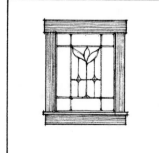

## PLANNING CONSIDERATIONS

When enlarging an existing window, or adding a new one, consider the following factors to help you decide the size, shape, style and placement of the new window or group of windows.

1. SUN

   Windows are sources of substantial heat loss and gain. While east and south-facing windows can take advantage of the sun's warmth in the winter, southwest and west-facing windows, if not properly shaded and ventilated, can overheat a space in the summer.

2. LIGHT

   To maximize the daylighting of a room, place windows near corners so that adjacent wall surfaces are washed with light. Whenever possible, provide windows on at least two walls of a room for balanced daylighting.

3. VIEW

   Windows should be placed to frame views. Their sill and head heights should not cut off a view for those sitting or standing in the room. Neither should a heavy mullion or framing member bisect a view.

   A new window should not sacrifice the degree of privacy desired for the room.

4. APPEARANCE

   Consider how new or altered windows will affect the exterior appearance of your house. New windows should have a similar scale and proportion to that of the existing windows. Their placement should not disrupt the existing pattern and composition.

5. CONSTRUCTION

   A window opening whose width is increased may require a larger, more substantial header or lintel to carry the load of the floor or roof above the opening.

   Try to salvage the exterior and interior trim removed during the alteration so that they can be reused. Otherwise, the new trim, if necessary, should match the existing trim.

6. WIND

   A window should open up to desirable breezes for ventilation in warm weather. Avoid exposing or facing windows to cold, winter winds.

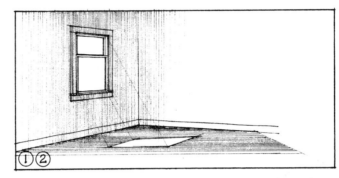

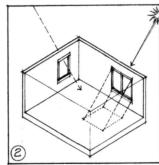

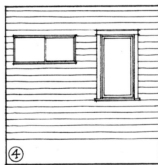
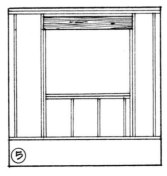
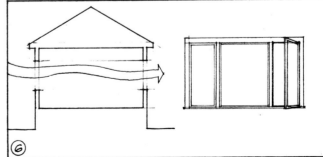

# WINDOWS

Once you have decided what general size and shape window you need, and where it should be located, a specific make of window must be selected that satisfies your design criteria and budget. This should be done prior to preparing the rough opening so that the required size of the opening can be verified.

Residential windows are manufactured units, fully-assembled in the factory. They usually arrive complete with frame, sash, glazing and hardware. In addition to the nationally-known brands, there may be available regional makes that offer the same features at less cost.

As you shop around, check for the following features:

1. Available sizes and proportions.
2. Frame material, strength, profile, and available finishes.
3. Type of operation, quality of hardware, and ease of use.
4. Type and insulation-value of glazing.
5. Quality of weather-stripping and overall weathertightness.

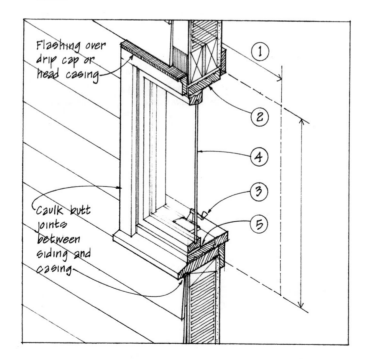

Flashing over drip cap or head casing

Caulk butt joints between siding and casing

## FRAMES

Residential window frames are either of wood or metal. Wood frames are warm and handsome in appearance, have good insulation value, and are generally weathertight. They can be factory-finished (painted, stained, or primed for painting), but they require a moderate amount of maintenance. To minimize the need for maintenance, some manufactured wood frames are clad with vinyl or bonded to acrylic-coated aluminum sections that require no painting. These linings also help eliminate the sticking of windows whose frames might swell when wet.

Metal frames require no painting. Unlike wood, they do not swell when wet. On the other hand, they lack the warm appearance of wood and offer little resistance to heat transfer. Some metal frames are now made with a thermal break that inhibits the transfer of heat through the metal frame. Metal frames can be of aluminum, steel, or stainless steel. They may be left the natural color of the metal, be anodized or vinyl-coated, or be treated to resist corrosion.

## GLAZING

Most windows are available with single glazing (a single sheet of glass) or with insulating glass (two sheets of glass, separated by a hermetically-sealed air space). Although more expensive, insulating glass does offer greater resistance to heat transfer. But an insulating glass window will not come close to approximating the insulating value of a well-insulated wall section. Compare the 2.75 R-value of an insulating glass window with the 19 R-value of an insulated wall.

In very cold climates, you might consider triple glazing, where a storm sash is installed in addition to the insulating glass sash. Carefully weigh the additional cost against the potential savings in heating fuel and the added comfort gained.

## WEATHER TIGHTNESS

Perhaps more important than the insulating value (R-value) of a window is its weathertightness. Air can leak around a closed sash when driven by wind and the normal heat flow due to the difference between inside and outside air temperatures. This leakage of air can lose more heat than the amount conserved with an insulating glass window. The air infiltration factor, measured in cubic-feet-per-minute (CFM), is a function of how well made a window is, and how effectively it is weather-stripped. The industry standard is 0.5 CFM.

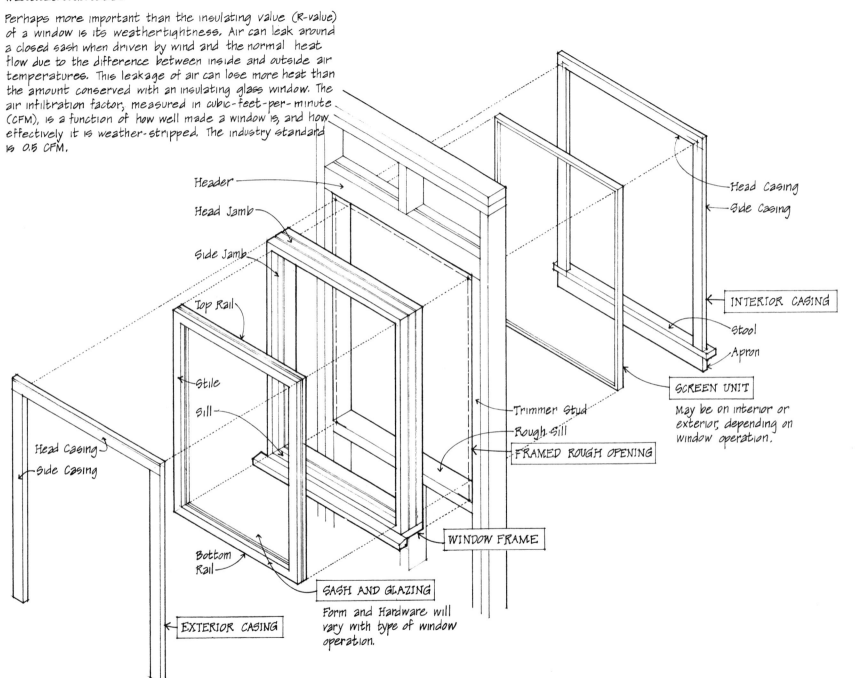

Header

Head Jamb

Side Jamb

Top Rail

Stile

Sill

Head Casing

Side Casing

Bottom Rail

EXTERIOR CASING

SASH AND GLAZING

Form and Hardware will vary with type of window operation.

WINDOW FRAME

FRAMED ROUGH OPENING

Trimmer Stud

Rough Sill

SCREEN UNIT

May be on interior or exterior, depending on window operation.

INTERIOR CASING

Stool

Apron

Head Casing

Side Casing

# WINDOW OPERATION

Windows are usually typed according to how they open. Fixed windows do not open at all and offer the greatest degree of weathertightness. Windows that do open – for ventilation, cleaning and emergency exit from a room – have operating sashes that slide, swing or pivot. The following are the main types of operating windows.

## SIZES

Each manufacturer has standard, modular or coordinated sizes for its own window units. Unfortunately, there are no industry-wide standards for sizes as there are for doors. Custom sizes are usually available at extra cost.

## 1. DOUBLE-HUNG WINDOWS

Double-hung windows have sashes that slide vertically. The sashes are held in position by a friction fit with the frame or by a counter-balancing device. 50% of the window area can be opened.

Single-hung windows are similar except that one sash is fixed.

## 2. SLIDING WINDOWS

Sliding windows consist of two sashes (one fixed, one sliding or both sliding) or three sashes (central one fixed). The operating sashes slide horizontally in tracks. A spring action may be supplied so that the sashes can be removed for cleaning. 50% to 66% of the window area can be opened.

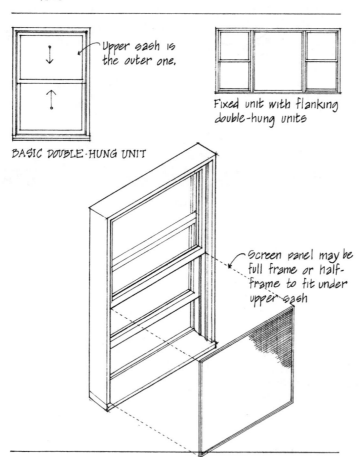

Upper sash is the outer one.

Fixed unit with flanking double-hung units

BASIC DOUBLE-HUNG UNIT

Screen panel may be full frame or half-frame to fit under upper sash

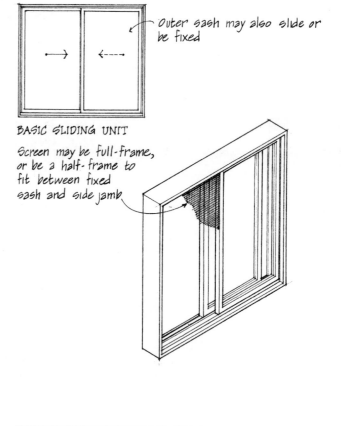

Outer sash may also slide or be fixed

BASIC SLIDING UNIT

Screen may be full-frame, or be a half-frame to fit between fixed sash and side jamb

## PROPORTIONS

Since operating sashes usually swing or slide along their longer dimension, the proportion of a window unit is related to how it operates. Casement or double-hung windows usually have square or vertical proportions, while awning and sliding windows have horizontal proportions.

## 3. CASEMENT WINDOWS

Casement windows have one or two operating sashes that are side-hinged and swing outward. Many casement windows are operated with a crank mechanism, although small casements may have a simple friction hinge. The direction of swing can direct incoming air flow or ventilation which is available through almost the entire area of the window.

## 4. AWNING AND HOPPER WINDOWS

These are similar to casement windows except that their sashes are hinged at the top (awnings) or at the bottom (hoppers). They can be stacked vertically or be combined with fixed window units. Unlike casements and hoppers, awning windows can provide some rain protection when opened.

## 5. JALOUSIE WINDOWS

Jalousie windows consist of horizontal slats that operate similarly to an awning window. The slats or louvers may be opaque or translucent. Since they cannot be sealed tightly, jalousie windows are more often used in warm climates where the control of light and ventilation is required along with visual privacy.

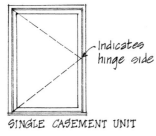

— Indicates hinge side

SINGLE CASEMENT UNIT

PAIR OF CASEMENTS

Hinged sash meet at a vertical joining mullion

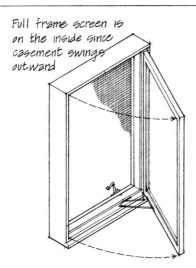

Full frame screen is on the inside since casement swings outward

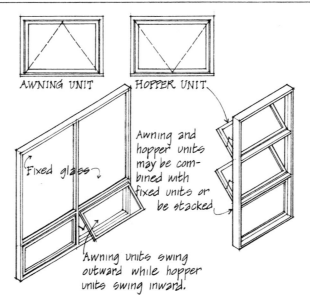

AWNING UNIT     HOPPER UNIT

Fixed glass

Awning and hopper units may be combined with fixed units or be stacked

Awning units swing outward while hopper units swing inward.

# PREPARING WINDOW OPENINGS

To install a new window in a room, an opening must be prepared and framed in the existing wall. To enlarge a window, the existing trim and window unit must be carefully removed before preparing the larger opening.

On the interior wall surface, mark the rough location of the new opening. Check if any plumbing or heating lines run through the location by inspecting the wall from the basement or crawl space. It is often easier to move the window location than to re-route these pipes or ductwork. Electrical wiring, however, is relatively easy to relocate if necessary.

Locate the studs on either side of the new opening, and cut through the wall material on the inner edge of each stud from floor to ceiling. Remove the baseboard and any wall trim before cutting. Use a saber or circular saw set to the thickness of the wall material. Do not cut through the sole plate.

> IMPORTANT: Before doing any cutting, disconnect any electricity to the area.

Remove the studs in the new opening by cutting them at their centers and carefully prying them from the exterior wall sheathing. If the new opening is 3½ feet or wider, temporary support for the ceiling or roof above should be provided before removing any studs in a bearing wall.

Install new outer studs and trimmer studs to frame the sides of the new opening. The required width of the opening is determined by the width of the window unit plus about a ½" for clearance. The height of the trimmer stud that supports the header over the opening is determined by the height of the window unit off the floor plus about a ½" for clearance. Verify the required rough opening with the window manufacturer.

Build and install the required header over the opening. (See pg. 221 for header sizes and framing.) Fit cripple studs between the top of the header and the top plate at each point a stud was removed.

Toenail a sill at the bottom of the opening, again checking the required rough opening for the window unit you are installing. Install cripple studs between the bottom of the sill and the sole plate at each point a stud was removed.

Mark rough opening required for new window.

Remove baseboard and any other wall trim.

Remove wall finish to inner face of studs on either side of rough opening.

Remove studs without damaging exterior sheathing.

Save any insulation for reuse.

Top Plate

Existing Studs

Wall Finish

Exterior Sheathing

Sole Plate

Existing Floor

**INTERIOR VIEW OF NEW OPENING**

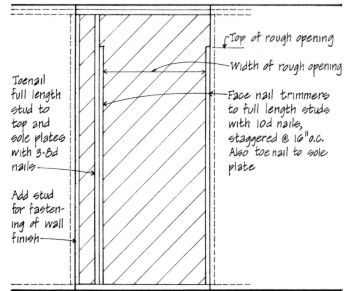

Toenail full length stud to top and sole plates with 3-8d nails.

Add stud for fastening of wall finish.

Top of rough opening

Width of rough opening

Face nail trimmers to full length studs with 10d nails, staggered @ 16"o.c. Also toenail to sole plate

Using pilot holes drilled at the corners of the framed opening to get started, cut through the exterior sheathing and siding material. This can be done from either the inside or the outside.

If the replacement or new window unit has exterior casing trim that projects beyond the window frame to butt up against bevel or lap siding, the siding material must be cut back. The amount of this cutback can be determined by placing the window frame temporarily in the opening and marking the siding around the casing trim.

If you are using a window unit that has projecting fins that slip in between the exterior sheathing and siding material - as in new construction - the siding material will have to be removed around the opening and be replaced after the window is installed.

If the window unit does not have projecting fins, it is a good practice, when the exterior is horizontal siding, to slip a strip of building paper or asphalt felt between the siding and the sheathing around the window opening to seal the joint against wind and rain.

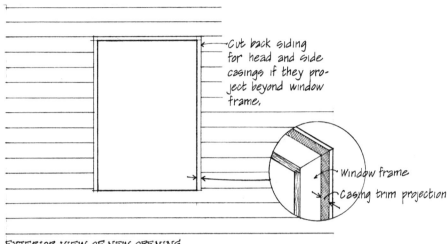

Cut back siding for head and side casings if they project beyond window frame.

Window frame

Casing trim projection

EXTERIOR VIEW OF NEW OPENING

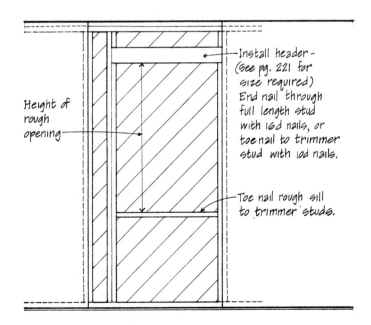

Height of rough opening

Install header - (see pg. 221 for size required) End nail through full length stud with 16d nails, or toe nail to trimmer stud with 10d nails.

Toe nail rough sill to trimmer studs.

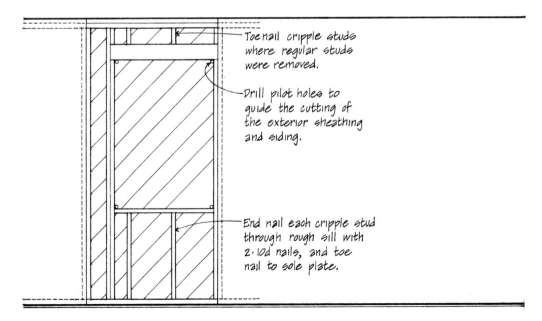

Toe nail cripple studs where regular studs were removed.

Drill pilot holes to guide the cutting of the exterior sheathing and siding.

End nail each cripple stud through rough sill with 2·10d nails, and toe nail to sole plate.

# 2

## WINDOW INSTALLATION

Before installing a window unit, ensure that the rough framed opening is the proper size and is both level and plumb. The rough opening, as specified by the window manufacturer, allows space around the window frame for leveling and shimming the unit.

Be aware of exactly where within the wall thickness the window unit will fit. If your exterior wall is framed with 2"x6"s, the window unit, made for a 2"x4" stud wall, may be placed flush with the exterior sheathing and require deeper sill and jambs. Use jamb extensions if necessary.

After lifting the window unit into place, check its levelness. If the window unit is not level, use shims (pieces of wood shingles) to level it. When leveled and plumbed, tack the unit temporarily in place. Check that the window frame is square and the sash operates smoothly.

Nail the window into place with aluminum or galvanized casing nails at about 16" o.c. Be sure to nail through the shim material. Use nails long enough to penetrate well into the wall frame.

Fill any gaps around the window with insulation before patching and repairing the interior wall finish.

## WINDOW TRIM

Window trim serves the purpose of concealing and finishing the joint between the window frame and the surrounding wall finish. It also helps to seal the gap against air infiltration.

Although there may be exceptions, the style of window trim generally matches the trim around interior door frames. In new construction, there are a variety of trim styles to suit your taste.

In remodeling work, the trim found in older houses will vary considerably with the age, style, and quality of the house. Since the original trim may no longer be available, remove existing pieces carefully when altering windows and doors so that they can be re-used. Small millwork shops can provide custom trim to match your existing trim but it is very expensive. Some specialty millwork supply firms do provide old-style trim material.

Window units are generally installed from the outside.

If the window unit comes with diagonal bracing to keep the frame square, do not remove it until the unit has been secured.

If not already primed, prime or seal the frame before installation.

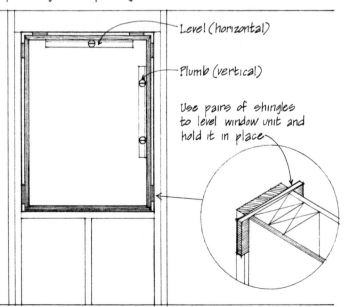

Level (horizontal)

Plumb (vertical)

Use pairs of shingles to level window unit and hold it in place

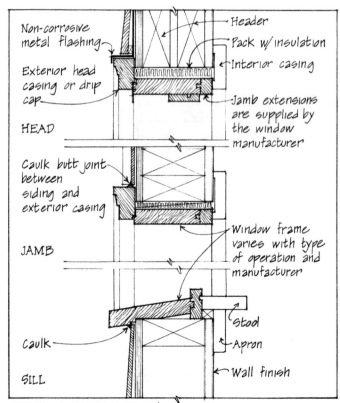

Non-corrosive metal flashing

Exterior head casing or drip cap

HEAD

Caulk butt joint between siding and exterior casing

JAMB

Caulk

SILL

Header

Pack w/ insulation

Interior casing

Jamb extensions are supplied by the window manufacturer

Window frame varies with type of operation and manufacturer

Stool

Apron

Wall finish

TYPICAL WINDOW DETAILS

The window stool, the bottom horizontal trim that over-laps the sill and extends beyond the side casing, is installed first. It is notched to fit around the edge of the wall finish.

The side and head casing members are installed next. They are usually set back from the face of the jambs from 1/8" to 3/16". If the head and side casing trim have the same molding shape, they must meet at a mitered joint. If the casing material is square-edged, a butt joint can be used.

The apron, the trim piece that finishes the joint between the stool and the wall finish below, is installed last. Its length is equal to the distance between the outer edges of the side casing.

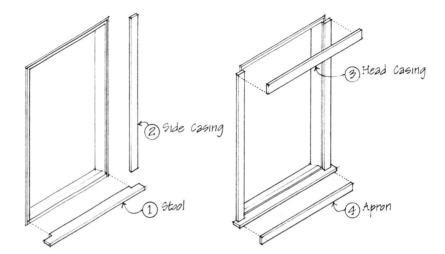

③ Head Casing

② Side Casing

① Stool

④ Apron

SEQUENCE FOR APPLICATION OF INERIOR CASING

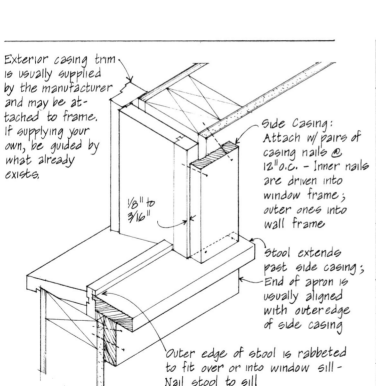

Exterior casing trim is usually supplied by the manufacturer and may be attached to frame. If supplying your own, be guided by what already exists.

1/8" to 3/16"

Side Casing: Attach w/ pairs of casing nails @ 12"o.c. - Inner nails are driven into window frame; outer ones into wall frame

Stool extends past side casing; End of apron is usually aligned with outer edge of side casing

Outer edge of stool is rabbeted to fit over or into window sill - Nail stool to sill

STOOL AND APRON DETAIL

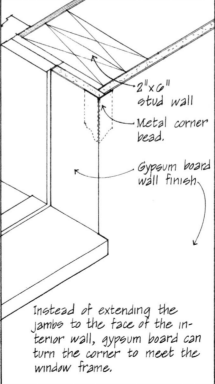

2"x 6" stud wall

Metal corner bead.

Gypsum board wall finish.

Instead of extending the jambs to the face of the interior wall, gypsum board can turn the corner to meet the window frame.

WINDOW IN A DEEP WALL

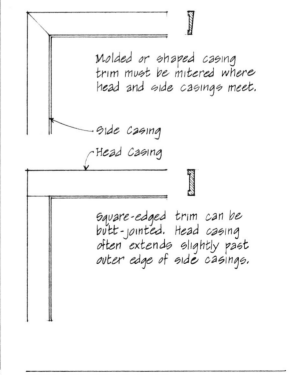

Molded or shaped casing trim must be mitered where head and side casings meet.

Side Casing

Head Casing

Square-edged trim can be butt-jointed. Head casing often extends slightly past outer edge of side casings.

HEAD AND SIDE CASINGS

## ALTERING DOORWAYS

If a doorway is creating a traffic path through a room and disrupting its layout and activities, you may be considering closing up the doorway and cutting in a new one. If a room has too many entrances and not enough traffic-free area or wall space, you may be considering eliminating one or more of the doorways. When planning to remove, move or add doorways in your remodeling or addition, consideration should be given to:

1. The door location.
2. The door size needed.
3. The door operation.
4. The frequency of use.
5. Requirements for weathertightness, acoustical privacy and ventilation.

## PLANNING CONSIDERATIONS

1. LOCATION

The placement of a doorway affects our pattern of movement within a room. A door that is centered along a wall visually divides the wall in half and isolates the corner areas that flank the doorway. A door at the corner of a room will encourage movement along the side of the room and leave the central area free for furnishings and activities. If a doorway is offset from a corner, the wall area between the doorway and the corner should be usable space.

2. SIZE

Doorways in a home should be large enough to permit easy access and allow for the movement of furnishings and equipment. The standard door height is 6'-8". Entrance doors and sliding glass doors may be 7'-0" or 8'-0" high.

Exterior doors are usually at least 3'-0" wide; bedroom doors are 2'-8" or 2'-6" wide; bathroom doors, 2'-6" or 2'-4" wide. Closet doors, such as sliding or bi-fold doors, are wider, 3'-0" to 12'-0", to permit access into as much of the storage space as possible.

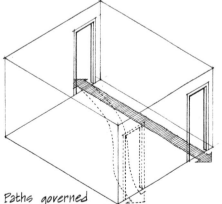

Keep doorways to a minimum. If other factors permit, locate doorways close to each other and keep traffic paths short and direct.

Paths governed by doorways should not pass through and disrupt a room's quiet or work areas.

DOOR LOCATIONS

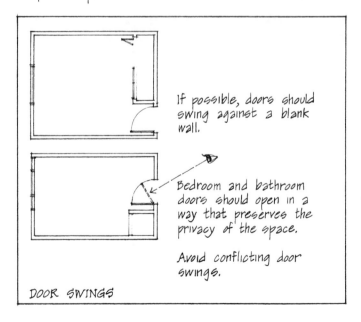

If possible, doors should swing against a blank wall.

Bedroom and bathroom doors should open in a way that preserves the privacy of the space.

Avoid conflicting door swings.

DOOR SWINGS

## 3. OPERATION

The most common type of door operation is, of course, the swinging door. It is the most natural to use, and is durable enough for high-frequency use. Consideration should be given to how the direction of swing affects how you enter a room, the use of the space, and the furniture layout. Exterior doors generally swing in while storm or screen doors swing out. Interior doors swing in the direction of entry into a room, and against a blank wall if possible.

If a door swing interferes with the furniture placement in a room, or with other door swings, a sliding or pocket door can be used. Pocket doors are particularly appropriate for doorways that are kept open most of the time since they have a clean, finished appearance when open.

By-pass sliding and bi-fold doors are used to close the wide openings of closet and storage spaces. If floor space is at a premium, sliding doors are preferred because they do not take up any of the space they open on to. Bi-fold doors, however, provide more access than do sliding doors, and take up only a minimal amount of floor space.

## 4. SPECIAL REQUIREMENTS

How much use a door will have, and requirements for weathertightness, acoustical privacy, and ventilation, affect the type of door construction and hardware used.

Since exterior doors are exposed to weather, they are usually of solid-core wood construction. Metal-clad doors, with a rigid insulation core, are also used for their high insulation value. Durable weather-stripping, in either case, is important to make exterior doors weathertight.

If a high degree of acoustical privacy is desired, solid-core wood doors with weather-stripping are used. Most interior doors, however, are of hollow-core construction. For the ventilation of rooms and storage spaces, louvered doors or doors with louvered panels are used.

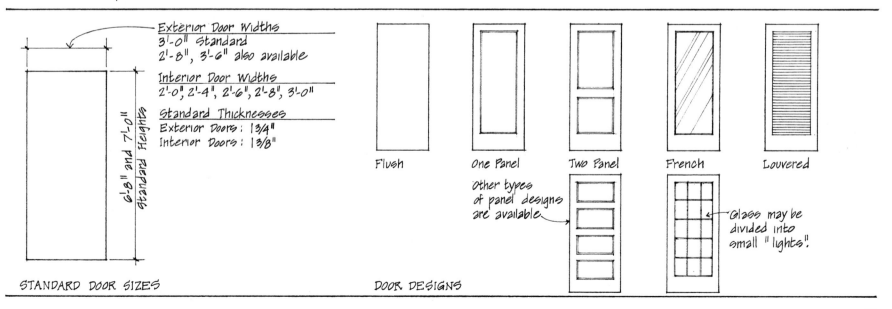

**Exterior Door Widths**
3'-0" Standard
2'-8", 3'-6" also available

**Interior Door Widths**
2'-0", 2'-4", 2'-6", 2'-8", 3'-0"

**Standard Thicknesses**
Exterior Doors: 1 3/4"
Interior Doors: 1 3/8"

6'-8" and 7'-0" Standard Heights

STANDARD DOOR SIZES

DOOR DESIGNS

Flush     One Panel     Two Panel     French     Louvered

Other types of panel designs are available.

Glass may be divided into small "lights".

## DOOR TYPES

Doors may be classified according to:

1. Type of operation.
2. Material and type of construction.
3. Surface appearance and design.
   *(See previous page)*

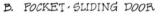

## 1. TYPES OF OPERATION

**A. SWINGING DOOR**
- Door is hinged on the side jamb
- Suitable for interior or exterior use
- Most convenient for entry and passage
- Most effective for isolating sound and for weathertightness
- Requires space for swing

**B. POCKET-SLIDING DOOR**
- Door is hung on a track, and slides into a pocket within the width of the wall
- Used where normal door swing would in interfere with use of space
- Doorway has a finished appearance when door is fully recessed

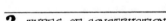
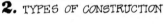

## 2. TYPES OF CONSTRUCTION

Doors, like windows, are factory-manufactured units. Many come "pre-hung", pre-assembled with door frame, hinges, and other necessary hardware.

Most doors for residential use are of wood, of either flush or panel construction. Flush doors have perfectly flat faces and either solid or hollow cores.

Flush solid-core doors have an interior construction of wood blocking or particle board, and are faced with two plies of veneer. They are used primarily as exterior doors or where increased fire-resistance, sound isolation, or dimensional stability is required.

Flush hollow-core doors have an interior of honeycombed wood strips or corrugation, and are faced with plywood and veneer. Hollow-core doors, much lighter than solid-core doors, are suitable for interior use only. They can be used as hinged or pocket-sliding doors.

For vision or ventilation requirements, glass or louvered inserts for flush doors are available.

Premium-grade veneers are used for natural, transparent finishes, while good or sound grades are for stain or paint finishes.

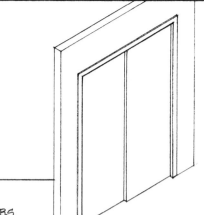

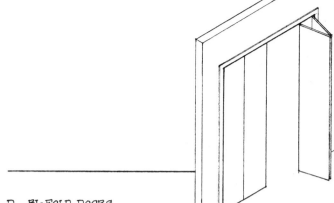

**C. BY-PASS SLIDING DOORS**
- Doors are hung from and slide along an overhead track (with floor guides), or roll along a floor-mounted track (with an overhead guide track).
- Used indoors primarily for screening of closet and storage spaces.
- Sliding glass doors are used for passage to outdoor spaces.

**D. BI-FOLD DOORS**
- Consists of hinged door panels that slide of an overhead track.
- Primarily for interior use as a visual screen to close off closet and storage spaces.

Wood panel doors consist of an exposed, supporting framework of vertical (stile) and horizontal (rail) members that hold solid wood or plywood panels. These filler panels can also be glazed if vision through the door is desired.

Panel doors may have one or more panels, with various trim and panel designs.

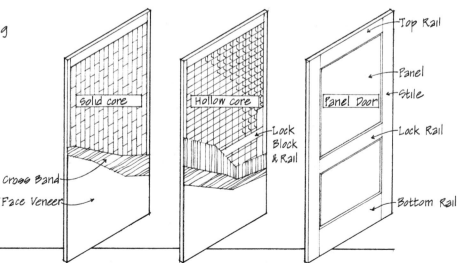

# PREPARING DOOR OPENINGS

The rough opening for a new doorway is prepared in a manner similar to cutting a window opening in an existing wall. (See pg. 76.) In addition to the studs that stand in the way of the new opening, however, the sole plate is also cut and removed after the rough opening is framed.

The width of the rough opening is equal to the door width plus 2½" (for the thickness of the side jambs and a ½" clearance on each side). The height of the rough opening is equal to the door height plus 2½" (for the thickness of the head jamb, a ½" top clearance, the finish flooring, and the threshold, if any). If you are using a pre-hung door assembly, simply add a ½" around the door frame for top and side clearance.

If you are installing a special entrance door unit, or one with sidelights, verify the rough opening required with the door manufacturer.

## EXTERIOR DOORS

Any bevel or horizontal lap siding will have to be cut back to accommodate the exterior casing trim that overlaps the door frame and sheathing joint and butts up against the siding.

Over the doorway, a strip of aluminum or galvanized metal flashing must be slipped behind the siding material and shaped to fit over the top casing trim.

When the floor joists are parallel to the sill, a header and short support members are necessary to support the door sill.

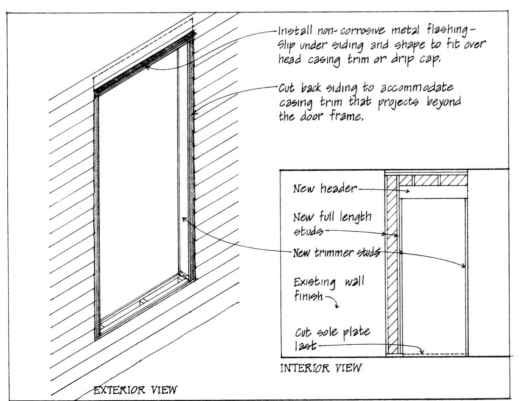

Install non-corrosive metal flashing—slip under siding and shape to fit over head casing trim or drip cap.

Cut back siding to accommodate casing trim that projects beyond the door frame.

New header

New full length studs

New trimmer studs

Existing wall finish

Cut sole plate last

INTERIOR VIEW

EXTERIOR VIEW

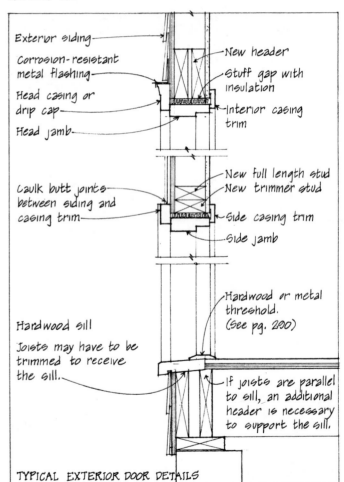

Exterior siding

Corrosion-resistant metal flashing

Head casing or drip cap

Head jamb

New header

Stuff gap with insulation

Interior casing trim

Caulk butt joints between siding and casing trim

New full length stud

New trimmer stud

Side casing trim

Side jamb

Hardwood sill

Joists may have to be trimmed to receive the sill.

Hardwood or metal threshold. (See pg. 200)

If joists are parallel to sill, an additional header is necessary to support the sill.

TYPICAL EXTERIOR DOOR DETAILS

## INTERIOR DOORS

Before cutting away the interior wall finish material, carefully remove the baseboard (and any casing trim for a door that is being moved) so that it can be re-used.

## LARGE OPENINGS

For exterior sliding glass doors, and for interior sliding, bi-fold, and pocket doors, larger openings spanned by stronger headers are required. When these wide openings are cut into bearing walls, the ceiling construction must be supported with bracing while the opening is being built. (See pg. 221 for header sizes and framing door openings in new partitions.)

IMPORTANT: Before doing any cutting, disconnect any electricity to the area.

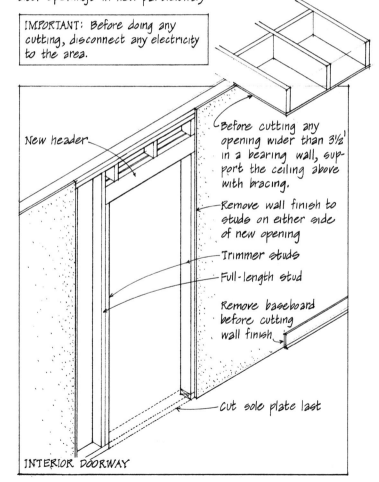

New header

Before cutting any opening wider than 3½' in a bearing wall, support the ceiling above with bracing.

Remove wall finish to studs on either side of new opening

Trimmer studs

Full-length stud

Remove baseboard before cutting wall finish

Cut sole plate last

INTERIOR DOORWAY

## CLOSING OPENINGS

To close up a doorway, remove the door from its hinges and pry off the casing trim around the doorway. Then use a hacksaw blade to cut through the nails that hold the door-frame in place. Remove the frame. If done carefully, the frame can be re-used.

Nail 2"x4" studs to both sides of the opening, and add 2"x4"s along the top and bottom as well. Toenail an additional stud in the center of the opening.

Apply the wall surfacing material to match the existing wall finish, and install the baseboard.

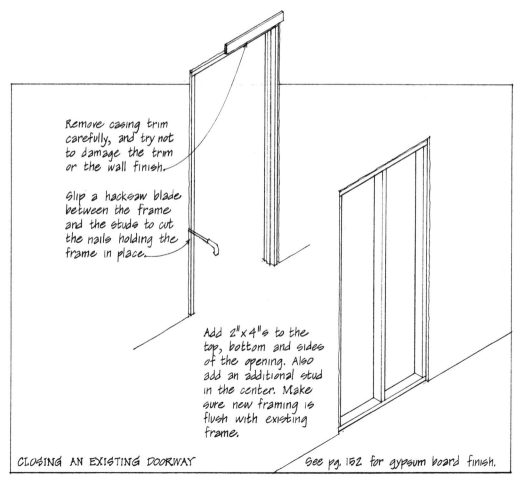

Remove casing trim carefully, and try not to damage the trim or the wall finish.

Slip a hacksaw blade between the frame and the studs to cut the nails holding the frame in place.

Add 2"x4"s to the top, bottom and sides of the opening. Also add an additional stud in the center. Make sure new framing is flush with existing frame.

CLOSING AN EXISTING DOORWAY

See pg. 152 for gypsum board finish.

# DOOR FRAMES

The frame for a swinging door consists of head and side jambs, with either integral or applied stops against which the door closes. The jambs are usually installed after the wall finish has been repaired, or in the case of new construction, after the wall finish has been applied.

Jambs can be fabricated from stock lumber, or purchased in pre-cut sets. They are also available pre-assembled, complete with stops and a pre-hung door. Pre-hung door assemblies may cost more, but they save you time and labor; are easy to install, and assure an accurate fit.

Some pre-hung door assemblies have casing trim already attached to one side of the door frame. Others have casing trim attached to both sides of a split jamb, each half being fitted into the opening from either side of the wall.

The jambs should be as wide as the overall wall thickness so that the casing trim can overlap the joint between the jambs and the surrounding wall finish.

To carry the weight of the door, exterior door frames should be at least 1⅛" thick (5/4" stock). To minimize air infiltration, the jambs should be rabbeted to form integral stops. The exterior casing trim should overlap the gap between the jambs and the exterior sheathing, and fit tightly. The gap itself should be stuffed with insulation.

The foot of an exterior doorway has a sill that is level with the finish floor and sloped outward to shed water. It may have an integral threshold that overlaps the finish floor, or have a wood or metal threshold applied separately over the floor and sill joint. Any wood used should be a hardwood to withstand the wear of traffic. Some metal thresholds have weather-seals to seal the gap at the door bottom. (See pg. 290.)

Thresholds are also required at interior doorways where a change of flooring height or material occurs.

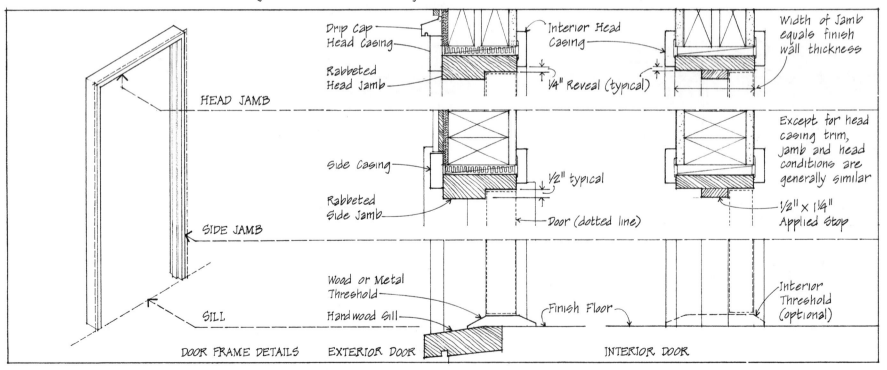

DOOR FRAME DETAILS          EXTERIOR DOOR                    INTERIOR DOOR

PRE·HUNG DOOR ASSEMBLIES

To install a pre-hung door assembly, set it into the pre-pared opening. Check to ensure that 1/16"-1/8" clearance between the door and jambs is evenly maintained with cardboard or wood strips. Use wood shims, or metal clips that may be supplied with the door kit, to align and level the unit. Use a level to make sure the side jambs are plumb. Check that the head jamb is square with the side jambs.

Shims should be inserted in two places along the top, and at least three places along each side. On the hinge side, shim just below each hinge and at the middle.

Once the door and frame assembly is properly aligned, nail the jambs through the shims into the rough wall frame. Use pairs of 8d casing or finishing nails. Additional nailing should be done at 12" o.c.

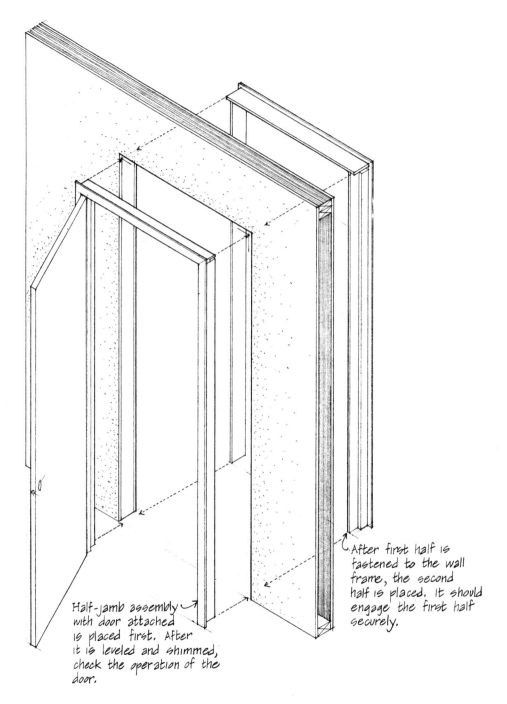

After first half is fastened to the wall frame, the second half is placed. It should engage the first half securely.

Half-jamb assembly with door attached is placed first. After it is leveled and shimmed, check the operation of the door.

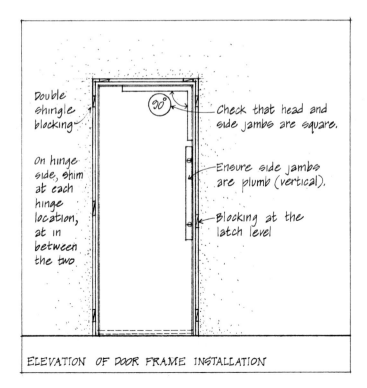

Double shingle blocking

On hinge side, shim at each hinge location, at in between the two

Check that head and side jambs are square.

Ensure side jambs are plumb (vertical).

Blocking at the latch level

ELEVATION OF DOOR FRAME INSTALLATION

## DOOR FRAMES

If you cannot use a pre-hung door assembly, you can re-use the frame from a doorway that has been closed up or fabricate your own.

Standard jambs are made from nominal 1" material. They are as wide as the overall thickness of the wall. Some jambs are kerfed or grooved to minimize their tendency to cup or warp. Stops, 1/2" thick and 1 1/2" to 2 1/4" wide, are not set until after the door is hung.

The head and side jambs can meet at a simple butt joint and be fastened with three 8d casing or finishing nails. For tighter joints, the side jambs can be dadoed or notched to receive the head jamb.

The door frame is installed in a manner similar to setting a pre-hung door assembly. Set the door frame in the opening. Place a 1"x6" spreader, equal to the length of the head jamb, between the side jambs at floor level. Center the door frame and secure it with double-shingle wedges at the top and bottom of the side jambs. On the latch side, place additional wedges at the latch level and in between the head jamb and the latch. On the hinge side, place additional wedges at the hinge locations and one set in between.

Use a level to ensure the side jambs are plumb and the frame is square. Adjust the wedges as necessary. When the frame is level and square, secure it with two 8d finishing nails at each wedged area. Locate one of each pair of nails so that the door stop will conceal it.

To make the job of setting the door frame in place easier, you can also pre-hang the door first so that it serves as a jig for the frame.

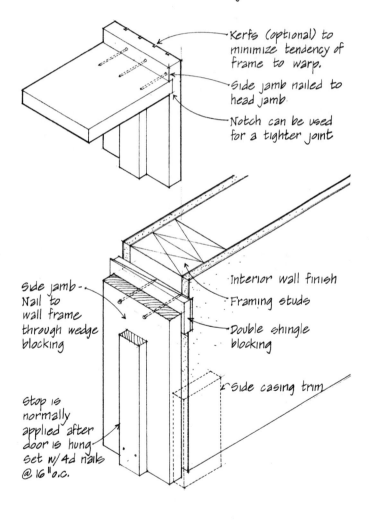

Kerfs (optional) to minimize tendency of frame to warp.

Side jamb nailed to head jamb.

Notch can be used for a tighter joint

Side jamb - Nail to wall frame through wedge blocking

Interior wall finish

Framing studs

Double shingle blocking

Side casing trim

Stop is normally applied after door is hung. Set w/ 4d nails @ 16" o.c.

DOOR FRAME AND INSTALLATION

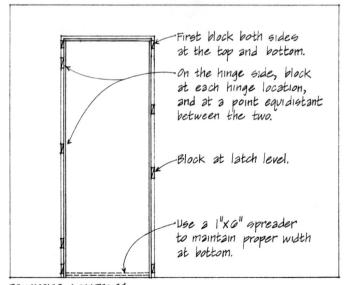

First block both sides at the top and bottom.

On the hinge side, block at each hinge location, and at a point equidistant between the two.

Block at latch level.

Use a 1"x6" spreader to maintain proper width at bottom.

BLOCKING LOCATIONS

## DOOR TRIM

Casings are the edge trim material around interior doorways and the room sides of exterior doors and windows. Door casing trim covers the gap between the door frame and the surrounding wall finish. It also helps to secure the door frame to the wall frame and make the jambs more rigid.

Depending on their width and finish, door casings visually set off a doorway from the wall in which it is set. They can be simple or ornate, thin or heavy. The simplest treatment consists of two square-edged side casings that butt up against a head casing. If the profiles of the head and side casings are irregular, the corner joints where they meet must be mitered.

The thickness of casings may vary from 1/2" to 3/4", but they should be at least as thick as the baseboard for which the side casings act as stops.

Door casings are normally set back from the face of the jambs 3/16" or 1/4". Use 4d or 6d finishing nails to fasten the casings to the jambs, and 6d or 8d finishing nails to fasten the outer edge of the casings to the studs. Space each pair of nails about 16" apart.

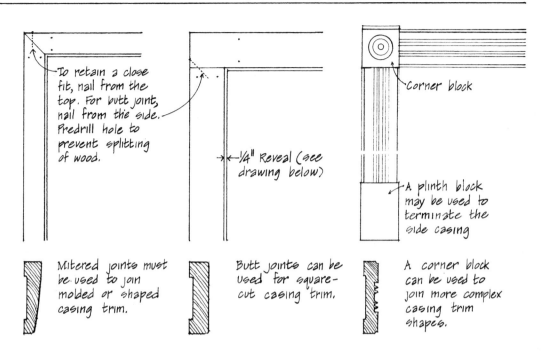

To retain a close fit, nail from the top. For butt joint, nail from the side. Predrill hole to prevent splitting of wood.

1/4" Reveal (see drawing below)

Corner block

A plinth block may be used to terminate the side casing

Mitered joints must be used to join molded or shaped casing trim.

Butt joints can be used for square-cut casing trim.

A corner block can be used to join more complex casing trim shapes.

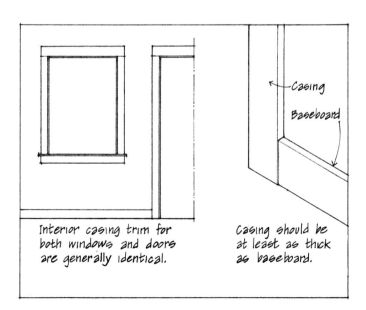

Casing

Baseboard

Interior casing trim for both windows and doors are generally identical.

Casing should be at least as thick as baseboard.

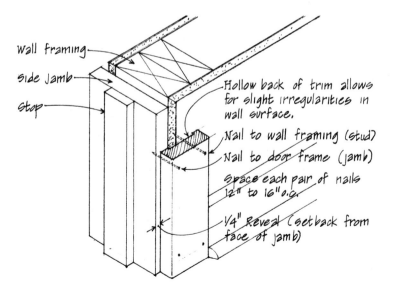

Wall framing

Side Jamb

Stop

Hollow back of trim allows for slight irregularities in wall surface.

Nail to wall framing (stud)

Nail to door frame (jamb)

Space each pair of nails 12" to 16" o.c.

1/4" Reveal (setback from face of jamb)

DOOR CASING TRIM

# HANGING THE DOOR

Full-size swinging doors hang on butt hinges. The most common type of butt hinge is the full-mortise hinge. It requires a mortise or recess in both the door edge and the side jamb into which the leaves of the hinge fit. This results in a clean installation since, when the door is closed, only the pins of the hinges are exposed.

Butt hinges are specified by first, their height (not including their tips) and second, their width when open. The height of a hinge is determined by the thickness and width of the door being hung, while its width is determined by the door thickness and its frequency of use.

For 1 3/8" thick doors, use 3 1/2" x 3 1/2" butt hinges; for 1 3/4" thick doors, use 4" x 4" butt hinges. For most lightweight interior doors, two hinges are sufficient. For exterior doors and others that are wider or heavier than normal, use three hinges.

Use loose-pin hinges so that the door can be easily removed when necessary. You might consider a fixed-pin hinge only if an exterior door happens to swing outward and the pins are exposed on the outside.

Before being hung, the door must be measured and cut to size if necessary. The door should fit into the finished opening of the frame with a 1/16" - 1/8" clearance along the top and latch side, a 1/32" - 1/16" clearance along the hinge side, and at least a 1/4" clearance along the bottom (more if the door is to swing over carpeting or a threshold). The lock side of the door should be planed to bevel slightly toward the stop and allow the door to swing clear of the jamb.

Use small wedges to hold the door in place with the proper clearances, and mark both the door and jamb simultaneously with a chisel for the hinge locations. Position one set of hinges 7" from the top of the door, and the other 11" from the bottom. Center a third set of hinges, if required, between the other two.

Remove the door from the opening, and install the hinges on the door first. Allow for a 3/16" or 1/4" backset. Outline the required mortise, using the hinge leaf as a guide. The barrel of the hinge should clear the face of the door. The thickness of the hinge leaf is also noted on the door edge.

Use a router to cut the required mortise. If using a chisel, first cut in the outline and then make shallow cuts to clean out the mortise to the required depth. Drill the required holes and screw the hinge into place. Make sure the hinge is flush with the door edge and square with the face. If the mortise is too deep, it can be shimmed with cardboard.

Replace the door in the opening and re-check the hinge locations on the jamb. Rout out the jamb for the other hinge leafs and fasten them into place. The door can then be repositioned and the hinge pins slipped into place. Adjustments can be made if the door does not operate smoothly. The door edges can be planed, or the hinges shimmed with narrow strips of cardboard.

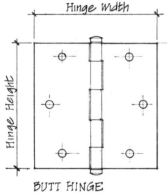

BUTT HINGE

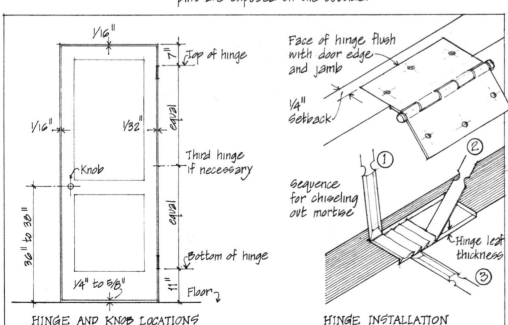

HINGE AND KNOB LOCATIONS    HINGE INSTALLATION

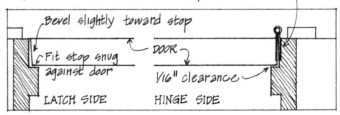

LATCH SIDE    HINGE SIDE

# DOOR LOCKSETS

Door locksets vary according to their locking ability, their construction and installation requirements, and the style of their handles. The primary lockset security choices include the following.

Passage sets have no locks, but have a latch bolt that is operable at all times by knobs on both sides. Privacy locks for bathrooms and other interior private rooms are operable by knobs on both sides, but can be locked by a push-button or a turn on the inside. Deadlatch entrance locks are used for lockable exterior doors. Manually or key operated deadbolt locks are often used in addition to deadlatch entrance locks for increased security.

Types of lockset construction and installation include the following. Mortise locks, rectangular units that are concealed in the edge of the door, are the most secure and are used primarily on exterior doors. Cylinder locks, the most commonly used on interior doors, are inexpensive and easy to install. Unit or integral locks, pre-assembled units that fit into a notch or mortise, combine the security of a mortise lock with the economy of a cylinder lock.

The primary style choices for locksets are knobs, levers, and handles with a thumb lever. These come in a variety of finishes (stainless steel, bright chrome, satin bronze, etc.) and designs (with rose or escutcheon plates). A style should be chosen to match the existing hardware in your house.

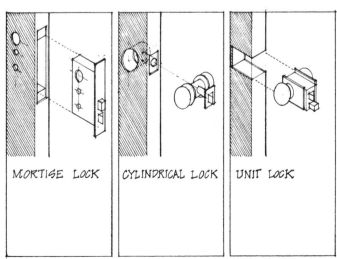

MORTISE LOCK     CYLINDRICAL LOCK     UNIT LOCK

INSTALLING A CYLINDER LOCKSET

Some doors come pre-drilled for a cylinder lockset. If yours is not, a manufacturer's template is usually included with the hardware to provide the precise locations for the two holes necessary. The hole for the cylinder lock case, located 36"-38" above the floor or to match the height of other knobs, is cut with a hole saw. Be sure to drill through the door only until the guide drill bit comes through the other side. Complete the hole by drilling from the opposite side to prevent splitting the door surface. The hole for the latch unit is drilled from the door edge into the cylinder hole as indicated by the template. It is important to have the door held in a fixed position with a wedge or other means so that the latch hole can be drilled as straight and level as possible.

Insert the latch unit into its hole and outline its face plate on the door edge. Chisel out the wood within the outline to a depth equal to the thickness of the face plate. Install the knob and latch according to the manufacturer's instructions.

Locate the center of the strike plate the same distance above the floor as is the center of the cylinder hole. The front edge of the strike plate hole must be the same distance from the stop as the face of the door is from the opposite side of the latch. Drill a hole in the jamb for the latch and inset the strike plate so it is flush with the face of the jamb.

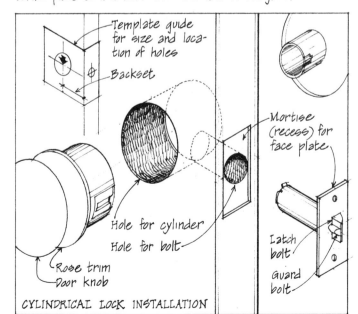

Template guide for size and location of holes

Backset

Mortise (recess) for face plate.

Hole for cylinder

Hole for bolt

Rose trim
Door knob

Latch bolt

Guard bolt

CYLINDRICAL LOCK INSTALLATION

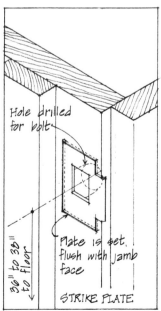

Hole drilled for bolt

36" to 38" to floor

Plate is set flush with jamb face

STRIKE PLATE

## SPECIAL DOOR TYPES

Bi-fold, by-pass sliding and pocket sliding doors require special hardware for their installation and operation. This hardware, along with instructions for its use and installation, is usually supplied by the manufacturer of the door kit. Some, such as bi-fold and sliding glass doors, come with door panels. Others, such as pocket doors, may require the separate purchase of standard doors.

The following section describes these types of doors and offers general guidelines for their installation. Always verify sizes and installation requirements or limitations with the manufacturer's instructions.

Since these door types utilize wider framed openings than those for normal swinging doors, larger headers are required. See pg. 221 for sizing these headers.

## BI-FOLD DOORS

Bi-fold doors consist of narrow panels that are hinged to one another. The door panels that are adjacent to the side jambs pivot on fixed pins at the top and bottom, while the others slide along an overhead track.

Unlike by-pass sliding doors, bi-fold doors open up to expose virtually all of the enclosed space. They do require some clearance for their operation, though not as much as swinging doors.

The standard height for bi-fold doors is 6'-8". Two-door units are available for openings 2' to 3' wide. Four-door units come in widths of from 3' to 6'.

The door panels may be of wood or metal, of flush or panel design. Flush panels may have natural or painted finishes, or have mirrors attached to them. Panel doors often are louvered for ventilation of the closet or storage space they enclose.

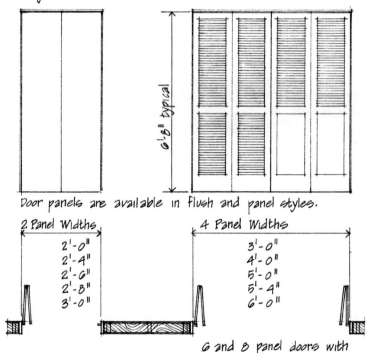

6'-8" typical

Door panels are available in flush and panel styles.

| 2 Panel Widths | 4 Panel Widths |
|---|---|
| 2'-0" | 3'-0" |
| 2'-4" | 4'-0" |
| 2'-6" | 5'-0" |
| 2'-8" | 5'-4" |
| 3'-0" | 6'-0" |

6 and 8 panel doors with heavy-duty hardware are available up to 12' wide.

BI-FOLD DOOR SIZES

Before the overhead track is secured to the header, the top pivot brackets are inserted into the track along with the rubber or plastic bumper that cushions the meeting door panels.

After the overhead track is secured, the top pivot brackets are positioned against each side jamb. The bottom pivot brackets are positioned on the floor directly below the top ones. Use a plumb bob for proper alignment, if necessary.

The door panels are folded, and the door's bottom pivot placed in the bottom socket. The top pivot brackets are slid along the track to meet the door's top pivot. As the door panels are moved back to the sides of the opening, the door slide guides are slipped onto the track.

Most bi-fold door assemblies have vertical and horizontal adjustment bolts which can be used to properly align the doors.

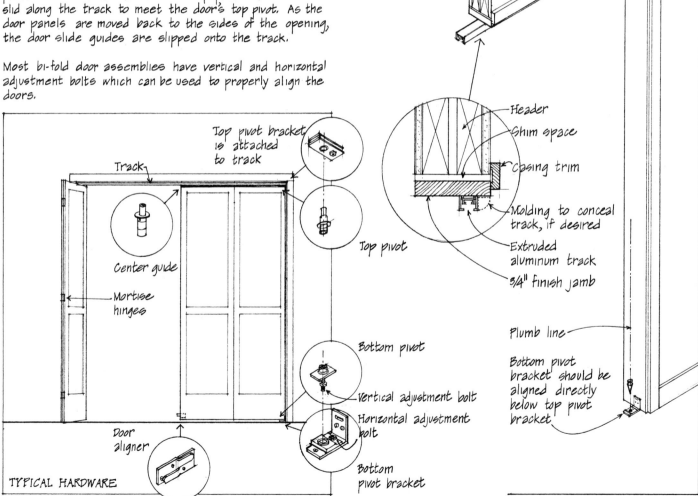

Header
Shim space
Casing trim
Molding to conceal track, if desired
Extruded aluminum track
3/4" finish jamb
Plumb line
Bottom pivot bracket should be aligned directly below top pivot bracket

Top pivot bracket is attached to track
Track
Center guide
Mortise hinges
Top pivot
Bottom pivot
Vertical adjustment bolt
Horizontal adjustment bolt
Bottom pivot bracket
Door aligner
TYPICAL HARDWARE

## BY-PASS SLIDING DOORS

By-pass sliding doors are hung from and roll along an overhead track. To prevent the door panels from swinging too freely and to keep them aligned, metal or nylon guides are mounted on the floor.

Since by-pass sliding doors cannot be sealed tightly, they are used primarily to screen closet or storage areas. Their main advantage is they can be used in tight areas where there is insufficient space for a swinging or bi-fold doors. Their disadvantage is they allow you to have only partial access to the enclosed space at any one time.

The doors are standard-size panel or flush type, usually hung in pairs. The width of the finished opening is equal to the total width of the pair of doors minus an inch for overlap where the doors meet. For the width of the rough opening, add to the finished opening the thickness of the side jambs.

The minimum height for the finished opening is the door height plus 1½" for the track and roller assembly. If a standard interior door frame is used and the track is mounted below the head jamb, the height of a standard door must be reduced and a trim strip installed to conceal the hardware.

Once the finished opening is prepared, the overhead track is secured to the head jamb with the open sides facing into the space being enclosed. It is essential that the track is aligned correctly.

The roller assemblies are attached to the tops of each door about 2" in from each end. The roller assembly plates usually have screw slots to allow the doors to be leveled after installation.

The doors are lifted onto the overhead track by tilting them slightly. Some tracks have key openings that indicate where to attach the roller assemblies.

After the doors have been installed and leveled, attach the floor guides.

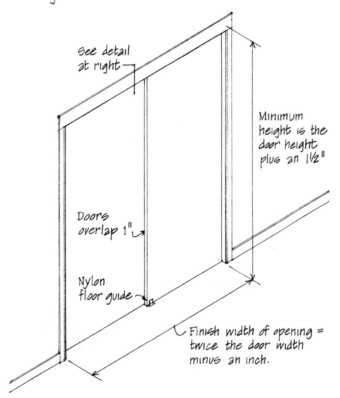

See detail at right

Minimum height is the door height plus an 1½"

Doors overlap 1"

Nylon floor guide

Finish width of opening = twice the door width minus an inch.

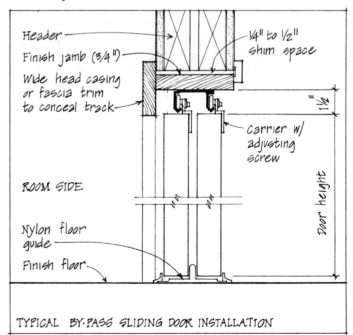

Header

Finish jamb (3/4")

Wide head casing or fascia trim to conceal track

¼" to ½" shim space

Carrier w/ adjusting screw

1½"

ROOM SIDE

Nylon floor guide

Finish floor

Door height

TYPICAL BY-PASS SLIDING DOOR INSTALLATION

## POCKET-SLIDING DOORS

Pocket-sliding doors consist of a single or pair of flush or panel doors that are hung from and roll along an overhead track. They differ from by-pass sliding doors in that, when opened, they disappear into pockets framed within the thickness of a stud wall.

Pocket doors have a clean, finished appearance, and are especially useful for doorways that are kept open most of the time. They are also used as passage doors when there is insufficient space for a swinging door.

The rough framing for a pocket door requires a header that spans across both the finished opening and the pocket itself. The width of this rough opening, therefore, is twice the width of the door plus 1¼". Verify this dimension and the height of the rough opening with the manufacturer of the door hardware.

The pocket door frame assembly consists of an overhead track/header that does not require a normal framed header for support. The track/header is supported instead by end brackets and the split metal jamb and stud that also serve to frame the pocket.

Some pocket frame assemblies have nailing strips along the header and the split jamb and stud so that the finish wall material can be attached directly to the frame.

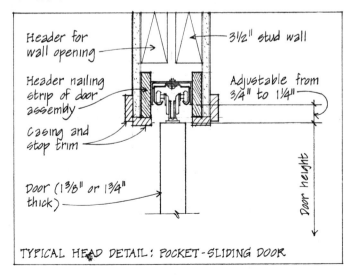

- Header for wall opening
- Header nailing strip of door assembly
- Casing and stop trim
- Door (1⅜" or 1¾" thick)
- 3½" stud wall
- Adjustable from ¾" to 1¼"
- Door height

TYPICAL HEAD DETAIL: POCKET-SLIDING DOOR

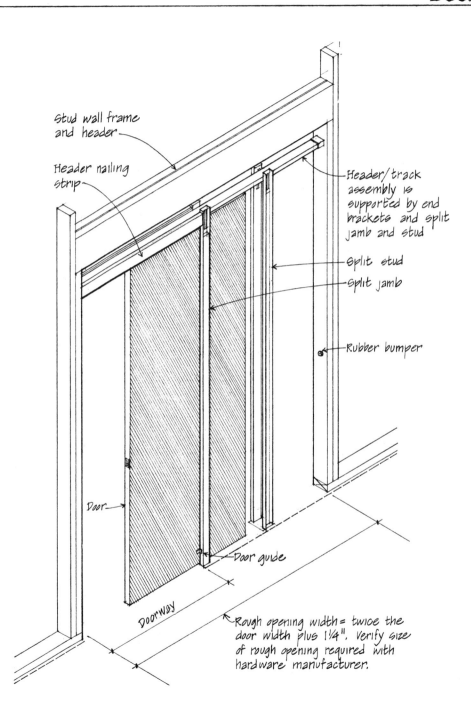

- Stud wall frame and header
- Header nailing strip
- Header/track assembly is supported by end brackets and split jamb and stud
- Split stud
- Split jamb
- Rubber bumper
- Door
- Door guide
- Doorway
- Rough opening width = twice the door width plus 1¼". Verify size of rough opening required with hardware manufacturer.

# SLIDING GLASS DOORS

Sliding glass doors allow a room to open up, visually and physically, to an outdoor living space. Because of their large glass area, they should be located and oriented carefully.

If oriented south or west and not shaded properly, a sliding glass door can overheat a room on a sunny day or create a glare problem. In cold weather, the glazing can be a source of substantial heat loss. The view seen through a sliding glass door is expansive and should be desirable, and not cause a loss in privacy.

A well-landscaped yard, fenced patio area, or an outdoor deck are ideal companions to sliding glass doors, and can help solve any daylighting and privacy problems that may exist.

Sliding glass doors are also points of entry and egress, and affect the traffic pattern in the room onto which the doors open. In addition to taking up a lot of wall space, the doors often restrict or limit the placement of furniture close to it.

Sliding glass doors are standard units offered by window manufacturers. In fact, they operate very much like sliding window units. They can have either wood or metal frames, usually with tempered insulating glass. They come in nominal 6'-8", 7'-0", and 8'-0" heights, and are available in widths from 5' to 12'. The door units contain at least one fixed and one operating panel. For widths greater than 9', the units may have three or four panels, with the end panels being fixed and the center ones operable.

Sliding glass doors are installed similar to regular exterior doors. Because of their width, openings for sliding glass doors require large headers to support the floor or roof loads above. (See pg. 221.) If the door unit is being installed into an existing wall, the ceiling framing above the new opening must be braced before you cut the opening.

Pay particular attention to the sill detail. The sill, of either wood or metal with metal tracks, usually rests directly on the subfloor so that it is flush with the finish floor. For the glass door to slide smoothly, the sill must be set level and straight.

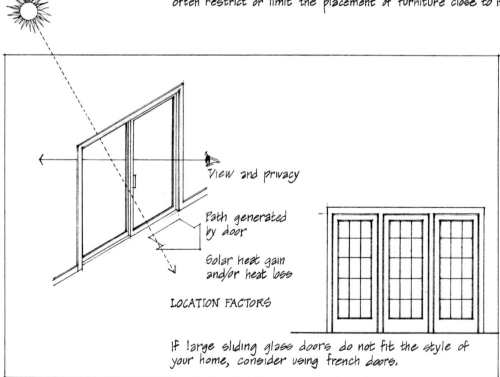

View and privacy

Path generated by door

Solar heat gain and/or heat loss

LOCATION FACTORS

If large sliding glass doors do not fit the style of your home, consider using french doors.

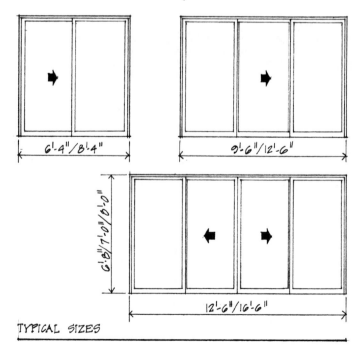

6'-4"/8'-4"

9'-6"/12'-6"

6'-8"/7'-0"/8'-0"

12'-6"/16'-6"

TYPICAL SIZES

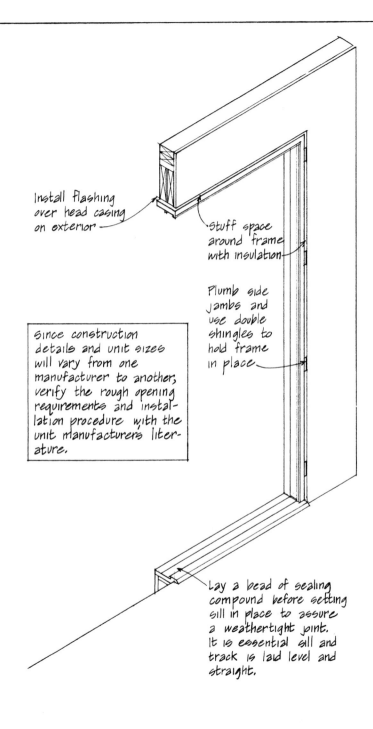

Install flashing over head casing on exterior

Stuff space around frame with insulation

Plumb side jambs and use double shingles to hold frame in place

Since construction details and unit sizes will vary from one manufacturer to another, verify the rough opening requirements and installation procedure with the unit manufacturer's literature.

Lay a bead of sealing compound before setting sill in place to assure a weathertight joint. It is essential sill and track is laid level and straight.

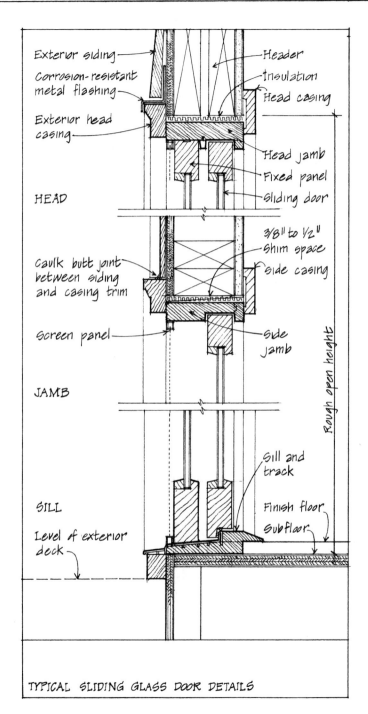

Exterior siding
Corrosion-resistant metal flashing
Exterior head casing
Header
Insulation
Head casing
Head jamb
Fixed panel
Sliding door

HEAD

Caulk butt joint between siding and casing trim
3/8" to 1/2" shim space
Side casing

Screen panel
Side jamb

JAMB

Rough open height

Sill and track
Finish floor
Subfloor

SILL

Level of exterior deck

TYPICAL SLIDING GLASS DOOR DETAILS

## RE-ARRANGING SPACE

If re-designing or altering the use of a space does not satisfy your needs, then you may want to consider changing the room's physical boundaries – its walls, floor or ceiling.

Removing an existing wall can transform two small rooms into a single large space. By removing and adding a set of walls, you can also consolidate wasted space into a usable room, eliminate awkward corners and tight spots, and simplify your room arrangements. Removing a wall is also necessary when adding on new space to an existing room.

Adding new walls is most often necessary when re-arranging a set of rooms or when converting an attic or basement into living spaces. A new partition can also define an entry foyer, help direct traffic around a living area, or create a private space within a larger room. Before deciding to build any permanent walls, however, consider the use of furnishings to create the spatial division you want without the permanence of a built-wall. Furnishings, such as vertical storage units, allow you to try out different arrangements of enclosure and alter them as your needs change.

If you do not need or want a total separation of space, new partitions can be half-walls or walls with interior window openings that allow space to flow over or through them. The same effect can be achieved by removing only a portion of an existing wall.

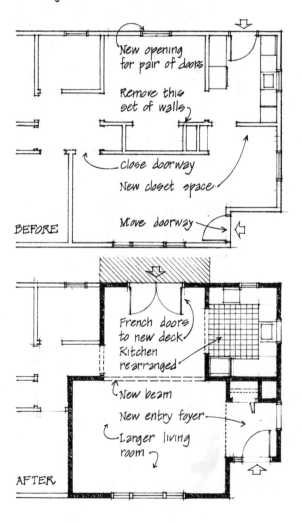

New opening for pair of doors

Remove this set of walls

Close doorway

New closet space

Move doorway

BEFORE

French doors to new deck

Kitchen rearranged

New beam

New entry foyer

Larger living room

AFTER

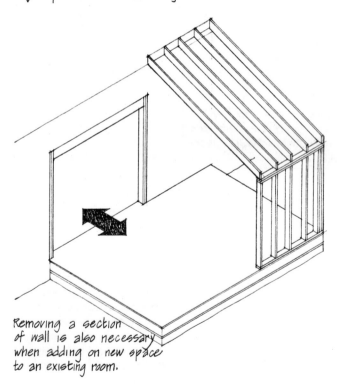

Removing a section of wall is also necessary when adding on new space to an existing room.

## PLANNING CONSIDERATIONS

Before making any firm decisions about removing or adding any walls, there are important planning and techical factors to consider.

Having the right amount of square footage is not the sole criterion for a workable space. Of equal, if not greater, importance is a room's proportion - its width to length to height relationships. These dimensions determine the scale of a room, what furniture groupings will fit into it, how much clearance you will have between pieces, and how much usable floor area there will be.

As you consider altering the size and shape of a room, study the effects of the changes on paper first. Layout possible furniture arrangements in the new space. See if the existing traffic pattern is improved or made more difficult. Consider how any changes might affect the existing pattern of windows and doorways in the room. Always avoid cutting a window in two with a new partition. If a new partition deprives a habitable space of natural light and ventilation, a new window will have to be installed.

Particularly when you are considering adding a wall in a room, hanging sheets of cloth from the ceiling in the position of the new wall can help you visualize the effect of the change on the existing space.

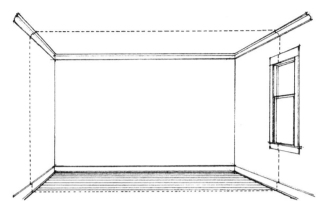

If a room has an ornate cornice, avoid building a full height partition that would visually interfere with the continuity of the trim.

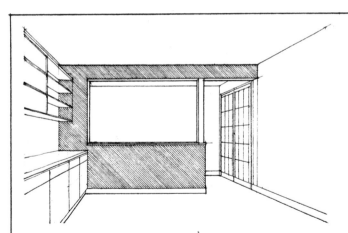

A partial wall can define a space without making it feel cramped. The solid portion can serve as a backdrop for furnishings; openings expose views beyond the room and enable it to borrow light from an adjacent space.

ALTERNATIVES TO BUILDING A PERMANENT PARTITION

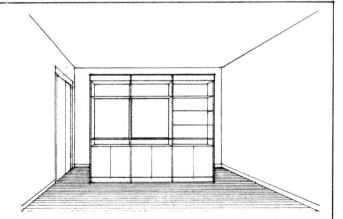

Wall storage units, whether purchased or modified from standard storage cabinets, make efficient space dividers. They can be as opaque or open and transparent as you wish.

## TECHNICAL CONSIDERATIONS

When considering removing any walls, review the structural system of your house. (See pg. 19) Try to make changes without disturbing bearing walls. If a bearing wall must be altered or removed, the load that it carries from the floor or roof framing above must be borne by a new beam or girder with post supports. These posts must transfer the beam loads down in a continuous manner to the structure or foundation below.

Also check if a wall to be removed contains any utility lines. A heating duct dead-ending in a register can be capped; an electrical circuit that terminates in the wall at an outlet can be removed back to a junction box. Any lines, pipes or ducts that rise continuously through the wall, however, will have to be re-routed. This can be a costly undertaking and should be avoided. In these cases, perhaps you can remove most of the wall and leave the portion that contains the utility lines in place.

If the wall you are removing contains wiring, disconnect the electrical circuit before you begin work and remove any outlet and switch cover plates. If you discover any wiring you do not understand, a professional electrician should help you re-route the cables.

## REMOVING A NON-BEARING WALL

Begin by removing the baseboard and other wall trim carefully. First break any paint seals with a utility knife and use a putty knife to pry the trim off. Salvage any trim you can to patch gaps after the wall removal.

The finish wall surface is removed next. Since this is messy work, protect adjacent areas with canvas or drop-cloths. Wear goggles and a respirator, especially when removing plaster or gypsum board. Gypsum board can be cut away in sections, while plaster can be removed with a hammer and crowbar.

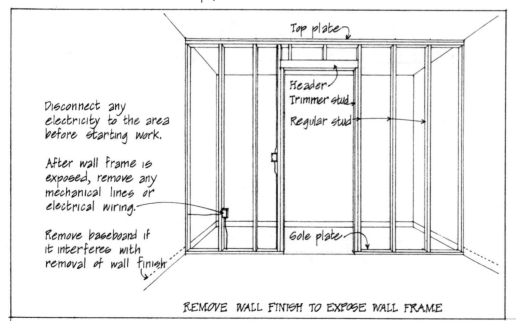

Disconnect any electricity to the area before starting work.

After wall frame is exposed, remove any mechanical lines or electrical wiring.

Remove baseboard if it interferes with removal of wall finish

Top plate
Header
Trimmer stud
Regular stud
Sole plate

REMOVE WALL FINISH TO EXPOSE WALL FRAME

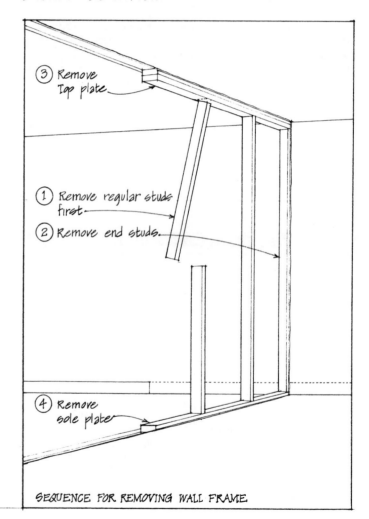

③ Remove Top plate
① Remove regular studs first
② Remove end studs
④ Remove sole plate

SEQUENCE FOR REMOVING WALL FRAME

After the wall frame is exposed, it can best be removed by sawing the studs in half and prying them from the top and bottom (sole) plates. You may have to use a crow bar to remove the end studs that are nailed to a pair of studs in the connecting wall.

The top and sole plates are likewise removed with a crow-bar from the ceiling joists and the subflooring. Cutting and removing a section of each plate can help you get a grip on them. Use a scrap 2"x4" as leverage and to protect the finish surfaces around the wall being removed.

After the wall is removed, the gaps in the ceiling and the adjoining walls must be patched to match their adjacent surfaces - plastering to the same thickness, or cutting strips of gypsum board to fit and finishing with tape and joint compound.

The gap in the finish flooring can be finished with the same species of wood, or a thickness of wood to provide a smooth and level surface for tile or carpeting. If the flooring in the two rooms being joined differs, the flooring in one or both rooms should be redone.

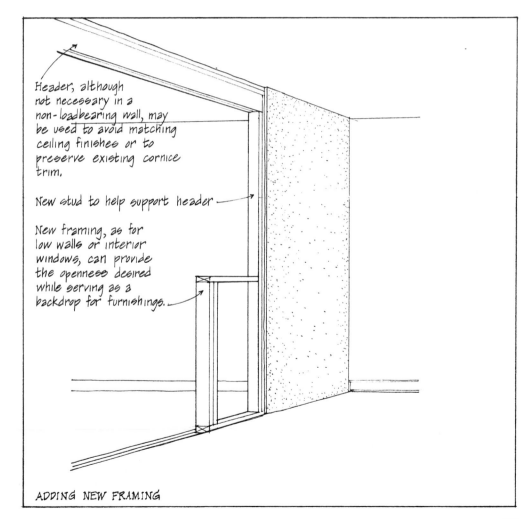

If cornice trim is to remain, or if ceiling materials differ, leave top plate in place.

If existing wall finish can be matched, remove only what is necessary.

Remove framing back to stud closest to the end of the wall section to be preserved.

Remove sole plate only at opening where flooring is to be continuous.

Preserving a portion of the wall may be desirable to avoid re-routing a vertical duct run or plumbing.

REMOVING A PORTION OF A WALL

Header, although not necessary in a non-loadbearing wall, may be used to avoid matching ceiling finishes or to preserve existing cornice trim.

New stud to help support header

New framing, as for low walls or interior windows, can provide the openness desired while serving as a backdrop for furnishings.

ADDING NEW FRAMING

# REMOVING A BEARING WALL

To prepare for removing a bearing wall, the ceiling framing above must be braced with temporary supports until the new beam is in place. This support can be provided with blocking and adjustable jacks, or a 2"x4" stud wall with a 1"x4" diagonal brace, assembled with double-headed nails for easy disassembly. These supports should be placed on both sides of the wall being removed, and shimmed for a tight fit.

Once these temporary supports are in place, the wall is removed in a manner similar to non-bearing walls.

The size of the new supporting beam is determined by the span of the new opening, the floor or attic/roof area being supported, and the load per square foot. The beam/span table offers guidelines for estimating the size of the beam you need. (See pg. 215)

If the wall you are removing lies directly below another bearing wall, or if the span of the new opening is greater than 12', you should consult an engineer or architect to help you determine the size of the beam needed and its necessary supports.

To reduce the span, and consequently the size of the beam needed, freestanding posts can be used or a portion of the wall can remain.

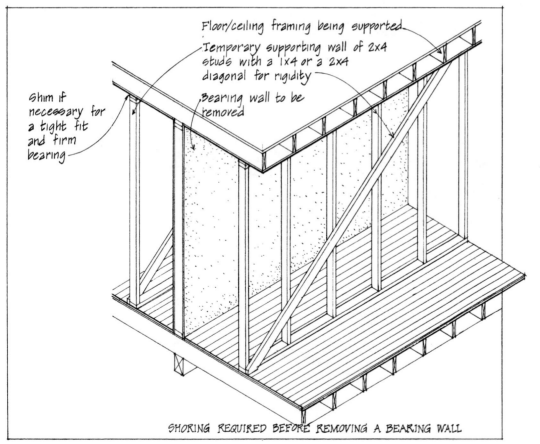

Shim if necessary for a tight fit and firm bearing

Floor/ceiling framing being supported

Temporary supporting wall of 2x4 studs with a 1x4 or a 2x4 diagonal for rigidity

Bearing wall to be removed

SHORING REQUIRED BEFORE REMOVING A BEARING WALL

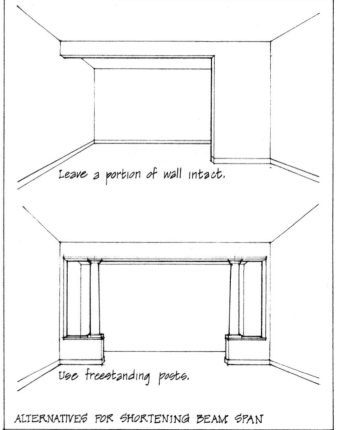

Leave a portion of wall intact.

Use freestanding posts.

ALTERNATIVES FOR SHORTENING BEAM SPAN

The new beam may be fabricated from 2" structural-grade lumber. Other options include glue-laminated beams, plywood box beams, and steel sections.

The end condition of the new beam depends on how it is supported. The beam supports are posts which may be free-standing, butted up against a wall, or built within a wall. For a simply-supported beam, each post carries half the beam load, a fairly concentrated load. Each post must therefore bear on either a bearing wall or girder below it. The base for each post must be solid and be able to transmit the post load down to the foundation system in a continuous manner.

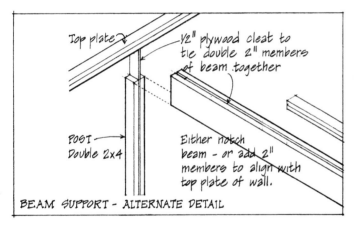

Top plate

½" plywood cleat to tie double 2" members of beam together

POST Double 2x4

Either notch beam - or add 2" members to align with top plate of wall.

**BEAM SUPPORT - ALTERNATE DETAIL**

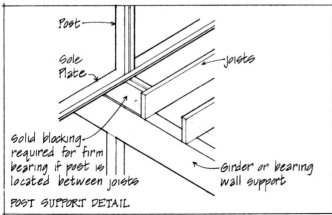

Post

Sole Plate

Joists

Solid blocking required for firm bearing if post is located between joists

Girder or bearing wall support

**POST SUPPORT DETAIL**

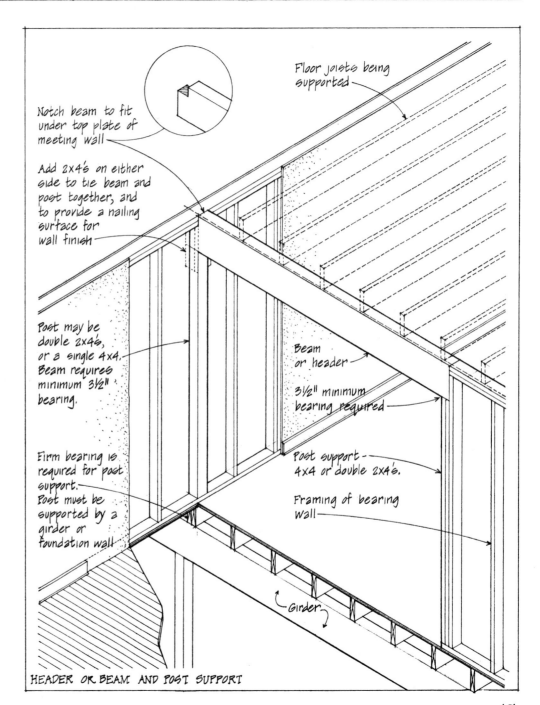

Floor joists being supported

Notch beam to fit under top plate of meeting wall

Add 2x4's on either side to tie beam and post together, and to provide a nailing surface for wall finish

Post may be double 2x4's, or a single 4x4. Beam requires minimum 3½" bearing.

Beam or header

3½" minimum bearing required

Firm bearing is required for post support. Post must be supported by a girder or foundation wall

Post support - 4x4 or double 2x4's.

Framing of bearing wall

Girder

**HEADER OR BEAM AND POST SUPPORT**

## ADDING WALLS

Framing a new wall for a room is much like building a wall in new construction. The wall consists of 2"x4" studs tied to top and sole (bottom) plates at 16" o.c. If the interior wall is not too long, and space is tight, 2"x3" studs can be used.

Once you have decided where the new wall will be located, mark its position on either the floor or the ceiling. In either case, use a plumb to align the top and sole plate positions.

Determine if the new wall will be perpendicular to or parallel with the floor joists below and the ceiling joists above. If the wall is perpendicular to the ceiling and floor joists, the top and sole plates can be nailed directly to these joists through the ceiling and flooring.

If the new wall is parallel with the ceiling and floor joists, try to position it directly under a ceiling joist and over a floor joist. If it falls between two joists, solid support blocking of the same dimension as the joists must be installed no more than 24" o.c. If the ceiling joists are not accessible through an attic space above, the ceiling material must be removed to allow this blocking to be installed from below. Similarly, blocking must be installed between the floor joists to support a new wall that lies between them.

Before building the new wall, remove the baseboard and other trim that the wall would meet. Whenever possible, pry off an entire section of trim without damaging it, and save it for re-use.

If you have enough room, fabricate the new wall frame on the floor. Measure and cut both the top and sole plates, and lay them side by side. Mark the locations of the studs on both of them simultaneously. Allow for any doorway or other openings you will have in the wall.

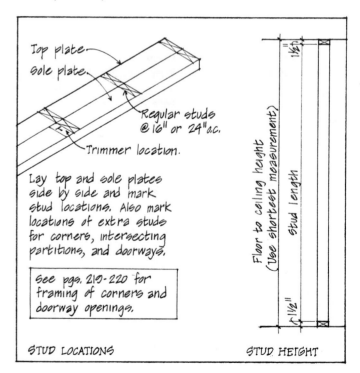

If possible, position partition directly under and over a joist.

Solid blocking

Use a plumb bob to properly align top and sole plates

If new partition is perpendicular to floor and ceiling joists, top and sole plates are nailed directly to the joists with 16d nails. Use a double top plate.

If new partition is parallel to joists, and lies between two joists, solid blocking is required no more than 24" o.c.

. PARTITION SUPPORT (See also pg. 200)

Top plate.
Sole plate.

Regular studs @ 16" or 24" o.c.

Trimmer location.

Lay top and sole plates side by side and mark stud locations. Also mark locations of extra studs for corners, intersecting partitions, and doorways.

see pgs. 210-220 for framing of corners and doorway openings.

Floor to ceiling height (Use shortest measurement)

Stud length

STUD LOCATIONS

STUD HEIGHT

Measure the distance from the floor to the ceiling or underside of the joists. Cut the studs 3" less than the shortest dimension to allow for the thicknesses of both plates.

Fasten the sole plate to the floor joists or the solid blocking between them with 16d nails. Nail the studs to the top plate, using two 16d nails for each stud, driven through the top plate into the ends of the studs.

Lift the partial frame into place and align the top plate. Nail the top plate to the ceiling joists or the blocking between them with 16d nails. Use goggles and a respirator when nailing upwards to protect your eyes and face from miss-hit nails and debris. When the top plate is secure, complete the frame by toenailing the studs to the sole plate with 8d nails.

If you want avoid toenailing, first build the entire frame, with both top and sole plates, 1½" less than the shortest floor to ceiling height. Nail an extra sole plate to the floor. Then lift the complete wall frame into place, and nail the two sole plates to each other.

The wall frame is then ready for the installation of electrical wiring, outlets and switches you may want, and for finishing and trim work.

End each stud through the top plate with 2-16d nails.

After top plate is nailed to studs and lifted into place, nail top plate to ceiling joists or solid blocking. Use 16d nails.

Sole plate is nailed first to floor joists or blocking between joists with 16d nails

Toe nail studs to sole plate with 8d nails, 2 on each side.

ERECTING PARTITION

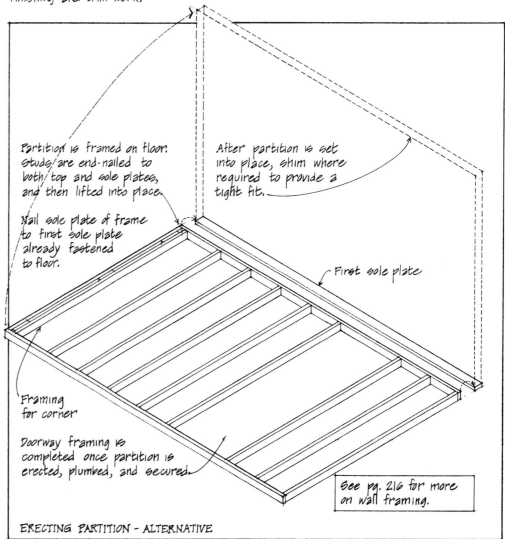

Partition is framed on floor: studs are end-nailed to both top and sole plates, and then lifted into place.

Nail sole plate of frame to first sole plate already fastened to floor.

After partition is set into place, shim where required to provide a tight fit.

First sole plate

Framing for corner

Doorway framing is completed once partition is erected, plumbed, and secured.

See pg. 216 for more on wall framing.

ERECTING PARTITION - ALTERNATIVE

# 2

## ALTERING CEILINGS & FLOORS

Since a remodeling project is usually generated by a desire for more space, it may seem odd to consider altering ceilings and floors. There may be, however, occasions when altering a floor or ceiling can enhance the form, scale and use of a space.

A portion of a floor can be dropped to accommodate a sunken tub while the lowered ceiling below creates a more intimate seating area. If the ceiling height permits, a portion of a room's floor can be raised to create built-in seating platforms with storage underneath.

As you consider raising a floor or dropping a ceiling, carefully measure the effect the change will have on the space immediately above or below the alteration. In particular, check your local building code for limitations on the height and area of dropped or furred ceilings, and the height of exposed beams in a space. (See pg. 40.)

In addition to dropping a ceiling to create a more intimate lounge or fireplace nook, a room's vertical dimension can be enhanced by raising its ceiling. This may be appropriate particularly when there is an unused attic space above. The ceiling material can be removed along with any ceiling joists not serving as structural ties for the roof system. The roof rafters or trusses may be finished or left exposed.

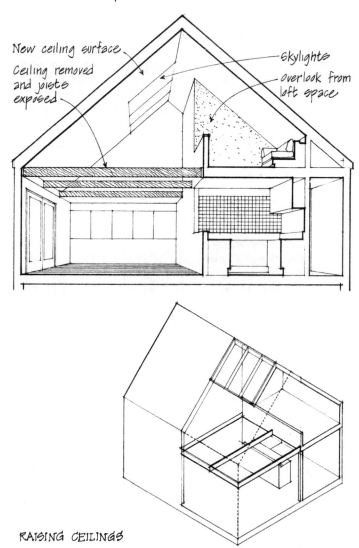

New ceiling surface

Ceiling removed and joists exposed

Skylights

overlook from loft space

Weight of filled tub is substantial, and must be structured carefully.

Lowering floor also lowers ceiling of space below. Check for minimum allowable ceiling height.

LOWERING FLOORS AND CEILINGS

RAISING CEILINGS

A raised floor or lowered ceiling can be supported by the existing floor or ceiling framing. A dropped floor or raised ceiling, however, requires that a portion of the existing framing be removed before the new floor or ceiling is built. The new framing must be constructed in such a way that it carries the loads of the new and remaining portions of the floor or ceiling to the building's bearing walls or foundation.

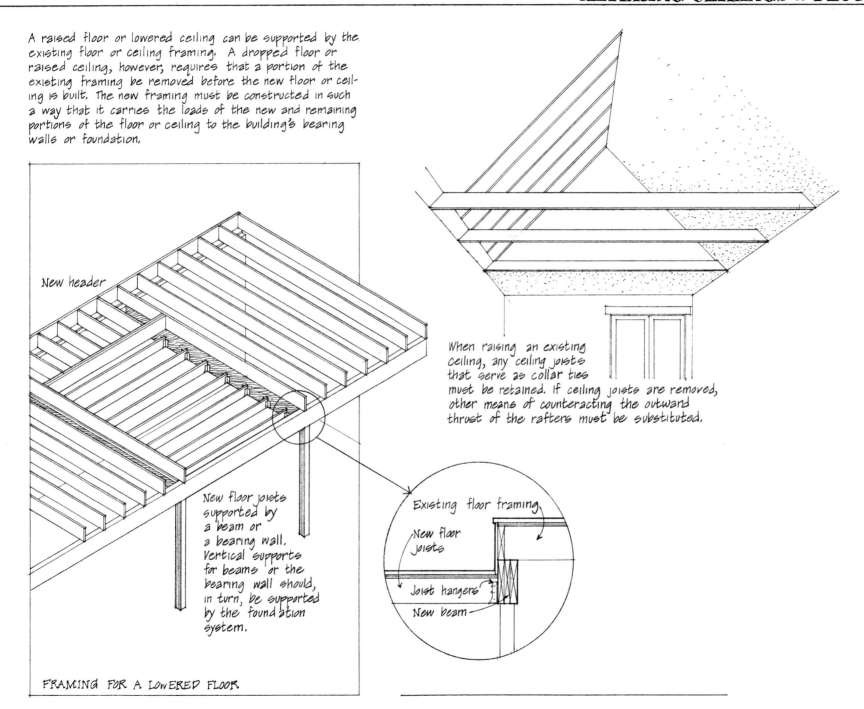

New header

New floor joists supported by a beam or a bearing wall. Vertical supports for beams or the bearing wall should, in turn, be supported by the foundation system.

FRAMING FOR A LOWERED FLOOR

When raising an existing ceiling, any ceiling joists that serve as collar ties must be retained. If ceiling joists are removed, other means of counteracting the outward thrust of the rafters must be substituted.

Existing floor framing

New floor joists

Joist hangers

New beam

# 3 CONVERTING UNUSED SPACE

A family's living needs seem to expand to fill available space. Regardless of the size of your house, there never seems to be enough space - space for informal gatherings, a work or hobby room, storage, additional bedrooms and bathrooms. If your main living levels are well laid out and the quality of their spaces are as you want them, and you simply need more space, consider the possibility of converting unused spaces in your home - your attic, basement, garage or porch. These spaces are already framed and enclosed. Although repairs and some exterior framing may be necessary, little or no foundation work or roof framing is required. Interior framing, finishing, and providing heat, light and ventilation can transform dark, damp areas into attractive living spaces.

## CONVERTING SPACE

Converting unused, unfinished spaces in your home is a viable, less expensive alternative to adding new space since the need for a foundation and exterior wall and roof framing is eliminated or greatly reduced. Furthermore, the size of your lot, your current lot coverage, and the setbacks required by code may not allow you to extend your house upward or outward. If you need more living space in your home, consider the following design possibilities.

If they have the necessary headroom and can be insulated and made weathertight, attic spaces can be converted into attractive bedroom and bath areas, with sunlight and views, or rooms for private, isolated activity.

If they have the necessary headroom and problems of darkness and dampness can be solved, basement spaces can be converted into workshops and hobby rooms. If it has access to adequate daylight and can be naturally ventilated, a basement can also be transformed into additional bedroom space.

Porches can be enclosed to allow an existing room to expand outward to a sunroom or study.

If the need for more living space is greater than for an enclosed space for your car, then your garage may be able to become a new living room or studio.

For each of these possibilities, there are important design, functional and technical factors that must be considered in their planning.

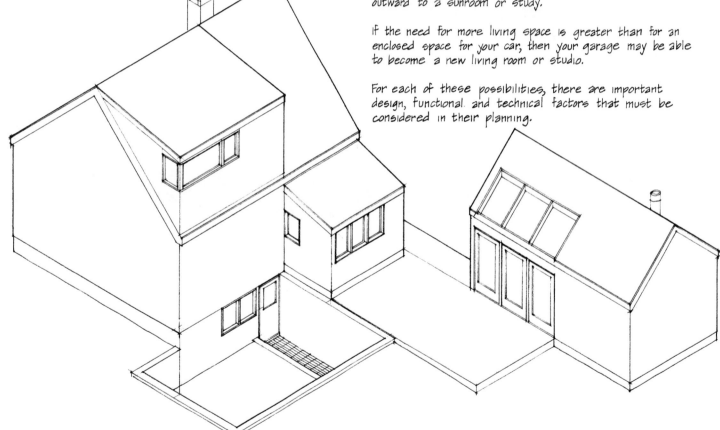

## PLANNING CONSIDERATIONS

When planning a conversion, analyze the existing space for:

1. HEADROOM:

   The space should have the necessary headroom as required by the building code. This is normally 7'-6" for habitable spaces, although 7'-0" may be allowable for some secondary uses. Check your local code.

2. DAYLIGHT AND AIR:

   Habitable spaces - those used for living, sleeping, eating or cooking - are required to have minimum levels of daylight and natural ventilation. See pg. 40

3. CIRCULATION:

   Consider what type of access is required for the converted space - stairs, halls, exterior doors - and how it ties into the rest of the house.

4. ZONING:

   Consider if the intended use of the converted space is appropriate for its location, relative to other spaces and their uses.

5. EMERGENCY EXITS:

   Bedrooms are required to have windows which can serve as emergency exits. See pg. 41.

6. UTILITIES:

   Consider what is necessary to heat, light and provide water, if necessary, to the converted space.

7. WEATHER TIGHTNESS:

   The existing space will have to be insulated, and repairs may be necessary to make it weathertight.

8. EXTERIOR APPEARANCE:

   If new windows are necessary to light and ventilate the existing space, and if new siding is required, consider their effect on the exterior appearance of your house.

9. STRUCTURE:

   Even though your house structure may be in good condition, additional loads may be imposed by the conversion and the structure may have to be reinforced accordingly.

## CONVERTING ATTIC SPACES

When considering converting an unused attic into livable space, first check its potential headroom. If your roof has a low pitch, or is framed with trusses, you may have to raise or re-frame the entire roof. This, in effect, would be adding space to your home.

Under a steep-pitched roof, however, there may be a substantial amount of space available for use. At least 50% of the floor area required by code should have a 7'-6" ceiling height. The actual floor area can extend under the roof slope, along the eave lines, where a 5' ceiling height is usually sufficient. Even lower heights may be acceptable over beds, bathtubs, and storage spaces.

If headroom is a problem, adding dormers can increase the usable floor area of an attic. Dormers can also accommodate the necessary windows for daylight, ventilation and views, add visual interest to the form of the attic space, and enhance the exterior appearance of your house.

Before laying out the rooms in your attic, consider the type and location of stairs that are required. If the attic will be used sparingly as storage, loft or overflow space, perhaps a spiral stair or ship's ladder that takes up little space can be used. If you plan to convert the attic into a family room or bedrooms, however, a standard stairway is required.

A standard stairway can take up a lot of space. A typical straight-run stair requires a space at least 3' wide and 10' long. A U-shaped stair requires a space about 6' wide and 7'-6" long. The stairway opening must also be structured carefully and be reasonably accessible from the lower living levels. For more on stairs, see pg. 124.

If your attic will constitute a third living level, check your local code requirements for emergency exits from that level in case of fire.

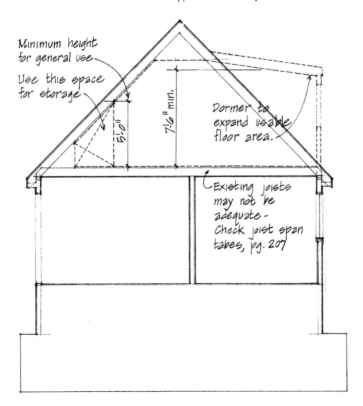

Minimum height for general use

Use this space for storage

5'-0"

7'-6" min.

Dormer to expand usable floor area.

Existing joists may not be adequate - Check joist span tables, pg. 207

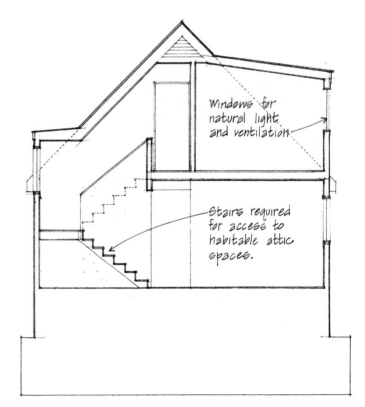

Windows for natural light and ventilation

Stairs required for access to habitable attic spaces.

To conserve heat in the winter, and help keep the finished attic space cooler in the summer, insulation must be installed around the walls and the ceiling of the converted space. To help control the formation of moisture, the space between the finished space and the roofing should be ventilated, and a vapor barrier installed. Any moisture collecting in this concealed space can lead to the deterioration of the insulation and roof structure.

Because heat naturally rises in a house, an attic space can become quite hot in the summer. Provisions should be made for ventilating the finished spaces. Windows, possibly assisted with an exhaust fan, should provide cross-ventilation to keep the attic rooms cool in hot weather.

If the stairway or attic area is open to the lower floors, build in the ability to circulate the hot air that collects in the higher spaces back down to the lower living areas. This heat destratification can be accomplished with a ceiling paddle fan, or a simple wall duct with a thermostatically-controlled fan, an inlet at the highest point, and an outlet at the lower floor level. If you have a forced-air furnace, you may also be able to extend a return-air duct up to the higher spaces.

If you plan on including a bathroom in your attic conversion, try to locate it above an existing bath or where it can use an extension of the existing water supply, waste and vent pipes.

A final but important point to check is the framing of the existing attic floor. Since many attic floors are framed with 2"x4"s or 2"x6"s, they will have to be reinforced to carry the live loads imposed by the change in their use.

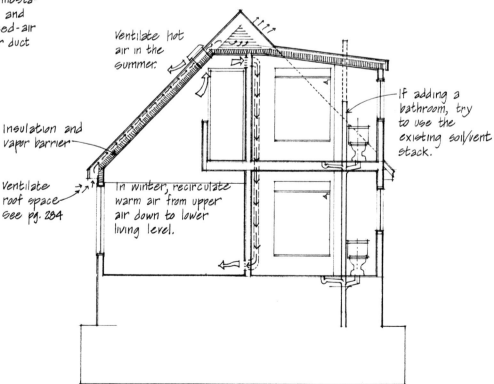

Ventilate hot air in the summer.

If adding a bathroom, try to use the existing soil/vent stack.

Insulation and vapor barrier

Ventilate roof space see pg. 284

In winter, recirculate warm air from upper air down to lower living level.

# ATTIC FLOOR FRAMING

The floor of an attic space converted to a habitable space must be able to carry a 40 lbs./s.f. live load in addition to the weight of any built-in furnishings and equipment. If the attic floor was originally intended only for light storage and framed with 2"x4"s or 2"x6"s, it will have to be reinforced.

The easiest way to reinforce an existing floor is to add new joists between the existing ones. For the size of the joists needed, refer to the joist/span table on pg. 207. The new joists should bear on the same surfaces as the existing ones - on the top plates of exterior walls and interior bearing walls.

It is often desirable to place spacers under each new joist to separate the joists from the existing ceiling surface below. This will decrease the possibility of damage to the ceiling as you build the floor and walls of the attic rooms.

In installing the new floor system, some existing wiring may need to be re-routed. Do not leave any wiring compressed between joists or between the existing ceiling and joist.

The existing structure of the house must be able to carry the additional loads imposed by the finishing of the attic space. Any interior walls that support the new attic floor framing should be continuous or transfer the floor loads down to the house foundation.

Rafters

Attic floor joists

Bearing walls

If new attic floor joists are necessary, they must be supported by bearing walls.

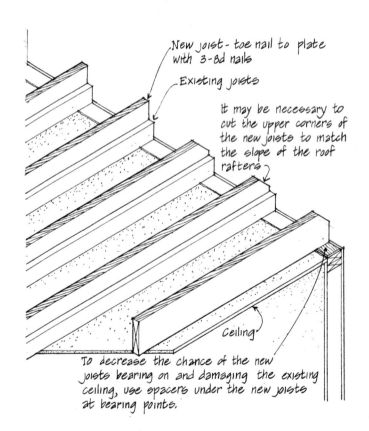

New joist - toe nail to plate with 3-8d nails

Existing joists

It may be necessary to cut the upper corners of the new joists to match the slope of the roof rafters

Ceiling

To decrease the chance of the new joists bearing on and damaging the existing ceiling, use spacers under the new joists at bearing points.

Once the new joists are in place, a new subfloor must be installed before any walls or partitions are erected. The subfloor should be continuous and provide a good working platform on which to assemble walls and finish the attic space.

The subfloor is usually of plywood, 5/8" or 3/4" thick, C-D grade, with the C-face or smoother side up. The plywood sheets should be laid with their face grain across the joists, and in such a way as to minimize cutting of the 4' x 8' sheets. Stagger the end joints so that they are not aligned along the same joist. Leave a 1/16" gap between adjoining sheets to allow for expansion and prevent their buckling. (See also pg. 211)

The plywood sheets are nailed directly to the floor joists with 8p coated box nails, 6" o.c. and 3/8" from the edges at the ends, and 10" o.c. on the interior of the sheets.

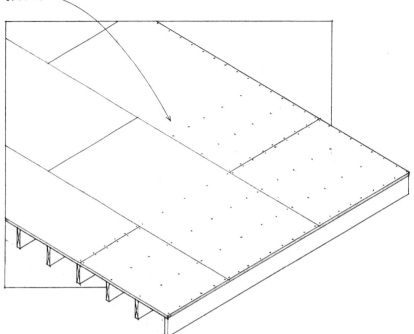

Plywood subflooring

New stairway opening. See next page.

Subflooring is required only over usable floor areas, including storage spaces.

See pg. 206 for general information on floor framing.

## ATTIC FLOOR OPENINGS

If a stairway is not already provided to your attic space, a new opening for a stairway must be framed into the attic floor. Openings may also be required for chimneys, large plumbing stacks, or heating ducts. A portion of the attic floor may even be removed to provide an overlook into a living space below.

It is generally easier to frame a new opening if its length is parallel to the attic floor joists. After marking the location of the opening on the ceiling side of the attic joists, remove the ceiling material and re-route any electrical wiring as required.

From above, double the floor joists on each side of the opening. Before cutting any existing joists, brace them temporarily from the floor below. Once braced, the joists are cut and headers are installed at each end of the opening.

A header equal to a double joist is usually adequate. Each header must be supported by the double trimmer joists. The cut or tail joists are in turn supported by the headers. Metal beam and joist hangers are often used to help support headers and tail joists of large openings.

If the new opening is perpendicular to the direction of the floor joists, a larger header may be needed to support the greater number of joists cut. The double trimmer joists must likewise be strong enough to carry the larger load. If this presents any difficulties, a new bearing wall or posts and a beam can be used to support the ends of the cut joists. See also pg. 210.

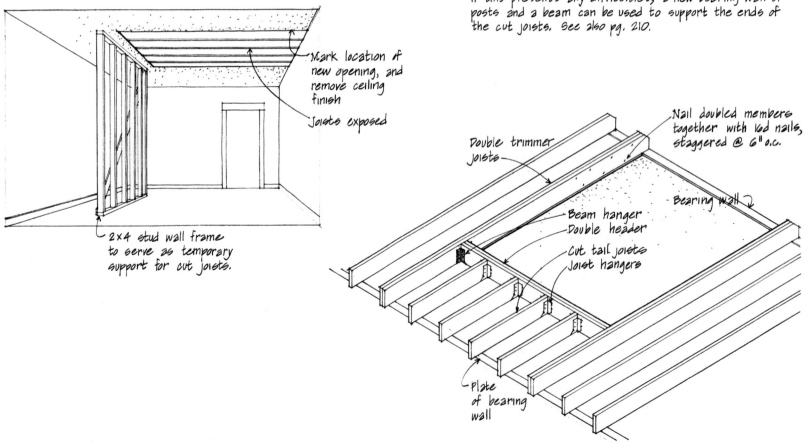

Mark location of new opening, and remove ceiling finish

Joists exposed

2×4 stud wall frame to serve as temporary support for cut joists.

Nail doubled members together with 16d nails, staggered @ 6" o.c.

Double trimmer joists

Bearing wall

Beam hanger
Double header

Cut tail joists
Joist hangers

Plate of bearing wall

## ATTIC CEILING FRAMING

If the roof structure consists of rafters tied together with collar beams, these collar beams can also serve as the framing for the attic ceiling. If used in this manner, the collar beams should be at least 7'-6½" from the floor.

If the collar beams are too low, new ones can usually be installed at a higher level. Do not remove collar beams unless you can verify that the attic floor joists are providing an adequate structural tie for the roof rafters. If you install a structural ridge beam supported by gable end walls and intermediate posts, no collar beams or structural ties are required.

If the roof rafters will also support the ceiling finish, check the rafter span table on pg. 225 to be sure that they can carry the added load. In addition, the rafters should be deep enough to allow adequate space for insulation and ventilation behind the new ceiling finish material. If the existing rafters are not very deep, thin rigid insulation panels (eg. extruded polystyrene) can be used instead of the thicker fiberglass blanket insulation. See pgs. 281 and 285.

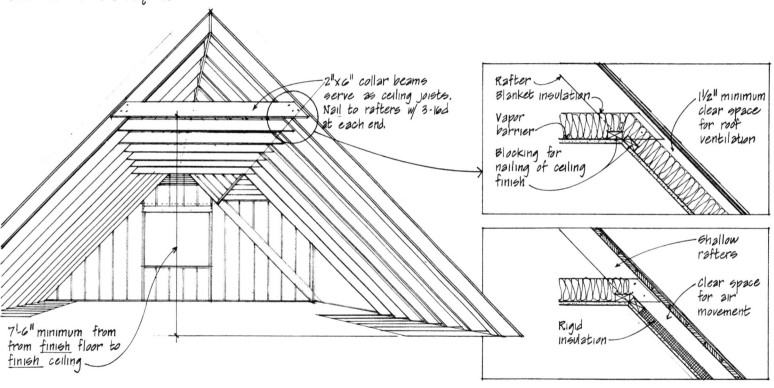

2"x6" collar beams serve as ceiling joists. Nail to rafters w/ 3-16d at each end.

7'-6" minimum from from finish floor to finish ceiling

Rafter
Blanket insulation
Vapor barrier
Blocking for nailing of ceiling finish

1½" minimum clear space for roof ventilation

Shallow rafters

clear space for air movement

Rigid insulation

## ATTIC WALL FRAMING

Once the attic floor is framed and the subfloor is installed, mark the position of new walls on the subfloor with chalklines. These walls should be coordinated with other changes necessary to make the attic space livable — dormers, skylights and new ceilings. These design elements will affect both the shape and height of new walls.

Knee walls along the eave sides of the attic should be built first. Measure in from the exterior wall line the necessary distance to arrive at the desired height of the knee walls.

Measure and cut the necessary length of the sole plates. Position the sole plates, and use a plumb bob to mark the positions of the studs under each rafter.

Measure and cut the studs, sloping their top ends so that they fit against the underside of the rafters. Nail the studs to each sole plate by driving two 16d nails through the plate into the ends of the studs.

Lift the sole plate and stud assemblies into position, and nail the studs to each rafter with two 10d nails. Nail each sole plate to the subfloor with 10d nails at 12" o.c. Use 16d nails when nailing into joists.

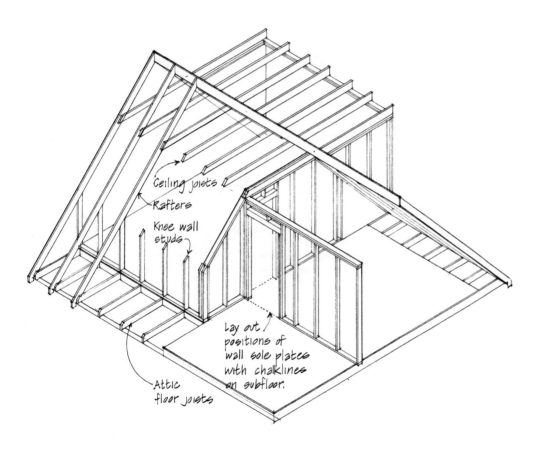

Ceiling joists

Rafters

Knee wall studs

Lay out positions of wall sole plates with chalklines on subfloor.

Attic floor joists

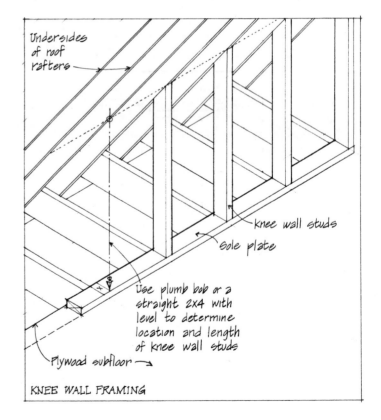

Undersides of roof rafters

knee wall studs

Sole plate

Use plumb bob or a straight 2x4 with level to determine location and length of knee wall studs

Plywood subfloor →

KNEE WALL FRAMING

Walls parallel with the roof rafters should, if convenient, lie directly under a rafter. If the dimensional requirements of a space do not make this desirable, blocking must be installed between the rafters to provide a nailing surface for the top plates of the new walls.

Frame and erect the central portions of walls first, those that lie under the flat portion of the ceiling. These partitions can be framed in the normal manner, assembled on the floor, and lifted into place.

Top plates of walls that frame into sloping surfaces can then be measured and cut to fit, and nailed to the undersides of rafters or blocking between the rafters. Thicken the rafters, if necessary with 2"x2"s or 2"x4"s to accept the top plates. Once these top plates are in place, studs can be cut to fit, and toenailed, between the sole plate and the sloping top plates.

Remaining walls and door openings are framed similarly to interior partitions in new construction. See pg. Special attention should be paid to walls that meet sloping surfaces, to corners, and to intersections of walls.

Provide blocking at intersections of walls and ceilings, and at transitions between flat and sloping surfaces, so that finish wall and ceiling materials have adequate nailing surfaces.

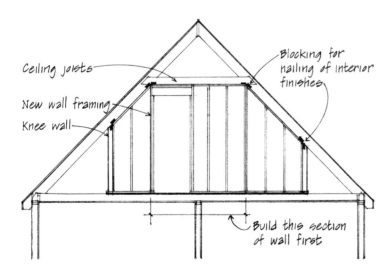

Ceiling joists

New wall framing

Knee wall

Blocking for nailing of interior finishes

Build this section of wall first

See pgs. 216-221 for general information on wall framing

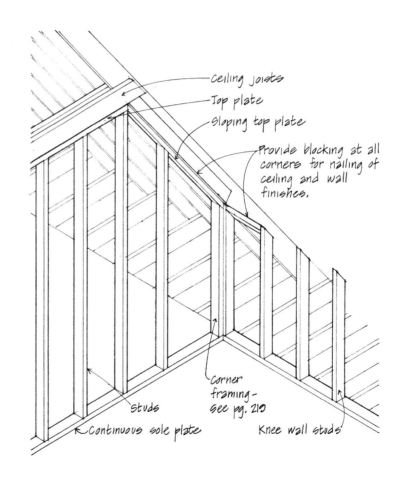

Ceiling joists

Top plate

Sloping top plate

Provide blocking at all corners for nailing of ceiling and wall finishes.

Studs

Corner framing- See pg. 210

Continuous sole plate

Knee wall studs

## DORMERS

Raising portions of your roof and constructing dormers can help you re-claim attic space and transform it into livable space. Dormers can not only increase the ceiling height and usable floor area of your attic. They also can conveniently incorporate windows in their vertical surfaces, and provide an attic space with needed daylight, ventilation and views.

Study a sectional view of your house, and mark the minimum ceiling height that is required. Extend this line outward to indicate the ceiling height of the dormer and where the dormer might meet the existing roof slope. Small window dormers need not have the required ceiling height if they are to be used simply as seating or daybed alcoves.

On an exterior view of your house, study the various roof forms the dormers could have, how each would fit into the overall form of the roof, and how much width each would allow for the dormers. Try to relate, if possible, any dormer windows to the windows in the exterior wall below.

Gable-roofed dormers are attractive and may be desirable for the exterior appearance of your house. They usually have the same pitch as the main roof and, therefore, are limited in size by the existing roof slope. Gable-roofed dormers are more useful for daylighting and ventilation than for increasing the usable floor area of an attic.

Shed-roofed dormers, unlike gable-roofed ones, can vary in width and greatly increase the usable floor area of an attic space. They are also easier to build since the dormer rafters are similar to common rafters and require no side cuts. The shed roof of a dormer will normally have a flatter pitch than the main roof, and can meet it at either the main ridge or an intermediate line framed by a double header or beam.

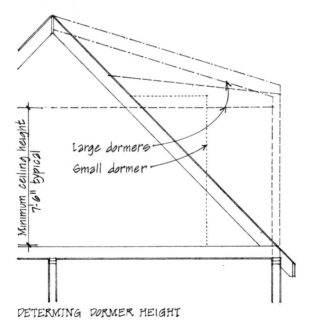

Minimum ceiling height 7'-6" typical

Large dormers
Small dormer

DETERMING DORMER HEIGHT

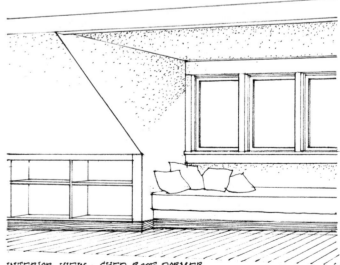

INTERIOR VIEW - SHED ROOF DORMER

Small dormers, 4' to 6' wide, are built around openings in the roof framing. These openings are first cut out and framed in a manner similar to openings in a floor frame. See pg. 236. The rafters or trimmers on each side of the opening are doubled to support the top and bottom headers. These headers, in turn, support the tail rafters, those that are cut to make the opening.

Within this opening, three stud walls, one front and two sides, are erected. These walls may rest on the attic floor or on the trimmer rafters and the bottom header. They are assembled like normal partitions, with top and sole plates.

The roof of the dormer can be a shed, gable, or hip form, and are constructed similarly to larger-scale roofs.

For a larger, wider dormer, structural support must be provided along the line where the dormer roof connects with the existing roof and along the outside edge. The support can be provided by a beam or by a bearing wall.

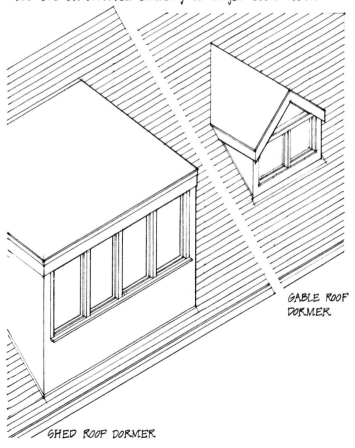

GABLE ROOF DORMER

SHED ROOF DORMER

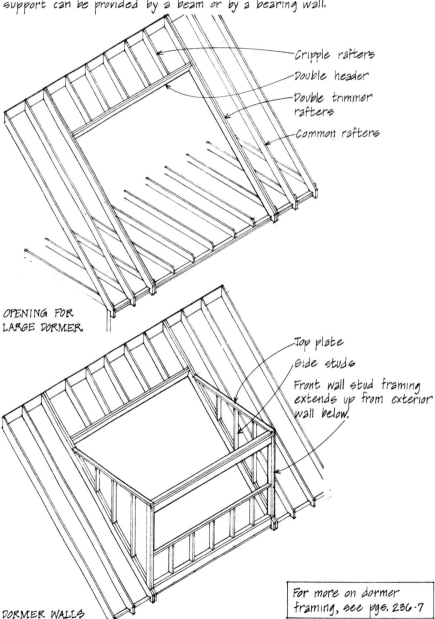

Cripple rafters
Double header
Double trimmer rafters
Common rafters

OPENING FOR LARGE DORMER

Top plate
Side studs
Front wall stud framing extends up from exterior wall below.

DORMER WALLS

For more on dormer framing, see pgs. 236-7

# SKYLIGHTS

Skylights can, even on cloudy or overcast days, brighten an interior space. Especially useful over windowless rooms, skylights can also be used to brighten dark corners, wash wall surfaces with light, and help balance the light in rooms already daylit with windows.

In determining the size, shape and location of skylights, consider the following factors:

1. LOCATION:

   The closer a skylight is to an interior wall surface, the more a space will benefit from the light entering since the wall surface will reflect the incoming light and become a light source in itself.

   A skylight more toward the center of a room may appear as a bright spot on the ceiling. To maximize the illumination from the skylight, increase the surface area perpendicular to and surrounding the skylight opening so that the surfaces serve as reflectors. Paint them flat-white for maximum reflectance.

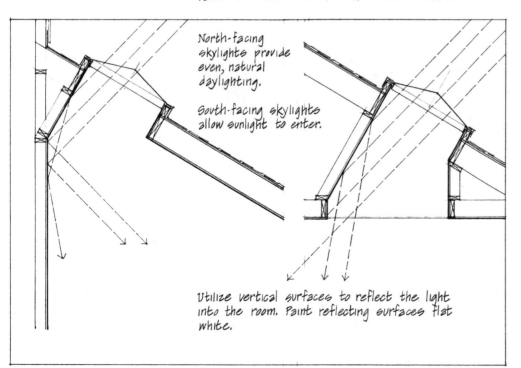

North-facing skylights provide even, natural daylighting.

South-facing skylights allow sunlight to enter.

Utilize vertical surfaces to reflect the light into the room. Paint reflecting surfaces flat white.

2. SIZE:

   Skylights and the glazing units used in fabricating skylights are factory-manufactured items. Their sizes, therefore, are standardized according to each manufacturer. Most skylights are modular units made to fit into the normal 16" or 24" o.c. spacing of roof rafters.

   The size of a skylight, along with its orientation, determines the type and quantity of daylight or sunlight admitted as well as the amount of heat gained or lost through the glazing.

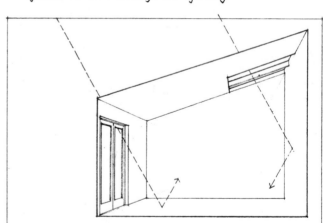

To provide a lighting level of about 120 foot-candles, a skylight should be between 4% and 12% of the room area. The actual percentage required depends on your geographic location. In addition, a room with light-colored walls and large windows will require less skylight area than a windowless room with dark-colored walls.

3. SHAPE:

Skylights are available in various shapes and forms. On sloping roofs, skylights can be quite visible, and their form and silhouette should be compatible with the style of the house.

4. CONSTRUCTION:

Since skylights are installed overhead in the roof framing, they are more directly exposed to the weather than windows in a wall. Their form and construction must shed water and melting snow efficiently without leaking. Their perimeter must be flashed so that water being shed by the surrounding roof area does not penetrate the opening.

To minimize heat loss through a skylight and control condensation on its surfaces, double-glazing should be used. Other means to control heat loss include operable shutters and insulating panels.

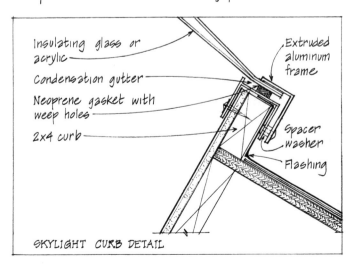

Insulating glass or acrylic

Condensation gutter

Neoprene gasket with weep holes

2x4 curb

Extruded aluminum frame

Spacer washer

Flashing

SKYLIGHT CURB DETAIL

5. GLAZING:

There are code requirements that regulate the type of glazing used in skylights. They are intended to protect persons walking on the roof as well as those inside from breaking glass. For safety, skylights are usually glazed with acrylic plastic, tempered glass, wire glass, or polycarbonates.

Clear glazing admits about 90% of available light, and affords upward views of overhead clouds and tall trees. Translucent glazing is used for privacy, to screen undesirable views, and to soften harsh or intense light.

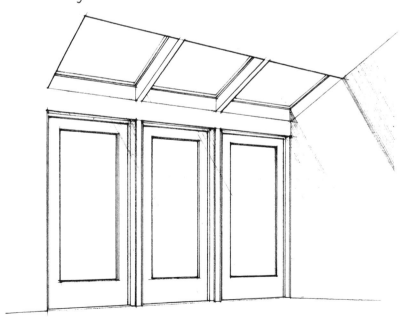

## SKYLIGHT UNITS

Pre-fabricated skylight units are available in a variety of shapes and sizes. They generally include the glazing, either acrylic plastic or tempered glass, and a metal frame with a flange for nailing or screwing the unit to your roof framing.

Skylights can also be built using stock double-glazed (with tempered glass) sash, or surplus glass sliding doors. With these, you have to prepare a curb of 2"x4"s around the opening. The glazing unit sits on top of the curb, caulked with glazing compound, and secured with wood stops that are nailed or screwed to the supporting curb frame. The entire perimeter must then be flashed.

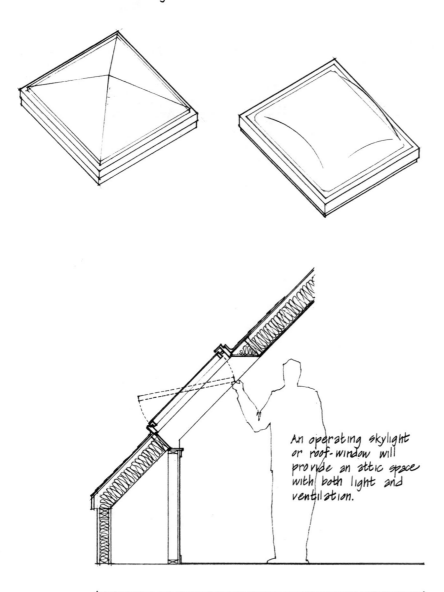

An operating skylight or roof-window will provide an attic space with both light and ventilation.

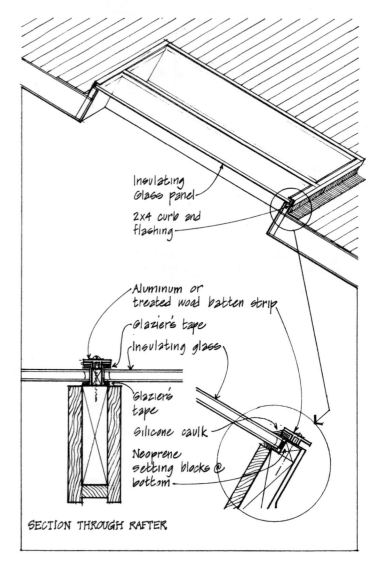

Insulating Glass panel

2x4 curb and flashing

Aluminum or treated wood batten strip

Glazier's tape

Insulating glass

Glazier's tape

Silicone caulk

Neoprene setting blocks @ bottom

SECTION THROUGH RAFTER

## PREPARING THE OPENING

When using a pre-fabricated skylight unit, verify the required rough opening with the manufacturer. When using window sash or sliding glass door units, determine the rough opening needed from the size of the glazing used.

Once you have determined the location of the skylight and verified the size of the rough opening required, shore up with temporary bracing the roof rafters to be cut. Then cut the rafters and tie the remaining portion to new headers that frame the top and bottom of the opening.

From the inside, mark the corners of the opening by driving long nails or drilling through the sheathing and roofing. From the outside, mark the outline of the opening with chalklines and cut the roofing away. Then saw through the sheathing material.

When installing the skylight unit, seal under the flanges before fastening them to the roof deck. New shingles can then be replaced over the flanges.

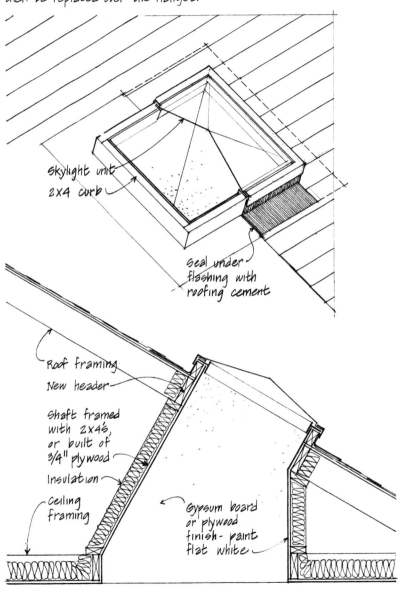

skylight unit
2x4 curb

Seal under flashing with roofing cement

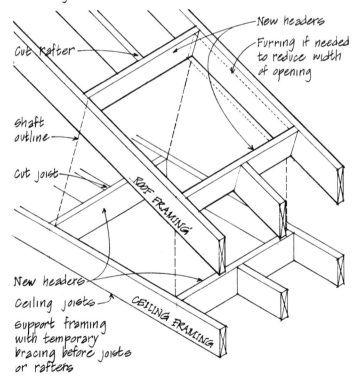

Cut rafter

New headers

Furring if needed to reduce width of opening

Shaft outline

Cut joist

ROOF FRAMING

New headers

Ceiling joists

CEILING FRAMING

support framing with temporary bracing before joists or rafters

Roof framing

New header

Shaft framed with 2x4's, or built of 3/4" plywood

Insulation

Ceiling framing

Gypsum board or plywood finish- paint flat white

## STAIRS

Stairs are important functional and design elements in any home with more than one living level. They are pivotal links in the pattern of movement between floor levels, and should be located for easy access without creating the need for long corridors or hallways.

As design elements, stairways may have different forms and treatments. They may be enclosed with walls, or be open and visible within a room. They may be attached to a wall, or be a freestanding, sculptural space divider.

Probably the two most important considerations in the design and construction of a stairway are safety and ease of travel. As a structural element, a stairway must be able to safely support the moving load of people on its steps. The weight and load of a stairway must in turn be supported by bearing walls, posts, or beams that transfer the loads down to the foundation.

For ease of travel, the treads, risers, width, and headroom clearance over a stair should be sized and proportioned carefully.

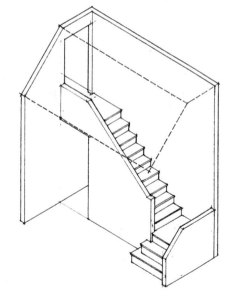

## STAIR DIMENSIONS

Stairs can be physically tiring as well as psychologically forbidding. They should be neither too steep nor too shallow. Experience has shown that certain proportions between the riser and tread dimensions of a stair work best. There are three rules-of-thumb that can be used to determine these proportions, in inches:

1. riser x run = 72 to 75
2. riser + run = 17 to 17½
3. (2x riser)+ run = 24 to 25

Building codes specify the maximum riser and minimum tread dimensions for all stairways. For private residential stairs, 8" is the maximum allowable rise and 9" the minimum allowable run. Stairs with this riser/tread ratio should be used only where space is extremely limited.

Comfortable riser/tread ratios for stairs are 7"/10¾" and 7½"/10". 6" risers and 12" treads are also acceptable, but usually require too much space.

For safety and comfort, it is important that all risers in a run of stairs be of the same height, and all treads be of the same depth. We generally assume this, and get used to a certain rhythm after the first few steps. Any variation in the riser or tread dimensions can cause one to trip and fall.

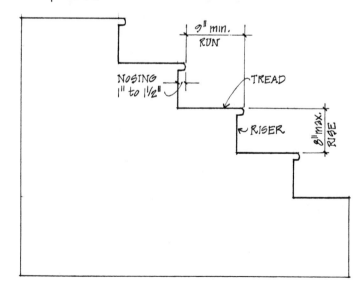

The riser and tread dimensions of a stair can be determined once the floor-to-floor height, or total rise, is known. This dimension is equal to the floor-to-ceiling height plus the total construction depth of the upper floor. The total rise, from one floor to the next, is divided by the estimated riser dimension. If this works out to be a whole number, that would be the number of risers needed, and the estimated riser dimension is the actual riser dimension.

If the result is a mixed number, round it off into a whole number (of risers), and re-divide the floor-to-floor height by this number to arrive at the actual riser dimension.

eg. For a total rise of 9' or 108", and an estimated riser dimension of 7½", divide 108 by 7.5 to get 14.4. If you use 14 risers, they will each have to be 108÷14 or 7.7" high, which is a bit steep. Using 15 risers, each of the risers would be 108÷15 or 7¼" high.

Using one of the rules-of-thumb for the riser/tread ratio, the tread dimension can be determined. Dividing 75 by 7.25, the tread can be 10¼" or 10⅜" deep. Since there is always one less tread than the number of risers, the total run would be 14 x 10.3" or 144.2" or 12'-0".

A main set of stairs should be at least 3'-0" wide. Considering that handrails can extend into a stairway about 3" on each side, many main stairs are built 3'-4" or 3'-6" wide for comfort and to make the moving of large furniture pieces easier. The minimum width for residential stairs is 2'-6", but stairs this narrow should be used only as secondary stairs.

The minimum headroom clearance, measured from the nosing of a tread vertically to any overhead construction, is 6'-6". While this may be the minimum required for physical clearance, it often does not feel comfortable. 6'-8" is a more reasonable minimum.

| Floor-to-Floor Height | Risers | | Treads | |
|---|---|---|---|---|
| | Nº | Dimension | Nº * | Dimension |
| 8'-6" | 14 | 7¼" + | 13 | 10¼" |
| 9'-0" | 15 | 7¼" - | 14 | 10⅜" |
| 9'-6" | 16 | 7⅛" | 15 | 10½" |
| 10'-0" | 17 | 7" + | 16 | 10¾" |
| 10'-6" | 18 | 7" | 17 | 10¾" |
| 11'-0" | 19 | 7" - | 18 | 10¾" |

* Every landing that occurs between floor levels counts as a tread.

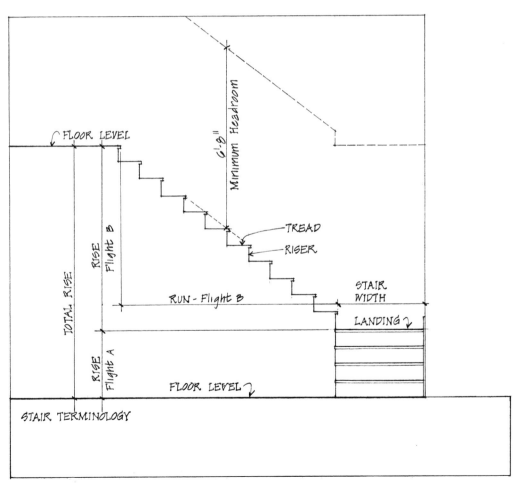

STAIR TERMINOLOGY

# STAIR PLANS

The type of stair plan you decide to use depends on the direction of access to the stair at both levels, and the proportion of the available space. Keep in mind that stairs, with the required overhead clearance, occupy a large volume of space. While a stairway should not restrict the size of adjacent rooms, spaces over or under the stairs can often be used for storage, sitting areas, etc.

Below are outlined three major types of stair plans. In addition to these basic forms, there are many variations that can be developed to fit into your specific situation. Several short flights of stairs can be connected by a series of landings, and wrap around a masonry fireplace. Landings can be enlarged into an overlook or reading alcove; stairs can be enlarged to double-function as seating.

## 1. STRAIGHT-RUN STAIRS

Straight-run stairs are the easiest to build. A long, straight run, however, can be tiring. Some building codes restrict the total rise of a straight flight of stairs between landings to 12'-0".

Any landings used to break a straight flight of stairs should be as deep as the stairs are wide.

When a door swings into a stairway at the top of the stairs, there should be a landing at least 2'-6" deep so that the door does not swing over the stairs.

## 2. L-SHAPED STAIRS

L-shaped stairs have two flights of stairs that turn 90° at a landing. These flights may be equal or unequal, depending on the desired proportion of the stairway opening. The landing that connects the two flights is sized according to the width of the stairs.

Where space is extremely limited, the landing may be omitted and winder treads used. This is generally not recommended since there is very little foothold at the corners of the winder treads. To increase the amount of foothold, the center of radius of the winders can be offset. The required tread width should be provided at a point no more than 12" in from the corner.

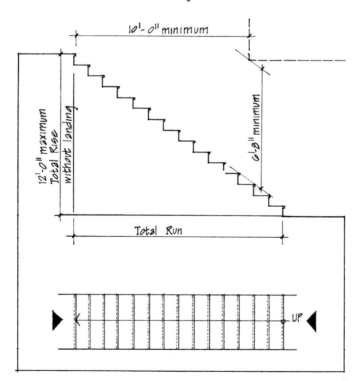

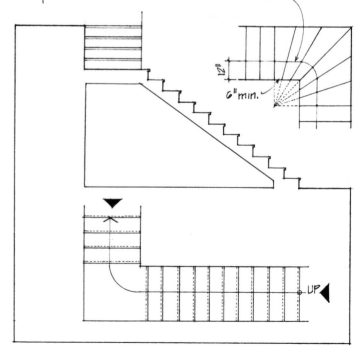

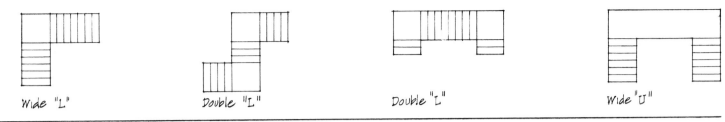

Wide "L"     Double "L"     Double "L"     Wide "U"

## 3. U-SHAPED STAIRS

U-shaped stairs also have two flights of stairs that turn 180° at a landing and end up parallel with each other. While the two flights are generally equal, they may also be unequal to fit into an elongated space. The landing should be as deep as the stairs are wide, and wider if large furniture pieces must be moved.

Where space is extremely limited and access is needed only to a loft or storage space, a ship's ladder or steep spiral stair can be used.

Spiral stairs are available in kit form with instructions for their assembly and installation. They generally consist of a center supporting post from which steel or wood winder treads are cantilevered. The center post does impose a concentrated load on the floor and should be adequately supported.

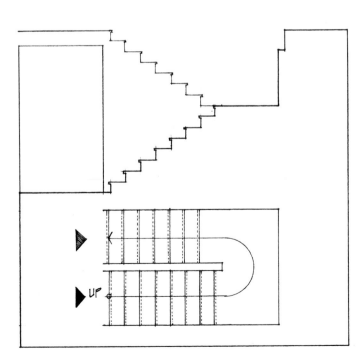

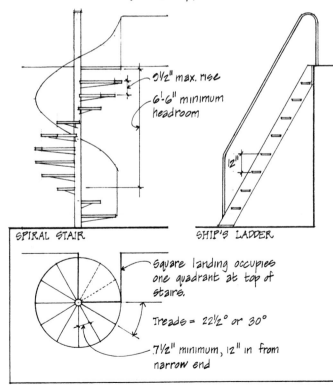

9½" max. rise

6'-6" minimum headroom

12"

SPIRAL STAIR          SHIP'S LADDER

Square landing occupies one quadrant at top of stairs.

Treads = 22½° or 30°

7½" minimum, 12" in from narrow end

## STAIR CONSTRUCTION

A stair is constructed of the following elements:

1. Carriages, or rough stringers, are the main framing members that support the stair treads and risers.
2. Stringers are the sloping side boards against which the risers and treads terminate. Stringers are usually finish members, although some may be housed to serve as a carriage and support the risers and treads.
3. Treads are the footways that act as small beams and span between the stair carriages.
4. Risers are vertical boards that also serve as mini-beams, and help make the stair construction rigid.

The stair carriages that carry the treads and support the stair load span between one floor and the next, or between a floor and an intermediate landing. At the upper level, the carriages can frame into a double header with joist hangers, or into a stud wall, bearing on a ledger board. At the lower level, the carriages can be secured to a kicker plate on the floor, or frame into a double header.

Two carriages of 2"x stock are used on the sides of the stair. An intermediate carriage is used when the tread material is less than 1" thick, and the stair is wider than 2'-6".

The stair carriages, or rough stringers, can be built in several ways. Perhaps the simplest is to use a 2"x12" from which a stepped pattern is cut for the risers and treads. A minimum effective depth of 3½" should remain. This notched carriage is secured to the supporting side wall, with a 2"x6" spacer that slopes with the stair between the carriage and the wall frame. This space allows the wall finish and a full, finish stringer to fit down beside the notched carriage. The risers and treads then are fastened to the supporting carriages.

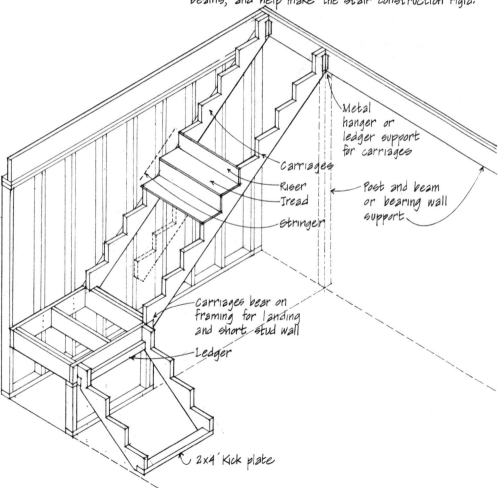

- Metal hanger or ledger support for carriages
- Carriages
- Riser
- Tread
- Stringer
- Post and beam or bearing wall support
- Carriages bear on framing for landing and short stud wall
- Ledger
- 2x4' Kick plate

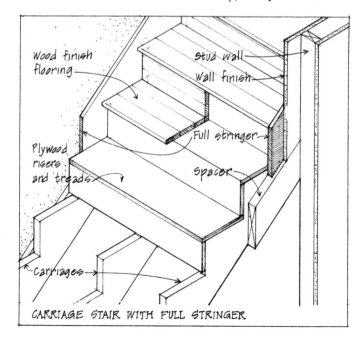

- Wood finish flooring
- Stud wall
- Wall finish
- Plywood risers and treads
- Full stringer
- Spacer
- Carriages

CARRIAGE STAIR WITH FULL STRINGER

The strongest stair and the most difficult to build uses housed stringers. These stringers are routed to create grooves into which the risers and treads fit. Space is allowed for wedges to which glue is applied. The wedges are then driven under the ends of the treads and in the backs of the risers. Shops that specialize in stair construction can fabricate these housed stringers, or an entire stair, to your specifications.

A stair may be open on one or both sides, and have open stringers that are cut to the profile of the stairs. This allows the treads to extend beyond the face of the stringers and form a tread return.

An open side of a stair can also be terminated with a curb stringer that is not notched. It is built and finished similar to a closed stringer against a wall, and often terminates a partition below the open side of a stair.

The riser and tread material for a stair may be cut from 2" clear stock, or be purchased pre-cut and pre-finished from a lumber yard. Finish wood treads should be of hardwood or vertical-grain softwood.

Rough treads and risers can also be cut from 3/4" or 1" plywood over which the finish surface of wood flooring or carpeting can be laid. For carpeting, the nosings of the treads should be chamfered to allow the carpeting to bend more easily over the tread.

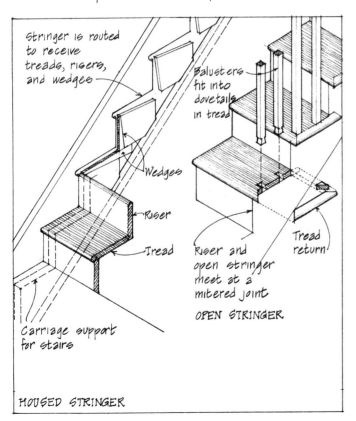

Stringer is routed to receive treads, risers, and wedges

Balusters fit into dovetails in tread

Wedges

Riser

Tread

Tread return

Riser and open stringer meet at a mitered joint

OPEN STRINGER

Carriage support for stairs

HOUSED STRINGER

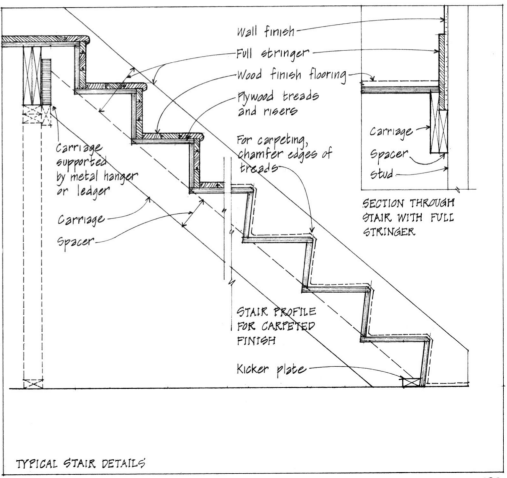

Wall finish

Full stringer

Wood finish flooring

Plywood treads and risers

For carpeting, chamfer edges of treads

Carriage supported by metal hanger or ledger

Carriage

Spacer

Carriage

Spacer

Stud

SECTION THROUGH STAIR WITH FULL STRINGER

STAIR PROFILE FOR CARPETED FINISH

Kicker plate

TYPICAL STAIR DETAILS

# OPEN-RISER STAIRS

An open-riser stair has an airy, light appearance, and provides a filtered view of what is below and beyond as we walk up the stairs. The openness of this type of stair may be appropriate where the visual separation of two spaces by the stairs is to be minimized, or where the stair is located, out of necessity, against an existing large window.

Because there are no risers to help support and stiffen the treads, the treads themselves must be thick enough to act as true beams that span between the stair carriages. While 2" thick plank material can be used for stairs up to 3'-0" wide, 3" material should be considered for greater stiffness and security.

The wood plank treads can rest on metal angle supports, or for a cleaner appearance, fit into slots or grooves routed into the stringer supports. If an open-riser stair is visible from below, the detailing of the tread/stringer connection should be neatly and cleanly executed.

In commercial construction, open-riser stairs are often built with steel pans and a concrete fill, or with steel grating, that span between steel channel stringers. You may want to consider this alternative because of the clean, slender lines steel stairs offer.

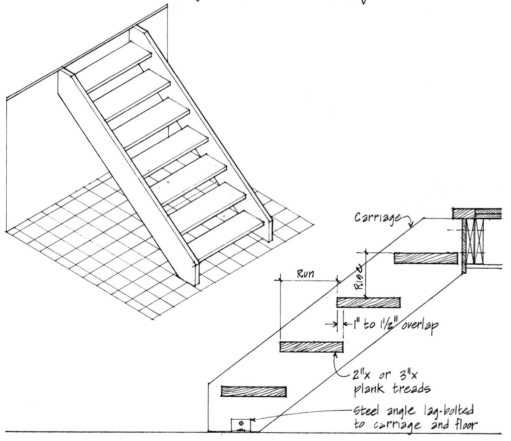

Carriage

Run

Rise

1" to 1½" overlap

2"x or 3"x plank treads

Steel angle lag-bolted to carriage and floor

LONGITUDINAL SECTION

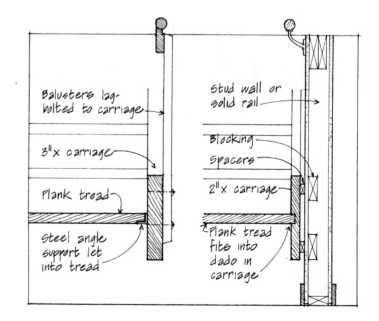

Balusters lag-bolted to carriage

3"x carriage

Plank tread

Steel angle support let into tread

Stud wall or solid rail

Blocking

Spacers

2"x carriage

Plank tread fits into dado in carriage

PARTIAL CROSS-SECTIONS

# HANDRAILS & RAILINGS

Handrails are required on at least one side of any stair with more than three risers. If the stair is open on one or both sides, a protective railing must be provided on the open sides. The handrail should be continuous and be from 2'-6" to 2'-10" above the nosing of the treads, following the slope of the stair.

When projecting from a wall, the handrail should be at least 1½" away from the wall surface to allow space for a handhold. The handrail itself should be between 1¼" and 2" wide, and have a smooth surface with no corners.

Handrails often continue into protective railings required at landings and balconies that open onto the space below. These railings should be 3'-0" to 3'-4" high, and be firmly anchored to resist overturning when leaned on.

Handrails and railings may be of closed or open design. Closed railings are easier to build and the stronger of the two. They consist simply of extensions of the wall that supports the stair carriages, and are cut off at the desired height. The handrail can be set on top of, or be hung from the railing wall with brackets.

Open railings may be designed and constructed in several ways. Vertical balusters can be fit into holes cut or drilled into the stair treads, or be fastened to the side of the stair stringer. Newel posts, used to turn the corners of and terminate balustrade railings, must be securely anchored to the building frame or starting step. A handrail can then be fastened to the top of the balusters. All of these are available as stock parts through millwork or lumber dealers.

Several larger vertical supports, spaced further apart and securely anchored to the stair stringer, can also be used. In this case, a top handrail and intermediate rails can be fastened to these supports. Another option is to fill the openings between the vertical supports and the top handrail with pre-fabricated panels or screens.

Building codes usually require that the width or height of any opening in a railing be 9" or less.

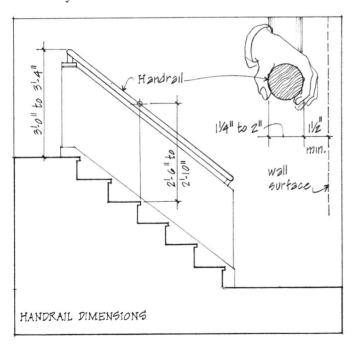

HANDRAIL DIMENSIONS

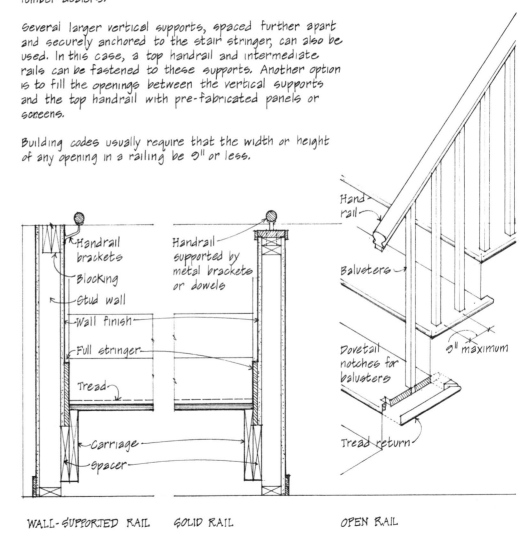

WALL-SUPPORTED RAIL    SOLID RAIL    OPEN RAIL

# 3

# CONVERTING BASEMENTS

When considering the conversion of a basement into livable space, first check the available headroom. It should be at least 7'-6" from the floor slab to the underside of the first floor joists.

If the basement is to be used as a living room or for sleeping, check your local code for daylight, ventilation and emergency exit requirements. The glazing area of windows for habitable spaces should be at least 10% of the usable floor area, with at least half of that area being operable for ventilation. Most codes also require that if a window is to serve as an emergency exit, it must have a minimum net opening of 5 to 6 s.f., a minimum opening height of 24" and opening width of 20", and a sill no more than 44" above the floor.

If the basement has no windows, the space may still be usable as a recreation room, hobby room, or workshop. Artificial lighting and mechanical ventilation become important in these cases.

As you plan the layout of the basement space, note which areas must be reserved for utilities and storage. Mark the locations of, and allow access to, the furnace, hot water heater, laundry, the main electrical service panel, and the main shutoffs for the water and gas lines.

Also study the access requirements for the intended use of the basement space. If you intend to use part of the basement as a family or group space, the existing stair may have to be refurbished or reinforced, if not for structural reasons, for appearance.

Keep the floor plan layout as open as possible, especially if there is insufficient daylight, so that inner portions of the basement have at least some access to daylight.

Plan for any special construction you may want, such as extra thick walls around the furnace, workshop or laundry room to isolate their sounds and keep them from disturbing adjacent areas.

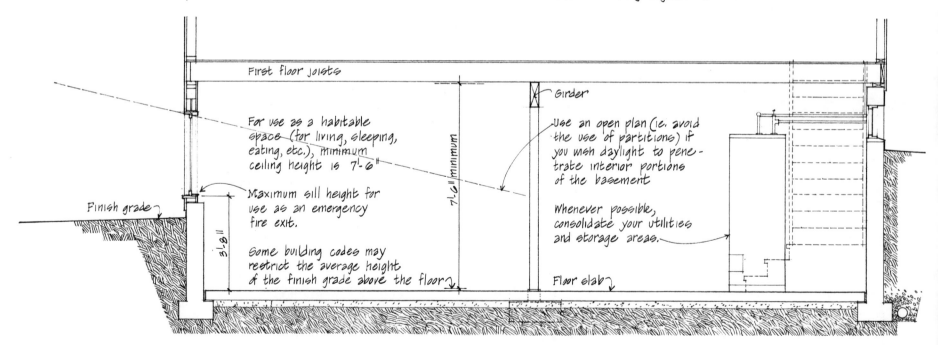

First floor joists

Girder

For use as a habitable space (for living, sleeping, eating, etc.), minimum ceiling height is 7'-6"

Use an open plan (ie. avoid the use of partitions) if you wish daylight to penetrate interior portions of the basement

Maximum sill height for use as an emergency fire exit.

Whenever possible, consolidate your utilities and storage areas.

Finish grade

7'-6" minimum

3'-8"

Some building codes may restrict the average height of the finish grade above the floor.

Floor slab

Before converting a basement space, any watertightness or dampness problems must be corrected. If condensation forms on the basement walls or pipes due to excessive humidity in the air, improve the ventilation of the basement space and install a dehumidifier.

If surface water is seeping through pores, mortar joints or expansion joints of a basement wall, check the roof and surface drainage around the house. Ensure that downspouts from roof gutters are channeling water away from the house to a drywell or storm sewer. Also see that the exterior grade slopes away from the foundation wall.

Once the surface drainage is improved, minor seepage problems can be treated with an interior sealer. If major seepage or leakage problems persist, the ground around the foundation wall must be excavated, the foundation wall waterproofed from the outside, and a system of drain tiles installed.

Minor dormant cracks can be repaired by routing out the crack area and resealing with an epoxy-cement compound. Active cracks, those that continue to grow, should be filled with an elastic sealant that will remain pliable so that it can deform along with any movement in the crack. (First, solve the cause of the cracking. If it indicates continuing structural settlement, consult an engineer.)

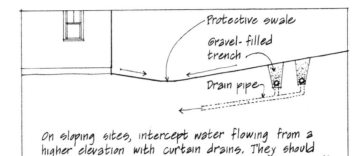

Protective swale
Gravel-filled trench
Drain pipe

On sloping sites, intercept water flowing from a higher elevation with curtain drains. They should lead water around the house to a drywell or runoff.

For any water leakage problem, first check the following:
- Grade should slope away from the house.
- Downspouts should channel water away from the house foundation, and lead to a drywell or storm sewer

- For minor seepage problems, seal the interior of the basement wall with a cement- or epoxy-based coating, or use a rubber-base paint.

- For cracks, use a quick-hardening, ex expansive cement, or an epoxy-based compound.

- If improving your surface drainage and sealing the interior of your basement walls do not solve leakage problems, the exterior of the basement walls must be waterproofed with an asphalt coating.

Coarse gravel or crushed stone

- To drain subsurface water away from the foundation walls, perforated plastic (ABS) drain pipe is required. The drain line should be sloped properly (1" in 20'), and lead to a dry well or storm sewer at a lower elevation.

# BASEMENT FLOORS

If the basement floor slab is reasonably smooth and remains dry, it is a suitable base for a variety of floor coverings - tile, wood, or carpeting. For additional protection against dampness, a clear, waterproof coating is always advisable before the flooring material is laid.

Linoleum, cork and particleboard tiles should not be laid directly over a concrete ground slab.

If the concrete slab is too uneven for a tile floor, or if moisture and condensation periodically dampens the slab, a vapor barrier can be laid over the slab and a 2" to 3" topping of concrete can be added.

For the same conditions as well as comfort and warmth, a raised wood platform laid over the slab is preferred. The concrete slab, which must be dry, is first waterproofed with a coating of tar or asphalt mastic. A layer of polyethylene film is then laid and pressed into the mastic. (If dampness is not a serious problem and the slab remains dry, substitute a coating of clear waterproofing.)

2"x4" wood sleepers, treated with a wood preservative, are laid flat in a coating of tar or asphalt mastic and spaced 12" to 16" o.c. These sleepers need not be full length lumber. They can be spare pieces 18" to 48" long. If concrete nails are used to secure the wood sleepers, use only as many as needed to keep the sleepers in place until the subflooring or wood strip flooring is installed.

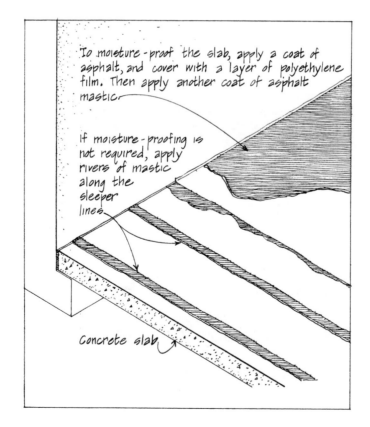

To moisture-proof the slab, apply a coat of asphalt, and cover with a layer of polyethylene film. Then apply another coat of asphalt mastic.

If moisture-proofing is not required, apply rivers of mastic along the sleeper lines.

Concrete slab

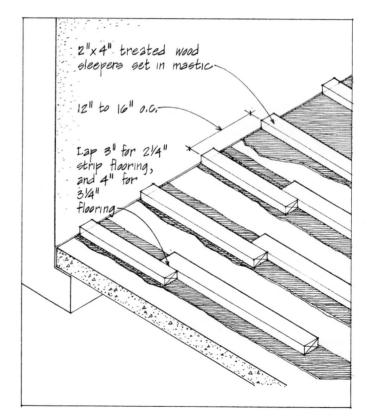

2"x4" treated wood sleepers set in mastic.

12" to 16" o.c.

Lap 3" for 2¼" strip flooring, and 4" for 3¾" flooring

To help keep the basement floor warm, lay a two-foot width of rigid polystyrene insulation around the perimeter of the floor within the depth of the wood sleepers. This is especially important when the exterior grade is low and close to the basement floor.

A vapor barrier of 4-mil polyethylene is laid over the wood sleepers. Wood strip flooring can then be laid directly across the sleepers, or a subfloor of 3/4" exterior-grade plywood installed for tile or carpet flooring.

An alternate system of wood sleepers for wood strip flooring consists of treated 1"x3"s or 1"x4"s, spaced 12" to 16" o.c., laid in mastic. Shim as required to provide a level base. A vapor barrier of 4-mil polyethylene is then laid, and a second set of 1"x3"s or 1"x4"s nailed to the first set.

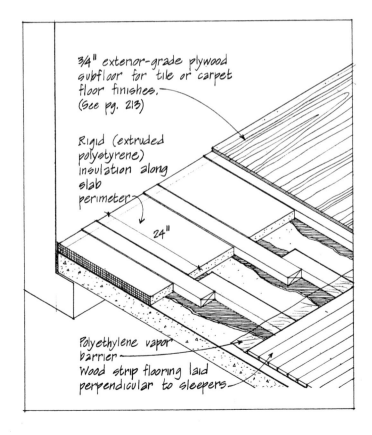

3/4" exterior-grade plywood subfloor for tile or carpet floor finishes. (See pg. 213)

Rigid (extruded polystyrene) insulation along slab perimeter

24"

Polyethylene vapor barrier

Wood strip flooring laid perpendicular to sleepers

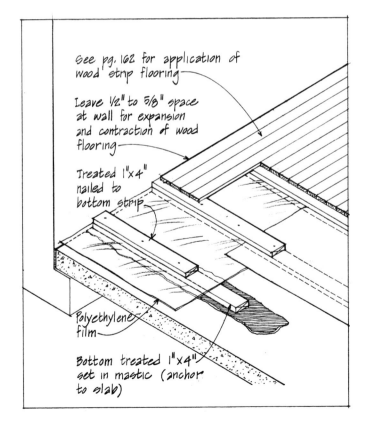

See pg. 162 for application of wood strip flooring

Leave 1/2" to 5/8" space at wall for expansion and contraction of wood flooring

Treated 1"x4" nailed to bottom strip

Polyethylene film

Bottom treated 1"x4" set in mastic (anchor to slab)

# BASEMENT WALLS

If the surface drainage around your house works, and the outside of your basement walls has been waterproofed, a variety of wall finishes can be applied to the interior surfaces. They can be painted a fresh new color, or if a more finished appearance is desired, gypsum board or other wall paneling can be applied over wood furring or rigid insulation.

If there is a chance of water penetrating the basement wall, however, coat the interior surfaces with a waterproof coating or masonry paint. Follow the manufacturer's recommendations. Some coatings may not be suitable for use over walls that have already been painted.

To prepare a basement wall for an interior finish, furring strips, 2"x2" or larger, are used to form a supporting frame.

2"x2" horizontal plates are first secured to the top and bottom of the basement walls. The bottom plate is secured to the floor with masonry nails or construction adhesive. The top plate is nailed to the underside of the joists or, when parallel to them, to blocking between the joists.

2"x2" vertical furring strips are then placed at 16" or 24" o.c., depending on the requirements of the wall finish material. These again are secured with masonry nails or construction adhesive. Before anchoring these furring strips permanently, check their spacing and make sure they are plumb.

Remember to frame around any window and door openings in the basement wall.

Once the furring strips are in place, any electrical work required along the basement walls should be done.

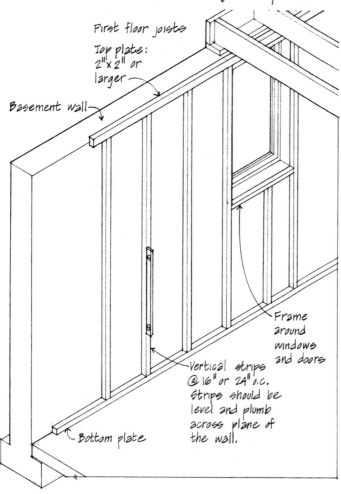

First floor joists

Top plate: 2"x2" or larger

Basement wall

Frame around windows and doors

Vertical strips @ 16" or 24" o.c. Strips should be level and plumb across plane of the wall.

Bottom plate

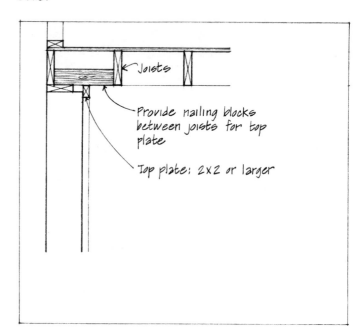

Joists

Provide nailing blocks between joists for top plate

Top plate: 2x2 or larger

Before applying the wall finish, place insulation in between the furring strips. If a blanket type of insulation is used, the vapor barrier should face into the room. The furring strips may have to be deeper to accept the thickness of the blanket.

Rigid foam insulation panels that are moisture-resistant (eg. extruded polystyrene) can also be glued or friction-fit in between the furring strips. Since these panels are combustible, they must be covered or sheathed with a fire-resistant material, such as ½" gypsum board.

If your basement walls are rough and uneven, an additional layer of 1"x 2" or 1"x 3" furring can be laid horizontally across the vertical strips and shimmed to provide a level base for the wall finish.

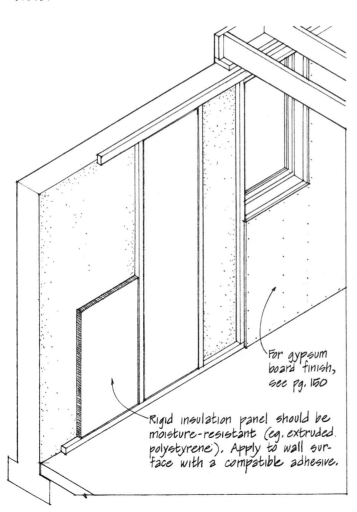

For gypsum board finish, see pg. 150

Rigid insulation panel should be moisture-resistant (eg. extruded polystyrene). Apply to wall surface with a compatible adhesive.

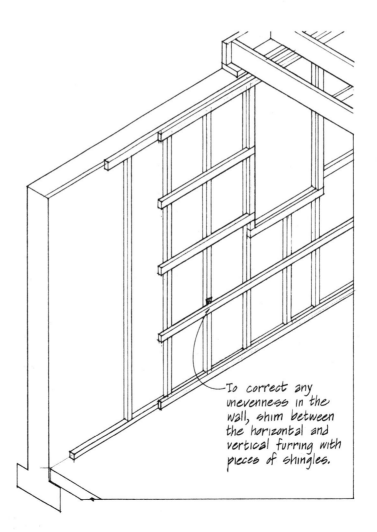

To correct any unevenness in the wall, shim between the horizontal and vertical furring with pieces of shingles.

## BASEMENT WALLS

Lightweight, rigid foam insulation panels can also be applied directly to the surface of basement walls with construction adhesive. The insulation panels should be vapor- and water-resistant (eg. extruded polystyrene) to eliminate need for a separate vapor barrier.

For this type of application, the surface of the basement walls must be smooth and level without any protrusions. If the surfaces are too uneven, first erect a framework of furring strips as described in the previous section. The wall surfaces must also be dry, clean, and free of grease or loose paint. Clean with a wire brush and fill any small voids with concrete caulk as necessary.

Lumber, 2" nominal width and as thick as the insulation used, is first secured with construction adhesive to the bottom of the walls and around any window or door openings. Another strip is nailed to the underside of joists or to blocking along the top of the basement walls. No vertical strips are required.

After any required electrical work is done, the insulation panels are applied with adhesive. The adhesive is usually applied in ribbon form. To achieve a better bond, the panels can be pressed into place, pulled off, and then re-applied in a few minutes. When using adhesives, follow the manufacturer's recommendations and instructions carefully.

The panels can be cut easily with a utility knife and applied either vertically or horizontally, whichever is easier for you. Work around any pipes you may encounter.

Because plastic foam is combustible, keep the panels away from hot surfaces and pipes. In addition, the insulation must be covered with a fire-resistant material such as 1/2" gypsum board. These can also be applied with drywall adhesive, and nailed to the top and bottom plates.

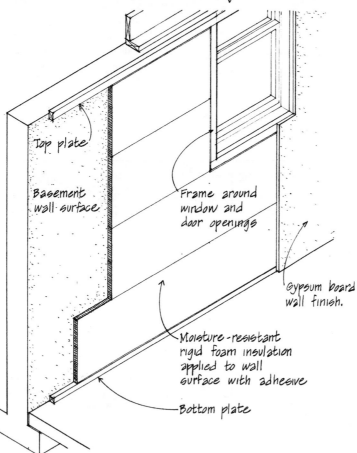

Top plate

Basement wall surface

Frame around window and door openings

Gypsum board wall finish.

Moisture-resistant rigid foam insulation applied to wall surface with adhesive

Bottom plate

## BASEMENT CEILINGS

Ceilings of basements can be finished similarly to ceilings of rooms above grade. Finishes such as gypsum board, ceiling tile, and wood can be applied directly to the undersides of the joists or be suspended from them.

Before applying any ceiling finish, all electrical, heating, and plumbing work in the ceiling space should be done. Cold water pipes should be insulated to prevent their sweating and dripping during periods of high humidity. If exposed electrical, heating or plumbing lines are hung from the joists, they can be concealed by a suspended ceiling.

When considering a suspended ceiling, check that the finished floor-to-ceiling height will be at least 7'-6" for a living or sleeping space, and at the very minimum, 7' for other spaces. If the headroom clearance is tight, and a suspended ceiling is not feasible, try to box in the utility lines, re-routing them as necessary.

Suspended ceilings are usually packaged and purchased as a system, including the tiles, the supporting grid, and detailed instructions for installation.

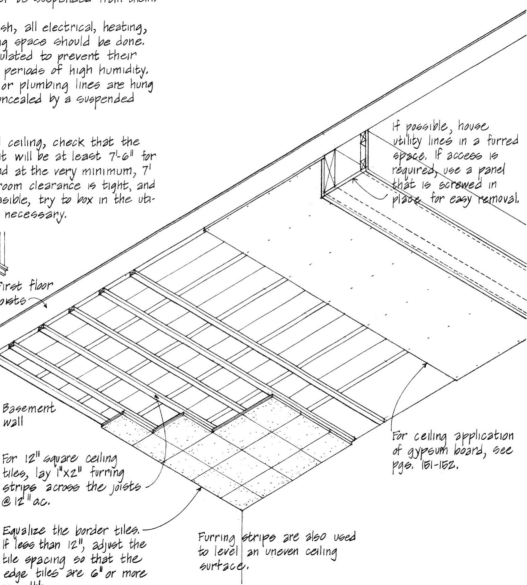

If possible, house utility lines in a furred space. If access is required, use a panel that is screwed in place for easy removal.

First floor joists

Basement wall

For 12" square ceiling tiles, lay 1"x2" furring strips across the joists @ 12" o.c.

Equalize the border tiles. If less than 12", adjust the tile spacing so that the edge tiles are 6" or more in width.

Furring strips are also used to level an uneven ceiling surface.

For ceiling application of gypsum board, see pgs. 151-152.

# GARAGE CONVERSIONS

A garage, if not needed for car storage, can be converted into a considerable amount of living space at a moderate cost. The structure is essentially complete. If the garage is attached to the house, utilities are close by. Assuming the exterior frame, siding and roof are in good condition, all that is needed, other than some structural modifications for new windows and closing of the existing garage doorway, is the insulation and finishing of the floor, walls and ceiling.

Even if the garage is detached, a new space can be built to serve as a new entry as well as a connection between the converted garage and the main house.

If you have a two-car garage, perhaps half of it could remain a garage while the other half is converted into usable space.

The open expansiveness of garage spaces is well suited for living or family rooms, studios, or workshop spaces. As you plan a garage conversion, consider carefully how you can best use the size and proportion of the space, and how it will relate to the rest of the house.

A new entry may be needed to enable the converted space to be reached without passing through the rest of the house. New patio or french doors may be desirable to connect the converted space to an outdoor living area.

New windows or skylights should satisfy code requirements for natural light and ventilation. Plan the size and location of any new windows carefully as you would in any new room. Consider the path of the sun, daylight requirements, views, wind, and the need for privacy.

Don't forget to check the zoning code to ensure it is possible to eliminate the garage parking space, and that the garage conversion satisfies the setback requirements of your lot.

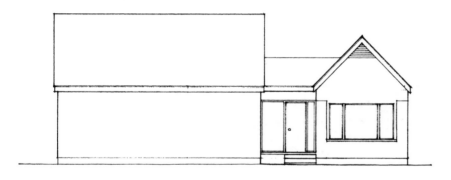

Be sure the garage has a concrete foundation under its walls. Many garages built before 1940 were constructed with their wood walls setting directly on the soil.

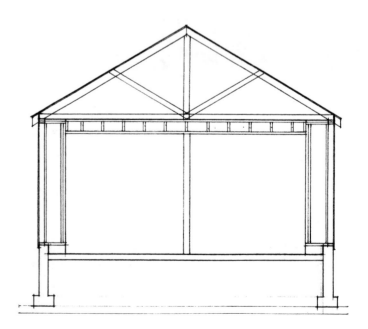

## GARAGE FLOORS

The concrete floor slab of a garage can be finished with vinyl sheet, tile or carpet flooring if it remains dry, and is reasonably level and smooth. Otherwise, a plywood subfloor over wood sleepers should be installed as over a basement floor slab. See pg. 134.

If the ceiling height of the garage allows, or if the garage and house ceilings are at the same level, a new wood joist floor can be built over the concrete slab. The space between the floor joists and the slab can be used for new electrical, heating and plumbing lines and eliminate any need to excavate for their placement.

The new floor joists can be supported either on the sole plate that rests on the foundation wall, or on 2"x4" ledgers secured to the existing exterior wall studs. Consult the floor joist span tables on pg. 207. for joist sizes. Where intermediate supports are needed to reduce the spans and sizes of the floor joists, a short cripple stud wall can be used.

Insulation can be placed around the perimeter of the garage floor slab between the wood sleepers. If wood sleepers are not used, an alternative is to apply moisture-resistant, rigid foam insulation panels directly to the outer face of the garage foundation wall, extending the insulation down to the footing. In this latter case, adjustments to the exterior wall finish may be necessary where it meets the insulation.

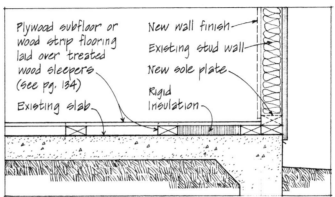

Plywood subfloor or wood strip flooring laid over treated wood sleepers (see pg. 134)

Existing slab

New wall finish

Existing stud wall

New sole plate

Rigid Insulation

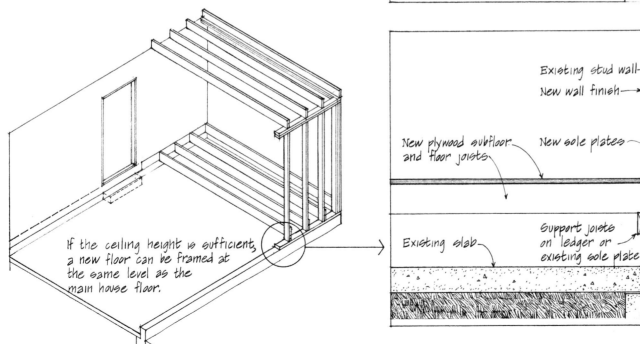

If the ceiling height is sufficient, a new floor can be framed at the same level as the main house floor.

Existing stud wall

New wall finish

New plywood subfloor and floor joists

New sole plates

Existing slab

Support joists on ledger or existing sole plate

## GARAGE WALLS

The existing walls of the garage are insulated and finished as in new construction. See pgs. 150 and 276. Modifications of these walls are needed to close up the garage doorway and to create openings for new windows and doorways.

The existing garage door must be removed along with any trim that surrounds the opening. The existing header over the opening is left in place. A new sole plate, along with sill sealer, is secured to the garage slab edge with concrete or masonry nails. Use a termite shield if it is necessary in your area.

If oriented properly, the existing opening can be framed to accept large windows or french doors.

If, however, a large window would interfere with the use or layout of the converted space, or with the desired degree of privacy, then the opening should be blocked up with standard 2"x4" stud framing, sheathed and sided to match or complement the existing siding material.

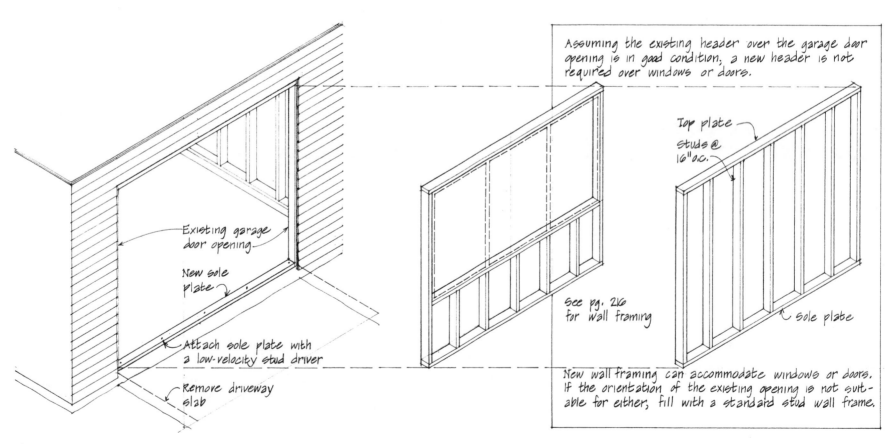

Existing garage door opening

New sole plate

Attach sole plate with a low-velocity stud driver

Remove driveway slab

Assuming the existing header over the garage door opening is in good condition, a new header is not required over windows or doors.

Top plate

Studs @ 16" o.c.

See pg. 216 for wall framing

Sole plate

New wall framing can accommodate windows or doors. If the orientation of the existing opening is not suitable for either, fill with a standard stud wall frame.

## GARAGE CEILINGS

Your garage roof may be framed with trusses, rafters, or a system of planks and beams. These framing systems open up various design possibilities for finishing the ceiling of a converted garage space. In each case, the ceiling space should be well insulated. If a space is created between the ceiling and the roof during the remodeling, it should be ventilated as well.

Flat ceilings of gypsum board, ceiling tile, or wood can be installed in the normal manner. Each ceiling material may have specific framing or furring requirements, but they can be secured to the bottom chords of trusses or regular ceiling joists that span across the garage space.

The roof structure of rafters, beams or trusses can be left exposed as design elements in the space. They can be painted, stained, or clad in a finish material. The finish ceiling material and a layer of rigid insulation can be applied directly to the underside of the roof sheathing. In this way, the form of the roof can be preserved and reflected in the on the interior.

Skylights and lighting fixtures can help to animate the exposed roof structure and brighten the interior portion of the garage space.

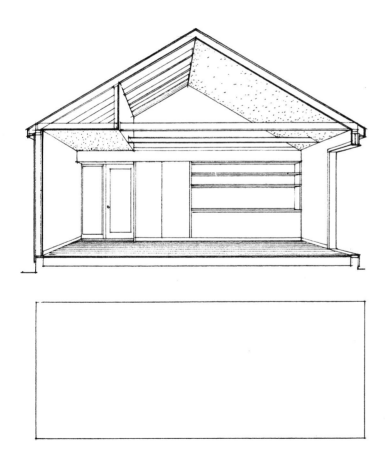

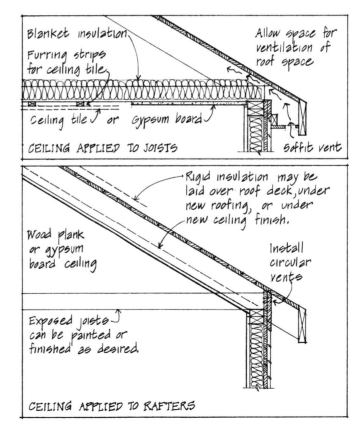

Blanket insulation

Furring strips for ceiling tile

Allow space for ventilation of roof space

Ceiling tile or Gypsum board

CEILING APPLIED TO JOISTS

Soffit vent

Rigid insulation may be laid over roof deck, under new roofing, or under new ceiling finish.

Wood plank or gypsum board ceiling

Install circular vents

Exposed joists can be painted or finished as desired.

CEILING APPLIED TO RAFTERS

## PORCH CONVERSIONS

A porch that is used sparingly or not at all can be enclosed, insulated and finished to extend or expand an existing room in your house. A small porch can become a sunroom or fireplace alcove; a larger porch can become a separate study or bedroom.

The advantage of a porch conversion over a room-sized addition is that it already has a basic structure - foundation, floor, posts and a roof. Since a porch is exposed to the weather, however, these elements should be inspected for signs of decay or deterioration, and repaired if necessary, before any remodeling work is done.

As with a room addition, several factors must be considered in the planning and design of a porch conversion. The new use of the space must be compatible with the adjacent rooms, and enclosing the porch should not block the required daylighting and ventilation of these rooms.

To prepare for the porch conversion, remove the existing ceiling finish, railings and any trim that will interfere with the construction of new exterior walls. If the porch stairs will lead to a new entry door, they can remain. If a new doorway will be located elsewhere, and the stairs are not needed, remove them as well.

Inspect the condition of the foundation, support posts, and the roof. The foundation should be strong enough to carry the additional load imposed by the new construction and the new use of the converted porch.

Check the floor joist size, spacing and span against the joist span table on pg. 207. Add additional joists if required.

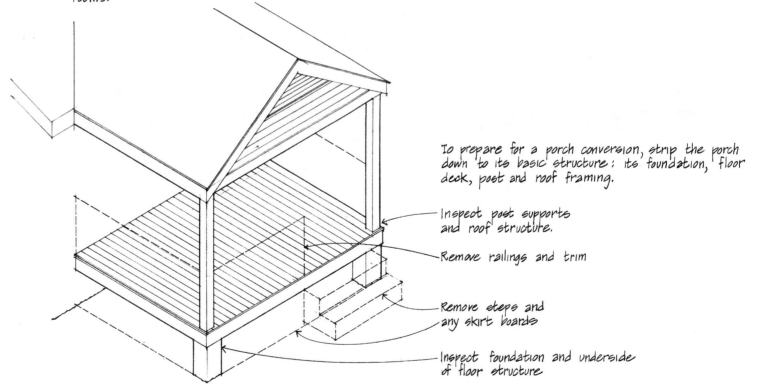

To prepare for a porch conversion, strip the porch down to its basic structure: its foundation, floor deck, post and roof framing.

Inspect post supports and roof structure.

Remove railings and trim

Remove steps and any skirt boards

Inspect foundation and underside of floor structure

If the porch deck is flat, at the same level as the house floor, and in good condition, a new 1/2" plywood subfloor can be laid directly over the deck.

If the porch deck slopes to drain any rainwater that falls on it, wood joists or sleepers should be placed over it. These are ripped or cut lengthwise to fit the slope and provide a level supporting framework for the new subfloor. Place them at 16" o.c., and tie them together with headers at the outer edge of the porch and where the porch meets the house.

They should be as deep as is necessary to bring the level of the porch floor up to the level of the house floor, minus the thickness of the plywood subflooring.

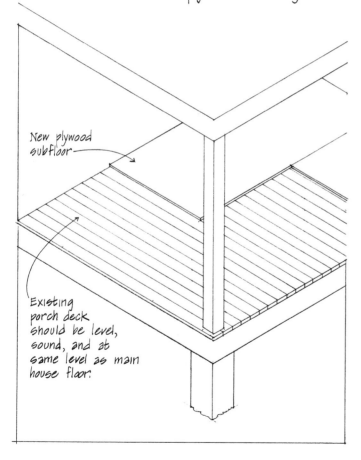

New plywood subfloor

Existing porch deck should be level, sound, and at same level as main house floor.

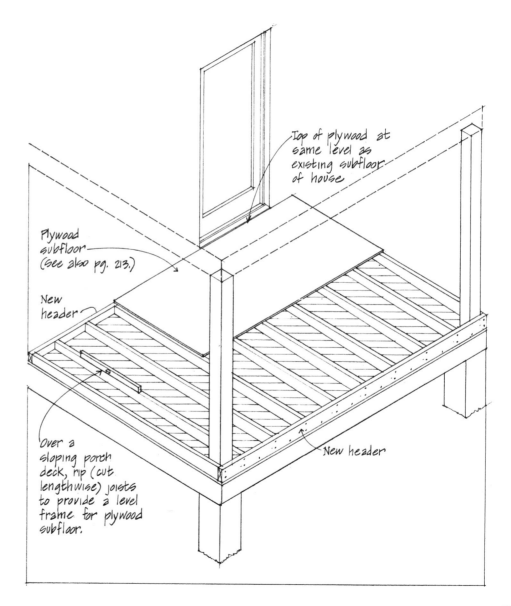

Top of plywood at same level as existing subfloor of house

Plywood subfloor (see also pg. 213.)

New header

Over a sloping porch deck, rip (cut lengthwise) joists to provide a level frame for plywood subfloor.

New header

Along the edges of the porch deck, and between the existing posts, exterior wall frames are built as in new construction. The outer face of the studs should ideally be aligned with the outer surface of the posts so that the wall sheathing is continuous and overlaps both the studs and the posts.

When enclosing a porch and converting it into usable space, the room that opens onto the porch will also have to be altered to some degree. If the existing exterior finish is not acceptable as an interior finish for the converted porch, it will have to be removed and replaced. The existing doorway can either be moved or enlarged to open the room up further to the converted space. An existing window can be eliminated, enlarged into a doorway, or be kept simply as interior pass-through.

See pgs. 217-221 for wall framing details.

If posts are set back from the edge of the porch floor frame, set the wall framing flush with the floor edge and add blocking to the posts.

Edge of floor frame

Post

Blocking

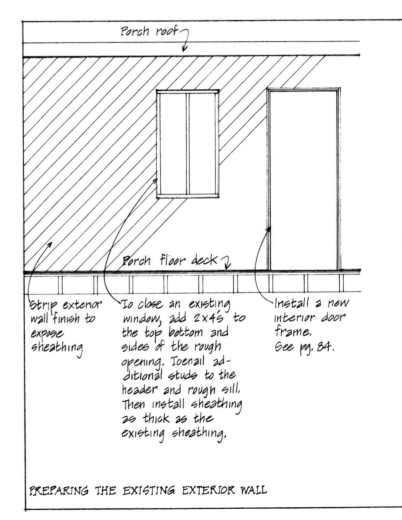

Porch roof

Porch floor deck

Strip exterior wall finish to expose sheathing

To close an existing window, add 2x4's to the top, bottom and sides of the rough opening. Toenail additional studs to the header and rough sill. Then install sheathing as thick as the existing sheathing.

Install a new interior door frame. See pg. 84.

PREPARING THE EXISTING EXTERIOR WALL

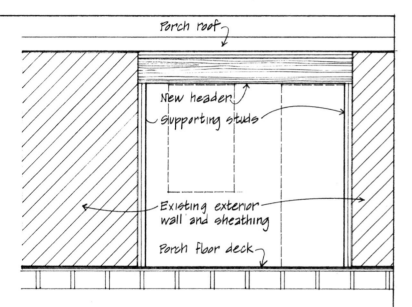

Porch roof

New header

Supporting studs

Existing exterior wall and sheathing

Porch floor deck

The existing doorway opening can be enlarged to open the enclosed porch space to the main house. The procedure for creating the new opening is similar to that described for windows on pgs. 74, 75. See also pg. 100 for removing a bearing wall, and pg. 221 for sizing the new header required.

## INTERIOR FINISHES

This section outlines common materials and methods used to provide the interior finish for walls, floors, and ceilings. Unlike exterior siding and roofing, interior finishes need not be weather-resistant. Rather, they must be suitable for the use and appearance of the individual rooms in a house.

Some activities may subject walls and floors to more use (or abuse) than others. Some rooms, like bathrooms, require finishes that are moisture-resistant. High-traffic areas require flooring that is durable and offers the safety of a non-slip surface. Ceilings, while generally immune from direct wear and tear, might be affected by moisture, dirt or grease.

In addition to durability and ease of maintenance, other factors to consider in selecting an interior finish material include the type of support or backing the material requires, its ease of application, and how it can be finished.

While rigid materials can often be laid over open framing on walls and ceilings, thin sheet and tile materials require a solid base, especially on floors. Some materials are pre-finished, while others require a separate coating or covering for durability, resistance to wear, and appearance qualities. Some materials are self-aligning and can be applied simply with adhesive, while others require carpentry tools and skills.

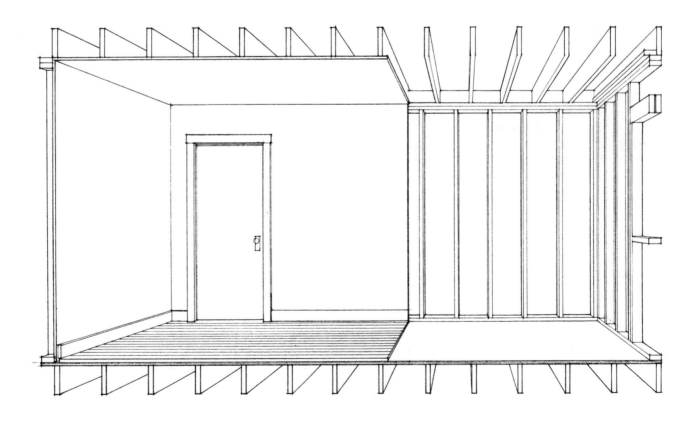

The finish floor, wall and ceiling surfaces are important visual design elements in any space. Their color, value, texture and pattern affect a room's scale, proportion and character. They establish the setting for the furnishings within the room.

Some materials have a clean, monolithic appearance, while others have a fine, natural texture. Some materials require special joint treatments. Others are modular and their layout must be coordinated with a room's dimensions and other visual elements in the space, such as windows and doors.

Finally, the interior finish work and trim are the most visible part of any construction. Whatever care has been taken during the rough framing can be negated by finish work that is not carefully done. And any mistakes in finish work can be difficult to correct.

If you are not sure of how to execute any phase of finish work, consider hiring a specialist. It may cost you more but it can save you the expense of having to do a badly done job over again. Keep in mind that even builders often use finish work specialists because they can do the job faster and better. If you do decide to do any finish work yourself, allow sufficient time for the work; select the right materials for the situation; use the proper tools and equipment. Above all, exercise care and patience.

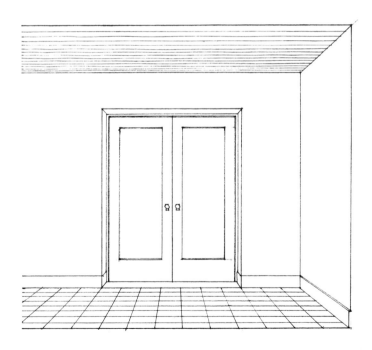

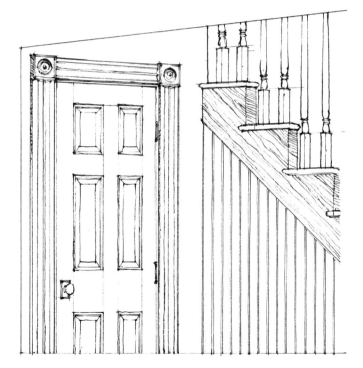

# GYPSUM BOARD

Gypsum board has surpassed plaster as the most common type of wall and ceiling finish. Although plaster remains a desirable finish, has a beautiful texture, and is well-suited for curved surfaces and decorative work, it is difficult for the homeowner to apply well. In addition, gypsum board, because of its large sheet size, is a more economical material and requires less time and labor to install.

Gypsum board is a sheet material that consists of a gypsum core faced on both sides with tough, durable paper. It is dense, durable and dimensionally stable. It can be used in wall and ceiling construction that is resistant to fire or sound transmission. It can be primed and painted, or serve as a base for ceramic tile, paneling, or a variety of wall coverings.

Gypsum board sheets are normally 4' wide by 8' long. Other lengths up to 16' are available for horizontal applications. The 4'x8' sheet size corresponds well to the 12", 16" and 24" spacing of studs and ceiling joists.

Standard gypsum board sheets are available in 3/8", 1/2" and 5/8" thicknesses. The choice of a board thickness depends on the spacing of the supporting framework, and the direction of the sheets relative to the framing. In new construction, 1/2" thickness is recommended. 3/8" thickness, the minimum required for 16" stud spacing, is more often used in remodeling and repair work over an existing wall. 5/8" thickness may be used for greater strength, or for greater resistance to fire or sound transmission.

Standard gypsum board is suitable for most wall and ceiling applications in dry locations. For special conditions, other types are available. These include:

1. Moisture-resistant board is used as a base for ceramic tile in baths, showers, or other wet areas.

2. Type-X board has a core of glass fibers and other additives to make it fire-resistant. Used in fire-rated construction, it can also be moisture-resistant or have a foil backing.

3. Foil-backed board is faced on one side with aluminum foil that serves as a vapor barrier and reflective insulator. It is used on the interior side of exterior walls.

4. Backing board is used as a base where a double layer of gypsum board is called for, as in fire-rated or sound control construction. Its surface is not suitable for painting or wallpapering.

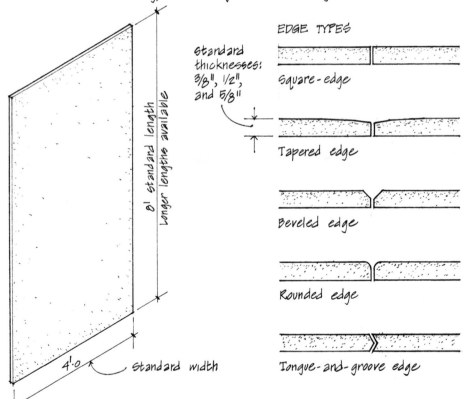

Standard thicknesses: 3/8", 1/2", and 5/8"

8' standard length
Longer lengths available

4'.0  ← Standard width

EDGE TYPES

Square-edge

Tapered edge

Beveled edge

Rounded edge

Tongue-and-groove edge

Gypsum board sheets are available with different edge conditions. They may have square, tapered, rounded or beveled edges. Tapered or rounded edges that allow for taping and filling are generally preferred for stronger, smoother joints. Some pre-finished boards have bevel edges, while gypsum board used as exterior sheathing has tongue-and-groove edges.

The supporting studs or ceiling joists should be aligned well to provide a smooth, even frame for the gypsum board. The supporting frame should also be structurally sound and rigid enough to prevent the gypsum board from buckling or cracking. If the wood framing has a high moisture content, allow it to reach its in-use moisture content before applying any gypsum board.

Gypsum board can be applied to new framing or to furring over an existing wall or ceiling that is too rough or uneven for direct application.

If ceiling joists are not properly aligned, or if the existing plaster ceiling is too uneven, use 2"x 2" or 2"x 3" wood furring laid perpendicular to the ceiling joists. Nail the furring with two 10p nails at each joist, using shims where necessary to provide a level base. Also install furring under all end joints.

Over existing wall finishes that are uneven, use standard 1"x 2" furring installed horizontally at 16" or 24" o.c., depending on the thickness of the gypsum board. Remove any existing base trim, and the trim around windows and doorways. Install additional furring around all openings and anywhere a vertical joint will occur. Shim as required to provide a level base for the gypsum board.

Instead of installing furring, badly cracked or loose wall and ceiling finishes can be removed, and the gypsum board applied directly to the existing framing.

If the existing wall or ceiling finish is smooth and level enough, gypsum board can be nailed or glued directly to the existing surface. The gypsum board can be fairly thin, 1/4" or 3/8" thick, since it is supported by a solid base material.

Although gypsum board can be applied directly to masonry or concrete, application over furring is generally preferred to keep the gypsum board from contact with any moisture that might be present in the masonry.

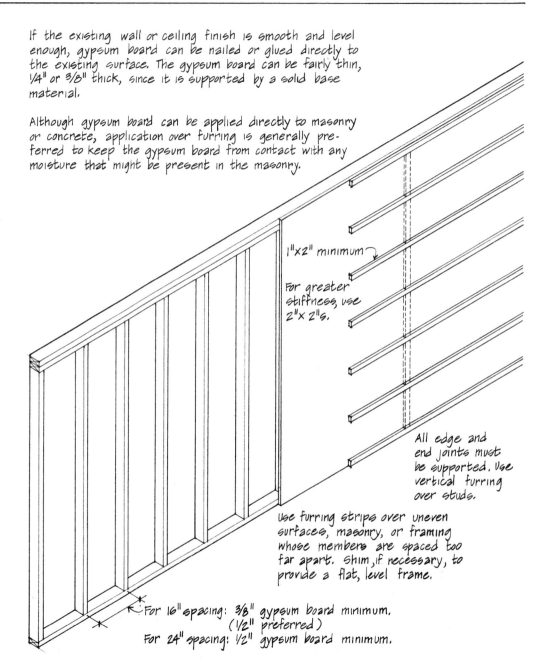

1"x2" minimum

For greater stiffness, use 2"x 2"s.

All edge and end joints must be supported. Use vertical furring over studs.

Use furring strips over uneven surfaces, masonry, or framing whose members are spaced too far apart. Shim, if necessary, to provide a flat, level frame.

For 16" spacing: 3/8" gypsum board minimum.
(1/2" preferred)
For 24" spacing: 1/2" gypsum board minimum.

# GYPSUM BOARD APPLICATION

Although the gypsum board core is dense, it can be cut easily. For full length or width cuts, use a metal straight-edge and a utility knife to score the face paper. Cut slowly and firmly through the paper and partially into the core. Snap the core, using a 2"x4" for leverage. Finally, cut through the back paper. Any rough edges can be smoothed with coarse sandpaper or a medium-tooth wood file or rasp.

Smaller cuts and openings for electrical outlets and plumbing lines can be made with a keyhole saw once holes are drilled at the corners.

Cover adjacent areas when installing gypsum board, and when taping and sanding joints, to protect them from the fine, powdery dust. It is also advisable to wear a respirator when sanding joint compound that may contain asbestos fibers.

Gypsum board may be installed horizontally (the long dimension perpendicular to the framing members) or vertically (parallel to the framing members). While horizontal application results in greater stiffness, it is best to apply gypsum board in a manner that will result in the fewest number of joints. In particular, minimize the number of butt end joints and stagger them well.

All edges and ends of gypsum board sheets should be supported by framing. Install additional blocking or furring if necessary.

Gypsum board sheets are loosely butted for light contact only. Cut sheets short rather than long since their edges will crumble if forced together. Measure carefully before cutting, especially when fitting corner sheets.

Use 1 5/8" ring-shank drywall nails for 3/8" and 1/2" gypsum board, and 1 7/8" nails for 5/8" thicknesses. Space nails 7" o.c. for ceilings and 8" o.c. for wall applications. Nails should be at least 3/8" in from the edge.

Double-nailing, for greater rigidity and fire-resistance, consists of sets of nails, 2" apart and spaced 12" o.c. in the middle of the panels.

To avoid the possibility of nails popping, Type-W drywall screws can be used. The screws are spaced, for 16" o.c. framing, 12"o.c. for ceilings and 16" o.c. for walls. With 24" support spacing, the screws are spaced 12" o.c. for both walls and ceilings.

For the strongest, most rigid system, the gypsum board can be both glued and nailed to the framing.

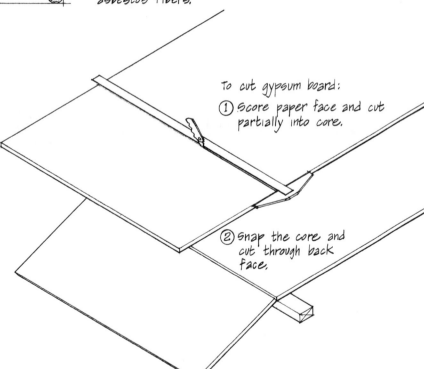

To cut gypsum board:

① Score paper face and cut partially into core.

② Snap the core and cut through back face.

When nailing, drive the nails perpendicular to the gypsum board and flush with the surface. With the last blow, form a dimple without breaking the board's paper surface.

Gypsum board is applied to the ceiling first since ceiling installations are more difficult, and any gaps between the ceiling board and the wall framing can be concealed with the wall layer. Since a gypsum board sheet can weigh up to 60 lbs., use bracing to help hold up the panels. Work from the center outward to the edges.

When applying gypsum board to walls, start at a corner. If a room is fairly narrow, it might be worthwhile to get sheets longer than 8' so they can be applied horizontally from corner to corner without any vertical end joints. If a gap is necessary, it should be at the base so that it can be concealed by the baseboard trim.

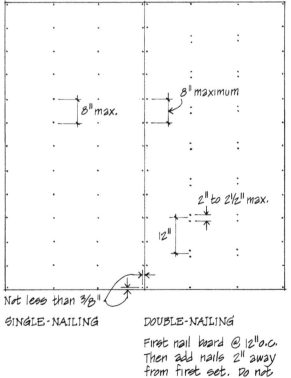

8" max.

8" maximum

2" to 2½" max.

12"

Not less than 3/8"

SINGLE-NAILING

DOUBLE-NAILING

First nail board @ 12" o.c. Then add nails 2" away from first set. Do not double-nail edges.

VERTICAL APPICATION ON WALLS

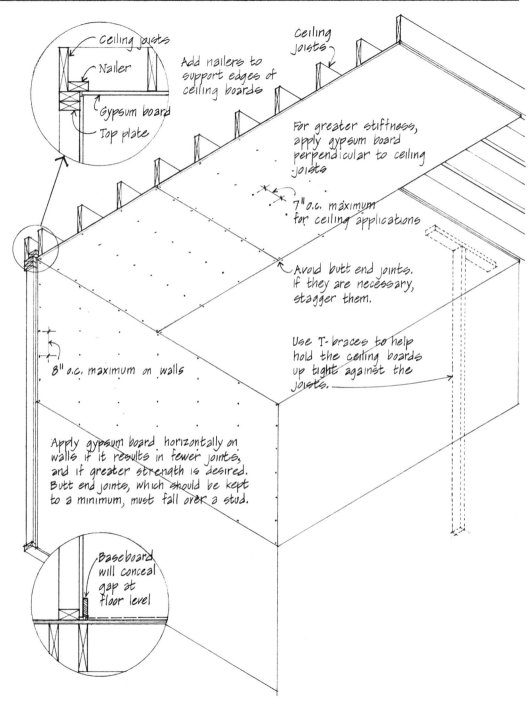

Ceiling joists

Nailer

Gypsum board

Top plate

Add nailers to support edges of ceiling boards

Ceiling joists

For greater stiffness, apply gypsum board perpendicular to ceiling joists

7" o.c. maximum for ceiling applications

Avoid butt end joints. If they are necessary, stagger them.

Use T-braces to help hold the ceiling boards up tight against the joists.

8" o.c. maximum on walls

Apply gypsum board horizontally on walls if it results in fewer joints, and if greater strength is desired. Butt end joints, which should be kept to a minimum, must fall over a stud.

Baseboard will conceal gap at floor level

# GYPSUM BOARD TAPING

The object of taping and spackling the joints of gypsum board installations is to provide a smooth, inconspicuous and monolithic surface when finished.

For every 200 s.f. of surface, about one gallon of joint compound and 75 ft. of tape is needed. The joint compound is available in powdered form (to be mixed with water into a paste) or ready-mixed. The tape used to reinforce the joints is of perforated fiber paper or mesh.

The joint compound is first applied with a 4" or 5" knife to the trough formed by the butting tapered edges of the gypsum board. The tape is pressed onto the joint with the drywall knife until the compound oozes through the perforations or mesh. Squeeze out any excess compound and work out any wrinkles in the tape. Make as smooth a joint as possible, feather the outer edges, and allow the compound to dry for about 24 hours.

At this time, the depressions or dimples at nailheads, and other imperfections, are filled with joint compound with a broad knife, leveled and feathered.

If the first coat is too rough, it can be lightly sanded or wiped with a damp sponge. Be careful not to roughen up the paper surface. After the first coat is dry, a thin second coat is applied and feathered about 2" to 4" beyond the tape.

Allow the second coat to dry, smooth out any irregularities with light sanding, and apply a thin third coat. Feather its edges 2" to 4" beyond the second coat and blend smoothly with the gypsum board surface. Let dry and lightly sand or sponge if necessary.

In a similar manner, apply second and third coats to nailhead dimples and other imperfections.

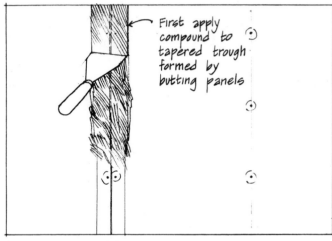

First apply compound to tapered trough formed by butting panels

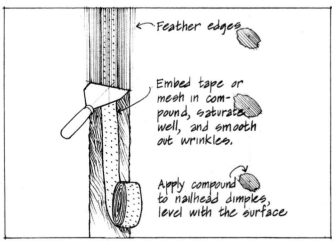

Feather edges

Embed tape or mesh in compound, saturate well, and smooth out wrinkles.

Apply compound to nailhead dimples, level with the surface

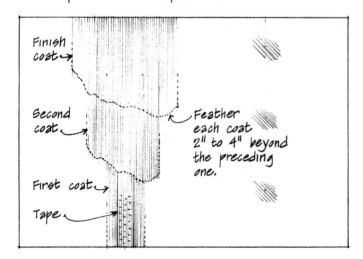

Finish coat

Second coat

First coat

Tape

Feather each coat 2" to 4" beyond the preceding one.

At inside corners, fill any cracks with joint compound and spread the compound to both sides about 1½". Cut the joint tape to the proper length, fold down the middle, and embed the tape in the compound. Then finish in a similar manner to flush joints. An inside corner tool can be used to apply and smooth out the second and third coats. If unavailable, use a regular drywall knife on one side of the corner, let the compound dry, and then work the other side.

Exterior corners and exposed edges of gypsum board must be protected against impact damage. Metal corner and edge beads are used for this protection. They are nailed through the gypsum board into the supporting framework every 5" or 6". Be careful not to dent the nosing of the beading.

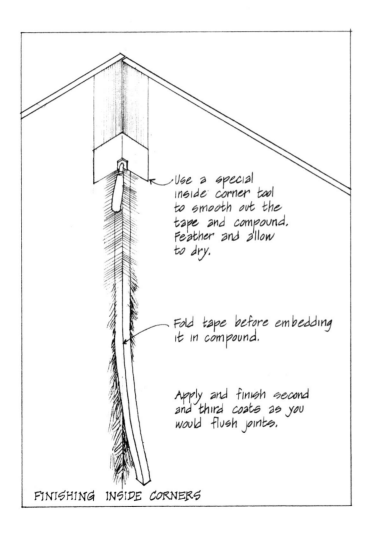

Use a special inside corner tool to smooth out the tape and compound. Feather and allow to dry.

Fold tape before embedding it in compound.

Apply and finish second and third coats as you would flush joints.

FINISHING INSIDE CORNERS

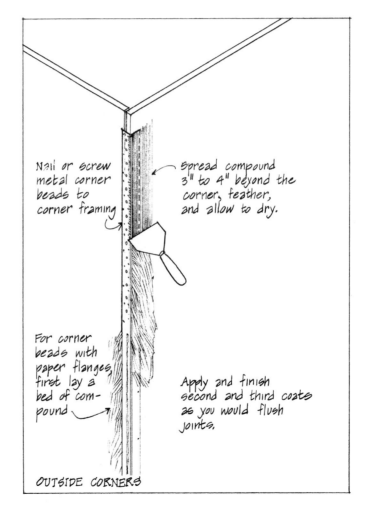

Nail or screw metal corner beads to corner framing

Spread compound 3" to 4" beyond the corner, feather, and allow to dry.

For corner beads with paper flanges, first lay a bed of compound

Apply and finish second and third coats as you would flush joints.

OUTSIDE CORNERS

## WOOD PANELING

Wood is a warm, attractive, durable material that is well-suited for wall and ceiling finishes. If finished properly, it requires little maintenance and ages well.

There is a great variety of woods available. Your choice will be based on cost, where the wood is to be used, and how much wear it will have. In addition, the color, grain and texture that make wood so visually appealing must be considered. Too much paneling in a room can give the space too much texture and make it appear too dark.

Wood may be applied to walls and ceilings as plywood sheets or as individual boards. While wood boards have a richer texture and can be laid in various patterns, plywood paneling is easier and quicker to install.

## PLYWOOD PANELING

Plywood is available with softwood or hardwood face veneers. The best grades for interior paneling are N (for natural finishes) and A (suitable for painting). In addition to flush panels, there is decorative paneling with striated, grooved, and rough-sawn textures and patterns. Less expensive plywood paneling may be surfaced with wood-grain vinyl. For walls that require a durable finish, consider using exterior plywood siding.

Plywood paneling is normally 4' wide. The most common length is 8', although 7' and 10' lengths are also available. The thickness of the paneling ranges from 1/8" to 3/4".

Thin 1/8" and 1/4" paneling can appear quite wavy when laid over open framing. For a better appearance, use thin paneling over a suitable existing wall finish or a new base of 3/8" gypsum board.

Plywood paneling, 3/8" and thicker, can be laid over new framing, or over an existing frame that has been stripped of its finish. As with gypsum board, the framing members should be aligned properly to provide a level base. Any irregularities in the framing may show up in the paneling.

If the support framing is uneven, or when installing paneling over a masonry wall, use furring strips and shims to provide a smooth, level frame.

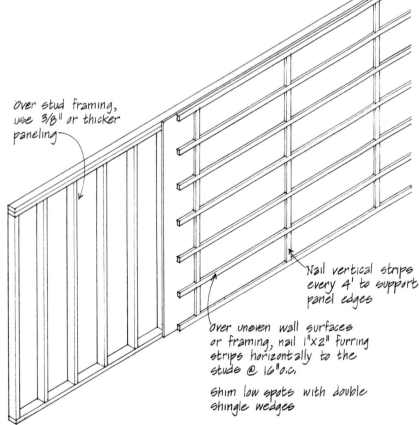

Over stud framing, use 3/8" or thicker paneling

Nail vertical strips every 4' to support panel edges

Over uneven wall surfaces or framing, nail 1"x2" furring strips horizontally to the studs @ 16"o.c.

Shim low spots with double shingle wedges

SUPPORT REQUIRED FOR PLYWOOD PANELING

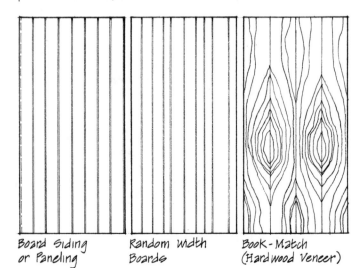

Board Siding or Paneling    Random Width Boards    Book-Match (Hardwood Veneer)

TYPICAL PLYWOOD PANELING PATTERNS

Before being installed, plywood and other wood materials should be acclimated to the conditions of the finished room. Purchase and stack them in the room several days before installation.

Plywood paneling may be installed vertically or horizontally, but all edges must be supported by framing and a 1/32" space between sheets should be provided. The orientation of plywood paneling depends on its face grain and texture, but is usually vertical.

Paneling with vertical board patterns have concealed edge joints that need no further treatment. On the other hand, the joints between paneling with flush faces can be treated in several ways. The joints may be beveled, recessed, or have a raised panel effect. Corners may be mitered or be accented with trim or moldings.

If the joints in plywood paneling are to be accentuated, the layout of the sheets should be studied beforehand on graph paper. Coordinate the joints with other wall elements, such as window and door openings.

When cutting plywood paneling, use a fine-tooth blade. Cut the paneling face down with portable circular and saber saws; cut face up with hand or table saws.

Plywood paneling may be fastened to the support framing with nails or adhesives. Adhesives are especially desirable for rigidity and to avoid marring the paneling surface with nails. When gluing paneling to support framing, follow the adhesive manufacturer's recommendations.

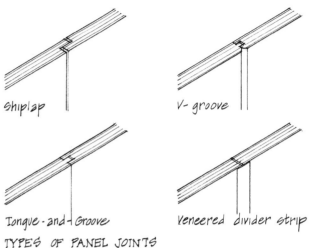

Shiplap       V- groove       Recessed

Tongue - and - Groove      Veneered divider strip      Batten or Raised Panel

TYPES OF PANEL JOINTS

Coordinate visible joints with door and window openings.

PLYWOOD PANEL LAYOUT

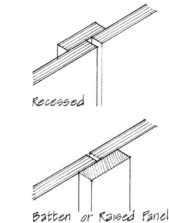

ↄ Allow 1/32" edge and end distance between panels

A 1/2" clearance between the panel bottoms and the floor will make it easier to adjust, level and plumb the panels.

When nailing, use 1¼" finishing nails @ 8"o.c. For paneling thicker than 1/2", use 2" nails.

INSTALLATION

## HARDBOARD PANELING

Hardboard paneling is less expensive than plywood panel-ing. It consists of compressed wood fibers with a vinyl or paper overlay. This overlay material gives the paneling its appearance. Various patterns and colors are available. Some have photographic overlays of wood grain to simulate real wood paneling.

The hardboard should be at least 1/4" thick if laid over support framing that is spaced 16" o.c. Hardboard 1/8" thick should be applied only over a solid base, such as an existing wall finish, or a new layer of 3/8" gypsum board.

Hardboard is installed in much the same way as plywood paneling. The panels can be applied with special adhesive, or be nailed in place. With the denser types of hardboard, it is advisable to drill the nail holes. Some prefinished paneling is available with moldings and nails that match the finish of the paneling.

As with plywood paneling, acclimate hardboard panels to the room conditions for at least 48 hours before application.

## WOOD BOARD PANELING

For a richer and more varied texture than plywood, solid wood boards can be used as the finish material for walls and ceilings. They can be laid vertically, horizontally, or diagonally, and create patterns such as herringbones or checkerboards. Wood board paneling, however, does re-quire more labor and carpentry skills than does plywood paneling and other sheet goods.

The boards used can vary from exotic and expensive hardwoods to recycled materials such as barn siding. They range in thickness from 3/8" to 3/4". The edges may be square-cut, tongued-and-grooved, or shiplapped. The boards come in standard lengths and widths. Boards wider than 8" should not be used unless the edges are matched or have long tongues for support.

The minimum board thickness is 3/8" for supporting studs or furring spaced 16" o.c.; 1/2" thickness for 20" support spacing; 5/8" thickness for 24" support spacing. Use 6d finishing nails. Narrow (up to 6" wide) tongue-and-groove boards can be blind-nailed. Others are face-nailed.

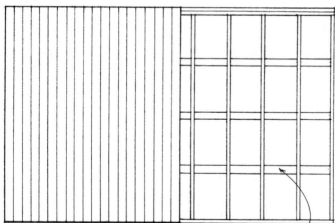

For vertical applications, furring or 2"x4" blocking between the wall studs is required at least 24" o.c.

When applied on an exterior wall, board paneling should be backed by an effective vapor barrier and insulation.

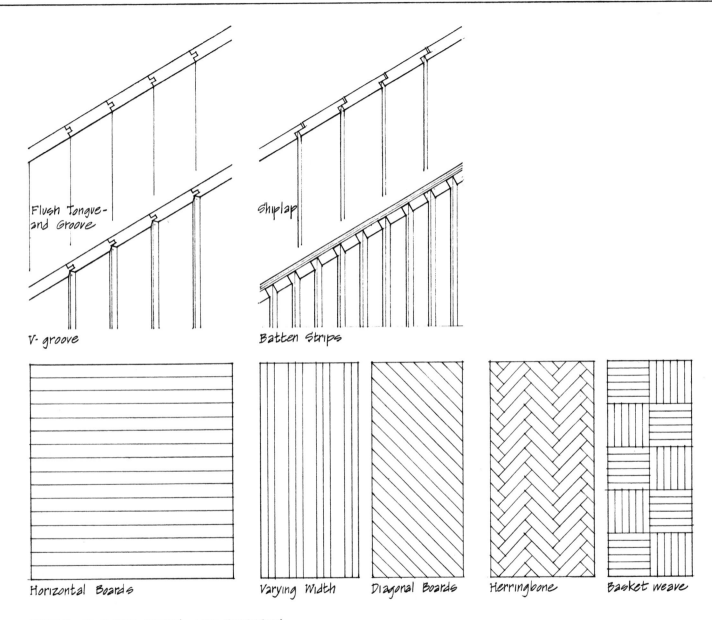

Flush Tongue-and Groove

Shiplap

V-groove

Batten Strips

Horizontal Boards

Varying Width

Diagonal Boards

Herringbone

Basket Weave

TYPES OF BOARD JOINTS AND PATTERNS

# WOOD FLOORING

Wood flooring combines durability and wear-resistance with comfort and warmth. It also has attractive qualities of color, grain and subtle patterns, depending on the type of wood used, and how it is laid.

Durable, hard, close-grained species of both softwood and hardwood are used for flooring. Softwoods, while less dense and more susceptible to wear and abrasion than hardwoods, can be used effectively in bedrooms and other light-traffic areas. Common types of softwood used for flooring include southern pine, Douglas-fir, and hemlock. The heartwood of redwood, because of its decay-resistance, is often used for porches and outdoor decks.

Hardwoods used for flooring include oak, maple, birch and pecan. Of these, oak has always been a favorite.

All wood flooring is appearance-graded, but not according to the same standards. Clear and select are the best grades of oak. First-grade is the best grade of many hardwoods like maple and birch. Select is the best grade of western softwoods like Douglas-fir. A sound, service-able floor can be had at less cost if slight surface imperfections are acceptable and lower grades of flooring used.

How wood flooring is sawn affects both its appearance and wear-resistance. Plain-sawn flooring (flat grain) has noticeable grain patterns, and can wear unevenly. Quarter-sawn flooring (edge or vertical grain) has more even grain patterns, and is generally preferred for better wearing qualities under hard usage.

There are three basic types of wood flooring: strip, plank, and block flooring. Of these, strip flooring is the most widely used. The strips are normally 25/32" thick and 1½", 2", or 2¼" wide. For remodeling work or use over a solid base, 3/8" x 2" strips are available. The strips are random length, varying from 2' to 16' or more.

*

The strips are tongued-and-grooved and end-matched, and their faces are slightly wider than their bottoms so that tight-fitting joints can be made. They have hollow backs so that their edges can bear firmly and allow for slight irregularities in the subfloor surface.

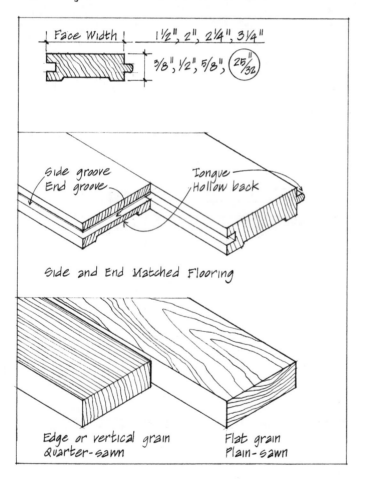

Face Width | 1½", 2", 2¼", 3¼"

3/8", ½", 5/8", 25/32"

Side groove
End groove

Tongue
Hollow back

Side and End Matched Flooring

Edge or vertical grain
Quarter-sawn

Flat grain
Plain-sawn

Plank flooring consists of random length boards that range in width from 3½" to 8". The widths are coordinated so that two or three narrow boards can match the width of a wide one. This allows the boards to be laid in a random width pattern. They may be blind-nailed, or face-nailed or screwed and then plugged. Some new plank flooring systems can be laid with mastic or adhesive.

Wood block flooring consists of factory-assembled tiles, 6" to 12" square or even larger, and 1/8" to 25/32" thick. Unit blocks are assembled from short lengths of strip flooring that are splined together. Laminated blocks have three or more plies of hardwood bonded together with water-resistant glue for dimensional stability. Slat blocks consist of slats that form larger blocks which, in turn, form block or parquet patterns.

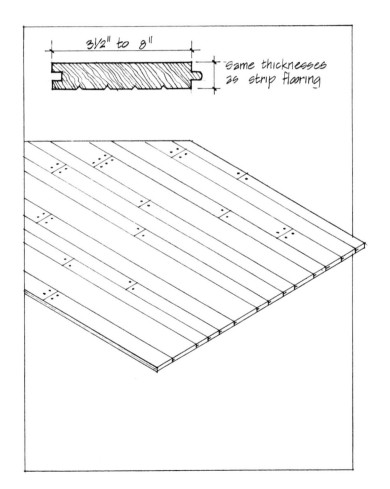

3½" to 8"

Same thicknesses as strip flooring

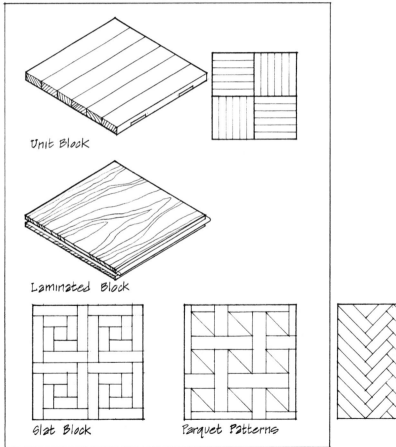

Unit Block

Laminated Block

Slat Block

Parquet Patterns

## INSTALLING WOOD FLOORING

Finish flooring is generally installed only after the ceiling and walls have been completed, and windows and doors installed. This is to prevent the flooring from being marred or damaged as the other finishes are being applied.

Before laying any wood flooring, let the material become acclimated to the conditions of your house. Order the flooring a few days in advance, and spread it out in the room in which it is to be laid.

Wood strip flooring may be laid over a level, clean board or plywood subfloor. Prepare the subfloor by sweeping it well and re-setting any nails that may have popped. When laying over an existing board subfloor, any dips should be repaired by shimming between the floor joists and the subfloor. Loose boards should be nailed or replaced; raised edges should be leveled; any openings should be filled.

Over board subflooring, a layer of building paper is usually laid to make the floor draft-tight. This layer can also help exclude moisture from below and smooth out slight irregularities in the subflooring.

Wood strip flooring should not be laid directly atop a concrete slab. The wood strips require a system of treated wood sleepers spaced 12" to 16" o.c., and a vapor barrier of 4-mil polyethylene. See pg. 134.

## WOOD STRIP FLOORING

Wood strip flooring is laid perpendicular to the floor joists or wood sleepers. If an existing board subfloor has been laid perpendicular to the joists, lay the strip flooring across the grain of the boards.

Since wood expands and contracts with changes in humidity, a 1/2" gap is left between the wood flooring and the wall around the perimeter of the room. This gap is more critical parallel to the strip flooring since wood will expand and contract more across its grain or across the width of the strips.

Start by laying the first strip 1/2" away from the wall, with the grooved edge facing the wall. For 25/32" thick flooring, use 8d flooring nails. Face nail this first strip close enough to the grooved edge so that the nails can be concealed by the base or shoe molding. Then blind nail, through the tongue at a 45° angle, every 10" to 12". Use a nail set to set the nails and avoid damaging the flooring.

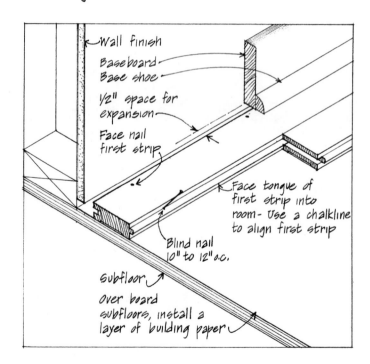

Wall finish

Baseboard
Base shoe

1/2" space for expansion

Face nail first strip

Face tongue of first strip into room- Use a chalkline to align first strip

Blind nail 10" to 12" o.c.

Subfloor

over board subfloors, install a layer of building paper

Succeeding strips are blind nailed only, at intervals of 10" to 12". Whenever possible, nail through the subfloor and into the floor joists. Before nailing, drive each strip tight against the others. Use a scrap piece of flooring to protect the tongues of the flooring strips.

As you lay the strips, select lengths so that end joints are well staggered, and at least 6" apart from each other. Check periodically that the courses remain parallel and straight. Crooked pieces may be wedged and forced into alignment, or be cut and used at the ends of courses.

As you reach the other wall, the last strip may have to be ripped (cut along its length) to allow for the ½" gap. To pull the last course tight, use a pry bar and a wood scrap to protect the wall surface. This last strip is face nailed like the first.

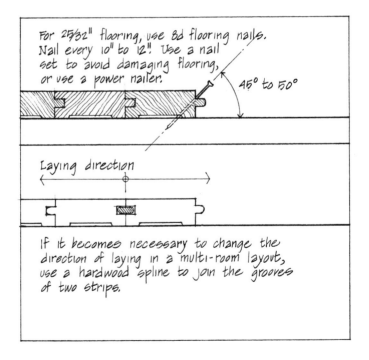

For 25/32" flooring, use 8d flooring nails. Nail every 10" to 12". Use a nail set to avoid damaging flooring, or use a power nailer.

45° to 50°

Laying direction

If it becomes necessary to change the direction of laying in a multi-room layout, use a hardwood spline to join the grooves of two strips.

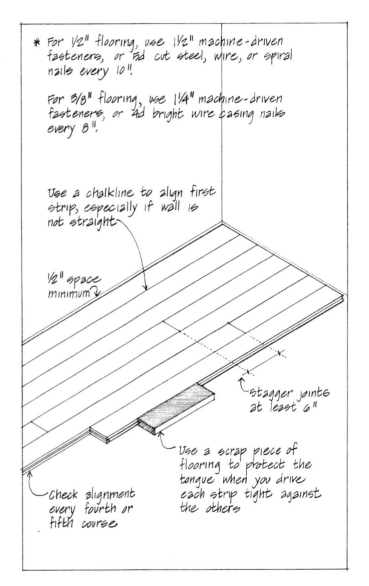

\* For ½" flooring, use 1½" machine-driven fasteners, or 5d cut steel, wire, or spiral nails every 10".

For 3/8" flooring, use 1¼" machine-driven fasteners, or 4d bright wire casing nails every 8".

Use a chalkline to align first strip, especially if wall is not straight.

½" space minimum

stagger joints at least 6"

Use a scrap piece of flooring to protect the tongue when you drive each strip tight against the others

Check alignment every fourth or fifth course

# WOOD BLOCK FLOORING

Wood block flooring is usually laid over a plywood subfloor or underlayment. It can also be laid over an existing floor, such as linoleum, that is sound, smooth, level and dry. Although wood block tiles can be applied to the surface of dry concrete slabs, it is best, especially in basements, to lay the flooring over a plywood subfloor and a vapor barrier set on treated wood sleepers. See pg. 134.

Thick wood block tiles with tongue-and-groove edges can be blind nailed to a plywood subfloor. Most wood block flooring, however, is laid with adhesives. Since block flooring and adhesives vary somewhat with different manufacturers, always follow the installation procedures recommended by the manufacturer of the products being used.

Some wood block tiles have a pressure-sensitive adhesive backing. The paper backs are simply removed and the tiles pressed into place.

Wood block flooring tiles can be laid in various patterns. Work your floor pattern out on paper beforehand. Solid wood unit blocks are usually laid with alternating tiles changing their grain direction to minimize the effect of their shrinking or swelling.

To begin laying out the block flooring in a normal square pattern, determine the centerpoint of the floor. This is located by the intersection of two diagonals that connect the corners of the room. Snap chalklines perpendicular to each other through the centerpoint.

Space out the dry tiles along the chalklines, from the centerpoint, to determine if the tiles must be cut along the room's perimeter. If the border tiles are less than half their width, shift the row of whole tiles a half width. This is to increase the size of the fractional border tiles, and avoid having to install narrow tiles.

In laying the block tiles, work in pyramid fashion from the centerpoint of the room. Lay the tiles into place with a minimum of sliding. Tap the edges lightly to assure a tight fit between the tiles.

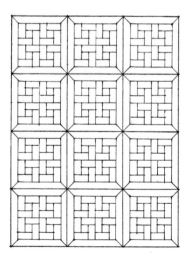

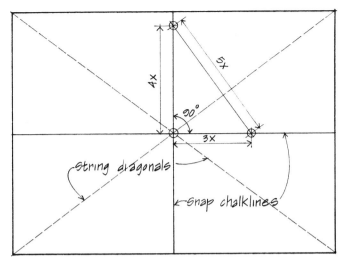

To locate the center of a room, string two diagonals from the corners. From the center, snap two chalklines to the midpoints of opposite walls. Check with a 3·4·5 right triangle to ensure the chalklines are perpendicular to each other.

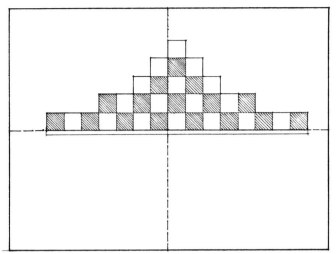

Lay tiles in one half of the room first. Work outward from the center in pyramid fashion. If desired, you can use a straight length of 1x2 to help keep the first row properly aligned.

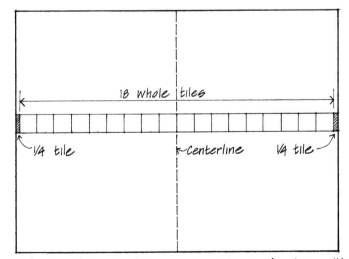

If fractional border tiles are less than half a tile width......

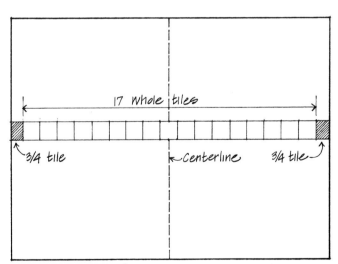

shift the row a half width. This will reduce the number of whole tiles by one, and make the fractional tiles more than half a tile width.

# CERAMIC TILE

Ceramic tiles are relatively small, modular surfacing units made of clay or other ceramic material that has been fired in a kiln at very high temperatures. The result is a durable, tough, dense material that is water-resistant and difficult to stain. Its colors generally do not fade. Ceramic tile is easy to clean, making it attractive as a wall and floor finish in kitchens and bathrooms.

Ceramic tile is available glazed or unglazed. Glazed tile has a face of ceramic material fused into the body of the tile, and may have glossy, matte, or crystalline finishes in a wide range of colors. Unglazed tiles are hard and dense, and derive their color from the body of the material. These colors tend to be more muted.

Ceramic tile is available as individual pieces or in sheet form for easier installation. Ceramic mosaic tiles may be faced with paper or backed with mesh to form 1'x1' or 1'x 2' sections with the proper tile spacing. Both ceramic wall and mosaic tiles are also available in large sheets with flexible, synthetic grouting. These are more expensive but offer the easiest installation.

Field tile refers to the square or rectangular flat pieces that cover the wall or floor surface. Trim pieces are required to turn corners and round off edges of tiled surfaces. Bullnose and edging caps are used to finish top edges. Cove bases are used where vertical tile surfaces meet floor tile. There are also special corner pieces to turn internal and external corners.

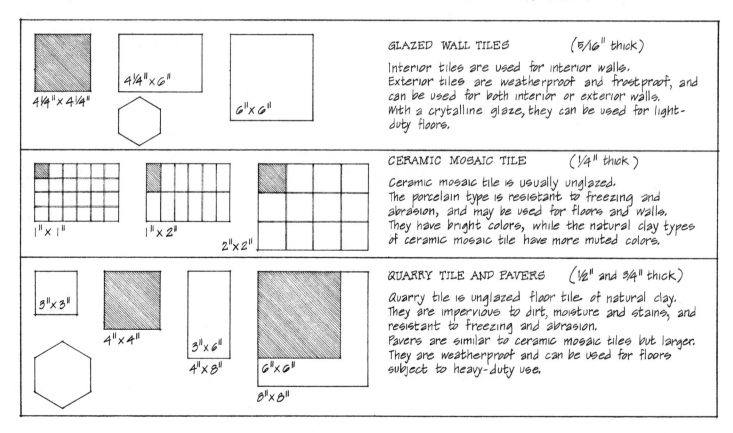

GLAZED WALL TILES          (5/16" thick)

Interior tiles are used for interior walls.
Exterior tiles are weatherproof and frostproof, and can be used for both interior or exterior walls.
With a crystalline glaze, they can be used for light-duty floors.

4¼" x 4¼"    4¼" x 6"    6" x 6"

CERAMIC MOSAIC TILE        (¼" thick)

Ceramic mosaic tile is usually unglazed.
The porcelain type is resistant to freezing and abrasion, and may be used for floors and walls.
They have bright colors, while the natural clay types of ceramic mosaic tile have more muted colors.

1" x 1"    1" x 2"    2" x 2"

QUARRY TILE AND PAVERS     (½" and 3/4" thick)

Quarry tile is unglazed floor tile of natural clay.
They are impervious to dirt, moisture and stains, and resistant to freezing and abrasion.
Pavers are similar to ceramic mosaic tiles but larger. They are weatherproof and can be used for floors subject to heavy-duty use.

3" x 3"    4" x 4"    3" x 6"    6" x 6"    4" x 8"    8" x 8"

Ceramic tile can be applied with either cement mortar or mastic adhesives over a dimensionally stable base material. Although many builders still prefer cement-based mortar, mastic adhesives make the job much simpler for the homeowner.

Ceramic tile may be applied with adhesive to any plaster, gypsum board or plywood surface that is smooth, sound, firm and stable. Any gypsum board or plywood used as a base, however, should be moisture-resistant or an exterior grade material. New gypsum board surfaces need not have their joints taped and spackled, but they should be sealed with a thin coat of adhesive.

When installing ceramic tile over an existing wall surface, remove any wall coverings such as wallpaper, or scrape away any loose paint. If the existing surface is glossy, sand it lightly for better adhesion.

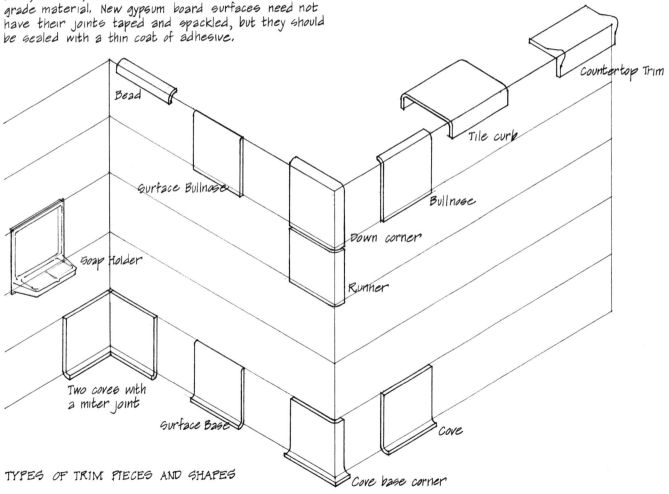

Bead

Countertop Trim

Tile curb

Surface Bullnose

Bullnose

Down corner

Soap Holder

Runner

Two coves with
a miter joint

Surface Base

Cove

Cove base corner

TYPES OF TRIM PIECES AND SHAPES

## CERAMIC WALL TILES

To prepare the layout of ceramic tile on a wall surface, measure and draw elevations of the walls to be covered. Work out the design pattern, and select the type and size of tile to be used. At this time, decide if you want any special decorative border or horizontal band treatments.

Locate the lowest point along the walls to be tiled. Draw a level horizontal line one tile height above this point. Also draw a plumb, vertical line at the wall's midpoint.

On a long length of wood, mark off a series of tile widths. Use this as a measuring stick to determine the tile spacing across the wall. If fractional tiles are required at each edge of a wall-to-wall installation, they should be equal. If they are less than half a tile width, shift the tile spacing a half tile width (so that the fractional tiles are more than a half tile width).

There are different types of adhesives - epoxies, latex mortars, and organic types. Follow the tile manufacturer's recommendations for the type of adhesive to use and its application. Type I adhesives are generally used for walls around bathtubs and showers. Type II is used for areas subject only to intermittent wetting.

Start by laying the cove or base row of tile first. Use a notched trowel to spread the adhesive and press firmly against the backing surface. The notches ensure a uniform and correct amount of adhesive is spread while any excess is scraped away. Apply the tile pieces firmly, twisting them slightly to adhere them to the surface. To avoid pushing the adhesive up onto the tile faces, do not slide them into place.

Work up from the base in horizontal rows. Allow about a 1/16" space between the tiles for grout. Some tiles have lugs to ensure they are spaced evenly. After each course or row is laid, check it with a level. After several rows have been laid, gently tap them down, using a flat board to ensure they lie in the same plane. Complete the entire field of whole tiles before installing edge tiles and trim pieces. As you do the field, leave space for any wall accessories you wish to install.

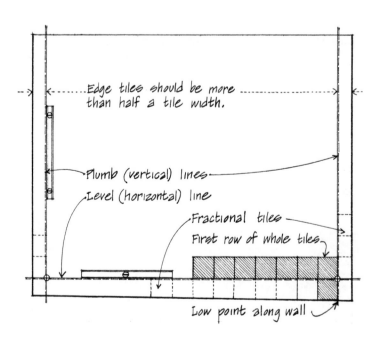

Edge tiles should be more than half a tile width.

Plumb (vertical) lines

Level (horizontal) line

Fractional tiles

First row of whole tiles

Low point along wall

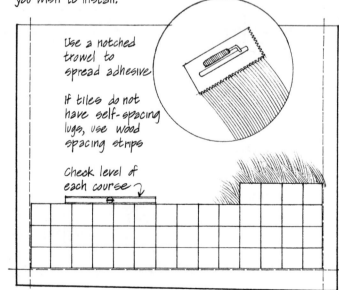

Use a notched trowel to spread adhesive

If tiles do not have self-spacing lugs, use wood spacing strips

Check level of each course

A tile cutter, rented from the tile distributor, can help you cut the tile easily. A glass cutter can also be used. First score the tile with the glass cutter, using a square as a guide. Place the score over the edge of a 2x4, or a wood dowel, and snap the tile downward. Smooth the cut edge with a wood file or whetstone and water.

Curved cuts are made with tile nippers. Work slowly and nip off only small bits at a time. To fit tile around pipes, cut a whole tile along the centerline of the required opening. Then cut out semi-circular notches from each piece with the tile nipper.

After the tiles are set, prepare the grout according to the manufacturer's instructions. Use a rubber-surfaced trowel or a squeegee to spread the grout over the tile surface, using an arc-like motion and working diagonally. Pack the grout firmly into the tile joints, and wipe off any excess grout.

After 10 to 15 minutes, use a tool with a rounded end to compact the grout. After all the joints have been tooled, wipe the tile surface free of grout with a damp sponge. Polish the tiles with a dry cloth.

Allow about two weeks for the grout to fully cure. The grouted joints can then be waterproofed and protected against dirt and mildew with a silicone sealer.

Score with glass cutter

Wood dowel

CUTTING TILE

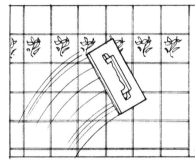

Snap tile downward over dowel

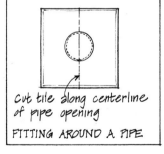

Cut tile along centerline of pipe opening

FITTING AROUND A PIPE

Cut notch from each half with tile nipper

Use a squeegee or rubber-surfaced trowel to spread and pack the grout firmly into the joints.

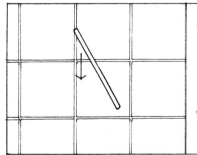

After grout has partially set, use a tool with a rounded end to compact the grout in the joints.

## CERAMIC TILE FLOORING

On floors, unglazed tile or glazed tile with dull or matte finishes are generally used. They are safer and less slippery than glazed tiles with glossy finishes, especially when wet. They are also less easily marred or scuffed from wear.

Because ceramic floor tiles and pavers are hard, inflexible, and somewhat brittle, they require a rigid, smooth base support. They can be laid over an existing floor if it is sound, level and firm enough. If the existing floor is rough or damaged, install ½" exterior-type plywood underlayment.

Ceramic tile can also be laid directly over a concrete floor slab if it is dry, clean and smooth. Fill any low spots with a latex or vinyl cement.

In most rooms, floor tiles are laid out so that full tiles run along the doorway. Some floor patterns that use a contrasting border tile may require that all edge tiles be equal, even at a doorway. Use a plan of the floor to work out your design pattern.

If you want full tiles at the doorway, snap a chalkline perpendicular to it. Lay out dry tiles along the chalkline, allowing for the thickness of the grout joints. At the wall opposite the doorway, and perpendicular to the chalkline, tack a straight-edged board to use as a guide. Lay out another row of dry tiles along the board, and adjust the row to equalize the border tiles.

Ceramic floor tile is laid and set like ceramic wall tiles. In selecting an adhesive, follow the tile manufacturer's recommendations for the type of tile used and the base material. The adhesive is spread with a notched trowel. If it sets quickly, spread only enough to cover a few square feet at a time.

The tiles are set, not slid, into place. Use thin wood strips, the thickness of the required grout joints, as row and tile spacers. Use a padded 2x4 and a hammer to set the tiles firmly in the adhesive and level them.

Border tiles are set last. Trim them as required with a tile cutter. After the tiles have set the proper amount of time, grout the joints with a type recommended by the tile manufacturer. Waterproof with a silicone sealer.

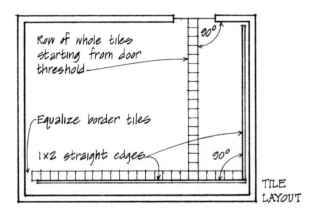

Row of whole tiles starting from door threshold

90°

Equalize border tiles

1x2 straight edges

90°

TILE LAYOUT

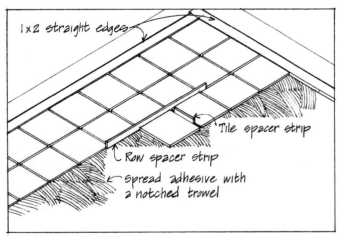

1x2 straight edges

Tile spacer strip

Row spacer strip

Spread adhesive with a notched trowel

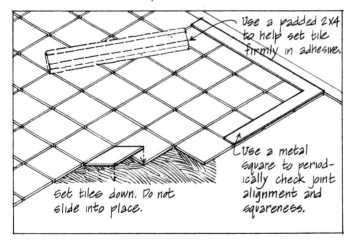

Use a padded 2x4 to help set tile firmly in adhesive.

Set tiles down. Do not slide into place.

Use a metal square to periodically check joint alignment and squareness.

## CERAMIC MOSAIC TILE

Ceramic mosaic tile is usually sold in sheet form, backed with mesh or faced with paper to maintain the proper tile spacing. These tile sheets are 1'x1' or 1'x 2' in size, making them easier to install than individual tiles. The small size of the tiles also makes equalizing the border tiles not as critical as when installing larger wall or floor tiles.

Mosaic tile sheets are laid out and set similarly to individual wall and floor tiles. As you lay the sheets, the edges of the sheets should be aligned and spaced the same distance as the tiles on the sheet. After several sheets have been laid, lay a piece of plywood over the tiles and tamp them gently to set the tiles firmly in the adhesive.

If border tiles must be cut, first remove them from the sheet, and then cut them as you would individual wall or floor tiles. Set them as individual tiles.

To fit a tile sheet around a pipe or other obstruction, cut the applicable tiles out from the sheet and lay the sheet. Cut the detached tiles to fit around the obstruction and set them individually.

Let the tiles set the proper amount of time. If the tiles are faced with paper, soak the paper with warm water and peel it off. Finish the tile joints with a grout that is recommended for the type of tile used.

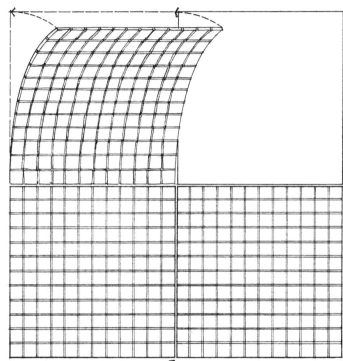

Space between sheets should be equal with the spaces between the tiles

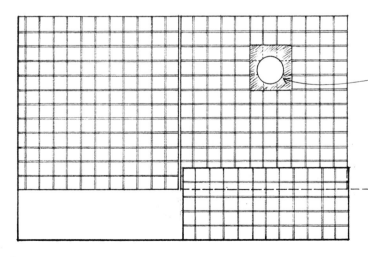

To fit around a pipe, cut the affected tiles out before laying the sheet. Then cut and fit individual tiles around the pipe.

To measure border sheets, lay a partial sheet down with whole tiles against the border edge. Cut along this line, where the sheets overlap. When laid, the cut tiles fit against the border.

# 3

# RESILIENT FLOORING

Resilient flooring is a class of thin floor coverings made from various combinations of resins, plasticizers, and fibers that are formed under heat and pressure. Although resilient flooring may not be as durable or as easy to maintain as ceramic tile, it is lower in cost, easier to install, and provides a fairly dense, non-absorbent surface with good durability. New finishes have also made some resilient flooring quite easy to maintain.

The flooring's resilience enables it to withstand permanent indentation and contributes to its quietness and comfort underfoot. How comfortable a resilient floor covering is, however, depends not only on its resilience but also its backing and the hardness of the supporting floor.

Resilient flooring is available as individual tiles or in sheet form. Individual tiles (6", 9", and 12" square) are less expensive and generally easier for the homeowner to install. Sheet goods (in 6', 9', and 12' widths) are more difficult to handle and must be cut to size and shape before their installation. Sheet flooring, however, does offer the advantage of a seamless floor and often has richer colors and more patterns to select from.

All resilient sheet flooring is made of vinyl, although the term linoleum is still used to describe resilient sheet goods. Solid vinyl sheet flooring is expensive but more durable and resistant to moisture, grease and alkali than most other types of resilient flooring. For added resilience and quietness, some solid vinyl sheet goods have an extra layer of foam cushioning. The thickness and weight of solid vinyl sheet flooring make it difficult for the homeowner to install. It should be laid by a professional.

Roto-vinyl sheet flooring has an inner core of vinyl foam over which is a printed design topped with a wear-layer of vinyl or polyurethane. The more expensive grades of roto-vinyl flooring are about as durable as vinyl-asbestos tiles. The less expensive grades have a thinner wear-layer, are less durable, and can often be laid loosely without adhesive.

Solid vinyl tiles are the most expensive and the best of the resilient tiles. They are very durable and offer excellent resistance to moisture, grease, alkali, and abrasion. They are available in 9" and 12" squares in a wide range of colors and patterns. Some have self-adhesive backings that make them easier to install.

Vinyl-asbestos tiles, consisting of vinyl resins and asbestos fibers, are probably the most popular flooring tile. Although not quite as resilient and durable as solid vinyl flooring, they still offer good resistance to grease, scuffing and burns. With self-adhesive backings, vinyl-asbestos tiles are quite easy to install.

Other resilient flooring materials that are available, but not used as often, include rubber, cork, linoleum and asphalt.

Rubber is a fairly expensive flooring material that offers excellent resilience, quietness and durability. The non-slip surface patterns of rubber flooring offer good graphic design possibilities for floors.

Cork tiles have a rich, natural appearance and are soft, warm and quiet underfoot. Some cork tiles have a vinyl coating for greater durability and ease of maintenance.

Linoleum tiles offer good resistance to grease and abrasion, but when subjected to water and detergents, they can become quite brittle and tear.

Asphalt tile is inexpensive and fairly durable, but has poor resistance to grease and can be difficult to maintain.

When shopping for or purchasing resilient flooring, check the conditions of the manufacturer's warranty. As always, follow the manufacturer's recommendations for the underlayment requirements, the type of adhesive to use, and the proper method of application.

## BASE PREPARATION

Resilient flooring should be laid over a level, dry and clean base that is free of grease, wax and dirt. In particular, the base should be smooth since any irregularities in its surface will show through the thin resilient material.

In new construction, a suitable base for resilient flooring can be either a single layer of subfloor/underlayment grade of plywood, or a separate layer of plywood or hardboard underlayment that is laid over the subfloor.

Vinyl, vinyl-asbestos, rubber and asphalt flooring can be laid over a level, dry concrete slab on or below grade. Linoleum and cork flooring should not be. (Follow the manufacturer's recommendations.) If the concrete slab is uneven or subject to dampness, install wood sleepers, a vapor barrier, and a plywood subfloor. See. pg. 134.

In remodeling work, any existing flooring that is rough, worn, or badly deteriorated should be removed or covered with new underlayment. To provide a smooth, clean base, underlayment grades of plywood, hardboard, or particle-board can be used. Plywood and hardboard underlayment should be at least 1/4" thick; particleboard underlayment should be at least 3/8" thick. Thicker underlayment may be desirable to match the floor height in an adjoining room. For easier handling, use 4'x4' size sheets.

In bathrooms and other areas subject to excessive moisture, use exterior-grade plywood underlayment. Do not use particleboard in such areas.

To prevent nailheads from popping, the underlayment should be acclimated to the conditions of the room for a few days before it is installed and the flooring laid.

The underlayment sheets should be laid in a staggered pattern so that their joints are not aligned. Their joints should also not fall over joints in the underlying subfloor. Allow about a 1/32" space between sheets, and an 1/8" space between the sheets and any vertical surface. Particleboard panels should be butted for light contact.

Use ring-shank, cement-coated or resin-coated nails. For 1/4" underlayment use 2d nails; for 3/8" underlayment, use 3d nails.

Minor indentations can be filled with a plastic-type filler used to level floors. Some manufacturers recommend the use of lining felt to help smooth out any irregularities in the underlayment. The felt, made especially for resilient flooring, is applied with adhesives, laid with edges butted, and rolled to iron out wrinkles. It should not be used on or below grade.

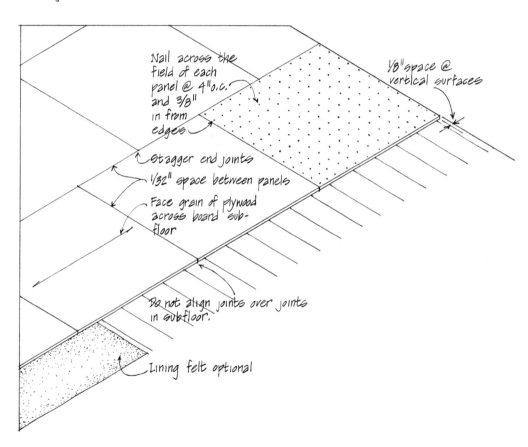

Nail across the field of each panel @ 4"o.c. and 3/8" in from edges

1/8" space @ vertical surfaces

Stagger end joints

1/32" space between panels

Face grain of plywood across board sub-floor

Do not align joints over joints in subfloor.

Lining felt optional

# LAYING RESILIENT TILE

To lay out the tile installation pattern, it is necessary to center and square off the floor of the room, and divide it into four equal quadrants. First locate the center of the floor by stringing two diagonals. Then snap two chalklines, perpendicular to each other, through the centerpoint to the walls.

For a square design, lay out the dry tiles along both chalklines. Shift the tiles as necessary to equalize the border tiles. If the border tiles are less than half their width, shift the line of tiles a half-tile width. Work for even margins.

Begin laying the tiles along one of the chalklines from the center of the room. If using tiles with a self-adhesive backing, simply remove the paper backing and press the tiles into place. Butt adjoining tiles carefully, and set them down firmly. Do not slide them into place since they are difficult to lift once they are set.

To lay tiles with adhesive, follow the directions supplied by the manufacturer. A notched trowel is usually used to spread the adhesive. The notches assure an even distribution of the right amount of adhesive. If the adhesive is too thinly spread, the tiles will not adhere properly; if it is too heavily laid, the adhesive will ooze up between the tile joints. Try not to conceal the chalklines with the adhesive. If necessary, snap new ones, or tack thin wood guide strips in their place.

Allow the adhesive to set the proper amount of time. Align and butt the tile joints carefully, and set the tiles firmly. To prevent the adhesive from being pushed up onto the tiles, do not slide them into place.

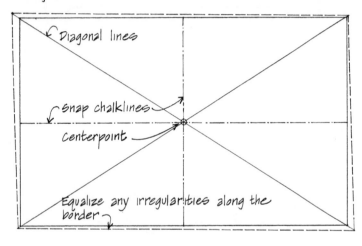

Diagonal lines

Snap chalklines

Centerpoint

Equalize any irregularities along the border

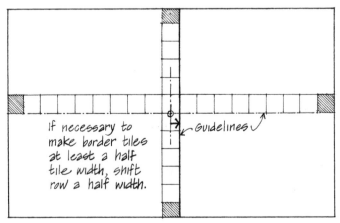

If necessary to make border tiles at least a half tile width, shift row a half width.

Guidelines

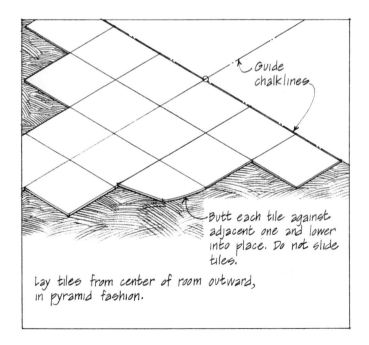

Guide chalklines

Butt each tile against adjacent one and lower into place. Do not slide tiles.

Lay tiles from center of room outward, in pyramid fashion.

Border tiles can be laid against the wall, marked where they overlap the last whole tiles, and be cut. Around door frames and other protrusions, scribe the border tile with a pencil compass. Cut the tiles with a utility or linoleum knife. Warming the tiles can sometimes make them easier to cut.

When laying tiles with a pattern or directional design, match them carefully. More elaborate designs can be achieved by laying the tile diagonally, using two-color designs, or by bordering the floor with a complementary color or pattern.

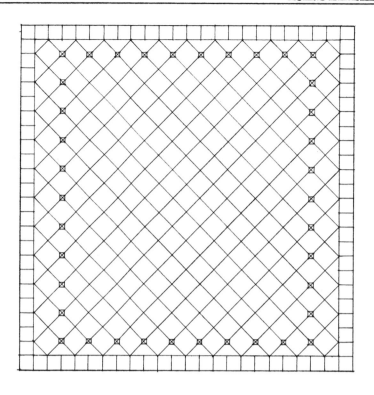

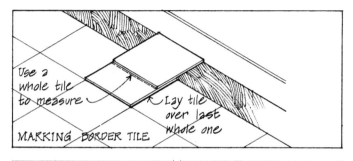

Use a whole tile to measure

Lay tile over last whole one

MARKING BORDER TILE

Mark one side first........ ...then the other

MARKING A CORNER TILE

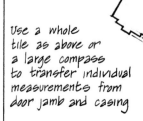
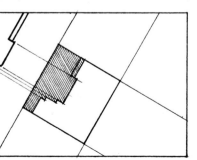

Use a whole tile as above or a large compass to transfer individual measurements from door jamb and casing

## LAYING SHEET VINYL

Laying resilient sheet goods is more difficult than laying tiles since the sheet flooring must first be laid flat, and the room's measurements transferred to the material. The material is then cut slightly larger than the required dimensions, loosely rolled, and carried into the room for installation. For sheet flooring that is laid with adhesive, this can be a tedious and difficult job. If using expensive solid vinyl sheet flooring, any mistakes can be quite costly.

There are, however, types of cushioned sheet vinyl, such as roto-vinyl sheet flooring, that are quite flexible and can be laid loosely without adhesive. The flooring lays flat, and is secured only along the perimeter of the room and at seams with adhesive.

Cushioned sheet vinyl is available in 6', 9', and 12' widths. For rooms up to 12' wide, therefore, a seamless installation is possible. For rooms wider than 12', purchase enough material to allow the pattern of the flooring to be matched along the seam. Drawing a plan of the floor can help you plan the installation and determine the amount of material you need.

Lay out the sheet flooring in a space that is larger than the room in which it is to be laid. If the outdoor and indoor temperatures are similar, you can work on an outside deck or patio.

Use the longest and straightest edge of the floor to be covered as a base line, and orient a long edge of the sheet flooring to this base line. If the edge of the sheet is not true, snap a chalkline and cut the flooring to form a new edge. From this base line, measure all dimensions of the floor and transfer them to the sheet flooring. Allow a few extra inches along the perimeter for adjustments as you lay the material. After re-checking all dimensions, cut the sheet flooring with heavy shears or a utility knife and straightedge.

Use longest and straightest edge of the floor as a baseline. Take all measurements from this baseline.

Baseline Measurement

When cutting, allow 2" to 3" extra material around the perimeter for fitting to wall irregularities.

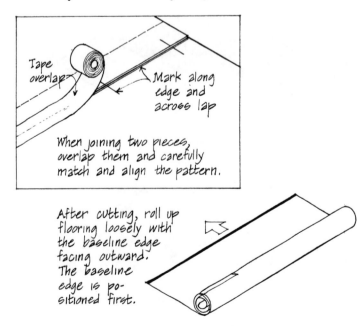

Tape overlap

Mark along edge and across lap

When joining two pieces, overlap them and carefully match and align the pattern.

After cutting, roll up flooring loosely with the baseline edge facing outward. The baseline edge is positioned first.

If two pieces have to be joined along a seam, overlap the two sheets and carefully match their patterns. Draw a line on the lower sheet where the upper sheet ends its overlap. Add a few marks perpendicular to and across the overlap, and tape the sheets together.

Once the sheet flooring material is cut, roll it up loosely with the base line edge facing outward. Inside the room, lay the base edge line down first. If there is a base shoe molding along the baseboard, remove it before laying the flooring down.

As you unroll the flooring, let the excess material curl up against the walls. After the flooring is laid out and pressed into place, the edges can be trimmed with a sharp utility knife. Allow an 1/8" clearance along the edges for expansion of the flooring material. Work carefully around door frames. To fit the flooring around an obstruction, such as a pipe in the floor, cut a slit from the wall to the object, and then cut carefully around it. The sheet is then pressed back together.

At seams, check the alignment of the flooring pattern. Cut through both sheets simultaneously where they overlap with a sharp knife. Roll back the sheets and spread adhesive on the floor along the length of the seam. Press the adjoining sheets back into place.

Also secure the edges of the flooring with an adhesive recommended by the flooring manufacturer.

The final step is to replace the base shoe molding, or install a new cove base. The base shoe should be nailed to the baseboard and not the floor. Allow space between the flooring and the base shoe so that any movement between the wall and the subfloor will not affect the flooring.

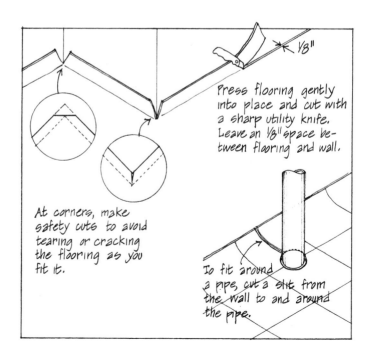

Press flooring gently into place and cut with a sharp utility knife. Leave an 1/8" space between flooring and wall.

At corners, make safety cuts to avoid tearing or cracking the flooring as you fit it.

To fit around a pipe, cut a slit from the wall to and around the pipe.

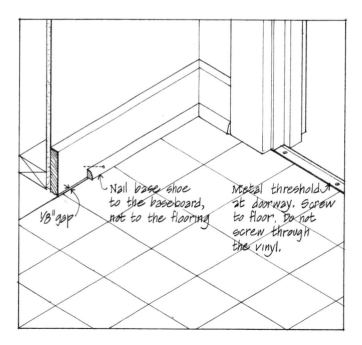

1/8" gap

Nail base shoe to the baseboard, not to the flooring

Metal threshold at doorway. Screw to floor. Do not screw through the vinyl.

# INTERIOR TRIM

Interior trim is normally installed after the finish walls, ceiling and flooring are in place. Although decorative in nature, interior trim also serves the function of concealing, finishing and perfecting the joints between interior materials. In many ways, trim pieces can be selected and installed to conceal mistakes made in cutting and fastening interior materials.

Common types of interior include:

1. CORNICES AND COVES

   Cornices and coves are used to finish the joint between ceilings and walls, especially when they are of different materials. Cornice and cove trim is now rarely used when the the ceiling and walls are of the same material.

2. DOOR AND WINDOW TRIM

   Head and side jamb casings conceal and finish the joint or gap between door and window frames and the surrounding interior wall surface. Stools and aprons are used to finish the joint between window sills and interior walls.

3. BASEBOARDS

   Baseboards and base shoes conceal and finish the joint between interior walls and the flooring.

Other interior trim, now rarely used but often found in older houses, include chair rails and picture moldings. Chair rails were originally used to protect plaster walls from being damaged by the backs of chairs. Dado caps are similar to chair rails and were used to cap off wood panel wainscots.

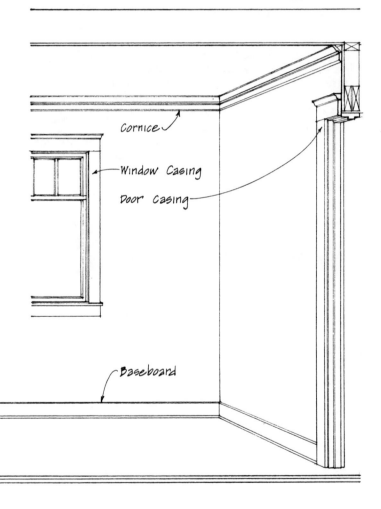

Cornice

Window Casing

Door Casing

Baseboard

Picture moldings are continuous projecting supports for picture hooks. Originally used when pictures were hung with cord and hooks, they were often integrated with cornice trim.

Elaborate trim work is often built up from a number of individual trim pieces. See the next two pages for examples of basic types of wood moldings.

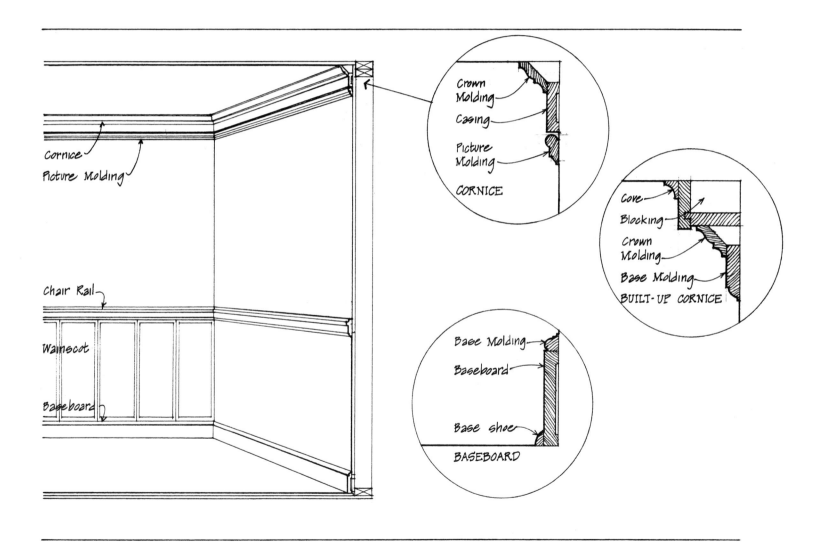

Cornice
Picture Molding

Chair Rail

Wainscot

Baseboard

Crown Molding
Casing
Picture Molding
CORNICE

Cove
Blocking
Crown Molding
Base Molding
BUILT-UP CORNICE

Base Molding
Baseboard
Base shoe
BASEBOARD

# WOOD MOLDINGS

Interior trim is almost always exposed woodwork. The type of wood used for trim depends on the type of finish to be applied to the woodwork. For painted finishes, the wood should be close-grained, smooth, and free of pitch streaks or other imperfections.

If the woodwork is to receive a transparent or natural finish, the wood should have a uniform color, an attractive grain figure, and a degree of hardness.

Any wood stock used for trim should be dry (6% - 11% moisture content) to prevent excessive shrinking and opening of joints after installation.

For use as trim, a variety of stock wood moldings are available at lumber yards and millwork shops. They vary in section, length, and species of wood. Some may be pre-finished. They can be used singly, or be combined to form more complex sections.

In addition to these stock sections, moldings and trim can be recycled from existing houses, or be milled to your specifications. The latter will, of course, be more expensive, but may be necessary in certain situations.

TYPES OF MOLDINGS AND USES

1. BASE . . . . . . . . . . . Where sidewalls meet floors, and for window and door casings.
2. CAP TRIM . . . . . . . Over windows, doors, and the tops of wainscots.
3. CASING . . . . . . . . To trim head and side jambs of windows and doors.
4. CHAIR RAIL . . . . . To protect a wall surface from the backs of chairs.
5. COVE . . . . . . . . . . At inside corners, and at surfaces that meet at 90°.
6. CROWN . . . . . . . . At the meeting of walls and ceilings, and for mantels.
7. HALF-ROUND . . . . To conceal vertical and horizontal joints in surfaces.
8. PICTURE . . . . . . . . To support picture hooks, and as a finishing line to upper part of wall.
9. SCREEN BEAD . . . To finish the raw edges of screening on windows and doors.
10. SEAM . . . . . . . . . . To conceal joints in paneling and other wide surfaces.
11. SHOE . . . . . . . . . . Finish base trim at the floor line.
12. SILL . . . . . . . . . . Bottom trim of door and window openings.
13. STOOL . . . . . . . . . Interior trim at the bottom of windows.
14. STOP . . . . . . . . . At window and door jambs, to guide windows or stop doors.

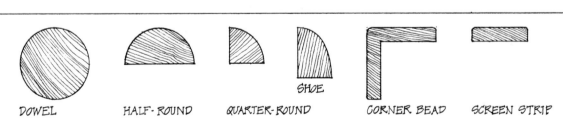

DOWEL     HALF-ROUND     QUARTER-ROUND     SHOE     CORNER BEAD     SCREEN STRIP

The molding types shown on this and the opposite page often come in several sizes. In some cases, profiles may vary slightly. Check with your local lumberyard or millwork shop.

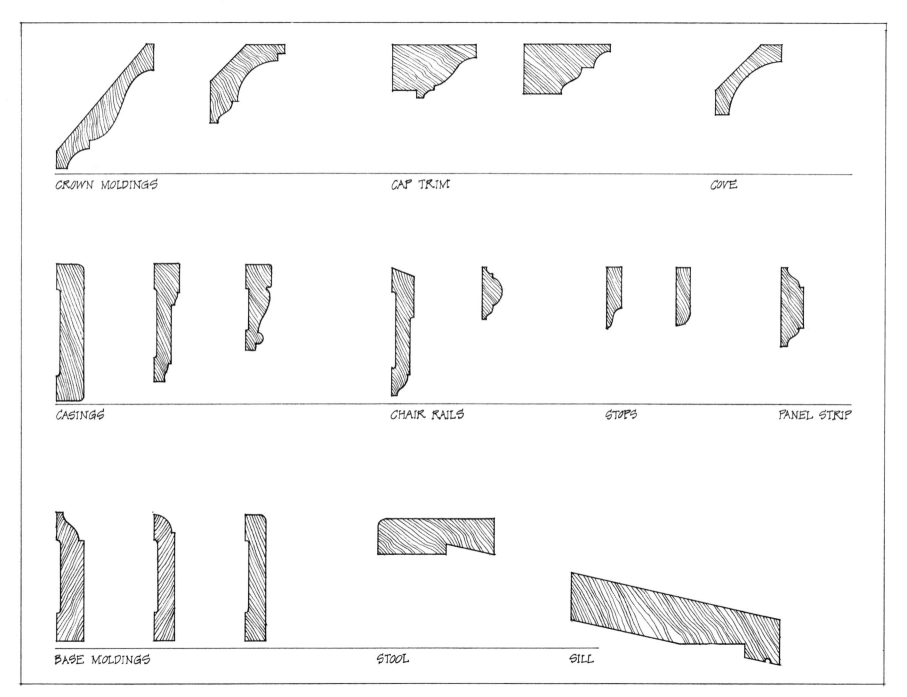

CROWN MOLDINGS        CAP TRIM        COVE

CASINGS        CHAIR RAILS        STOPS        PANEL STRIP

BASE MOLDINGS        STOOL        SILL

## TRIM DETAILS

Through history, the tendency in the treatment of surfaces has been toward simplification. Trim moldings, for example, are simplified versions of architectural elements that once were developed out of necessity. Today, the treatment of surfaces and joints are often the result of individual decisions or habit, based purely on functional requirements.

The homeowner-builder is often his or her own designer, and should, therefore, consider the choices in materials carefully. This is especially true since such a wide range of materials are available, and most of them perform well if used properly. In selecting the trimwork for a home's interior spaces, consider not only the function of the trim pieces but also their aesthetic impact on the surfaces of each room.

Even though the range of moldings and trim stock may seem limited, there are choices of size, scale and proportion. Window and door openings can be kept very simple by turning the wall material at the edges. They can also be trimmed neatly with 3/4" or 5/4" stock. They can even be emphasized with wider casings and a cap trim piece at the top.

In addition to the size and scale of the trim pieces, the finish used can also affect their visual weight. A light-colored wood with a natural or transparent finish can be used for subtle contrast. For greater contrast, the trim can be a darker wood, or be painted a contrasting color. The trim can also be painted the same color as the wall and visually become part of the wall surface.

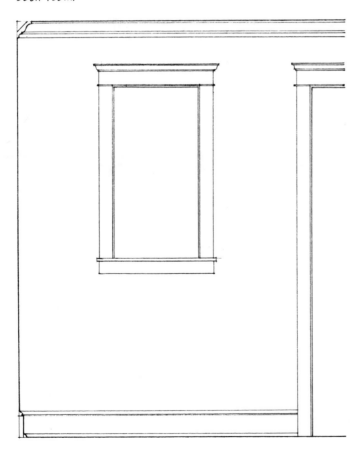

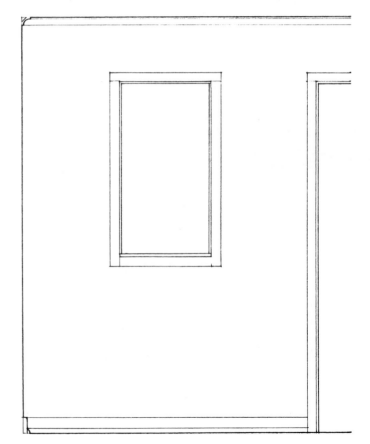

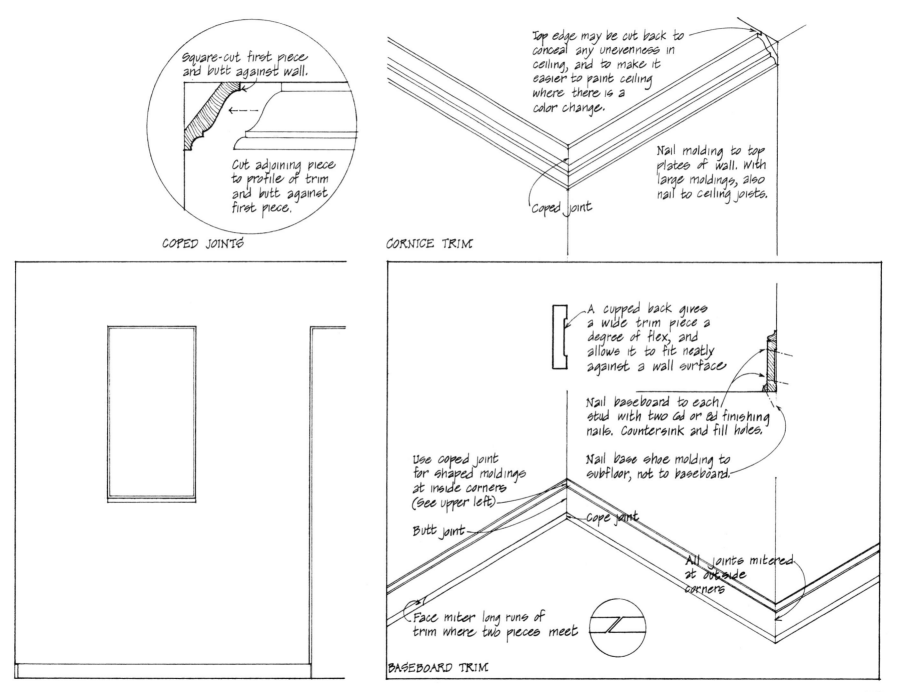

Square-cut first piece and butt against wall.

Cut adjoining piece to profile of trim and butt against first piece.

COPED JOINTS

Top edge may be cut back to conceal any unevenness in ceiling, and to make it easier to paint ceiling where there is a color change.

Nail molding to top plates of wall. With large moldings, also nail to ceiling joists.

Coped joint

CORNICE TRIM

A cupped back gives a wide trim piece a degree of flex, and allows it to fit neatly against a wall surface

Nail baseboard to each stud with two 6d or 8d finishing nails. Countersink and fill holes.

Nail base shoe molding to subfloor, not to baseboard.

Use coped joint for shaped moldings at inside corners (see upper left)

Butt joint

Cope joint

All joints mitered at outside corners

Face miter long runs of trim where two pieces meet

BASEBOARD TRIM

# 4 ADDING NEW SPACE

If your present home works well for you, and there are no possibilities for expanding within the existing structure, then adding on new space may be the only answer to your space needs. Additions to your home can range in scale from small window seats and dormers to larger one-room additions. Even adding another story or a two-story addition containing several rooms may be possible.

Although additions are the most expensive of the alternatives discussed thus far, they offer the greatest flexibility in their design and layout. They are not restricted as much by the house structure as are modifications and conversions of existing interior space. Code requirements, costs, and aesthetic considerations of appearance, however, often play a role in determining where and how much space can be added on to your house.

Additions usually employ the techniques of new construction in the building of their foundations, floors, walls and roofs. The unique part of planning and building an addition is making the connection - functionally, technically, and visually - between the new and the existing.

## ADDING SPACE

Adding on to your house may be the best and only way to satisfy your need for more living space. It can also be expensive, although not as expensive as building a new home. To make the most of what time, effort and money you do spend, an addition, no matter how small or large, should be carefully planned and designed.

In considering an addition, try to develop a solution that solves several problems with the new construction. In addition to gaining more space, perhaps your design can also improve the appearance of your house, or make it more energy-efficient. An extension to your house might also be able to create and define a new outdoor living area. A new second story might, with skylights, also help to brighten a dark interior.

To begin planning your addition, first determine how much space you really need, where it is needed, what it is to be used for, and how it should relate to or fit in with the rest of your house. The outline on pgs. 188-192 can help you review these and other factors during the planning and design of your addition.

During this review, consider the various forms the addition can have. The following section illustrates several design possibilities for you to explore. You may not find exactly what you're looking for, but you may be able to adapt one to suit your specific needs. At the very least, they can stimulate your thinking.

## SMALL-SCALE ADDITIONS

Small-scale additions can often be built without a new foundation being required. Instead, they can be cantilevered out from the existing floor framing or be hung from an exterior wall. They can extend from the first or second story level, or be built over an existing balcony.

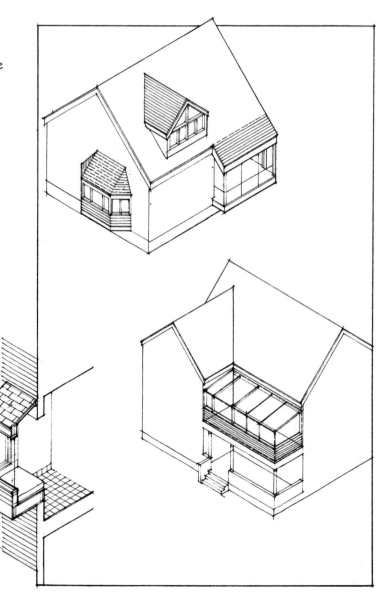

Small-scale additions can dramatically improve the quality of an existing room while increasing its usable space. Even an addition of two or three feet along the width of a room can, with a row of windows, brighten a space and visually expand it. Within this space, a built-in seat, daybed, or desk area can be provided along with needed storage.

From an exterior view, small additions can help improve the appearance of your home. Bay windows and dormers can add visual interest and character. Linear extensions can help unify a house that has already been added on to, or conceal aesthetic defects.

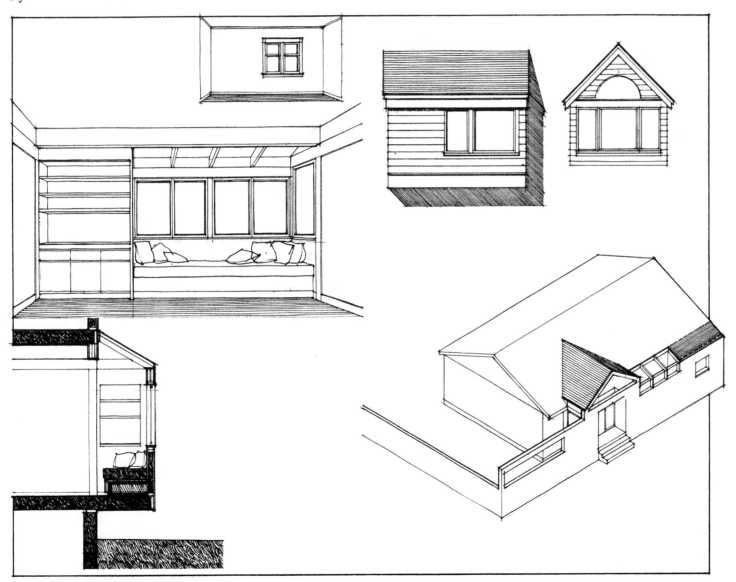

# ROOM ADDITIONS

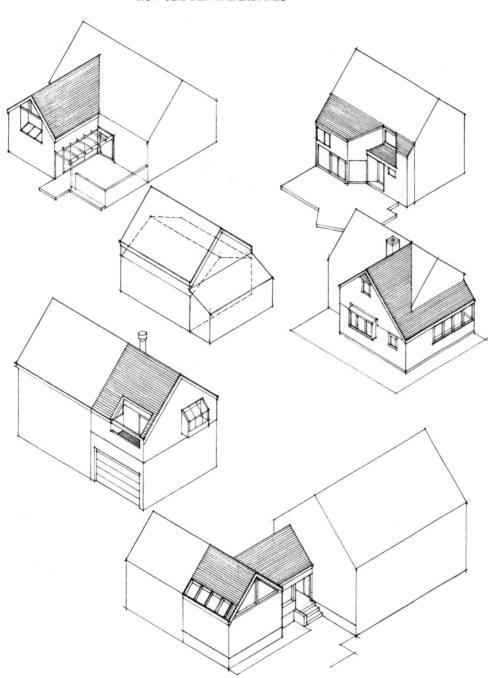

# PLANNING & DESIGN FACTORS

In planning and designing your addition, the following factors should be reviewed.

1. SIZE

   Carefully consider how much space you really need for the intended use. While the size of an addition may be limited by zoning restrictions, site conditions, and your budget, don't lose sight of your long-range goals. It may be possible to build the shell first, and then complete the interior in stages.

   In determining the size of your addition, remember that its proportions are as important as its square-footage in deciding its usefulness and impact on the appearance of your house.

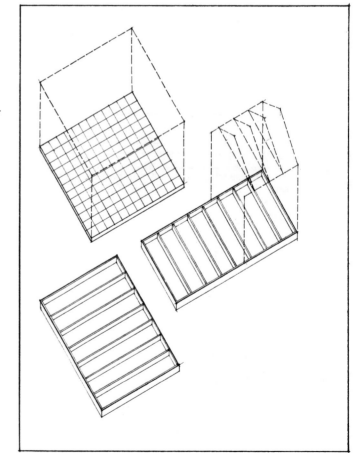

## 2. USE

Because of the expense involved, use the addition for your most critical needs. If space and money are tight, consider a multi-use room, one that can be used for two or more activities.

Before making a firm decision, list all possible uses for the addition. For each, study its requirements for furnishings, lighting, access, and privacy. This can help you decide which use fits best with the size and location of the addition.

## 3. LAYOUT

Once you have decided on the best use for the addition, determine where it should be located relative to other spaces and activities in your house. Consider where the addition would least disrupt the existing layout and activity zones of your house.

For access, the addition should related to an existing hallway, circulation path, or entrance foyer. Avoid creating a new hallway just to gain access to the addition.

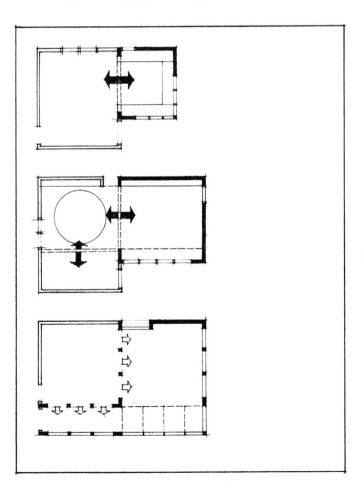

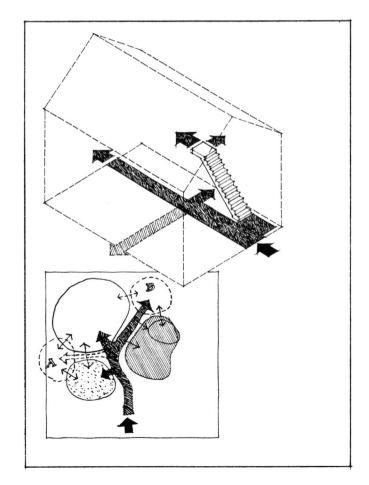

# PLANNING & DESIGN FACTORS

## 4. CODES

Check your local building, zoning and land-use regulations carefully. Any addition, whether it extends up or outward from your house, will have to comply with local code restrictions on setbacks, height and lot coverage. Mark these restrictions on your site plan, and you will have a picture of your buildable area. If your addition must extend beyond the limits established by the code, you may be able to obtain a variance.

If your addition is large, some building codes require that the entire house be brought up to code.

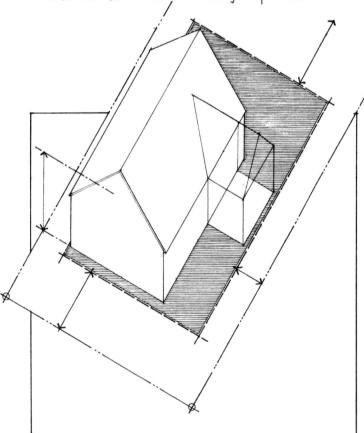

## 5. SITE

In addition to code restrictions, the character of your site and any underground utilities will affect the size and location of your addition. The addition should not adversely affect your site drainage, or require the removal of significant landscaping elements. Nor should it be built over a fuel tank or septic tank and drain field.

Consider also how the size and location of the addition will affect your outdoor spaces, and how its orientation will infuence the quality of its interior. Perhaps the addition can help define a pleasant deck or courtyard space. To take advantage of a nice view, you may want to consider placing the addition at a second-story level.

If you plan to have a sunroom, orient it to the south or southeast. Will the addition be shaded most of the time by adjacent buildings or landscaping? Will it interfere with the sunlighting of another room or an outdoor deck?

6. APPEARANCE

The addition should appear to be intentionally de-signed to be where it is, not merely stuck on as an afterthought. The massing and proportions should complement the style of the existing house. If the addition has a sloping roof, it should have the same pitch as the existing roof.

If you cannot match the older siding material, select one that will complement it in color, texture, pattern and proportion. The horizontal lines of the roof, floor levels, and window and door headers can often help tie the addition visually to the house.

If you want the addition to contrast with what exists, provide a visual break between new and old with a setback, a tall window or landscaping.

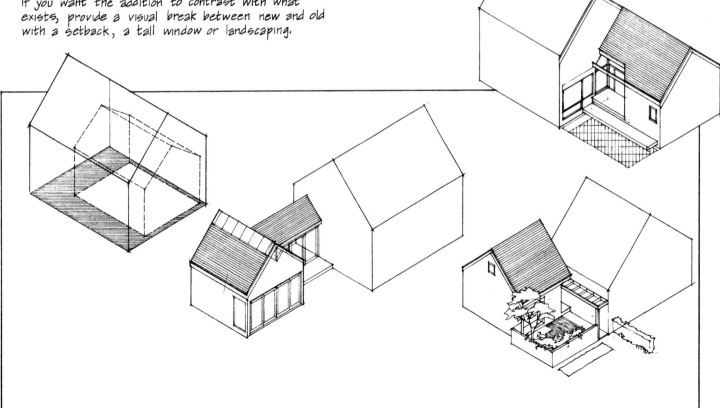

## 7. CONSTRUCTION

While small additions may be cantilevered from the existing structure, room-size additions at the first floor level require a foundation, floor and wall framing, and a roof structure. In effect, it is like building a small house except that it is connected in some manner to your existing house.

The most difficult connection is the meeting of new and existing roof forms. The meeting of a sloping roof and a vertical wall is usually easier to frame than the intersection of sloping roof planes. In either case, the roof forms should be compatible in appearance and not create any roof drainage problems.

A room addition will require a doorway be cut into the exterior wall of the house. If the addition is an extension of an existing room, an even larger opening is required. Whenever possible, use an existing window or doorway to reduce or eliminate the work involved in cutting through an existing wall.

Rooms can also be added over an existing garage, or atop a single story house. In both cases, the need for a foundation is eliminated, but the existing house structure and foundation must be able to support the additional load. If you are not sure of this, you should consult an engineer or architect.

## 8. UTILITIES

Heating, electrical and plumbing requirements for the addition should be considered in determining its location. If you intend to extend the utility lines, locate the addition as close as possible to the existing lines without sacrificing any desirable functional relationships.

Your furnace may be able to handle the additional heating load of the addition. If your furnace is too small, or too distant for the heating system to maintain its balance, supplementary heating can be installed in the addition.

Bathroom and kitchen additions will require new plumbing lines, while most other additions will not.

Small additions may not require any utilities at all, except perhaps a single baseboard heating unit and a couple of convenience outlets.

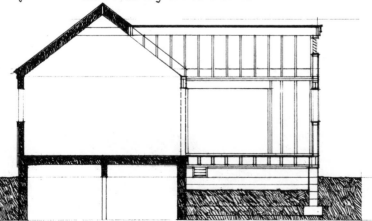

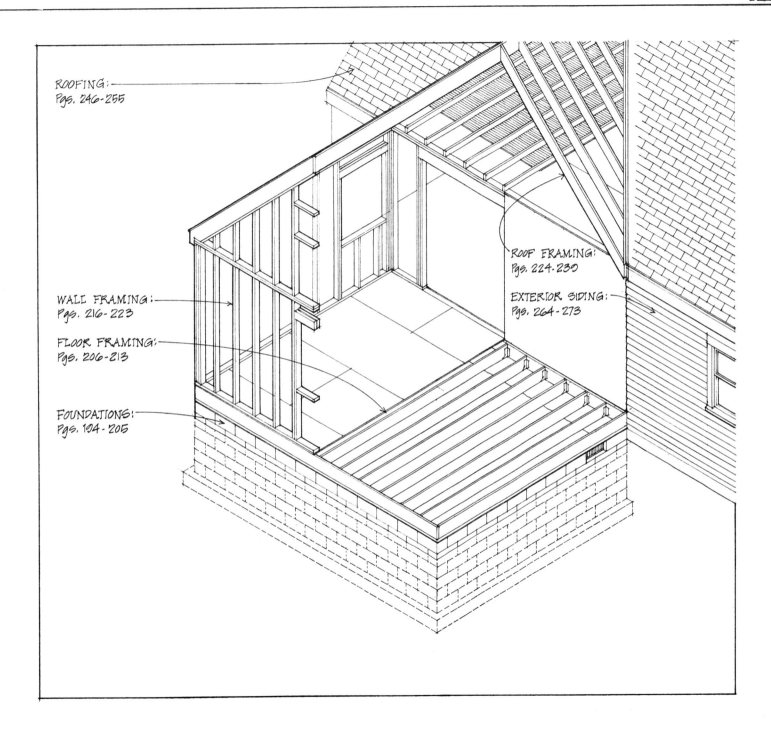

ROOFING:
Pgs. 246-255

WALL FRAMING:
Pgs. 216-223

FLOOR FRAMING:
Pgs. 206-213

FOUNDATIONS:
Pgs. 194-205

ROOF FRAMING:
Pgs. 224-230

EXTERIOR SIDING:
Pgs. 264-273

## FOUNDATION SYSTEMS

A new foundation is required for any large-scale addition that cannot be supported by the existing structure of your house. This section describes the parts of a foundation system and the types commonly used in residential construction. Bear in mind that the foundation of a house is probably its most critical component since, once it is built, there is little you can do to alter it. A foundation's form, dimensions and details should therefore be planned and constructed carefully to give a house or addition stability and permanence.

A foundation system is the substructure that supports the weight of a building's superstructure and any loads imposed on it, such as its occupants and furnishings, snow and wind. It consists of piers or walls that are laid out to transmit these loads to footings which, in turn, distribute the house loads directly to the supporting earth.

A foundation system must also, through its wall and floor connections, anchor a building against ground pressures and wind, and prevent it from lifting, shifting or rotating on its base.

A building can normally be expected to settle, to some degree, over a period of time. A foundation system, and its footings in particular, must be designed to minimize this settlement. Whatever settlement does occur should be equal under all parts of the building. Uneven settlement between the parts of a building, or between an addition and the existing house, can result in cracks in wall and ceiling finishes, sloping floors, and doors that bind. If excessive, foundation settlement can create serious structural problems leading to failure.

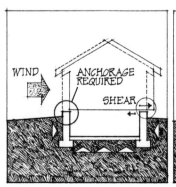

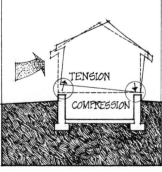

## FOOTINGS

Footings form the base of a foundation system that bears on, and transmits house loads directly to, the supporting soil. They are enlarged or spread to distribute the loads over a wide portion of soil and thus avoid exceeding the soil's bearing capacity.

The size of a footing is directly related to the loads being borne and the type of supporting soil. Because the loads encountered in residential construction are comparatively light, footing sizes are often estimated using the following guidelines.

For pier or post footings: $A = P/S$, where
$A$ = horizontal bearing surface of footing
$P$ = load in pounds
$S$ = soil bearing capacity in lbs. per sq.ft. (psf)

For foundation wall footings:
Width of footing = 2 × wall thickness
Depth of footing = wall thickness

Your local building code may also specify required footing sizes for various load and soil conditions. If you encounter a soil of low-bearing capacity or unusual load conditions, consult a structural engineer.

| General Soil Type | Typical Bearing Capacity |
|---|---|
| Compact gravel, sand-gravel.... | 4,000 psf |
| Gravel and sand............ | 2,000 psf |
| Sand; silty sand............ | 1,500 psf |
| Clay .................... | 1,000 psf |
| Organic Soils.............. | Not Suitable |

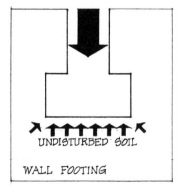

WALL FOOTING

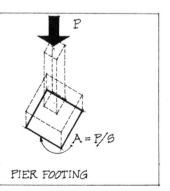

PIER FOOTING

Footings should always be placed on firm, undisturbed soil. Uncompacted fill is susceptible to compaction after the foundation is in place, leading to uneven settlement and cracks in the foundation and structure. Fill any excessive depth in the footing excavation with concrete; do not replace with soil.

Also avoid placing footings on wet clay or organic soils since these may shrink. Also do not place footings on frozen ground that can displace as it thaws.

Footings should be placed at a depth at least 12" below the frost line (the deepest penetration of frost) in your area. Local building codes usually specify this depth. This is to ensure the footing will not be subject to the heaving action of moisture in the soil as it freezes during the winter.

If you have an older home, any weaknesses or deficiencies in its foundation have probably already manifested themselves. Older homes have had time to settle in, and further problems are unlikely unless a new condition arises, such as clogging of the drain tile system or improper excavation during the construction of an addition. Any problems that do exist can be costly to correct. If excessive settlement has occurred, have the situation evaluated by a structural engineer.

If your house foundation is in good condition and has performed well, use it as a model for selecting the type and size of foundation for your addition. Current local practice can also provide useful guidelines for a successful foundation in your neighborhood.

The two basic types of foundations you can use for your addition are the pier foundation and the wall foundation. Pier foundation systems use a series of columns and footings to support the house loads at various points. Wall foundation systems use a perimeter wall and footing around the house or addition to support the loads along a continuous line.

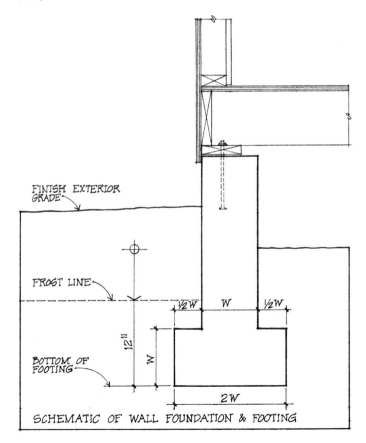

FINISH EXTERIOR GRADE

FROST LINE

½W  W  ½W

12"

W

BOTTOM OF FOOTING

2W

SCHEMATIC OF WALL FOUNDATION & FOOTING

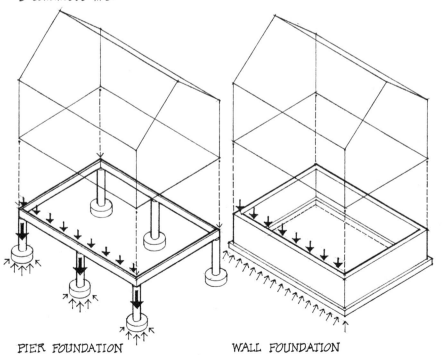

PIER FOUNDATION        WALL FOUNDATION

## PIER FOUNDATIONS

Pier foundation systems use concrete, masonry or treated wood piers to transfer house loads to the supporting soil at various points. The grid pattern of piers is directly related to the posts and beams that rest on these piers and support the floor, walls, and roof above.

Pier foundations cost less and take less time to build than wall foundations. They are well-suited for steep slopes or where minimal excavation is desired. The piers allow the main structure to be set off the ground and give it a light, airy appearance. This is ideal for ventilation of the space below the first floor, but also requires steps be taken to prevent animals and rodents from using the space.

The point loads created by a pier foundation are concentrated loads. To avoid excessive settling, the piers and footings must be carefully spaced, sized and constructed.

Lateral bracing must also be built into a pier foundation to provide adequate structural resistance against wind and earthquake forces. Integrated, reinforced concrete piers and footings, combined with side soil resistance, can usually provide the necessary lateral strength. Wood piers and concrete footings, on the other hand, may require additional cross-bracing to provide the necessary resistance to lateral forces.

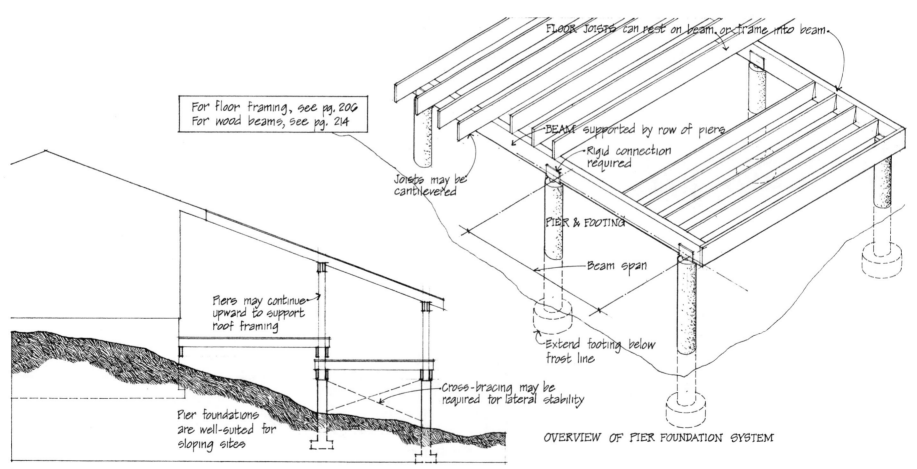

For floor framing, see pg. 206
For wood beams, see pg. 214

FLOOR JOISTS can rest on beam or frame into beam.

Joists may be cantilevered

BEAM supported by row of piers

Rigid connection required

PIER & FOOTING

Beam span

Extend footing below frost line

Piers may continue upward to support roof framing

Cross-bracing may be required for lateral stability

Pier foundations are well-suited for sloping sites

OVERVIEW OF PIER FOUNDATION SYSTEM

The spacing and layout of piers should be coordinated with the pattern of beams and joists of the floor system they support. Bearing walls, ideally, should lie directly over a beam supported by a row of piers.

Beams span between piers in one direction while joists span between the beams in the other. Beams are most efficient for a given size if they are continuous over two or more spans. When laid in this manner, adjacent spans can help limit the deflection in neighboring ones.

If floor joists are discontinuous, the spacing of the beams (and consequently the rows of piers) should be as even as possible so that the joists can economically be of the same length.

There is a great deal of flexibility in determining the number and pattern of piers. If a minimal number of piers is desired for appearance, cost, or the difficulty of placing them, then the beams and joists can be increased in size and span greater distances. On the othe hand, the number of piers can be increased with a subsequent reduction in the spans and sizes of beams and joists.

To best judge the relative economy of these alternatives, lay them out on paper, calculate the respective quantities of materials, and their costs. Using a greater number of members will require more connections and increase labor costs. Using fewer piers will increase the concentrated loading at each pier.

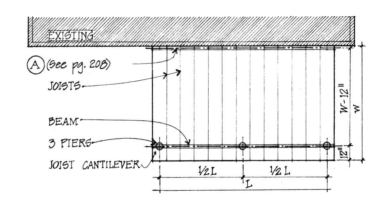

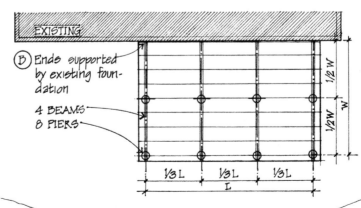

ALTERNATIVE PIER FOUNDATION & FRAMING PATTERNS

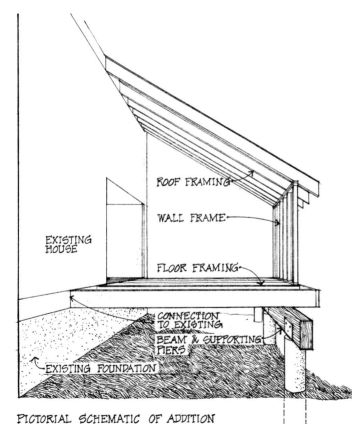

PICTORIAL SCHEMATIC OF ADDITION

## CONCRETE PIERS

While concrete piers are inherently stronger than concrete block piers, they also require more labor and are more expensive due to the cost of formwork and concrete.

The concrete is poured-in-place into formwork that should be tight and well-braced. This formwork can be built of 3/4" plywood or 1" stock lumber, nailed and tied together securely. You can also use cylindrical fiber-form tubes. These can be cut to the desired length, and are disposable. A section of clay or concrete sewer pipe will also work as formwork, and can be left in place.

Before the concrete is set, steel anchors or saddles are placed to secure posts or beams to the piers.

## CONCRETE BLOCK PIERS

Concrete block piers are less expensive and generally easier to build than concrete piers. The individual blocks are easy to handle, and they do not need to be set all in the same day.

To support the loads of a one-story addition, concrete block piers are more than adequate. For maximum strength, the cores of the block piers can be filled with concrete and reinforced with steel bars.

Because concrete block is a modular material, base the height of each pier, from the top of the footing, on the number of blocks required.

As with concrete piers, steel anchors or saddles are placed in the cores and set with concrete.

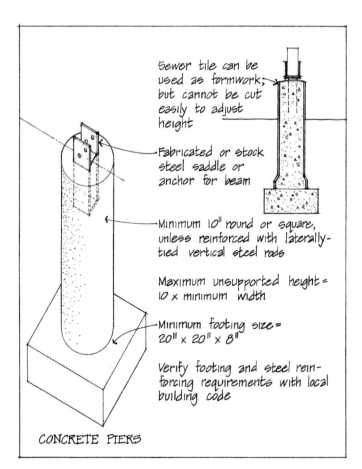

Sewer tile can be used as formwork, but cannot be cut easily to adjust height

Fabricated or stock steel saddle or anchor for beam

Minimum 10" round or square, unless reinforced with laterally-tied vertical steel rods

Maximum unsupported height = 10 x minimum width

Minimum footing size = 20" x 20" x 8"

Verify footing and steel reinforcing requirements with local building code

CONCRETE PIERS

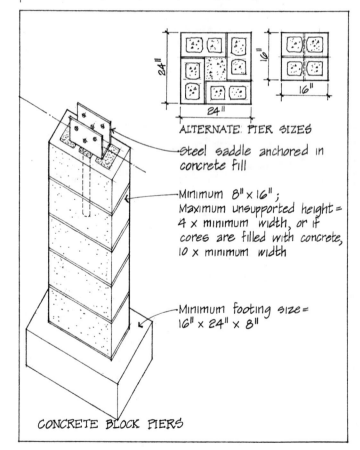

ALTERNATE PIER SIZES

Steel saddle anchored in concrete fill

Minimum 8" x 16"; Maximum unsupported height = 4 x minimum width, or if cores are filled with concrete, 10 x minimum width

Minimum footing size = 16" x 24" x 8"

CONCRETE BLOCK PIERS

## WOOD PIERS

Wood piers that are in close contact with or buried in the ground must be protected against insect damage and decay. This protection is best provided by pressure-treatment with a preservative, such as a water-borne salt solution or creosote. (See also pg. 202)

Wood piers are set atop concrete footings. Once the piers are plumb and braced temporarily, the post holes are back-filled and tamped in 6" layers.

Split or double wood beams are normally bolted to the top of each pier, one on each side. If round poles are being used, they are notched to form partial ledges for the wood beams. If the wood beams are set atop square or rectangular posts, metal connectors that can provide lateral stability for the beams are required.

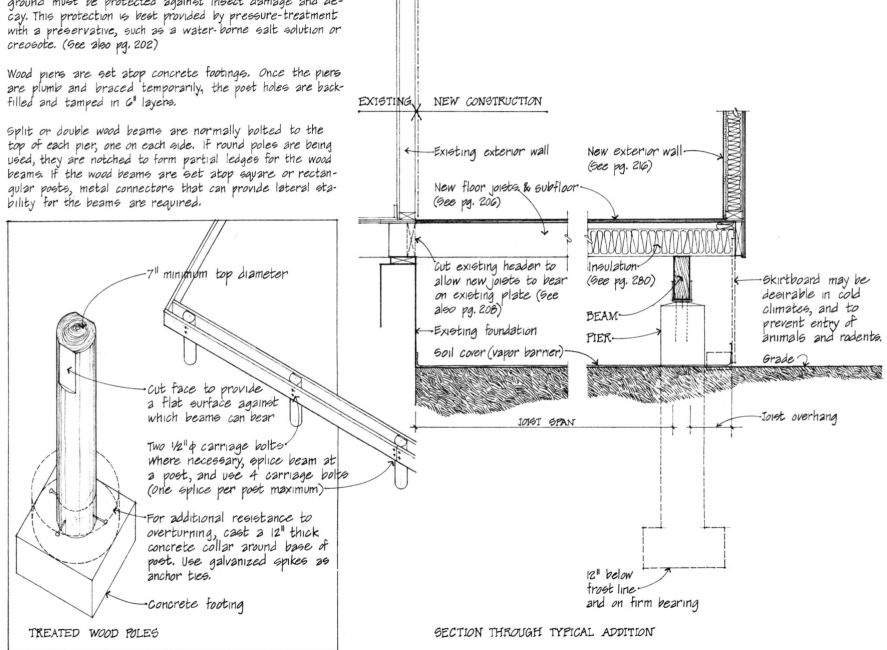

7" minimum top diameter

Cut face to provide a flat surface against which beams can bear

Two ½"⌀ carriage bolts. Where necessary, splice beam at a post, and use 4 carriage bolts (one splice per post maximum)

For additional resistance to overturning, cast a 12" thick concrete collar around base of post. Use galvanized spikes as anchor ties.

Concrete footing

TREATED WOOD POLES

EXISTING | NEW CONSTRUCTION

Existing exterior wall

New exterior wall (See pg. 216)

New floor joists & subfloor (See pg. 206)

Cut existing header to allow new joists to bear on existing plate (see also pg. 208)

Insulation (See pg. 280)

Skirtboard may be desirable in cold climates, and to prevent entry of animals and rodents.

Existing foundation

BEAM

PIER

Soil cover (vapor barrier)

Grade

JOIST SPAN

Joist overhang

12" below frost line and on firm bearing

SECTION THROUGH TYPICAL ADDITION

## WALL FOUNDATIONS

Wall foundations are the most common type of house foundation. The foundation walls and footings anchor the house structure and transmit house loads to the ground along a continuous line. The linear footings distribute the the loads more evenly over a greater area than pier foundations, and can be used over various soils and terrains.

The foundation wall is usually laid out along the perimeter of the new construction to support the floor and exterior walls above. If it is impractical for the floor system to span from one foundation wall across to another, interior posts and a beam can be used to shorten the span.

Wall foundations can enclose a basement or a crawl space. In both cases, the walls help to insulate the first floor from drafts. When they form basements, foundation walls must be able to withstand the lateral forces of the surrounding soil, and be waterproofed to prevent the penetration of moisture. In addition, surface and ground water must be drained away from the foundation.

Crawl space construction is well-suited for additions. Little or no excavation or grading is necessary within the foundation walls. With proper insulation and ventilation of the crawl space, the first floor framing can be kept warm and dry. Further, waterproofing of the foundation wall and installation of drain tiles are normally not required.

Foundation walls may be of concrete, concrete block, or pressure-treated wood. For additions requiring only a crawl space, concrete block is less expensive than concrete block and requires no formwork. A simple rectangular configuration is the most economical way to lay it out. Small-scale extensions of the first floor, such as bay windows and decks can be cantilevered over the foundation wall.

The outside face of the foundation wall is aligned with the outside line of the first floor framing. When laying out the actual dimensions of the perimeter wall, keep in mind the modular dimensions of concrete block. The lengths of concrete block walls should be a multiple of 8" so as to avoid having to cut the block at corners. Also locate any intersections and openings in the wall accordingly.

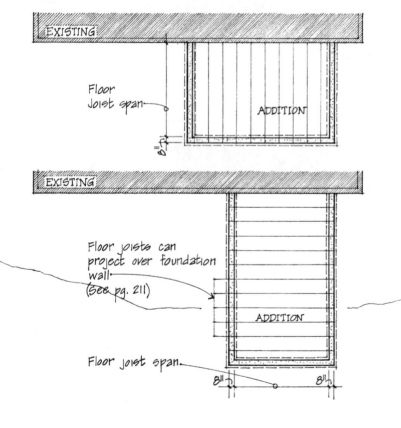

EXISTING

Floor Joist span

ADDITION

8"

EXISTING

Floor joists can project over foundation wall. (See pg. 211)

ADDITION

Floor joist span.

8"     8"

EXISTING

FLOOR JOISTS
HEADER
SILL

FOUNDATION WALL
FOOTING

OVERVIEW OF WALL FOUNDATION SYSTEM

EXAMPLES OF SCHEMATIC FRAMING PLANS

The poured-in-place concrete footings for a foundation wall should be placed at least 12" below the frost line, and on firm, stable, undisturbed soil. The top of the footings should be level all around, especially when concrete block is used for the foundation wall.

The height of the foundation wall is determined by a number of factors: (1) the required depth of the footing; (2) the desired height of the first floor above grade; and (3) the modular dimensions of the concrete block.

If inexperienced in laying concrete block with mortar, consider using a surface bonding technique. After the first course is laid, set and leveled on the footing with mortar, the remaining courses are laid or stacked dry. Both sides of the block wall are then troweled with a cement-glass fiber mixture that bonds the block together. This surface bonding cement is fairly easy to use, and produces a wall as strong, if not stronger, than a normally built wall with mortar.

To provide solid bearing for the first floor framing, the top course can be 4" solid cap blocks, or regular hollow core units filled with concrete. If greater lateral stability is required, a bond beam can be formed with concrete lintel blocks, filled with concrete and reinforced with a No. 3 or No. 4 steel bar.

Anchor bolts for the sill plate must be placed no more than 6' apart, and no more than 12" away from a corner. In areas of high wind, space the anchor bolts 4' apart or less. The 1/2" diameter anchor bolts, with a hook or large washer at their ends, should extend down through two courses and be set in concrete.

To protect the first floor framing members from decay due to ground moisture and humidity, the crawl space should be ventilated and the ground covered with a vapor barrier. The vents should be screened, and have a net area equal to 1 1/2 sq.ft. for each 25 lineal feet of foundation wall. The vents should be located as high as possible on each side of the crawl space to encourage cross-ventilation through the space.

Floor joist framing.
(See pgs. 206-208)

2"x6" treated sill

see next page

Exterior grade

1/2" Ø x 15" long anchor bolts @ 6' o.c. set in cores filled with concrete

For additional lateral stability, fill cores and reinforce with a Nº 4 steel rod @ 4' o.c. and at corners - Tie into footing

Vapor barrier

8" concrete block

8"x16" concrete footing. Check local building code for steel reinforcing requirements

12" below frost line and on firm bearing

TYPICAL FOUNDATION WALL

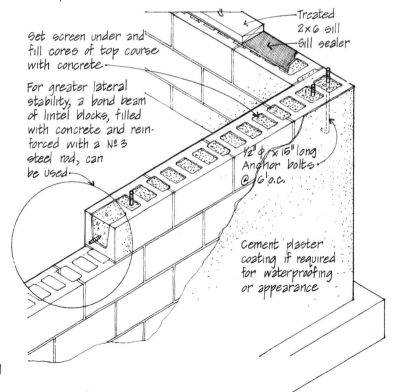

Set screen under and fill cores of top course with concrete

For greater lateral stability, a bond beam of lintel blocks, filled with concrete and reinforced with a Nº 3 steel rod, can be used

Treated 2x6 sill

Sill sealer

1/2" Ø x 15" long Anchor bolts @ 6' o.c.

Cement plaster coating if required for waterproofing or appearance

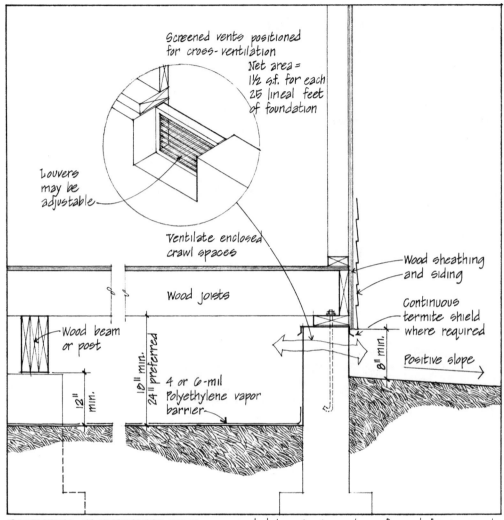

Screened vents positioned for cross-ventilation

Net area = 1½ s.f. for each 25 lineal feet of foundation

Louvers may be adjustable.

Ventilate enclosed crawl spaces

Wood joists

Wood sheathing and siding

Continuous termite shield where required

Wood beam or post

10" min. 24" preferred

8" min.

Positive slope

12" min.

4 or 6-mil Polyethylene vapor barrier.

PROTECTION OF UNTREATED WOOD is provided by:  1. Separation of wood from ground.
2. Ventilation and condensation control in enclosed spaces.
3. Positive site drainage.

## WOOD FOUNDATION SYSTEMS

Any wood that is in close contact with the ground is susceptible to insect damage and decay. This is particularly true of wood piers or foundation walls that are buried in the ground. Since the fungi that cause decay flourish best in warm, damp conditions, dry climates present less of a problem for wood foundations. Protection against termites and other insects is best afforded by treating the soil around the foundation.

While the heartwood of redwood and cedar is more decay-resistant than other species, it is expensive and may be difficult to obtain. The best choice, therefore, for any wood structural members in contact with the ground is wood that is commercially pressure-treated with a preservative.

Wood may be pressure-treated with water-borne salts, pentachlorophenol, or creosote. Water-borne salt preservatives are often used to treat wood for residential construction since they leave the wood clean, odorless, and easy to glue or paint.

Pentachlorophenol is an oil-borne preservative that is insoluble in water. It is also highly toxic to plants and animals. When dry, the treated wood is clean, relatively odorless, and paintable.

Creosote is both a water-repellant and a preservative often used to treat utility poles and other wood structural members that require the maximum amount of protection against decay and insect damage. Since it has a dark color and leaves an oily surface that cannot be painted, creosoted poles are used primarily as the underpinning for a structure.

Commercial water-repellant preservatives containing either pentachlorophenol or copper naphthenate are available. They can be applied with a brush, or for better protection, the wood being treated can be soaked for 24 hours. These treatments are suitable for wood that is exposed to weather above grade, but are not recommended for wood piers or foundations that are in contact with the ground.

Because of the development of preservative pressure-treatments that make wood highly resistant to decay, even when in contact with the ground, an all-wood foundation system has become viable and is now approved by some building codes. A major advantage of an all-wood foundation system is the speed with which it can be pre-fabricated and erected.

An all-wood foundation consists of 2"×6" studs at 16" o.c., end nailed to a single bottom and a single top plate. This frame is sheathed with ½" plywood, with the face grain running across the studs.

The foundation sections are set on a 2"×8" footing plate that rests on a 6" bed of fine gravel or crushed stone.

The plywood panel joints should have an 1/8" space for caulking with a suitable sealant. The outer face of the plywood is covered with a 6-mil polyethylene vapor barrier, with joints lapped 6" and sealed with a construction adhesive. The top of the vapor barrier, extending to the finish grade line, should be securely bonded to the plywood with an adhesive and treated wood strip.

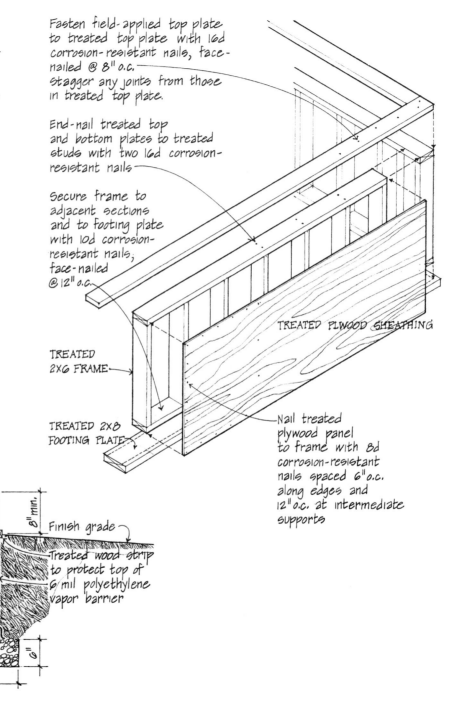

Fasten field-applied top plate to treated top plate with 16d corrosion-resistant nails, face-nailed @ 8" o.c. Stagger any joints from those in treated top plate.

End-nail treated top and bottom plates to treated studs with two 16d corrosion-resistant nails

Secure frame to adjacent sections and to footing plate with 10d corrosion-resistant nails, face-nailed @ 12" o.c.

TREATED PLYWOOD SHEATHING

TREATED 2X6 FRAME

TREATED 2X8 FOOTING PLATE

Nail treated plywood panel to frame with 8d corrosion-resistant nails spaced 6" o.c. along edges and 12" o.c. at intermediate supports

Field-applied top plate
Treated 2x6 top plate
Treated 2x6 studs @ 16" o.c.
Treated ½" plywood sheathing

18" min. to untreated joists

Vapor barrier

8" min.

Finish grade

Treated wood strip to protect top of 6 mil polyethylene vapor barrier

Treated 2x6 bottom plate
Treated 2x8 footing plate
Gravel base below frost line and on undisturbed soil

6"

1'-4"

CRAWL SPACE WITH TREATED WOOD FOUNDATION

## CONCRETE GROUND SLABS

For basementless additions, an alternative form of floor construction is a concrete slab placed directly on the ground. In warm climates, where frost penetration is not a problem, the concrete slab can be combined with the foundation by simply thickening its edge and reinforcing it as required. This footing, placed integrally with the slab, should rest on stable, firm, well-drained soil, and extend at least 12" below the natural gradeline.

In temperate and cold climates, the exterior walls of new construction must be supported by foundations that extend below the frost line to solid bearing soil. The concrete slab in these cases is usually separated from the perimeter foundation, and must itself rest on a stable base of undisturbed soil or compacted fill. This base should be free of sod, organic matter and debris.

To help control the capillary rise of subsoil moisture through the slab bed, a 4" to 6" base course of gravel or crushed stone is placed over the soil base.

If the finished elevation of the concrete slab must be raised to a desired height, or if the site slopes slightly, a well-compacted fill of coarse-grained soil can be added before the gravel base course is laid.

Even if surface drainage or ground water problems are not expected, it is good practice to install a vapor barrier under the slab. If a moisture problem does occur, it is virtually impossible to correct the problem once the slab is placed. The vapor barrier should be 6-mil polyethylene, with joints lapped 6" and sealed. Care should be taken not to puncture the vapor barrier while the concrete is being placed.

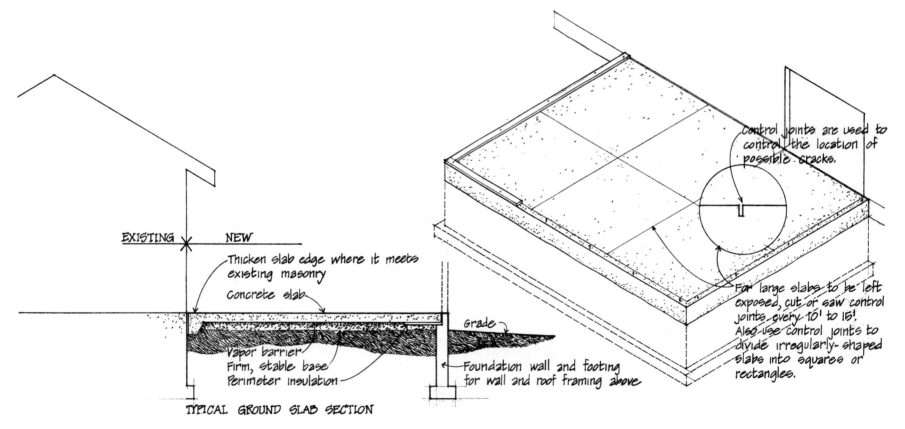

Control joints are used to control the location of possible cracks.

For large slabs to be left exposed, cut or saw control joints every 10' to 15'. Also use control joints to divide irregularly-shaped slabs into squares or rectangles.

EXISTING     NEW

Thicken slab edge where it meets existing masonry

Concrete slab

Grade

Vapor barrier
Firm, stable base
Perimeter insulation

Foundation wall and footing for wall and roof framing above

TYPICAL GROUND SLAB SECTION

A permanent, waterproof type of rigid insulation should be installed around the perimeter of the slab to reduce heat loss directly to the outside air or surrounding ground. The manner of installing the insulation, 2" thick and extending 24" vertically or horizontally, depends on the type of foundation used.

Any underground utility lines are placed while the slab bed and base course are being prepared. The lines should be brought up to a point above the finish floor level of the slab.

The concrete slab is normally 4" to 6" thick with 6x6 10/10 wire mesh reinforcement placed midway within the depth of the slab. This reinforcement controls the size of shrinkage cracking, and helps the slab withstand slight differential movement in the underlying soil.

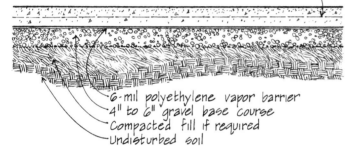

- 6-mil polyethylene vapor barrier
- 4" to 6" gravel base course
- Compacted fill if required
- Undisturbed soil

TYPICAL SLAB BED

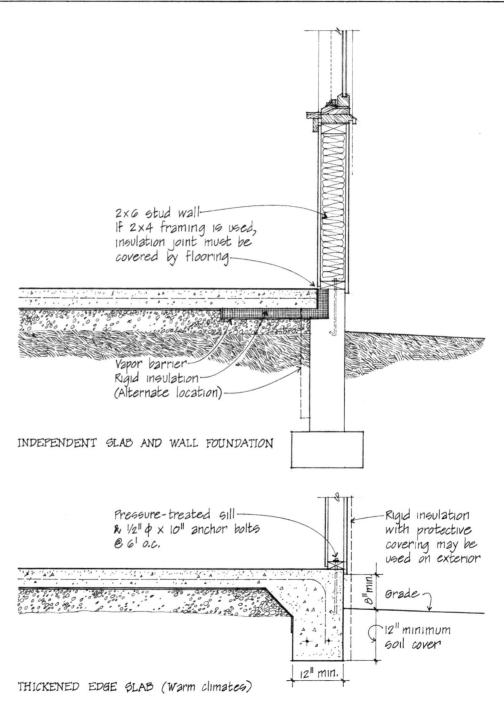

2x6 stud wall —
If 2x4 framing is used, insulation joint must be covered by flooring.

Vapor barrier —
Rigid insulation —
(Alternate location)

INDEPENDENT SLAB AND WALL FOUNDATION

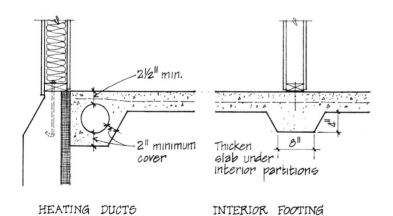

2½" min.

2" minimum cover

HEATING DUCTS

Thicken slab under interior partitions

8"

4"

INTERIOR FOOTING

Pressure-treated sill
& ½" ⌀ x 10" anchor bolts
@ 6' o.c.

Rigid insulation with protective covering may be used on exterior

Grade

8" min.

12" minimum soil cover

12" min.

THICKENED EDGE SLAB (Warm climates)

# WOOD FLOOR FRAMING

For floors above grade, over basements and crawl spaces, the most common construction is a wood joist framed platform. This platform must be smooth, level, and securely anchored. Most importantly, it must be designed and built to be strong enough to support imposed loads and transfer them horizontally to its supports.

The loads a floor must carry include the fixed, dead load of its composite weight and built-in equipment, as well as transient, live loads of occupants and furnishings. For a house, the dead load of a floor is usually assumed to be 10 lbs./s.f. Most building codes have established, for residences, 40 lbs./s.f. as the minimum live load that a floor system must be able to support safely.

Keep in mind that these design loads are guidelines that only set the minimum standards for household uses and furnishings. They also assume that the loads are fairly evenly distributed across a floor's surface. In cases where a heavier-than-normal load is anticipated, such as for an oversized bathtub, pottery kiln, or printing press, the floor framing must be reinforced. This can be done by reducing the span and spacing of the floor joists or increasing their size.

Common floor framing consists of evenly-spaced joists sheathed with a layer of plywood subflooring. This system is flexible and adaptable to various plan shapes because of wood's workability, the lumber sizes used, and the various means of fastening available.

The joists are nominal 2" thick lumber, spaced 12", 16", or 24" o.c. These spacings are related to the strength and size of the 4'x8' plywood sheets commonly used as the subflooring. With these spacings, the plywood sheets will always have a bearing and nailing surface along their end joints.

Of these, 16" is the most common spacing. 24" spacing can be used for light loads or with thicker, stronger plywood sheathing. 12" spacing can be used for heavier loads in certain areas without increasing the typical joist size, or where floor depth must be kept to a minimum.

The depth of the floor joists used depends on the:
1. Floor design load,
2. Spacing of the joists,
3. Joist span, and the
4. Species and strength of the wood used.

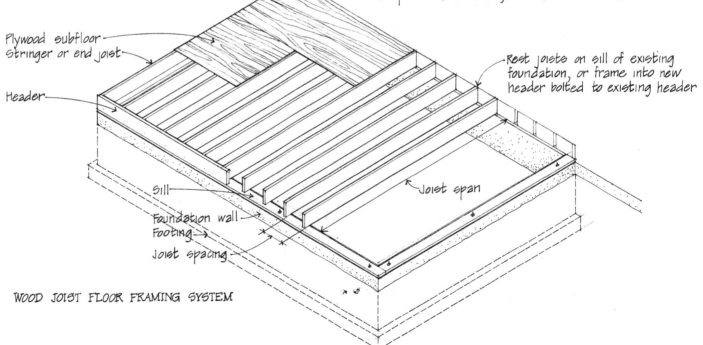

Plywood subfloor

Stringer or end joist

Header

Rest joists on sill of existing foundation, or frame into new header bolted to existing header

Sill

Foundation wall

Footing

Joist spacing

Joist span

WOOD JOIST FLOOR FRAMING SYSTEM

The joists and beams of a wood frame floor can be sized and spaced to span up to 20' without danger of the joists actually breaking. Stiffness, however, is as important a quality for a floor system as its strength. A floor should not bounce perceptibly or feel springy as you walk across its surface. In addition, the deflection of a floor should be limited so as to avoid damage to finish flooring and ceiling materials. For these reasons, deflection (limited to 1/360th of the span) rather than bending stress failure is the controlling factor in the structural design of a floor system.

If the total depth of a floor is not a critical factor, deeper joists spaced farther apart are more desirable for stiffness, and require less labor to frame, than shallower joists spaced closely together.

In planning the framing of your floor system, try to use a combination of the shortest spans with the fewest intermediate supports. Shorter spans require shallower joists, while fewer supports require less labor in framing. Also remember that lumber longer than 14' may be difficult to obtain, and if available, will be more expensive. Since yard lumber usually comes in 8', 10', 12' and 14' lengths, try to utilize these lengths fully to minimize waste.

Some building codes require cross-bridging or solid blocking be installed to prevent rotation or lateral displacement of the floor joists. For joists up to 2" x 8", headers, blocking, or other framing to hold the joist ends in place are sufficient. For 2" x 10" and 2" x 12" joists, bridging or blocking may be required at 8' intervals unless the top edges of the joists are supported adequately by the plywood subflooring, and their ends laterally supported by framing.

Any joists with a slight crook should be laid with the crown or camber on top.

SIMPLIFIED JOIST SPAN TABLE

| E (lbs./sq.in.) | | 1,000,000 | | 1,200,000 | | 1,600,000 | |
|---|---|---|---|---|---|---|---|
| Live Load (lbs./s.f.) | | 40 | 60 | 40 | 60 | 40 | 60 |
| Joist | | ← Allowable Spans → | | | | | |
| Size | Spacing | | | | | | |
| 2" x 6" | 12 (in.) | 9'-2" | 8'-1" | 9'-9" | 8'-7" | 10'-9" | 9'-6" |
| | 16 | 8'-4" | 7'-4" | 8'-10" | 7'-10" | 9'-9" | 8'-7" |
| | 24 | 7'-3" | 6'-6" | 7'-3" | 6'-10" | 8'-6" | 7'-7" |
| 2" x 8" | 12 | 12'-1" | 10'-9" | 12'-10" | 11'-5" | 14'-2" | 12'-7" |
| | 16 | 11'-0" | 9'-9" | 11'-8" | 10'-5" | 12'-10" | 11'-5" |
| | 24 | 9'-7" | 8'-7" | 10'-2" | 9'-2" | 11'-3" | 10'-1" |
| 2" x 10" | 12 | 15'-5" | 13'-6" | 16'-5" | 14'-5" | 18'-0" | 15'-10" |
| | 16 | 14'-0" | 12'-4" | 14'-11" | 13'-2" | 16'-5" | 14'-6" |
| | 24 | 12'-3" | 10'-10" | 13'-0" | 11'-6" | 14'-4" | 12'-8" |
| 2" x 12" | 12 | 18'-9" | 16'-4" | 19'-11" | 17'-4" | 21'-11" | 19'-1" |
| | 16 | 17'-0" | 14'-11" | 18'-1" | 15'-10" | 19'-11" | 17'-5" |
| | 24 | 14'-11" | 13'-1" | 15'-10" | 13'-11" | 17'-5" | 15'-4" |

Notes: 1. Design Load = 40 or 60 lbs./s.f. live load plus 10 lbs./s.f. dead load.
2. Deflection is limited to 1/360th of the span.
3. E = modulus of elasticity in lbs./sq.in.; varies with species and grade of wood.

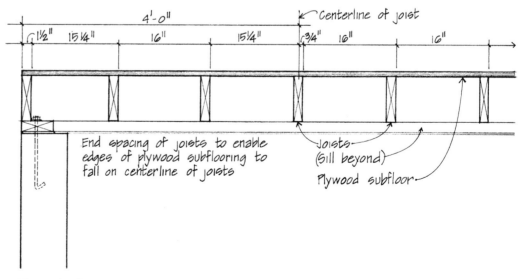

End spacing of joists to enable edges of plywood subflooring to fall on centerline of joists

Centerline of joist

Joists (Sill beyond)

Plywood subfloor

PARTIAL SECTION THROUGH WOOD JOIST FLOOR

## WOOD JOIST SUPPORTS

The platform of a wood joist floor system can be supported by either a foundation or exterior stud wall. Intermediate supports, if required to reduce the joist spans, can be interior stud partitions or beams that are supported in turn by posts or foundation walls.

Along a perimeter foundation wall, joists rest on a sill plate that is secured to the foundation wall with anchor bolts. The sill plate must be installed level and straight. It is usually laid over a strip of sill sealer to protect the joint against air infiltration, dust and insects. In termite-infested areas, a non-corrosive metal shield should also be installed under the sill plate.

If the floor joists of an addition are spanning perpendicular to the side or end of the house, the existing header can be notched so that the new joists can rest on the existing sill. If it is too difficult to cut through the existing header, bolt a new header to it. The new joists can then frame into the new header with joist hangers.

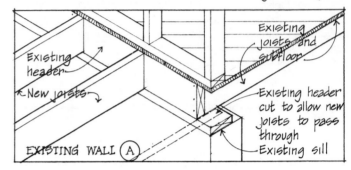

Existing header
New joists
Existing joists and subfloor
Existing header cut to allow new joists to pass through
Existing sill

EXISTING WALL (A)

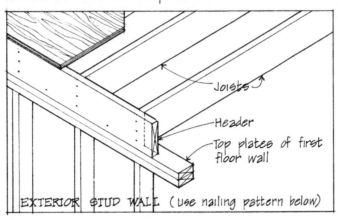

Joists
Header
Top plates of first floor wall

EXTERIOR STUD WALL (use nailing pattern below)

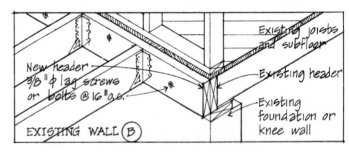

New header — 3/8"⌀ lag screws or bolts @ 16" o.c.
Existing joists and subfloor
Existing header
Existing foundation or knee wall

EXISTING WALL (B)

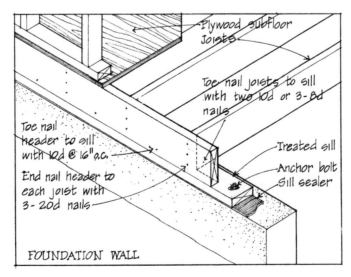

Plywood subfloor
Joists
Toe nail joists to sill with two 10d or 3-8d nails
Toe nail header to sill with 10d @ 16" o.c.
End nail header to each joist with 3-20d nails
Treated sill
Anchor bolt
Sill sealer

FOUNDATION WALL

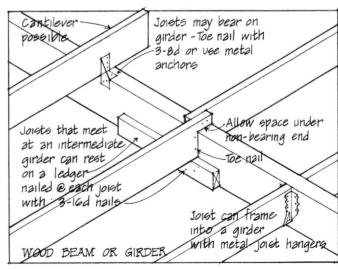

Cantilever possible
Joists may bear on girder - Toe nail with 3-8d or use metal anchors
Joists that meet at an intermediate girder can rest on a ledger nailed @ each joist with 3-16d nails
Allow space under non-bearing end
Toe nail
Joist can frame into a girder with metal joist hangers

WOOD BEAM OR GIRDER

## PARTITION CONNECTIONS

When supporting a partition, the floor framing should be reinforced to carry the additional load of the wall. If the partition runs parallel to the joists, a double joist is placed directly beneath it. To permit plumbing lines or a heating duct to pass through the floor and up the wall, the double joists can be spaced apart with solid blocking.

If a nonbearing partition is parallel to the joists, but positioned between the regular joist spacing, blocking can be inserted at 16" o.c. to transfer the partition load to the joists on either side of the wall.

For partitions perpendicular to the supporting joists, there is normally no need for additional framing. If the partition load warrants, or if a bearing partition lies directly over one below, structural continuity is provided by solid bridging inserted between the joists.

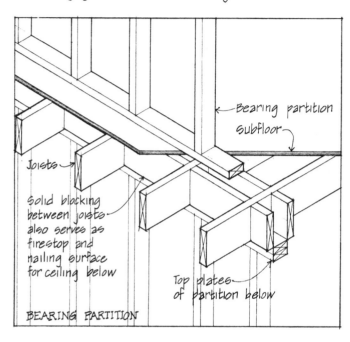

Bearing partition

Subfloor

Joists

Solid blocking between joists also serves as firestop and nailing surface for ceiling below

Top plates of partition below

BEARING PARTITION

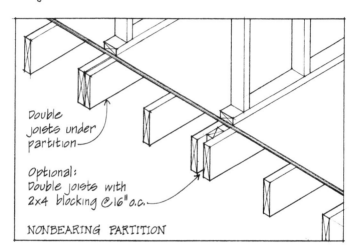

Double joists under partition

Optional: Double joists with 2x4 blocking @16" o.c.

NONBEARING PARTITION

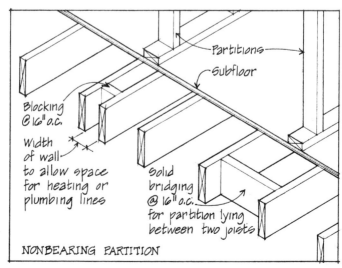

Partitions

Subfloor

Blocking @16" o.c.

Width of wall to allow space for heating or plumbing lines

Solid bridging @ 16" o.c. for partition lying between two joists

NONBEARING PARTITION

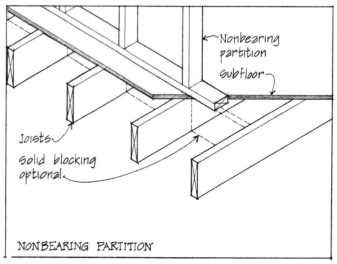

Nonbearing partition

Subfloor

Joists

Solid blocking optional

NONBEARING PARTITION

# FRAMING OPENINGS

Special conditions may occur in the design of your addition that will interrupt the normal, regular spacing of the floor joists. The addition may require a stairway to a second floor, or include a balcony or window seat that projects from the main body of the structure.

For a floor opening, the remaining portion of the cut or tail joists frame into cross-joists or headers. The headers, in turn, are framed into trimmer joists that run along the sides of the opening. For small openings, single headers and trimmer joists are usually adequate.

Larger openings for a stairway or sunken tub are framed by a box of double headers and trimmers. The tail joists frame into the double headers with metal joist hangers. The double headers frame into the double trimmers with metal beam hangers.

A large rectangular opening can have its length run either perpendicular or parallel to the floor joists. Of these, the latter option is preferred since its headers and trimmers are required to carry a lesser load.

If the length of an opening is perpendicular to the floor joists, a double header, designed as a beam, is limited to a 10' span. Additional support for the tail joists can be provided by a bearing partition or post and beam structure below.

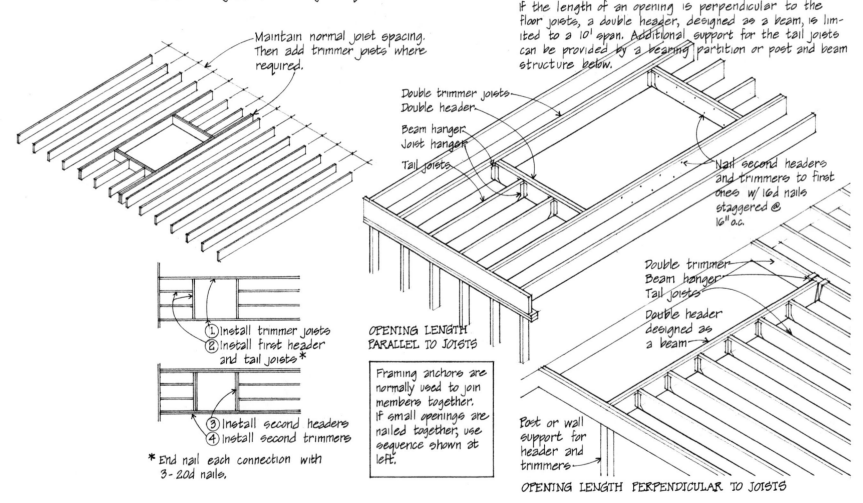

Maintain normal joist spacing. Then add trimmer joists where required.

Double trimmer joists
Double header
Beam hanger
Joist hanger
Tail joists

Nail second headers and trimmers to first ones w/ 16d nails staggered @ 16" o.c.

① Install trimmer joists
② Install first header and tail joists *

③ Install second headers
④ Install second trimmers

* End nail each connection with 3- 20d nails.

Framing anchors are normally used to join members together. If small openings are nailed together, use sequence shown at left.

OPENING LENGTH PARALLEL TO JOISTS

Double trimmer
Beam hanger
Tail joists

Double header designed as a beam

Post or wall support for header and trimmers

OPENING LENGTH PERPENDICULAR TO JOISTS

## FRAMING PROJECTIONS

A portion of the floor framing can be cantilevered beyond the perimeter support fairly easily if the length of the overhang or projection is not excessive. A helpful rule-of-thumb is to limit the cantilever to 1/4 of the fully-supported span, and to ensure that the cantilevered members are continuous across the outer support. Their non-cantilevered ends should be firmly anchored to prevent them from lifting when a load is placed on the cantilever.

For cantilevers parallel to the span of the floor joists, the joists are simply extended over the outer support. The end or stringer joists are normally doubled, and a header used to provide rigidity to the ends of the cantilevered joists. Solid blocking between the joists, directly over the support, helps keep the joists vertical, aids their rigidity, and closes off the floor construction.

For cantilevers perpendicular to the span of the floor joists, the cantilevered or stringer joists must be extended into and interrupt the normal framing pattern. For this reason, these cantilevers should be limited to 24", unless engineered for a greater projection. The stringers are supported at their uncantilevered ends by a double joist, and anchored with joist hangers. The interrupted or tail joists are framed into double stringer joists.

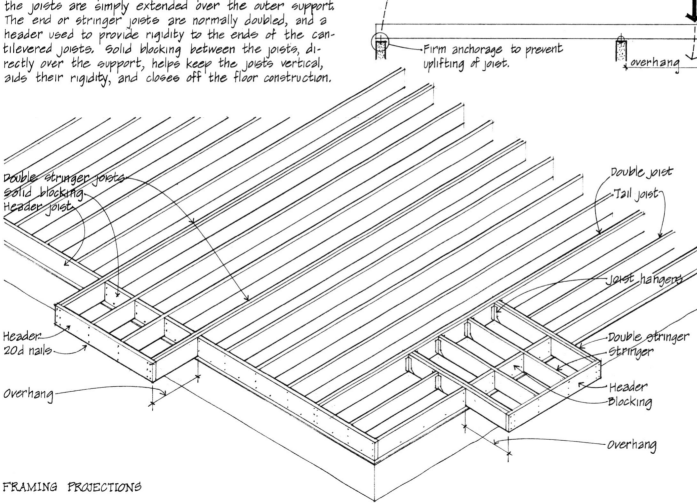

Firm anchorage to prevent uplifting of joist.

overhang

Double stringer joists
Solid blocking
Header joist

Double joist
Tail joist

Joist hangers

Header
20d nails

Double stringer
Stringer

Header
Blocking

Overhang

Overhang

FRAMING PROJECTIONS

## SUBFLOORING

The wood joist floor system has two layers built up over its frame - a subfloor or rough floor, and a finish floor of wood, tile, or carpeting. The subfloor is installed as soon as possible after the joists and any required bridging are in place to tie the entire assembly together. This platform then serves as a working base for wall construction.

In the past, 3/4" thick tongue-and-groove boards, 6" to 8" wide, were laid in a diagonal fashion to serve as the subfloor. More common practice today is to use plywood sheathing. Because of its cross-ply construction, plywood is extremely strong across its plane and imparts great rigidity to the platform floor. The modular 4'x8' size of plywood sheets also saves installation time and labor.

The plywood sheathing, joists, and headers are nailed together to form a single, cohesive structural unit. The plywood can also be glued and nailed to the floor joists for greater stiffness and strength.

Plywood is available in a variety of grades and thicknesses. For most subflooring, standard sheathing grades are satisfactory. Where a condition of prolonged exposure to moisture exists, such as in bathrooms, or when the subfloor will be exposed to the weather for a long period of time during construction, plywood bonded with exterior glue or an exterior-grade plywood should be used.

The panel identification index marking on a plywood sheet will indicate the allowable joist spacing over which the plywood will span. See next page.

A separate layer of underlayment grade plywood is used to provide a smooth base for resilient flooring and other non-structural flooring materials. Underlayment is not laid until after the interior wall and ceiling surfaces are complete, and just before the flooring is installed.

Plywood can also serve as a combined subfloor and underlayment, functioning both as a structural subfloor and a smooth substrate for the finish floor. When used in this manner, the plywood should have tongue-and-groove edges, or be blocked along all unsupported edges, and be protected during construction.

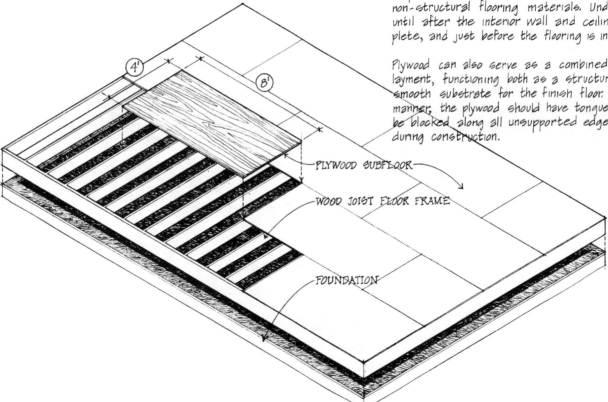

4'

8'

PLYWOOD SUBFLOOR

WOOD JOIST FLOOR FRAME

FOUNDATION

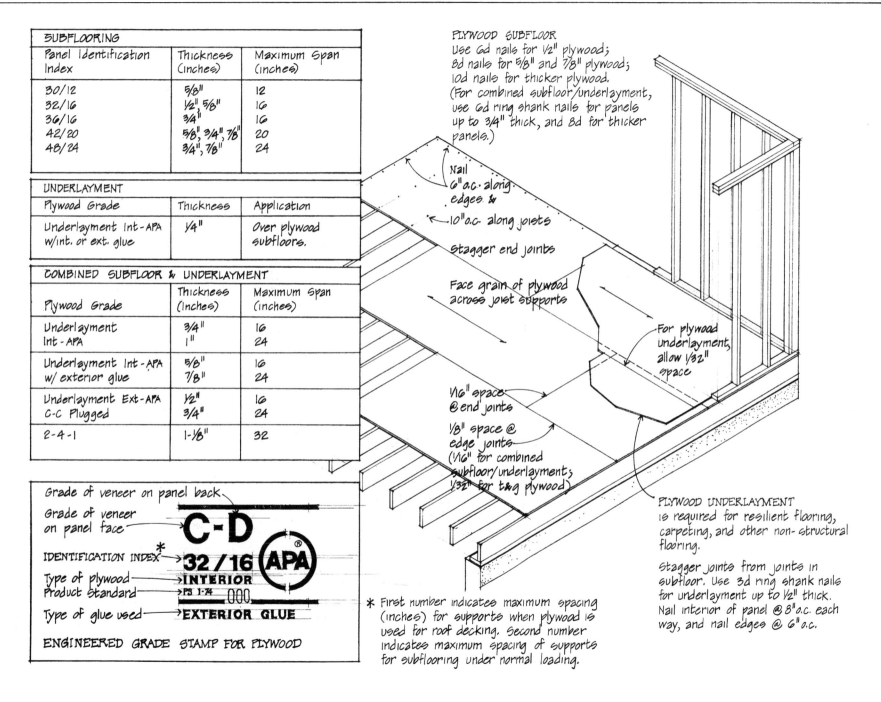

**SUBFLOORING**

| Panel Identification Index | Thickness (inches) | Maximum Span (inches) |
|---|---|---|
| 30/12 | 5/8" | 12 |
| 32/16 | 1/2", 5/8" | 16 |
| 36/16 | 3/4" | 16 |
| 42/20 | 5/8", 3/4", 7/8" | 20 |
| 48/24 | 3/4", 7/8" | 24 |

**UNDERLAYMENT**

| Plywood Grade | Thickness | Application |
|---|---|---|
| Underlayment Int-APA w/int. or ext. glue | 1/4" | Over plywood subfloors. |

**COMBINED SUBFLOOR & UNDERLAYMENT**

| Plywood Grade | Thickness (Inches) | Maximum Span (Inches) |
|---|---|---|
| Underlayment Int - APA | 3/4"  /  1" | 16  /  24 |
| Underlayment Int - APA w/ exterior glue | 5/8"  /  7/8" | 16  /  24 |
| Underlayment Ext-APA C-C Plugged | 1/2"  /  3/4" | 16  /  24 |
| 2-4-1 | 1-1/8" | 32 |

Grade of veneer on panel back

Grade of veneer on panel face

**C-D (APA)®**

IDENTIFICATION INDEX *
**32/16**

Type of plywood
Product Standard → **INTERIOR**
→ PS 1-74  000

Type of glue used → **EXTERIOR GLUE**

**ENGINEERED GRADE STAMP FOR PLYWOOD**

\* First number indicates maximum spacing (inches) for supports when plywood is used for roof decking. Second number indicates maximum spacing of supports for subflooring under normal loading.

PLYWOOD SUBFLOOR
Use 6d nails for 1/2" plywood;
8d nails for 5/8" and 7/8" plywood;
10d nails for thicker plywood.
(For combined subfloor/underlayment, use 6d ring shank nails for panels up to 3/4" thick, and 8d for thicker panels.)

Nail 6" o.c. along edges &

10" o.c. along joists

stagger end joints

Face grain of plywood across joist supports

For plywood underlayment, allow 1/32" space

1/16" space @ end joints

1/8" space @ edge joints
(1/16" for combined subfloor/underlayment; 1/32" for t&g plywood)

PLYWOOD UNDERLAYMENT
is required for resilient flooring, carpeting, and other non-structural flooring.

Stagger joints from joints in subfloor. Use 3d ring shank nails for underlayment up to 1/2" thick. Nail interior of panel @ 8" o.c. each way, and nail edges @ 6" o.c.

## WOOD BEAMS

The wood joists of a floor system are relatively slender, horizontal structural members that support the subfloor. Beams are heavier, spaced further apart, and carry greater loads than joists. They can support either the joists of a floor system or, without the joists, thick solid wood planking. In addition, they may be required to support additional wall, floor, or roof loads from above.

Since beams carry large loads, they (and the posts that support them) are critical to the structural integrity of your house or addition. It is important that a beam be sized adequately to carry its total load, and be securely fastened to its supports. The supporting posts, which carry a concentrated load, must bear directly on the foundation, or another support that leads to the foundation. To help you with these determinations, it is recommended that you consult a structural engineer.

Joist Span
Joist Span
Joist Span
Beam Span

TOTAL LOAD ON BEAM =
Beam Span x Load Width x
Total Floor Load in Lbs./S.F.

JS = Joist Span

Beam
Load Area

JS/2 · JS/2
Load Width

BEAM SUPPORTING
A FLOOR LOAD

ROOF LOAD:
Live Load = 10-30 psf.
Dead Load = 10-15 psf.

PARTITIONS:
Dead Load = 20 psf.

FLOORS:
Live Load: 40 psf.
Dead Load: 10 psf.

BEAM
POSTS

Girder/
Foundation
support

BEAM SUPPORTING
A WALL & TWO FLOOR LOADS

BEAM
POSTS

Foundation wall

BEAM SUPPORTING WALL, FLOOR & ROOF LOADS

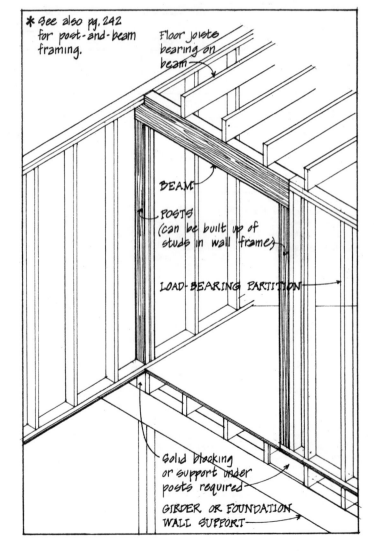

\* See also pg. 242
for post-and-beam
framing.

Floor joists
bearing on
beam

BEAM

POSTS
(can be built up of
studs in wall frame)

LOAD-BEARING PARTITION

Solid blocking
or support under
posts required

GIRDER OR FOUNDATION
WALL SUPPORT

Wood beams and girders can be either solid or built-up. Solid wood beams are simple and have a greater net area than built-up beams for a given cross-section. They also are more susceptible to shrinking and checking.

Built-up wood beams are more dimensionally stable than solid wood beams, and can be joined together to form longer lengths. They consist of two or more 2" lumber spiked together. Joints generally are made directly over a supporting post or at quarter points of the span. For appearance if exposed, the built-up beam can be clad with finish lumber or gypsum board.

Where a natural wood finish is desired for a beam exposed within a room, a glue-laminated beam can be used. Glue-laminated beams are factory-produced of 2" lumber that is glued together with casein or, for exterior applications, a waterproof glue. The beam is then dressed for a clean, smooth surface.

Another type of beam that is commercially available consists of a plywood web with top and bottom flanges of solid lumber. These beams are pre-engineered for certain spans and load conditions. Small sizes can be used as long-span joists, while larger sizes can be used as headers over large openings.

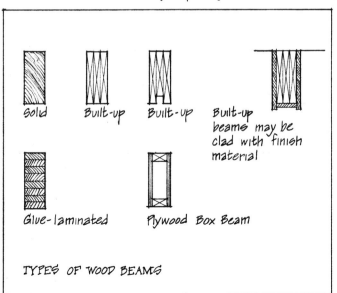

Solid  Built-up  Built-up  Built-up beams may be clad with finish material

Glue-laminated  Plywood Box Beam

TYPES OF WOOD BEAMS

## SIMPLIFIED BEAM SPAN TABLES

These beam span tables are to be used for estimating and preliminary sizing only.

| SOLID AND BUILT-UP BEAMS | | | GLUE-LAMINATED BEAMS | | |
|---|---|---|---|---|---|
| Span (feet) | Spacing (feet) | Size (nominal) | Span (feet) | Spacing (feet) | Size (inches) |
| 10 | 4 | 2 - 2 x 8 | 12 | 6 | 3 1/8 x 9 |
|  | 6 | 2 - 2 x 10 |  | 8 | 3 1/8 x 10 1/2 |
|  | 8 | 4 x 10 |  | 10 | 3 1/8 x 10 1/2 |
|  |  |  |  | 12 | 3 1/8 x 12 |
| 12 | 4 | 3 x 10 | 16 | 8 | 3 1/8 x 13 1/2 |
|  | 6 | 2 - 2 x 12 |  | 12 | 3 1/8 x 15 |
|  | 8 | 4 x 12 |  | 14 | 3 1/8 x 15 |
|  |  |  |  | 16 | 3 1/8 x 15 |
| 14 | 4 | 4 x 10 | 20 | 8 | 3 1/8 x 16 1/2 |
|  | 6 | 6 x 10 |  | 12 | 5 1/8 x 15 |
|  | 8 | 3 - 2 x 12 |  | 16 | 5 1/8 x 18 |
| 16 | 6 | 3 - 2 x 12 |  | 20 | 5 1/8 x 18 |
|  | 8 | 4 - 2 x 12 |  |  |  |
| 18 | 6 | 6 x 12 |  |  |  |
|  | 8 | 8 x 12 |  |  |  |
| 20 | 6 | 2 - 3 x 14 |  |  |  |
|  | 8 | 2 - 4 x 14 |  |  |  |

Notes:  1. Total live load = 40 lbs./s.f.
   2. E (modulus of elasticity)= 1,400,000 ; varies with species and grade of wood.
   3. Deflection limited to 1/360 of the span.

| SAFE DISTRIBUTED LOAD IN POUNDS FOR GIVEN SPAN | | | | |
|---|---|---|---|---|
| BEAM SIZE | 7 ft. | 8 ft. | 9 ft. | 10 ft. |
| 6 x 8 solid | 5500 | 5150 | 4580 | 4125 |
| 6 x 8 built-up | 4500 | 4200 | 3750 | 3375 |
| 6 x 10 solid |  |  | 6950 | 6600 |
| 6 x 10 built-up |  |  | 5700 | 5400 |
| 6 x 12 solid |  |  |  | 8400 |
| 6 x 12 built-up |  |  |  | 6900 |

Notes:  1. Fb (Extreme fiber stress) for wood = 1200 psi.
   2. E (Modulus of elasticity) = 1,600,000 psi.
   3. See pg. 221 for sizes of headers over window and door openings.

## WOOD STUD WALLS

The vertical components of your house or addition, its walls and columns, must be able to transfer their loads vertically to the foundation system. The exact determination of a wall's structural members, however, is not as critical as in the design of a floor or roof framing system. While floor and roof members span horizontally and are subject to bending stresses and deflection under loading, walls are subject primarily to compression under vertical loading. Masonry is extremely strong is compression. Wood, while not as strong as masonry, also handles well the compressive stresses encountered in residential construction. For these reasons, the design of a wall system is rarely calculated mathematically. More often than not, walls are built according to convention and tradition based on the sizes of the materials and the method of construction used.

In addition to vertical loads, walls may be subject to lateral loading - wind forces on exterior walls, or the lateral thrust of sloping roof rafters. In order to resist these forces, walls must be braced by other walls or horizontal members in a direction perpendicular to their plane.

Perhaps the easiest wall system for the homeowner to build is the wood stud frame wall. The sizes of the required pieces are fairly small, and can be easily handled and fastened together. The framing system itself is adaptable to any number of wall configurations, and can accept a wide range of finishes. The spaces created by the depth of the studs can accommodate insulation material, electrical and plumbing lines, as well as some mechanical ductwork.

The standard frame consists of 2"x4" studs spaced vertically at 16"o.c., and tied at the top and bottom with horizontal plates of the same cross-sectional dimension. This frame is sheathed with sheet material that gives the frame its rigidity.

2"x4" studs spaced 16"o.c. are more than adequate to handle typical residential floor and roof loads. The 16" spacing is common practice that is based on the 4' width of sheathing materials such as plywood and gypsum board. If this sheathing material is thick enough, the stud spacing can sometimes be increased to 24"o.c.

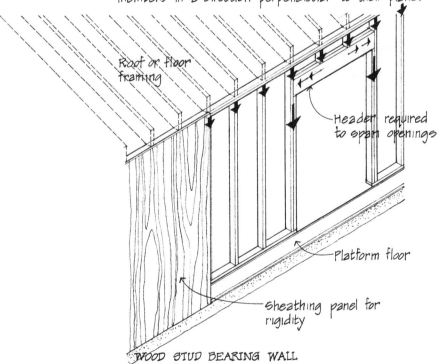

Roof or floor framing

Header required to span openings

Platform floor

Sheathing panel for rigidity

WOOD STUD BEARING WALL

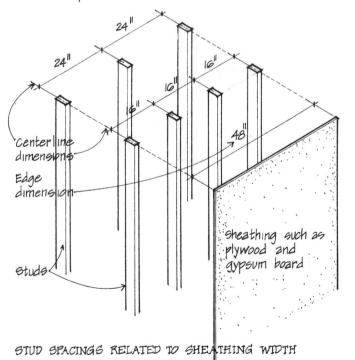

24"    24"    16"    16"    16"    16"    48"

Centerline dimensions

Edge dimension

Studs

sheathing such as plywood and gypsum board

STUD SPACINGS RELATED TO SHEATHING WIDTH

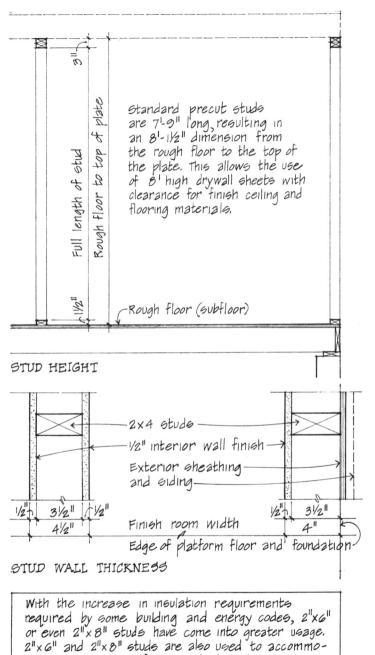

Standard precut studs are 7'-9" long, resulting in an 8'-1½" dimension from the rough floor to the top of the plate. This allows the use of 8' high drywall sheets with clearance for finish ceiling and flooring materials.

Rough floor (subfloor)

Full length of stud

Rough floor to top of plate

3"

1½"

## STUD HEIGHT

2x4 studs

½" interior wall finish

Exterior sheathing and siding

Finish room width

Edge of platform floor and foundation

½"  3½"  ½"
4½"

½"  3½"
4"

## STUD WALL THICKNESS

With the increase in insulation requirements required by some building and energy codes, 2"x 6" or even 2"x 8" studs have come into greater usage. 2"x 6" and 2"x 8" studs are also used to accommodate the passage of large plumbing lines.

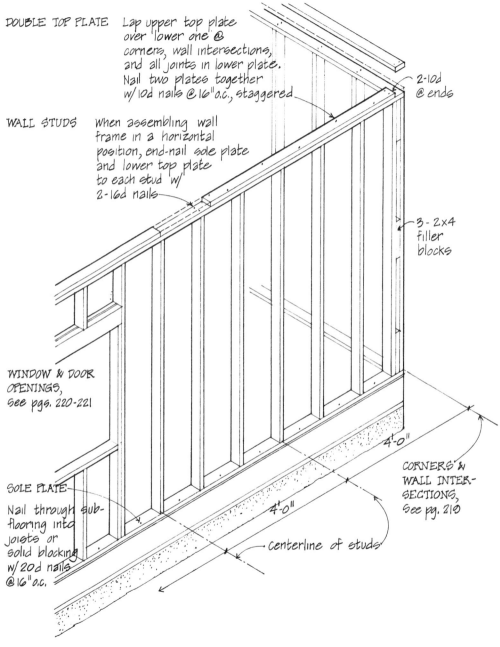

DOUBLE TOP PLATE   Lap upper top plate over lower one @ corners, wall intersections, and all joints in lower plate. Nail two plates together w/ 10d nails @ 16" o.c., staggered

WALL STUDS   When assembling wall frame in a horizontal position, end-nail sole plate and lower top plate to each stud w/ 2-16d nails

2-10d @ ends

3 - 2x4 filler blocks

WINDOW & DOOR OPENINGS, see pgs. 220-221

SOLE PLATE   Nail through sub-flooring into joists or solid blocking w/ 20d nails @ 16" o.c.

4'-0"

4'-0"

CORNERS & WALL INTER-SECTIONS, see pg. 210

centerline of studs

## WOOD STUD WALL FRAMING

## PLATFORM FRAMING

The most common type of framing in residential construction is platform framing where each story is assembled as a separate entity. The completed floor frame, together with the subflooring, forms a working platform on top of which the wall framing can be cut, assembled and nailed together. The wall frame sections can be built flat on the platform and then tilted up into place. Plywood sheathing for exterior walls can be applied either before or after the wall frames are in place.

Once all of the first floor wall framing is in place, the roof construction or, if there is a second story, the second floor framing can be built atop the wall framing.

Exterior walls are built first. When they have been erected, plumbed and braced, their sole plates are nailed, through the subflooring, to the floor joists, headers and stringers.

Interior walls that run perpendicular to overhead floor or ceiling joists and help support this framing are built similarly to exterior walls. Nonload bearing walls that run parallel to the direction of the joists are also, by convention, built with 2" x 4" studs. If space is at a premium, however, they can be built with 2" x 3" studs.

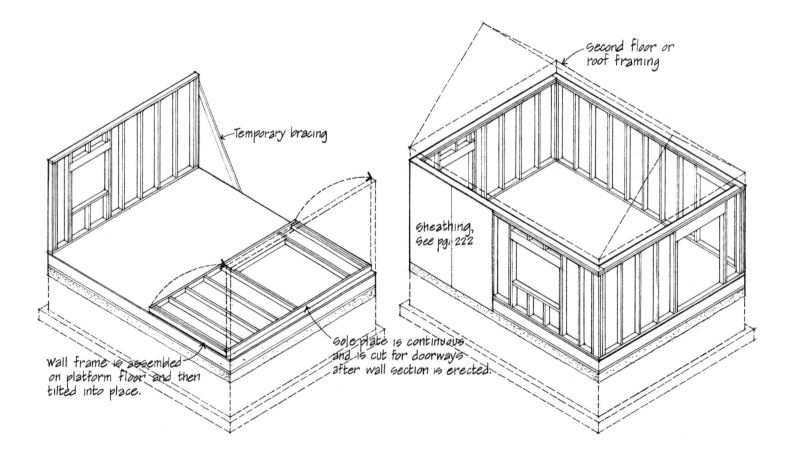

Temporary bracing

second floor or roof framing

sheathing, see pg. 222

Wall frame is assembled on platform floor and then tilted into place.

Sole plate is continuous and is cut for doorways after wall section is erected.

Corners and intersections of wood stud walls must be framed securely and in such a way that sufficient nailing surfaces are provided for the application of sheathing or the finish wall material.

The second top plate can be assembled with the rest of the wall frames in the horizontal position, or be nailed in place after the wall frames are tilted into place. In either case, the second top plate should overlap the first top plate at all corners and intersections, as well as all joints that may occur in the first top plate.

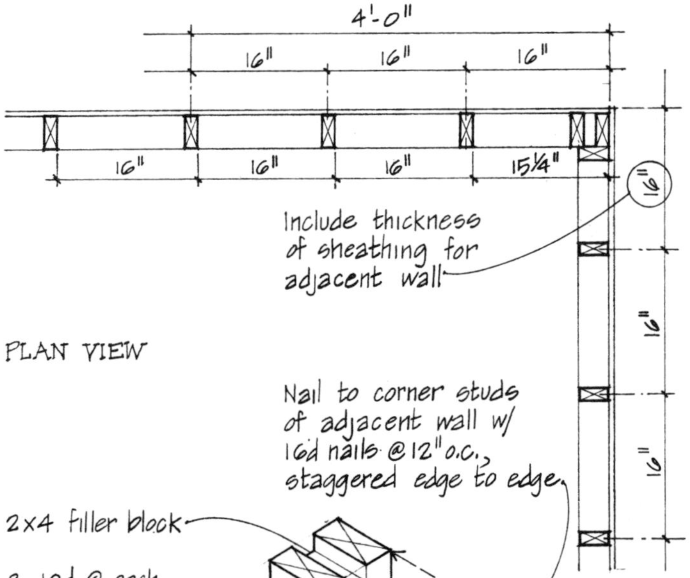

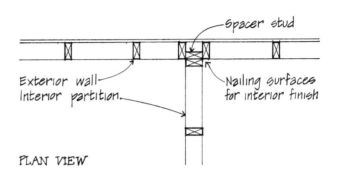

4'-0"

16"  16"  16"

16"  16"  16"  15¼"

Include thickness of sheathing for adjacent wall

PLAN VIEW

16"

16"

PLAN VIEW

Spacer stud

Exterior wall
Interior partition

Nailing surfaces for interior finish

Nail to corner studs of adjacent wall w/ 16d nails @ 12" o.c., staggered edge to edge.

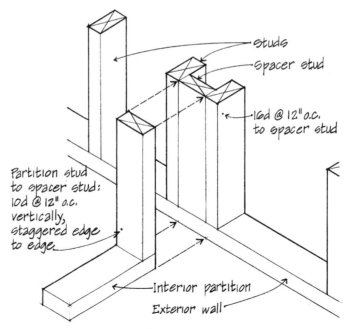

2×4 filler block

3-10d @ each filler block from both corner studs

Stud

Sole plate

1-10d to each filler block

If toe nailing studs to sole plate, use 4-8d nails

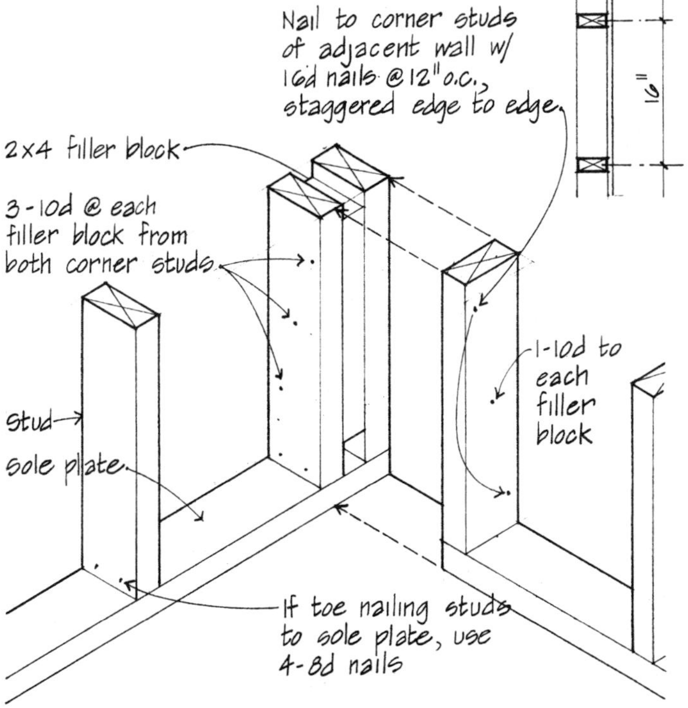

**OUTSIDE CORNER ASSEMBLY**

studs

Spacer stud

16d @ 12" o.c. to spacer stud

Partition stud to spacer stud: 10d @ 12" o.c. vertically, staggered edge to edge.

Interior partition

Exterior wall

**WALL INTERSECTIONS**

## WINDOW & DOOR OPENINGS

Window and doorway openings are framed within the standard stud spacing of the wall. The framing consists of a horizontal member (header) that spans the opening and rests on vertical studs (trimmers) that frame the sides of the opening. Short studs (cripples) continue the normal stud spacing above and below the opening.

The sizes and locations of window and door openings are normally determined in the design stage according to functional and aesthetic requirements. When laying them out within the wall frame, it is not necessary to disrupt the standard stud spacing. If the required width of an opening does not conform to the stud spacing, additional studs can be installed.

The rough openings should be large enough for the window and door units to slip easily into place, with sufficient space around the units to allow for their adjustment and leveling. Verify the required rough openings with the window or door manufacturer.

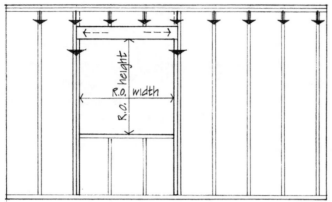

R.O. = rough opening

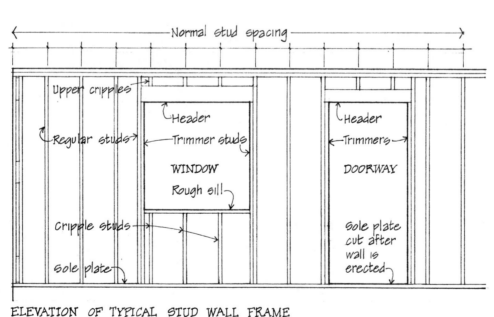

ELEVATION OF TYPICAL STUD WALL FRAME

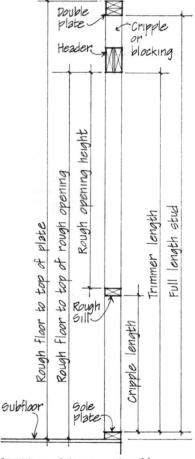

HEIGHT RELATIONSHIPS

The assembled frame must be strong enough to transfer superimposed wall loads around the opening without sagging or distorting. It must also be able to support the window or door unit, and provide sufficient nailing surfaces for the application of wall finish and trim materials.

The header is a small-scale beam that spans the width of an opening and transfers loads from the floor or roof above to the side frame. As the width of the opening increases, the depth of the header must also increase to support a greater superimposed load. The following can be used as a guide in sizing headers.

| | SIZE OF HEADER | |
|---|---|---|
| | Supporting a typical roof above | Supporting a typical floor and roof above |
| Up to 3' | 2 - 2" x 4" | 2 - 2" x 6" |
| 4' | 2 - 2" x 4" | 2 - 2" x 8" |
| 6' | 2 - 2" x 6" | 2 - 2" x 10" |
| 8' | 2 - 2" x 8" | 2 - 2" x 12" |
| 9'-6" | 2 - 2" x 10" | 1 - 4" x 12" |

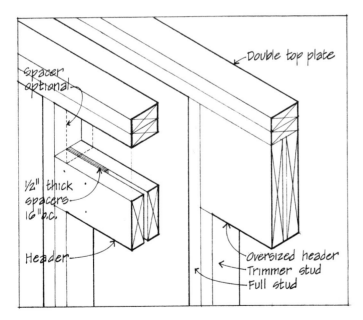

HEADERS

The header in a stud wall is typically made up of two 2"x members with 1/2" plywood blocking to bring its composite width to the 3½" depth of the wall studs. For 2"x6" stud walls, three 2"x members with two layers of 1/2" plywood can be used to make up the 5½" depth of the studs.

If the distance between the top plates and the header is too short to justify the use of cripple studs, the space can be completely blocked or a larger than necessary header installed.

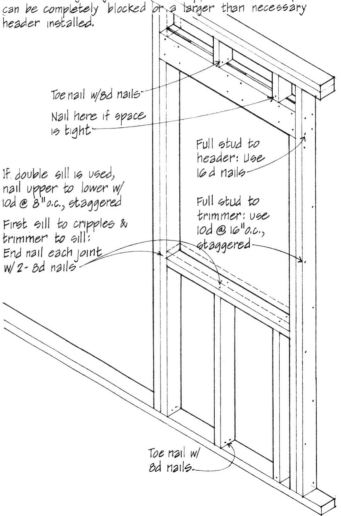

## WALL SHEATHING

Boards laid in a diagonal fashion were traditionally used to sheath the outside of exterior frame walls. Plywood sheets are now more commonly used because their strength imparts great rigidity to the wall frame, and their large size requires less time and labor to apply.

3-ply, 3/8" standard sheathing grade plywood is most often used, although 5/16" and 1/2" thicknesses may also be used. Plywood manufactured with an exterior glue (CDX) is preferred, and should always be used for severe exposures, or if the sheathing is to be exposed for a period of time during construction.

The plywood sheets may be applied vertically or horizontally. If the sheets are installed horizontally, their vertical joints should be staggered. Use blocking between studs, tongue-and-groove panels, or plyclips to support all horizontal edges. Leave a 1/16" space at the ends, and a 1/8" space at the edges of all sheets. Nail the sheathing at 6" o.c. along edges, and at 12" o.c. along intermediate supports, using 6d common or threaded nails for 3/8" plywood. For thicker plywood, use 8d nails.

When plywood sheathing is installed vertically at corners, corner bracing can be omitted. Increase the nailing to 4" o.c. along edges, and 8" o.c. along intermediate supports.

1/16" space @ end joints

Stagger vertical joints when face grain is laid across supports

1/8" space @ edge joints

Support horizontal edges with blocking or plyclips

For corner bracing, nail 4" o.c. along edges, and 8" o.c. along intermediate supports

12" o.c. and 6" o.c. along edges

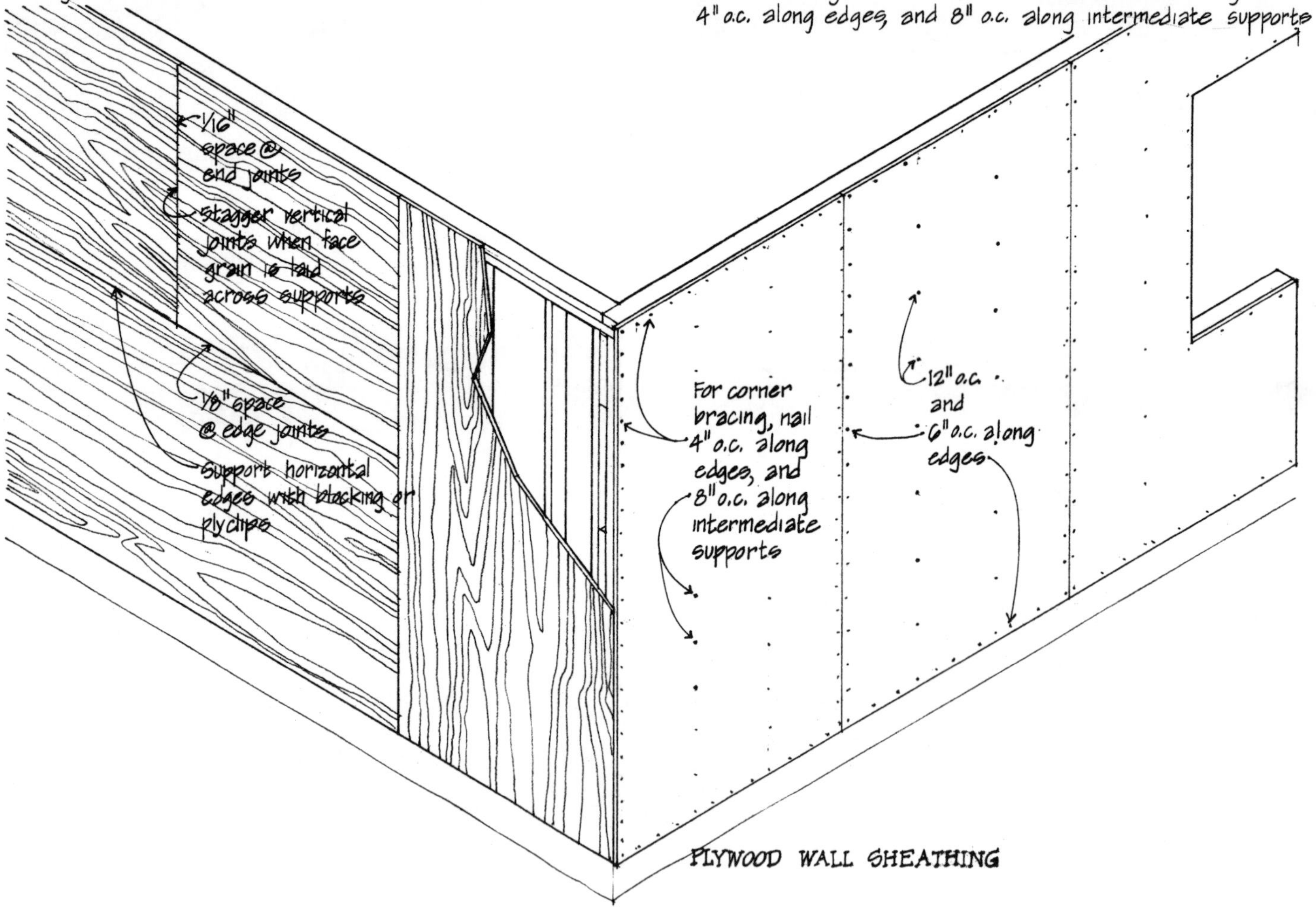

PLYWOOD WALL SHEATHING

Fiberboard, treated or impregnated with asphalt, can also be used as exterior wall sheathing. Because of its R-value (2.5 for ½" thickness), fiberboard is also called insulation board. It is available in regular, medium and high densities, and in ½" and 25/32" thicknesses. High-density fiberboard can be used as a nailing base for exterior wall finish materials.

Some building codes may allow wall corner bracing to be omitted if high-density fiberboard sheets, 4'x8' or longer, are applied vertically and nailed with № 11 gauge galvanized roofing nails at 3" o.c. along edges and at 6" o.c. along intermediate supports.

Because of their thermal insulation value, polystyrene and polyurethane panels are also used as exterior wall sheathing. These foamed plastic panels are available in 2'x4' and 2'x8' sheets with tongue-and-groove edges, in 3/4" and 1" thicknesses. Since the panels are not structural, corner bracing is required, or the panels can be applied over plywood sheathing. The exterior wall finish material must be nailed into the wall studs or horizontal furring.

These plastic insulating materials are combustible. The interior surfaces of exterior walls sheathed with these panels should have a gypsum wallboard finish.

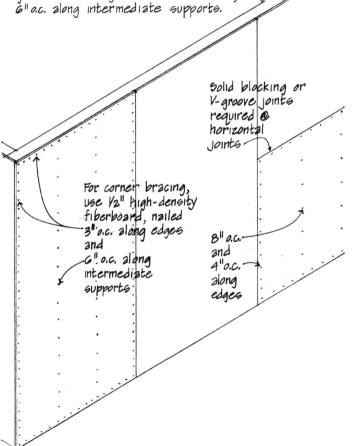

Solid blocking or V-groove joints required @ horizontal joints

For corner bracing, use ½" high-density fiberboard, nailed 3" o.c. along edges and 6" o.c. along intermediate supports

8" o.c. and 4" o.c. along edges

FIBERBOARD WALL SHEATHING

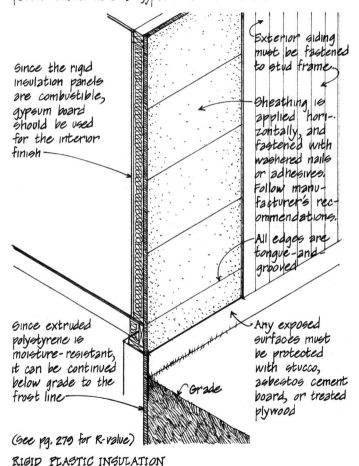

Since the rigid insulation panels are combustible, gypsum board should be used for the interior finish

Since extruded polystyrene is moisture-resistant, it can be continued below grade to the frost line

Exterior siding must be fastened to stud frame

Sheathing is applied horizontally, and fastened with washered nails or adhesives. Follow manufacturer's recommendations.

All edges are tongue-and-grooved

Any exposed surfaces must be protected with stucco, asbestos cement board, or treated plywood

Grade

(See pg. 279 for R-value)

RIGID PLASTIC INSULATION

# ROOF CONSTRUCTION

The roof construction, along with the exterior walls, shelters the interior spaces of your house or addition. The roofing must control the flow of water from rain and melting snow, and prevent its penetration into the interior. The roof assembly must be insulated to control the flow of heat and water vapor. Any enclosed space between the ceiling and the roof must be ventilated to control the formation of condensation.

While similar to floor systems in their structural framing, roof systems are inherently more complex because of the latitude you have in designing their forms, and the options you have in framing them.

Of the many roof forms in the vocabulary of architectural design, the most commonly used in residential construction are the gable, hip, gambrel and flat roofs. In addition to these major roof forms, smaller scale forms, such as dormers and shed roofs, can allow daylight to enter, and increase the headroom within, attic spaces. Of course, all of these forms may be combined into larger, more complex compositions. The discussion of roof forms, however, will be restricted to the basic types listed above.

All of the basic roof forms share a similar framing pattern. As with wood joist floors, the framing of the roof planes consists of evenly-spaced structural members called rafters (as differentiated from the joists of floors and flat ceilings). These rafters transfer their loads to larger supporting members - hip rafters, beams and exterior walls. The roof forms differ in the configuration of the roof planes, and the manner in which they meet at ridges, hips and valleys. See pgs 232, 234.

The load on a roof is somewhat lighter than floor loads. In addition to its own weight (10 to 15 lbs./s.f., depending on the roofing material), a roof structure must support the force of driving rain, the weight of accumulated snow, and the wind forces that can bear down on or tend to lift the roof.

Building codes normally specify the design live loads for a roof as average figures based on the roof slope. Since all roof live loads are assumed to act vertically upon an area projected on a horizontal plane, the span of a rafter is measured along its horizontal run, not along its length.

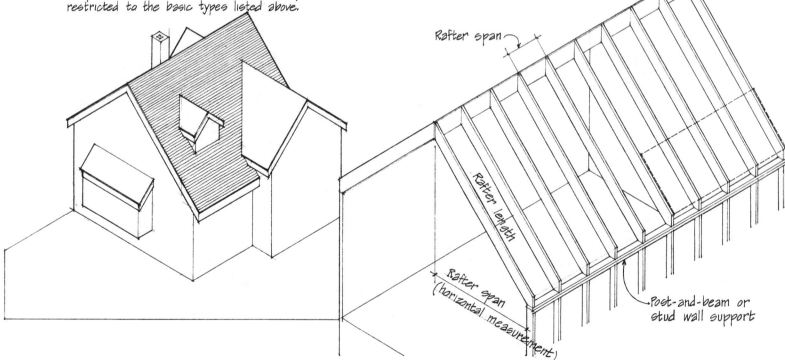

Rafter span

Rafter length

Rafter span
(horizontal measurement)

Post-and-beam or stud wall support

Where snow loads occur, their magnitude may govern the design of the roof structure. The lower the roof slope, the greater will be the amount of snow that can accumulate on the roof. Rafters for low-pitched and flat roofs must, as a consequence, be designed for greater snow loads than for those of steep roofs. Some codes may allow a reduction in the snow load for roof slopes above 4:12.

Roof structures and roofing must be able to withstand wind forces that create upward pressure on the roof surfaces. This can vary from 15 to 40 lbs./s.f., depending on local conditions. On the windward side of roofs with 7:12 slopes or greater, wind forces can bear down on the roof surface.

Consult your local building code for live load, snow load, and wind load requirements in your area.

## ROOF SLOPE

The slope of a roof plane refers to the ratio of its vertical rise to its horizontal run, and is most commonly expressed as inches of rise per foot of run. eg. A 6:12 slope means the roof plane rises 6" for every foot or 12" of run.

The slope of a roof affects the type of roofing used, underlayment requirements, eave flashing requirements, and the design loads for which the roof must be structured. (See Roofing, pgs. 246-247)

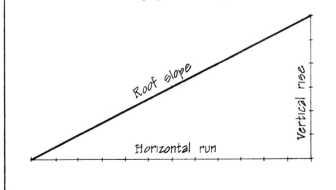

## SIMPLIFIED RAFTER SPAN TABLE

| RAFTER | | SPAN | |
| Size (nominal) | Spacing (inches) | Low or High Slope | Low Slope (3:12 or less) |
| --- | --- | --- | --- |
| 2" x 6" | 12 | 11' - 7" | 12' - 4" |
| | 16 | 10' - 0" | 10' - 8" |
| | 24 | 8' - 2" | 8' - 7" |
| 2" x 8" | 12 | 15 - 3" | 16' - 2" |
| | 16 | 13 - 3" | 14' - 0" |
| | 24 | 10' - 10" | 11' - 6" |
| 2" x 10" | 12 | 19' - 6" | 20' - 8" |
| | 16 | 16' - 11" | 17' - 10" |
| | 24 | 13' - 3" | 14' - 8" |
| 2" x 12" | 12 | 23' - 8" | 25' - 2" |
| | 16 | 20' - 6" | 21' - 9" |
| | 24 | 16' - 8" | 17' - 8" |

Notes: 1. Live load = 30 lbs./s.f.
2. Dead load = 15 lbs./s.f.
3. $F_b$ (allowable extreme fiber stress in bending) = 1200 psi.

High Slope (8:12 to 12:12)
- Less accumulation of snow
- Usable attic space
- Can use shingle or shake roofing

Medium Slope (4:12 to 7:12)
- Moderate accumulation of snow
- Can use shingle or shake roofing

Low Slope (2:12 to 3:12)
- Greater accumulation of snow
- Roll or continuous roofing generally used

Flat (1/4" per foot)
- Continuous membrane roofing required

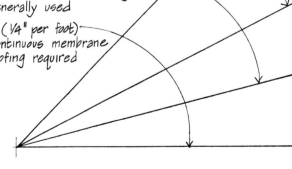

# ROOF FORMS

A gable roof consists of two inclined planes that meet at a peak or ridge, and slope down to two opposing supports, usually the top plates of stud walls or beams. The two triangular wall sections at the ends are gable ends that continue the framing pattern of the walls below.

Under loading, the roof rafters will tend to push outward at their supports. This tendency must be restrained by either ceiling joists or collar beams. Lateral wind forces must be resisted by the end walls or interior partitions perpendicular to the supporting walls.

For roof slopes over 3:12, the roof rafters bear against and support each other in pairs. The ridge board at which the rafters meet, therefore, is not structural. It merely serves to keep the peak in line.

A shed roof can be visualized as half a gable roof, and is similar in its structural framing. The major difference is that the peak must be supported by a high wall or the main body of the house.

A hip roof is similar to a gable roof except four rather than two inclined planes meet at four hips. These hips transfer the majority of the roof load to four corner posts. The tendency for the roof to push outward occurs at these corners in a balanced hip roof, and is resisted by the roof sheathing and the exterior wall plates. Thus the hip roof is theoretically a self-contained structural unit. If the hip roof form becomes elongated along a ridge, collar beams must be used as in the case of gable roofs.

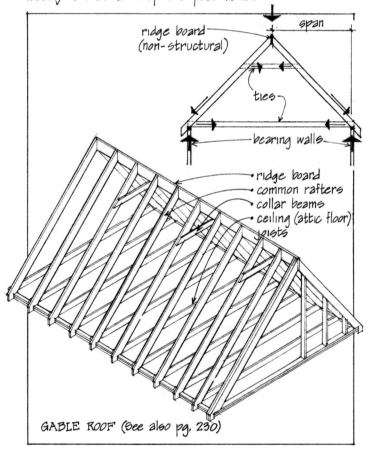

GABLE ROOF (See also pg. 230)

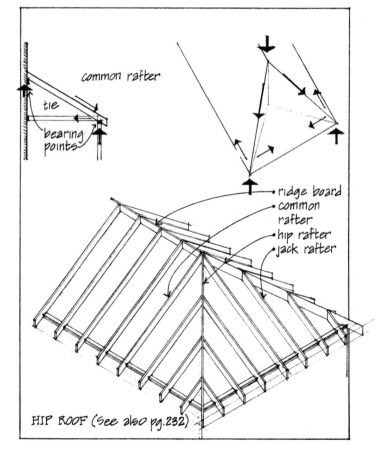

HIP ROOF (See also pg. 232)

The chief advantage of a gambrel roof is the additional space it provides without increasing the height of the ridge. The gambrel roof has four inclined planes, two on each side of the peak. The upper planes have fairly low pitches while the lower ones are more steeply pitched. The tendency for the rafters to spread occurs at the lower ends of both upper and lower rafters. Ties are therefore required at these points.

A flat roof performs structurally as a floor system. The roof joists double-function as ceiling joists that support the ceiling finish for the rooms below. When spanning low-sloping (3:12 or less) gable roofs, the roof joists require a center support.

Roof joists may be eliminated if solid wood decking supported by beams is used. See pg. 244.

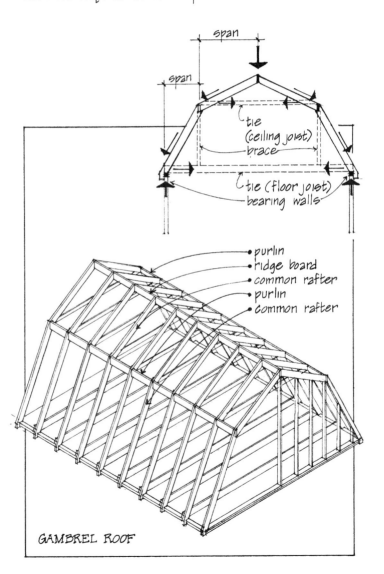

GAMBREL ROOF

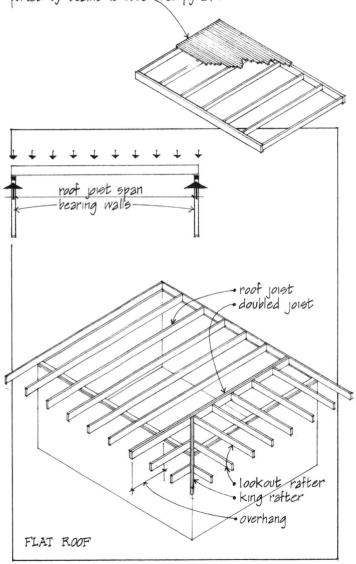

FLAT ROOF

## GABLE ROOF FRAMING

In pitched roof construction, the ceiling or attic joists are nailed in place after the exterior and interior wall framing is complete. This is done prior to erecting the roof rafters to prevent the rafters from pushing their supporting walls outward.

The ceiling joists are nailed to the supporting top plates directly over the wall studs. The locations of the rafters (12", 16", or 24" o.c.) are marked on the supporting plates as well as the ridge board that is laid down next to one of the plates. If two ridge boards are needed to make up the length of the roof, they should be joined at the intersection of two rafters.

After three common rafters are measured and cut, two are nailed to opposing wall plates and to the ridge board. The other end of the ridge board can be braced temporarily or, in the case of an addition, attached to the existing roof construction. With the two common rafters in place, verify the overall dimensions of the roofline, the headroom beneath the roof, and if necessary, the proper relationship to the existing roof. If the rafters are correctly cut, use the third rafter as a pattern piece to cut the remaining rafters.

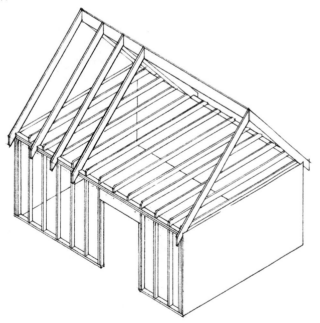

## COMMON RAFTERS

Common or full-length rafters are normally pre-cut and erected in pairs along the ridge board. The ridge board should be as straight as possible, of 1" or 2" stock and 2" deeper than the rafter size to provide a solid nailing surface for the rafters.

Common rafters must be cut to proper length, with the proper angle cuts at the ridge and eave ends, and with notches (bird's mouth cuts) for fitting onto the supporting top plate or beam. The length of a common rafter is the distance from the outer edge of its support to the centerline of the ridge. When cutting the rafter, half the width of the ridge board must be subtracted from the rafter length; any overhang must be added to the length.

The rafter length can be determined by using the Pythagorean theorem, where

$$L \text{ (rafter length)} = \sqrt{Rise^2 + Run^2}$$

The total run of the rafter is its horizontal span. Its total rise is the roof slope times the total run.

eg. For an 8:12 roof slope and a rafter span of 14', the total rise is (8/12 × 14' = 9.33'). The rafter length is ($L = \sqrt{14^2 + 9.33^2}$) or 16.8'.

The rafter length can also be found by using the first line of the table found on the framing square.

eg. For a roof slope of 8:12, look under the 8" mark. The length of a common rafter is 14.42" per foot of run. For a 14' run, therefore, the rafter length is (14 × 14.42" = 201.88"). Dividing by 12 to convert to feet, the rafter length is 16.82'.

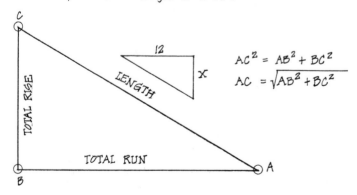

Once the rafter length is determined, subtract half the width of the ridge board, and add for any overhang desired. Lay the rafter stock for measuring with the camber or bow, if any, along the top edge of the rafter. Use a framing square to mark the plumb or square cuts at the ridge and eave ends, and the bird's mouth cut.

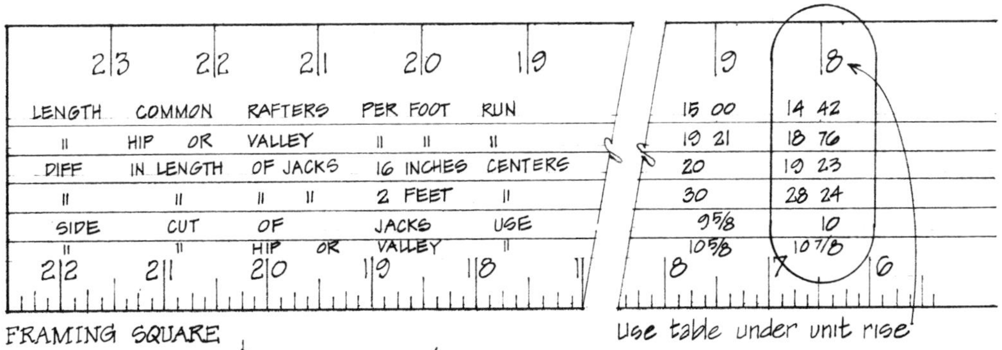

| 2 3 | | 2 2 | | 2 1 | | 2 0 | | 1 9 | | | | 1 9 | | 1 8 |
|---|---|---|---|---|---|---|---|---|---|---|---|---|---|
| LENGTH | COMMON | | RAFTERS | PER | FOOT | RUN | | | | | 15 00 | | 14 42 |
| " | HIP | OR | VALLEY | | " | " | " | | | | 19 21 | | 18 76 |
| DIFF | IN LENGTH | OF JACKS | | 16 INCHES | CENTERS | | | | | | 20 | | 19 23 |
| " | " | " | " | 2 FEET | " | | | | | | 30 | | 28 24 |
| SIDE | CUT | OF | JACKS | USE | | | | | | | 9 5/8 | | 10 |
| | | HIP | OR | VALLEY | " | | | | | | 10 5/8 | | 10 7/8 |
| 2 2 | | 2 1 | | 2 0 | | 1 9 | | 1 8 | | | | 8 | | 7 | | 6 |

FRAMING SQUARE

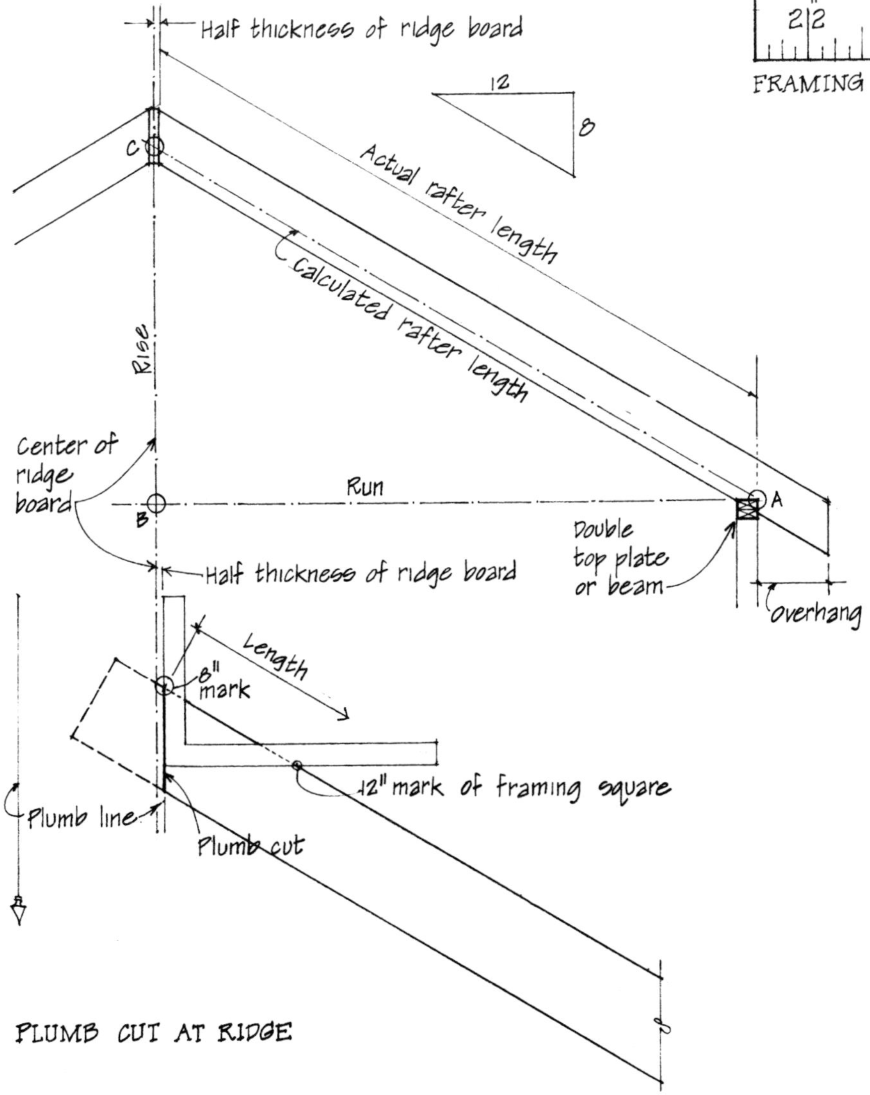

Use table under unit rise

**PLUMB CUT AT RIDGE**

- Half thickness of ridge board
- 12
- 8
- Actual rafter length
- Calculated rafter length
- C
- Rise
- Run
- Center of ridge board
- B
- A
- Half thickness of ridge board
- Double top plate or beam
- Overhang
- Length
- 8" mark
- 12" mark of framing square
- Plumb line
- Plumb cut

**BIRD'S MOUTH CUT**

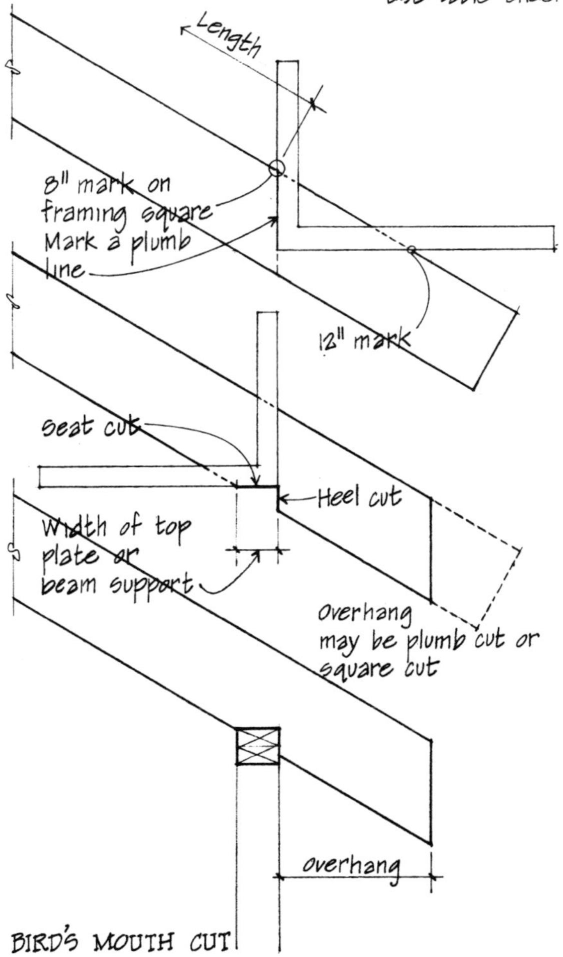

- Length
- 8" mark on framing square Mark a plumb line
- 12" mark
- Seat cut
- Heel cut
- Width of top plate or beam support
- Overhang may be plumb cut or square cut
- overhang

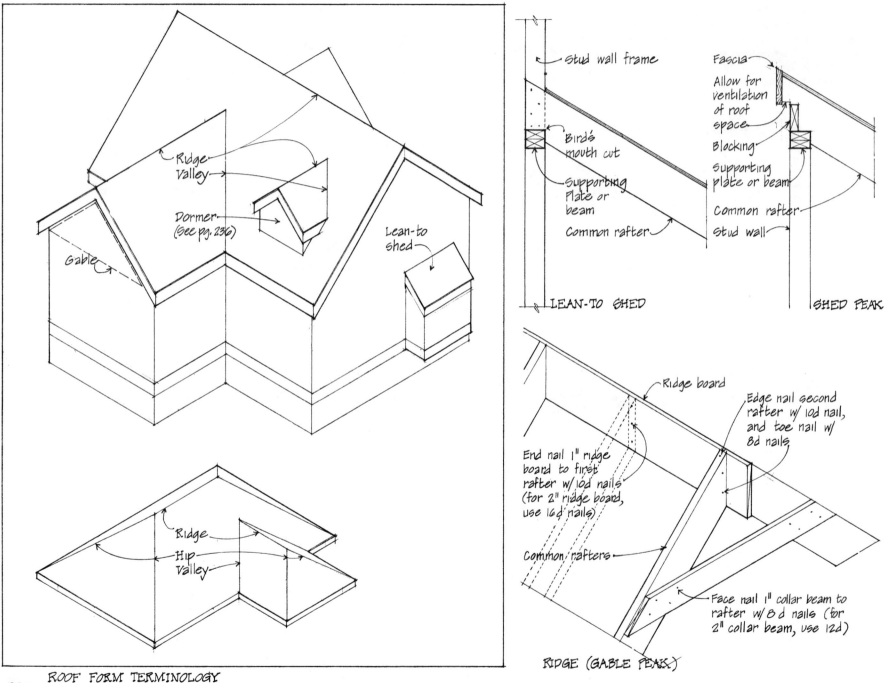

Ridge
Valley

Dormer
(See pg. 236)

Gable

Lean-to
shed

Ridge
Hip
Valley

ROOF FORM TERMINOLOGY

Stud wall frame

Bird's
mouth cut

Supporting
Plate or
beam

Common rafter

LEAN-TO SHED

Fascia

Allow for
ventilation
of roof
space

Blocking

Supporting
plate or beam

Common rafter

Stud wall

SHED PEAK

Ridge board

Edge nail second
rafter w/ 10d nail,
and toe nail w/
8d nails

End nail 1" ridge
board to first
rafter w/ 10d nails
(for 2" ridge board,
use 16d nails)

Common rafters

Face nail 1" collar beam to
rafter w/ 8d nails (for
2" collar beam, use 12d)

RIDGE (GABLE PEAK)

## COLLAR BEAMS

Collar beams are used to tie pairs of rafters together, keep them from pulling apart at the ridge during high winds, and to resist their outward thrust at the eaves. They are used to reinforce every pair of rafters in gambrel roofs and low-sloping gable roofs. Steep-pitched gable roofs and roofs with short rafter spans may require collar beams only at every third pair of rafters

1"x6" material can be used as collar beams. If, however, the attic space will be finished, use 2"x4" or 2"x6" material at each pair of rafters to support the ceilings of the finished rooms.

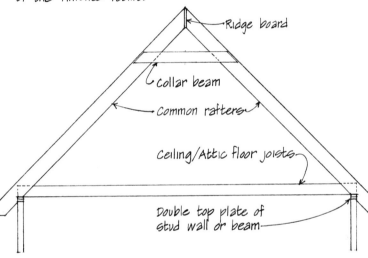

- Ridge board
- Collar beam
- Common rafters
- Ceiling/Attic floor joists
- Double top plate of stud wall or beam

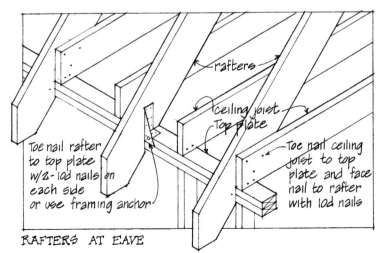

rafters

ceiling joist
Top plate

Toe nail rafter to top plate w/2-10d nails on each side or use framing anchor

Toe nail ceiling joist to top plate and face nail to rafter with 10d nails

RAFTERS AT EAVE

## OVERHANGS

Overhangs at eaves are created simply by extending the rafters the desired length beyond their supports.

Overhangs at gable ends, perpendicular to the rafter span, are constructed similarly to the framing of floor cantilevers. A doubled rafter is located back from the gable end wall at a distance twice that of the overhang. Lookout rafters form a ladder that frames into the doubled rafter, and rests on the top plate of the gable end wall.

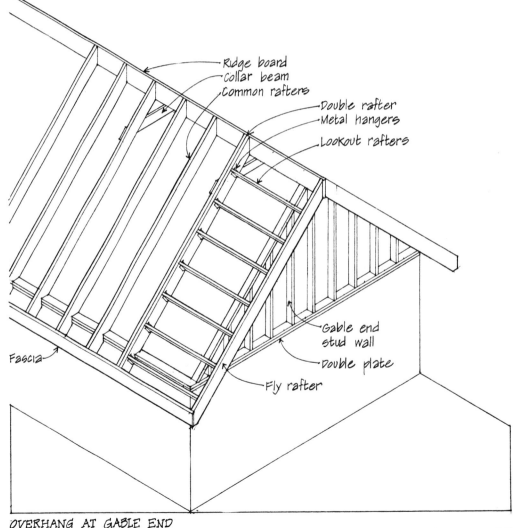

- Ridge board
- Collar beam
- Common rafters
- Double rafter
- Metal hangers
- Lookout rafters
- Gable end stud wall
- Double plate
- Fascia
- Fly rafter

OVERHANG AT GABLE END

## HIP RAFTERS

The central portion of a hip roof is framed similarly to a gable roof with common rafters. The ends, however, are framed with hip rafters that run from the ridge board at a 45° angle (in plan) to the outside corner posts or supports. Hip jack rafters then extend from the hip rafters to the supporting top plates of the exterior walls.

Most hip roofs have equal-pitch roof planes. Their end slopes are equal to their side slopes. The plan view of such a hip roof shows that the run of a hip rafter is the hypotenuse of a right triangle whose sides are equal to the run of a common rafter. The horizontal run of a hip rafter can then be calculated using the Pythagorean theorem, where H (run of the hip rafter) equals $\sqrt{R^2 + R^2}$, (R is the run of a common rafter.)

The rise of a hip rafter is identical to the rise of a common rafter. The length of a hip rafter can therefore be determined by finding the hypotenuse of a right triangle whose legs are the total rise and run of the hip rafter.

eg. For a hip-roofed structure 30' wide with an 8:12 roof slope:
1. The run of a common rafter = 30/2 = 15'.
2. The rise of a common rafter = rise of the hip rafter = 8/12 × 15' = 10'.
3. The run of the hip rafter = $\sqrt{15^2 + 15^2}$ = 21.21'.
4. The length of the hip rafter = $\sqrt{10^2 + 21.21^2}$ = 23.45'.

The hip rafter length can also be found by using the second line of the table found on the framing square.

eg. For the same situation as above, look under the 8" mark (for an 8:12 slope), down to the second line. The length of a hip rafter is 18.76" per foot of run (of a common rafter), or 18.76" × 15 = 281.4". Dividing by 12 to convert to feet, the length of the hip rafter is 281.4/12 = 23.45'.

Ridge
Common rafters
Hip rafter
Hip jack rafters

PARTIAL PLAN OF HIP ROOF

BD = Run of common rafter
BC = Rise of common rafter
CD = Length of common rafter

AB = Run of hip rafter
   = $\sqrt{BD^2 + BE^2}$
BC = Rise of hip rafter
AC = Length of hip rafter
   = $\sqrt{AB^2 + BC^2}$

UNIT RISES of hip and common rafters are identical.
UNIT RUN of any hip rafter = $\sqrt{12^2 + 12^2} = \sqrt{288} = 16.97 \rightarrow$ (17)

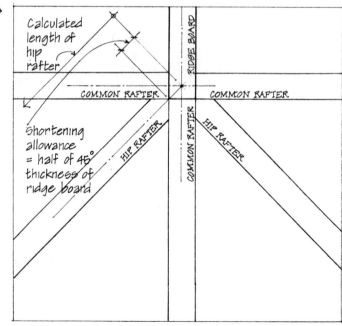

HIP RAFTER SHORTENING ALLOWANCE

Calculated length of hip rafter

Shortening allowance = half of 45° thickness of ridge board

RIDGE BOARD
COMMON RAFTER
COMMON RAFTER
HIP RAFTER
HIP RAFTER

As with common rafters, a shortening allowance must be made, depending on how the hip rafter frames into the ridge board and common rafters at the ridge end. This shortening allowance is ½ of the 45° thickness of the member (ridge board or common rafter) into which the hip rafter frames.

Since common rafters run perpendicular to the ridge, their ridge ends are cut square or 90° to the rafter length. A hip rafter joins the ridge at an angle and therefore requires a side cut. To determine this side cut, first measure for the required shortening allowance. Using a framing square set at the rafter cut, (eg. For the example on the previous page, set the square at 8, the unit rise, and 17, the unit run.) and mark a plumb line. From this line, mark another plumb line a distance equal to ½ of the hip rafter thickness.

On the top edge of the hip rafter, draw a centerline and the angle of the side cut as shown in the illustration. If the hip rafter frames into the ridge board, only a single side cut is necessary. If it frames into common rafters, a double side cut is required.

The tail of the hip rafter must also be side cut, but in the reverse direction.

An allowance is also required so that the top of the hip rafter is at the same level as the common rafters. This can be done by either beveling the top edge of the hip rafter or deepening the heel of the bird's mouth cut. To determine the amount of drop required, set the square to the cut of the rafter, and mark off along the edge of the square that indicates the unit run, a ½ thickness of the hip rafter.

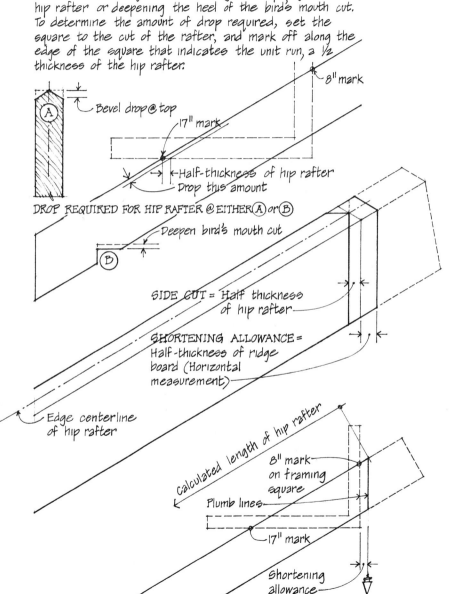

DROP REQUIRED FOR HIP RAFTER @ EITHER Ⓐ or Ⓑ

TAIL CUT

RIDGE CUT

# VALLEY RAFTERS

A valley is the internal angle formed by the intersection of two sloping roof planes, as between a main roof section and a gable-roofed addition or dormer. The supporting member is the valley rafter. To provide full contact for the jack rafters that frame into it, the valley rafter is normally 2" deeper than the common rafters. At the intersection of two equal-sized roof planes, the valley rafter is doubled to support the roof load.

In most situations, the intersecting roof planes have equal slopes, and the valley rafter makes a 45° angle (in plan) with the jack rafters they connect. Figuring the length of a valley rafter, therefore, is similar to that for a hip rafter. Use the second line of the table found on the framing square. (See top of pg. 220)

AD = Run of common rafter
    = BE = AF = AE

AB = Run of valley rafter
    $= \sqrt{AD^2 + AE^2}$

BC = Rise of common and valley rafters

AC = Length of valley rafter
    $= \sqrt{AB^2 + BC^2}$

Side cuts are laid out as they are for a hip rafter. Unlike hip rafters, valley rafters require no dropping of the bird's mouth cut. The shortening allowances depend on how the valley rafters are framed.

There are two ways to frame a gable-roofed addition whose width is less than that of the main roof. The first uses a full length valley rafter that spans from the supporting top wall plate to the ridge board. A shorter valley rafter is then framed into the longer one.

Another method is to extend the ridge board of the addition into the main roof and hang it from the main roof's ridge board. Two valley rafters of equal length then are framed into the ridge board of the addition.

Again using the second line of the table found on the framing square, find the unit length for the valley rafters under the unit rise of the roof slope. (eg. Look under 8" for an 8:12 slope.) Multiply this unit length by the total run of a common rafter of the roof to which the valley rafter belongs.

VALLEY RAFTER SHORTENING ALLOWANCE = Half of 45° thickness of main ridge board

INTERSECTING ROOFS OF EQUAL SPAN

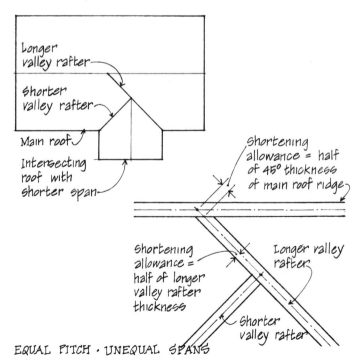

EQUAL PITCH · UNEQUAL SPANS

## JACK RAFTERS

A jack rafter is a part of a common rafter that is shortened to frame into a hip rafter, valley rafter, or both. It has the same cross-sectional dimension and spacing as a common rafter. It also has the same unit length for a given slope. Looking along the first line of the table on the framing square, the unit length of a jack rafter with an 8:12 slope (under the 8" mark) is 14.42" per foot of run.

The run of the shortest hip jack rafter at a corner is usually 16" or 24", depending on the rafter spacing. If spaced closer to the corner, the run is equal to the distance from the hip jack to the corner. The length of the shortest hip jack rafter with an 8:12 slope, 16" from the corner, would be 14.42" x 16"/12", or 19.23".

This length is also known as the common difference in length of jacks, and can be found on the third line of the table on the framing square. The length of the next hip jack would be (2 x 19.23"), the third would be (3 x 19.23"), etc. For 24" rafter spacing, use the fourth line of the table.

The lengths of valley jack and cripple jack rafters are found in a similar manner. Once their runs are determined from a framing plan, multiply their runs by their unit length to arrive at their total lengths.

Jack rafters have shortening allowances equal to ½ of the 45° thickness of the member into which they frame.

For side cuts, use the fifth line of the table on the framing square. eg. For an 8:12 slope, look under the 8" mark. For side cuts of jacks, use "10." Set the framing square, face up on the edge of the rafter, to "12" on the tongue and "10" on the blade, and draw the side cut line along the tongue.

The bird's mouth cuts and overhangs of jack rafters are identical to those of common rafters.

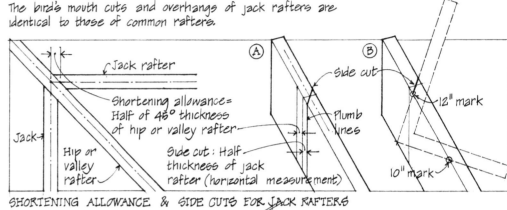

SHORTENING ALLOWANCE & SIDE CUTS FOR JACK RAFTERS

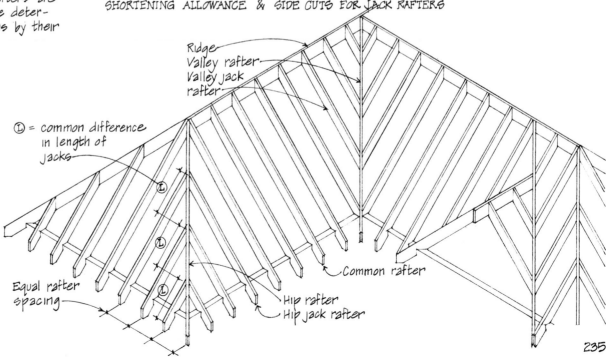

PARTIAL FRAMING PLAN

# DORMER FRAMING

Dormers are framed around openings in the roof plane. These openings, in turn, are framed similarly to those in floor framing. The trimmer rafters on each side of the opening are doubled, as are the top and bottom headers. If the opening extends to the ridge board or down to the exterior wall, the top or bottom headers may be omitted.

The opening for a large dormer may require additional structural support for the top and bottom headers. This support can be provided by a beam or bearing wall.

The side walls of a dormer consist of studs that rest on the trimmer rafters. The studs can also extend down past the trimmers to rest on a sole plate nailed to the attic floor joists and subflooring.

The front wall and any window openings are framed as in normal stud wall construction, and rest on the bottom header. The front wall can also lie directly above and be a continuation of an exterior wall.

A gable-roofed dormer is framed as a normal gable roof. The valley rafters that frame the intersection of the dormer roof and the main roof are tied to the top header.

The rafters of a shed-roofed dormer are measured, cut and erected as common rafters, except at a much lower slope.

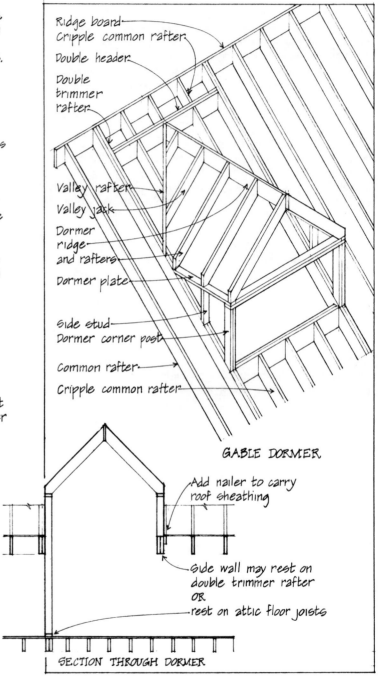

Ridge board
Cripple common rafter
Double header
Double trimmer rafter
Valley rafter
Valley jack
Dormer ridge and rafters
Dormer plate
Side stud
Dormer corner post
Common rafter
Cripple common rafter

GABLE DORMER

Add nailer to carry roof sheathing

Side wall may rest on double trimmer rafter
OR
rest on attic floor joists

SECTION THROUGH DORMER

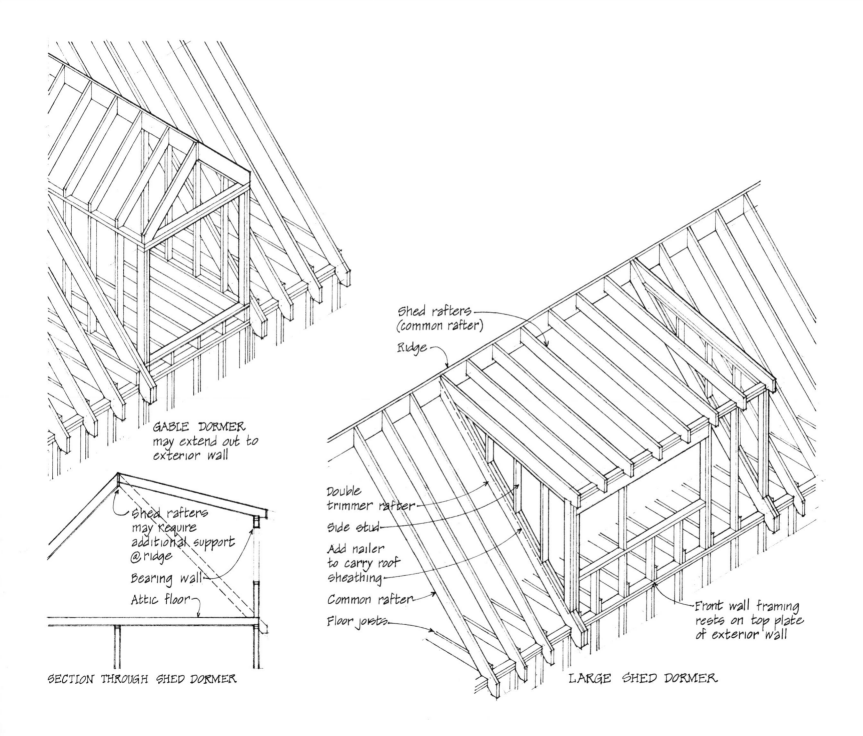

GABLE DORMER
may extend out to
exterior wall

Shed rafters
(common rafter)

Ridge

Shed rafters
may require
additional support
@ ridge

Bearing wall

Attic floor

SECTION THROUGH SHED DORMER

Double
trimmer rafter

Side stud

Add nailer
to carry roof
sheathing

Common rafter

Floor joists

Front wall framing
rests on top plate
of exterior wall

LARGE SHED DORMER

237

## ROOF SHEATHING

Plywood is normally used for structural sheathing over a wood-framed roof. It enhances the strength and rigidity of the roof frame, and serves as a solid base for the application and fastening of most roofing materials. (In damp areas not subject to blizzard conditions, spaced sheathing of 1"x3", 1"x4", or 1"x6" boards are used with wood shingle or shake roofing. (See pgs. 253-254)

Standard C-C, C-D, structural I and II grades of plywood can be used for roof sheathing. Plywood bonded with an exterior glue (CDX) or an exterior grade plywood is preferred for roof sheathing. If interior plywood is used, it should be bonded with intermediate glue, and any exposed edges along eaves and gable ends should be protected with trim.

PLYWOOD ROOF SHEATHING SPANS

| Panel Identification Index ✱ | Thickness (inches) | Span w/ Edges blocked (inches) | Allowable Live Load (lbs./s.f.) |
|---|---|---|---|
| 16/0 | 5/16 , (3/8) | 16 | 75 |
| 20/0 | 5/16 , 3/8 | 20 | 65 |
| 24/0 | 3/8 , (1/2) | 24 | 50 |
| 30/12 | 5/8 | 30 | 50 |
| 32/16 | 1/2 , 5/8 | 32 | 50 |
| 36/16 | 3/4 | 36 | 40 |

Although 5/16" thick plywood can be used with rafters spaced 16" o.c., and 3/8" plywood with 24" rafter spacing, it is recommended these be increased to 3/8" and 1/2" respectively to provide better penetration for roofing nails, increased resistance to racking of the roof plane, and a smoother roof appearance.

As with floor sheathing, plywood roof sheathing panels are laid with their face grain perpendicular to the roof rafters. End joints should lie over the center of a rafter, and be staggered by at least one rafter spacing. Unsupported edges should be blocked with framing, or be braced by the use of tongue-and-groove joints or plyclips. Allow an 1/8" space between panels along edges, and a 1/16" at end joints.

For plywood up to 1/2" thick, use 6d common or 5d threaded nails; for plywood up to an inch thick, use 8d common or 7d threaded nails. Nail the panels at 6" o.c. along edges and at 12" o.c. along intermediate supports.

✱ See pg. 213 for illustration of Engineered Grade Stamp on plywood sheathing panels.

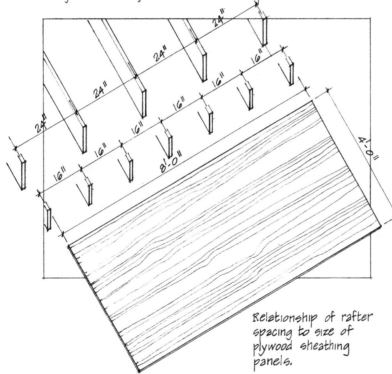

Relationship of rafter spacing to size of plywood sheathing panels.

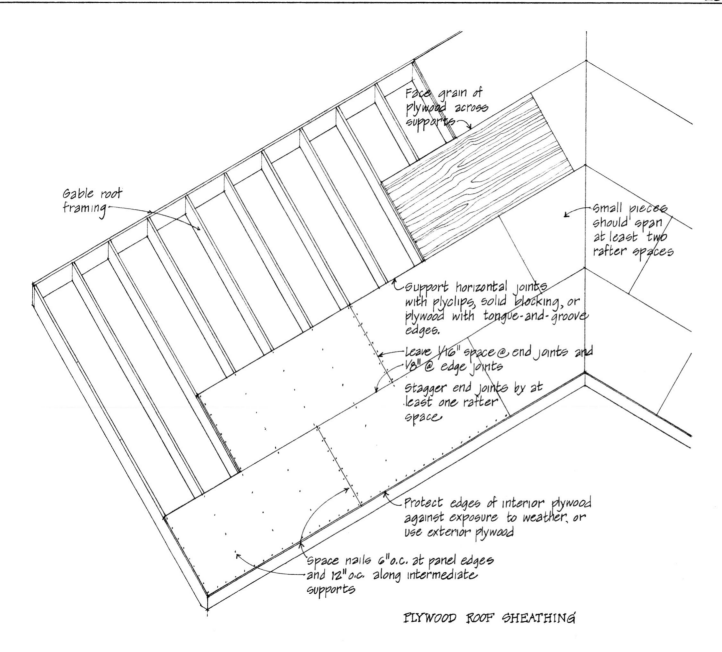

Face grain of plywood across supports

Gable roof framing

Small pieces should span at least two rafter spaces

Support horizontal joints with plyclips, solid blocking, or plywood with tongue-and-groove edges.

Leave 1/16" space @ end joints and 1/8" @ edge joints

Stagger end joints by at least one rafter space

Protect edges of interior plywood against exposure to weather, or use exterior plywood

Space nails 6"o.c. at panel edges and 12"o.c. along intermediate supports

PLYWOOD ROOF SHEATHING

# WOOD TRUSSES

A truss consists of framing members assembled in a triangulated configuration. The truss assembly forms a rigid structural unit that is capable of a long span without intermediate support. Trusses use material efficiently, can be erected quickly, and allow for flexibility in the layout of interior spaces. Interior partitions may be arranged without regard for structural considerations.

The development of lightweight wood trusses, pre-engineered and assembled in a factory to your design specifications, has made them feasible for residential construction. These trusses are best used when a rectangular plan requires long spans (over 18') and a quantity of a single type of truss.

Because the individual members of a truss are subject primarily to compressive and tensile stresses, and very little bending stress, they can be smaller than normal floor joists and roof rafters. Lightweight wood trusses usually consist of 2"x 4"s, and possibly 2"x 6"s for the top chords. The truss members must be rigidly connected b, special metal plates or plywood gussets. For heavy loads, split-ring connectors are used.

Fabricated wood trusses may have sloping or flat top chords. When spaced at 24" o.c., their bottom chords can be used to support the finish ceiling material. If the trusses are spaced further apart, furring strips may be necessary

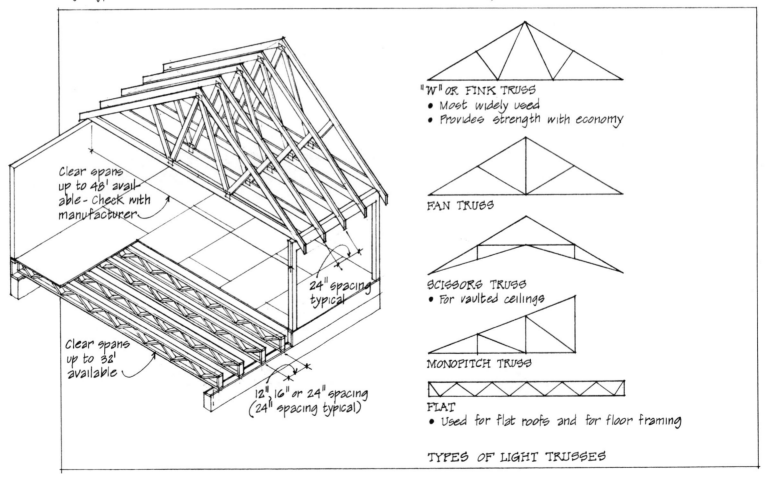

Clear spans up to 48' available - Check with manufacturer.

24" spacing typical

Clear spans up to 32' available

12", 16" or 24" spacing (24" spacing typical)

"W" OR FINK TRUSS
- Most widely used
- Provides strength with economy

FAN TRUSS

SCISSORS TRUSS
- For vaulted ceilings

MONOPITCH TRUSS

FLAT
- Used for flat roofs and for floor framing

TYPES OF LIGHT TRUSSES

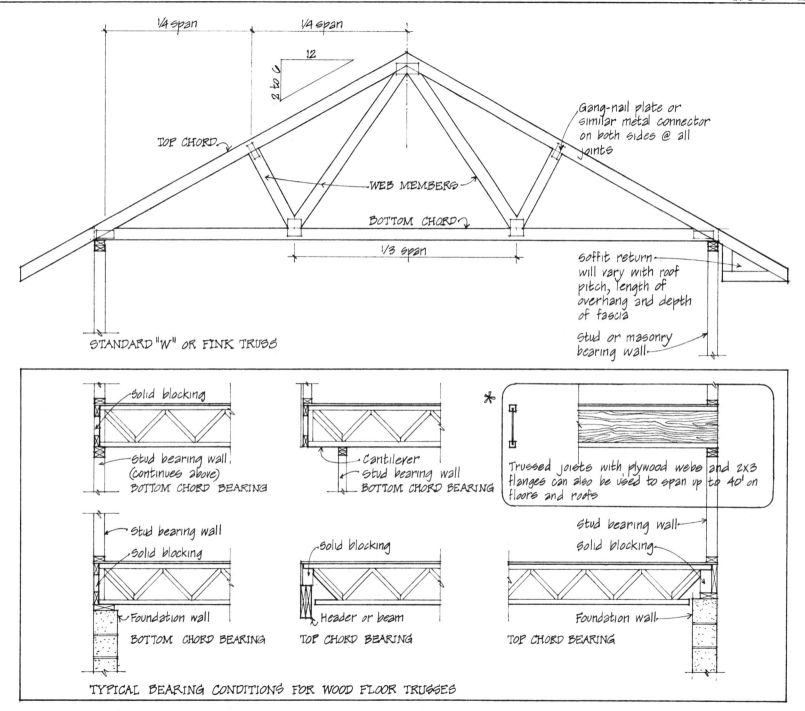

¼ span   ¼ span

12
2 to 6

TOP CHORD

Gang-nail plate or similar metal connector on both sides @ all joints

WEB MEMBERS

BOTTOM CHORD

⅓ span

soffit return will vary with roof pitch, length of overhang and depth of fascia

Stud or masonry bearing wall

STANDARD "W" OR FINK TRUSS

solid blocking

Stud bearing wall (continues above)
BOTTOM CHORD BEARING

Cantilever
Stud bearing wall
BOTTOM CHORD BEARING

\*

Trussed joists with plywood webs and 2x3 flanges can also be used to span up to 40' on floors and roofs

Stud bearing wall
Solid blocking

Foundation wall
BOTTOM CHORD BEARING

solid blocking
Header or beam
TOP CHORD BEARING

Stud bearing wall
solid blocking

Foundation wall
TOP CHORD BEARING

TYPICAL BEARING CONDITIONS FOR WOOD FLOOR TRUSSES

## POST & BEAM FRAMING

While joist, stud and rafter framing consists of many slender members, post and beam framing uses fewer but larger members that are spaced further apart and spanned with thick planking material.

The primary advantage of a post and beam framing system is its simple, straightforward expression of its structure. The planks and beams are often left exposed as the interior ceiling finish. The posts may also be partially exposed on the wall surface. In addition, because there are fewer members required, there is a potential savings in labor.

Each structural element in a post and beam system, however, is critical to the stability of the overall structure. Each element must be sized, installed, and connected to other members carefully. In contrast to this, a joist, stud and rafter frame, with plywood diaphragm surfaces and a continuous perimeter foundation, has many structurally redundant parts, enabling the system to absorb errors or weaknesses in the materials installed.

To take advantage of the system's economy, post and beam supports should be laid out in a modular grid pattern, and standard 8', 10', 12' and 14' lengths of lumber used. Windows, doors and wall sections should fit within and not disrupt the structural grid.

While post and beam framing is ideally suited for one-story structures, consider its use for an addition carefully. Its style may not be compatible with your house. Its structural pattern may not merge well with the existing house framing. On the other hand, the openness of its skeleton structure may be appropriate for the construction of a sunroom or solarium that requires large glass areas.

Finally, the exposing of structural members in an interior space requires the selection of good quality materials, careful attention to joint and connection details, and craftsmanship.

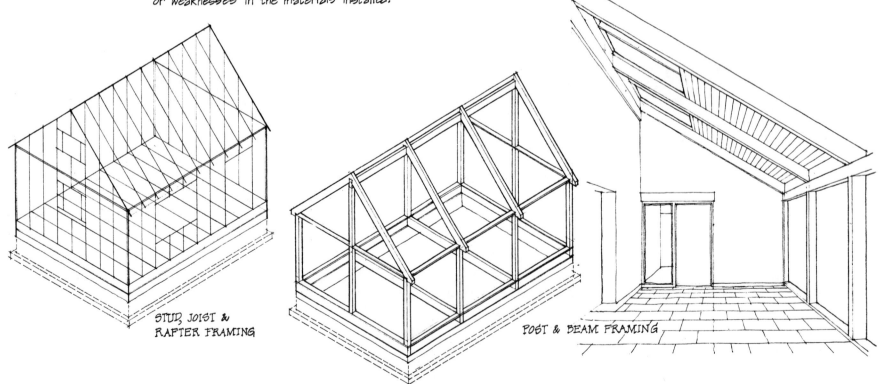

STUD JOIST & RAFTER FRAMING

POST & BEAM FRAMING

## WALL FRAMING

Post and beam framing is often used for walls with large window and door areas, and integrated with plank and beam roof framing. It consists of posts, spaced 4' to 8' o.c., that support roof beams and headers. The space between the posts are filled with window and door units, or with wall sections that are framed in the normal manner. Together, these elements serve as a weather barrier.

Even though the infill wall sections are not structural and theoretically carry no roof loads, they should be fully sheathed to provide lateral stability for the post and beam framework.

The posts may be solid 4"x4"s or 4"x6"s, or be built up from 2" members that are securely fastened together. The beams or headers supported by the posts may also be solid or built up. A minimum bearing of 3½" is normally required in the direction of the beam span, or 6" when two beams meet over a post support.

While the spacing of the posts is directly related to the size, strength and spacing of the beams they support, their spacing should also be coordinated with the standard sizes of the window and door units used.

Because there are fewer structural members and fewer connections in a post and beam structure, the loads and forces exerted on the structure are concentrated at these joints. Post and beam connections therefore require metal framing anchors or angle clips. These may be nailed or, for extra holding power, lag-screwed or bolted to the framing members. If the connections are to be left exposed, concealed fastening devices such as steel dowel pins are available.

Post connections to the foundation system and to the roof beams must also provide resistance to uplift forces.

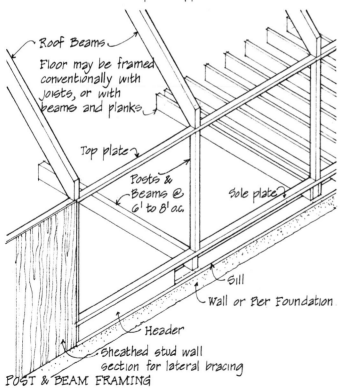

POST & BEAM FRAMING

Labels: Roof Beams; Floor may be framed conventionally with joists, or with beams and planks; Top plate; Posts & Beams @ 6' to 8' o.c.; Sole plate; Sill; Wall or Pier Foundation; Header; Sheathed stud wall section for lateral bracing

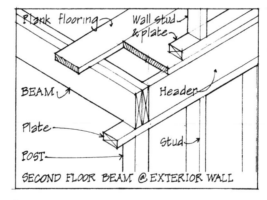

SECOND FLOOR BEAM @ EXTERIOR WALL

Labels: Plank flooring; Wall stud & plate; BEAM; Header; Plate; Stud; POST

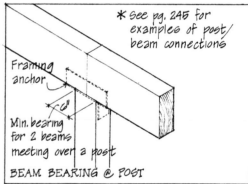

BEAM BEARING @ POST

Labels: ✱ See pg. 245 for examples of post/beam connections; Framing anchor; 6"; Min. bearing for 2 beams meeting over a post

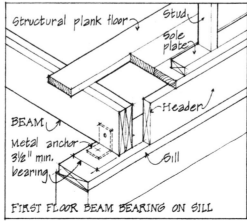

FIRST FLOOR BEAM BEARING ON SILL

Labels: Structural plank floor; Stud; Sole plate; BEAM; Header; Metal anchor 3½" min. bearing; Sill

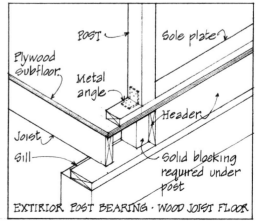

EXTERIOR POST BEARING · WOOD JOIST FLOOR

Labels: POST; Sole plate; Plywood subfloor; Metal angle; Header; Joist; Sill; Solid blocking required under post

# 4

# ROOF FRAMING

As an alternative to wood rafter or truss framing, plank and beam framing uses 2" or thicker planking to span between roof beams spaced 6' to 8' o.c. The underside of the planking and the roof beams are often left exposed as the ceiling finish.

Because there is no concealed roof space, any required insulation (in addition to the insulation value of the planking) must be installed over the planking. Rigid insulation panels, such as extruded polystyrene, are usually laid over a vapor barrier. The roofing material is secured with fasteners that are long enough to penetrate through the insulation well into the planking.

There also is no space to conceal any overhead ductwork, pipes, or electrical wiring, although spaced wood beams can sometimes be used to house wiring for overhead lighting.

The roof beams can be parallel to the roof slope, and be supported by exterior stud walls or a post and beam structure. The outward thrust of the beams must be counteracted by ceiling joists or collar beams which may be left exposed in the space. The exterior post supports can also be buttressed by interior partitions.

Unlike the ridge board of a gable roof framed with rafters, the ridge beam of a gable plank and beam roof must help support the transverse roof beams. The ridge beam itself is supported by posts in the end walls.

The roof beams may also run perpendicular to the roof slope, and be supported by interior posts, or by posts in the end walls.

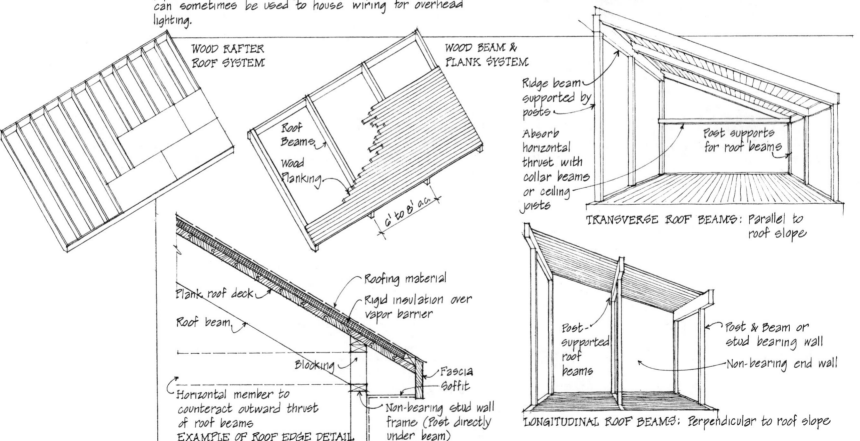

WOOD RAFTER ROOF SYSTEM

WOOD BEAM & PLANK SYSTEM

Roof Beams

Wood Planking

6' to 8' o.c.

Ridge beam supported by posts

Absorb horizontal thrust with collar beams or ceiling joists

Post supports for roof beams

TRANSVERSE ROOF BEAMS: Parallel to roof slope

Roofing material

Rigid insulation over vapor barrier

Plank roof deck

Roof beam

Blocking

Fascia

Soffit

Horizontal member to counteract outward thrust of roof beams

Non-bearing stud wall frame (Post directly under beam)

EXAMPLE OF ROOF EDGE DETAIL

Post-supported roof beams

Post & Beam or stud bearing wall

Non-bearing end wall

LONGITUDINAL ROOF BEAMS: Perpendicular to roof slope

2"x6" or 2"x8" solid wood planking with tongue and groove edges can span up to 8' and support normal roof loads. For longer spans, planking up to 4" thick is available.

For the most economical use of random length material, the planking can be laid as follows. The planking should be applied over not less than three continuous spans, with each individual plank bearing on at least one support. End joints should be staggered from those in adjacent pieces by at least 24".

If uniform lengths of planking are used, they should be laid in a continuous manner over two or three spans.

2" planking is usually only face-nailed to the supports. Thicker planking requires additional toe-nailing to the supports and edge-nailing to each other.

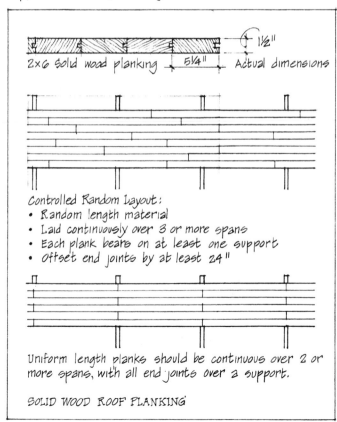

2x6 Solid wood planking — 5¼" — Actual dimensions — 1½"

Controlled Random Layout:
• Random length material
• Laid continuously over 3 or more spans
• Each plank bears on at least one support
• Offset end joints by at least 24"

Uniform length planks should be continuous over 2 or more spans, with all end joints over a support.

SOLID WOOD ROOF PLANKING

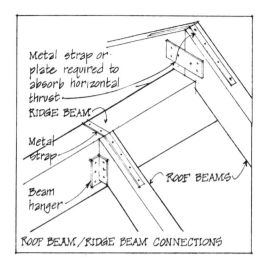

Metal strap or plate required to absorb horizontal thrust. RIDGE BEAM

Metal strap

Beam hanger

ROOF BEAMS

ROOF BEAM / RIDGE BEAM CONNECTIONS

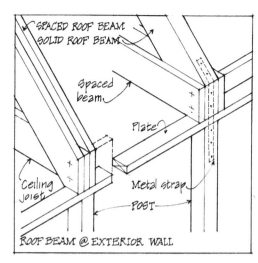

SPACED ROOF BEAM
SOLID ROOF BEAM

Spaced beam

Plate

Ceiling joist

Metal strap

POST

ROOF BEAM @ EXTERIOR WALL

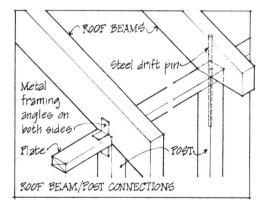

ROOF BEAMS

Steel drift pin

Metal framing angles on both sides

Plate

POST

ROOF BEAM / POST CONNECTIONS

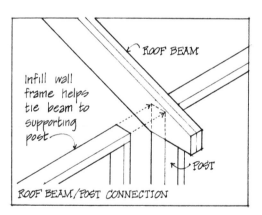

ROOF BEAM

Infill wall frame helps tie beam to supporting post

POST

ROOF BEAM / POST CONNECTION

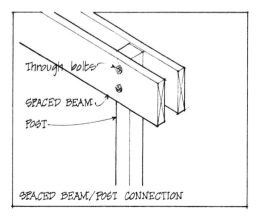

Through bolts

SPACED BEAM

POST

SPACED BEAM / POST CONNECTION

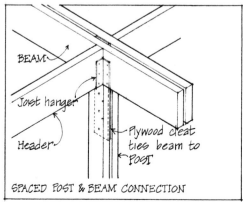

BEAM

Joist hanger

Header

Plywood cleat ties beam to POST

SPACED POST & BEAM CONNECTION

# ROOFING

The roofing material should provide a durable, weather-tight covering that will protect your house, addition and contents from rain, snow and wind. The type of roofing used and the method for its application depend first on the form of the roof structure and its slope. Other factors to consider in the selection of a roofing material are:

1. Initial cost
2. Durability and longevity
3. Wind-resistance
4. Fire-resistance
5. Local climate
6. Code requirements
7. Appearance: color, texture, pattern
8. Compatibility with style of house.

There are three major categories of roofing, each being suitable for use on certain roof slopes. Flat and low-sloping roofs that do not shed rain or melting snow easily require a continuous, waterproof membrane.

Normal and high-pitched roofs that do shed water quickly can be covered with either shingle or sheet roofing materials. The most common types of roofing used in residential construction are asphalt, fiberglass, or wood shingles and shakes. These will be discussed first, followed by an outline of other roofing types you may wish to consider.

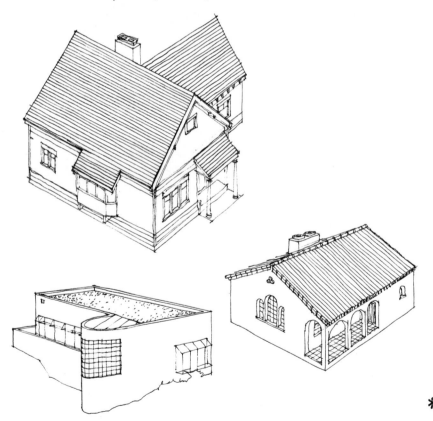

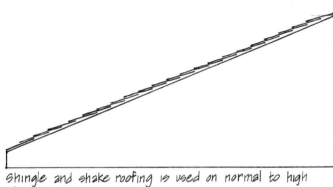

Shingle and shake roofing is used on normal to high slopes.

Roll roofing is used on low slopes.

Built-up or other continuous membrane roofing is used on flat roofs.

\* Cornices at eaves and rakes at gable ends are normally constructed before roofing is laid. For cornice and rake construction, see pgs. 262-263.

## UNDERLAYMENT

Roof underlayment is used on pitched roofs covered with asphalt, asbestos, slate or metal shingles, or with clay or concrete tiles. It protects the roof sheathing from moisture absorption until the roofing is applied, and provides additional protection from wind-driven rain.

Underlayment is not normally required for wood shake roofs except in areas subject to wind-driven snow and where solid sheathing is required. Similarly, underlayment is not required under wood shingle roofing unless protection for solid sheathing is desired.

The underlayment material, usually 15 lb. or 30 lb. asphalt-saturated felt, should have a low water vapor resistance to prevent moisture from accumulating between the underlayment and the sheathing. It should be applied as soon as possible after the roof sheathing is completed. Use only enough staples or nails to hold the underlayment securely in place until the roofing is applied.

The underlayment, 36" wide, is laid in long horizontal rows, perpendicular to the roof slope, to shed water. For single coverage, each row laps over the one below 2". End joints are lapped 4". For double coverage, the rows are lapped 19".

## EAVE FLASHING

For low-sloped roofs, and for all sloped roofs in areas subject to roof ice buildup, eave flashing is required. This flashing consists of two layers of 15 lb. asphalt-saturated felt, solidly cemented together, and extending from the eave up the roof to a point 24" inside the exterior wall line of the house or addition.

For wood shingle and wood shake roofs, this eave flashing should extend 36" inside the exterior wall line.

To help minimize the chance of water backing up and entering the exterior wall, effective ceiling insulation and good attic ventilation are both necessary. (See pg. 284)

Width required for cemented eave flashing (see illustration below)

24"

(36" for wood shake or shingle roofs)

EAVE FLASHING REQUIREMENTS

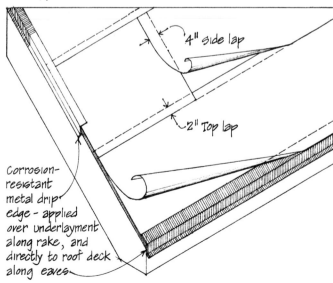

Corrosion-resistant metal drip edge - applied over underlayment along rake, and directly to roof deck along eaves.

4" Side lap

2" Top lap

UNDERLAYMENT FOR NORMAL SLOPE (4:12 and up)
(SINGLE COVERAGE)

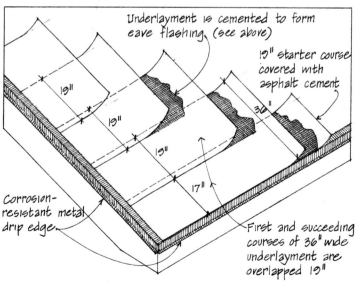

Underlayment is cemented to form eave flashing (see above)

19" starter course covered with asphalt cement

19"

19"

19"

30"

17"

Corrosion-resistant metal drip edge

First and succeeding courses of 36" wide underlayment are overlapped 19"

UNDERLAYMENT FOR LOW SLOPE (2:12 to 4:12)
(DOUBLE COVERAGE)

# ASPHALT & FIBERGLASS SHINGLES

Asphalt shingles are made of asphalt-impregnated organic felts coated with a layer of colored stone or ceramic granules for color and texture. Compared with other roofing materials, asphalt shingles are relatively inexpensive, easy to apply, and can last from 15 to 25 years.

Although individual shingle units are available, strip shingle units (12" x 36"), scored to look like individual shingles, are most commonly used. Since asphalt shingles are relatively thin, they have slim shadowlines. To appear more like wood shingles or slate, some asphalt shingles have thickened butt edges, embossed patterns, and color variations.

Asphalt shingles, having an organic felt base, have a moderate resistance to fire (UL Type Class C). Fiberglass shingles are similar in size, appearance, and application to asphalt shingles, but their inorganic base gives them excellent fire-resistance (UL Type Class A). Fiberglass shingles also have excellent resistance to rot, moisture and curling.

Wind-resistant asphalt shingles have factory-applied, self-sealing adhesive or integral locking tabs. These are used on low-sloping roofs and in areas subject to high winds. Also available are mildew-resistant shingles that are treated with chemicals designed to destroy mildew organisms.

The minimum roof slope for asphalt and fiberglass shingles is 4:12. They can, however, be used on low slopes, 2:12 to 4:12, if they are of the self-sealing type or if they are hand-sealed with roofing cement, and applied over two layers (double-coverage) of underlayment.

The shingles are generally laid with a 5" exposure and a 7" toplap. Before they are laid, all necessary flashing along the eaves and valleys, and at vertical walls, should be installed. In addition, a continuous, corrosion-resistant drip edge should be nailed along the eaves and rakes to protect the edges of the roof deck, and to allow water to drip free of the eave, fascia, or cornice.

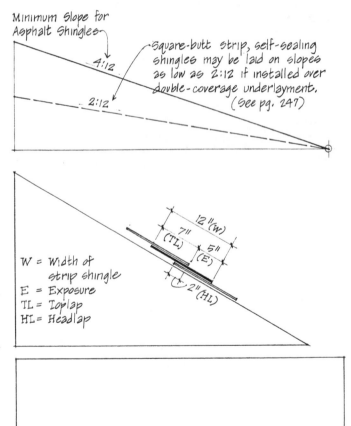

Minimum Slope for Asphalt Shingles

4:12

2:12

Square-butt strip, self-sealing shingles may be laid on slopes as low as 2:12 if installed over double-coverage underlayment. (See pg. 247)

12" (W)
7" (TL)
5" (E)
2" (HL)

W = Width of strip shingle
E = Exposure
TL = Toplap
HL = Headlap

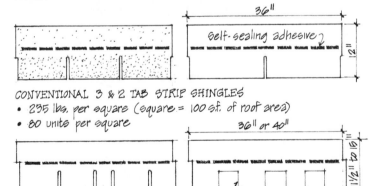

36"

Self-sealing adhesive

12"

CONVENTIONAL 3 & 2 TAB STRIP SHINGLES
- 235 lbs. per square (square = 100 s.f. of roof area)
- 80 units per square

36" or 40"

11 1/2" to 16"

WOOD APPEARANCE STRIP SHINGLES
- Various edge and surface textures
- 250 to 350 lbs/square; 67 to 90 units per square

(Thickness varies)

The flashing for an open valley consists of 90 lb. mineral-surfaced asphalt roll roofing laid as follows. An 18" wide strip is first laid face (mineral surface) down, and nailed (1" in from each edge) only enough to hold it in place. A second layer, 36" wide, is then laid and nailed face up. When splices are necessary, lap the strips 12" and secure with plastic asphalt cement.

The open valley should be 6" wide at the top and increase in width at the rate of 1/8" per foot downward to the eave. Chalklines should be snapped along each side of the valley to serve as a guide for trimming the shingles as they meet the valley. After each shingle is trimmed, the upper corner is cut at a 45° angle and cemented to the valley lining to help direct water into the valley.

Closed valleys, often used in reroofing work, are flashed with a 36" wide strip of 55 lb. roll roofing. Over this lining, strip shingles are woven, with each strip extending at least 12" beyond the centerline of the valley.

Where a rake meets a vertical wall, stepped corrosion-resistant metal flashing, 6" long and 2" wider than the shingle exposure, is bent so that it extends 2" onto the roof underlayment. The remaining portion extends up the wall and is secured with a nail in the top corner. The finish siding will be installed over the flashing.

Where a roof rises to meet a vertical wall, base flashing of a similar material is turned up, over the wall sheathing, at least 4". The finish siding then serves as a cap flashing over the base flashing.

For flashing stack vents, corrosion-resistant metal sleeves are available with adjustable flanges to fit the roof slope. After the shingles are laid to the face of the stack, the sleeve is fitted over the stack and its top turned into the pipe opening. The flange rests on the shingles below the stack, and shingles are laid over the flange above the stack.

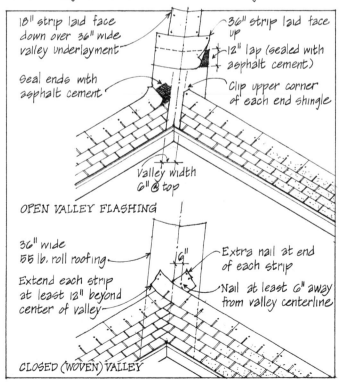

18" strip laid face down over 36" wide valley underlayment

36" strip laid face up

12" lap (sealed with asphalt cement)

Seal ends with asphalt cement

Clip upper corner of each end shingle

Valley width 6" @ top

OPEN VALLEY FLASHING

36" wide 55 lb. roll roofing

6"

Extra nail at end of each strip

Extend each strip at least 12" beyond center of valley

Nail at least 6" away from valley centerline

CLOSED (WOVEN) VALLEY

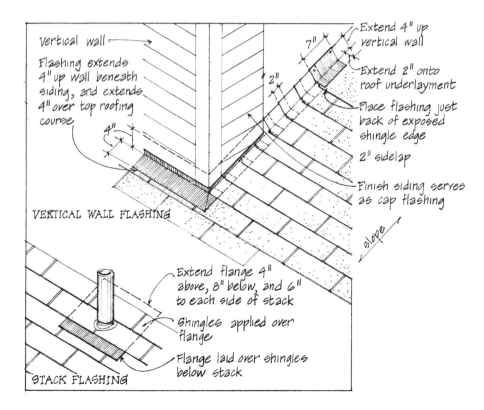

Vertical wall

Flashing extends 4" up wall beneath siding, and extends 4" over top roofing course

4"

Extend 4" up vertical wall

7"

2"

Extend 2" onto roof underlayment

Place flashing just back of exposed shingle edge

2" sidelap

Finish siding serves as cap flashing

VERTICAL WALL FLASHING

slope

Extend flange 4" above, 8" below and 6" to each side of stack

Shingles applied over flange

Flange laid over shingles below stack

STACK FLASHING

## ASPHALT SHINGLES

The starter course is a row of strip shingles laid with their tabs facing upward over the eave flashing strip. This starter course closes the gaps of the cutouts in the first row of shingles. Nails should be spaced so that they are not exposed at the cutouts of the first course.

The first course is laid directly over the starter course. For a roof where both rakes are visible, start at the center of the roof and work outward. For roof surfaces that are broken, start at the rake.

Each shingle strip receives four nails, driven about a ½" above the cutouts. Use galvanized, aluminum, or other corrosion-resistant nails with threaded shanks and large heads. They should be 1¼" long when nailing into 1" boards, or ⅞" long when nailing into ⅜" plywood. When reroofing over asphalt or wood shingles, use nails 1½" to 1¾" long.

Succeeding courses are laid so that 5" of each row is exposed. Use chalklines at 5" o.c. as a guide to lay the courses. The rows can have the pattern of tabs offset at either their third (4" offset) or their half (6" offset) points.

The ridge can be covered with individual 10" shingles or shingles cut from strip units. Start at the end opposite of the prevailing wind. Nail each piece about 1" in from each edge and, for a 5" exposure, about 5½" back from the exposed end.

Hips are covered in a similar manner, starting at the bottom of the hip and working upward.

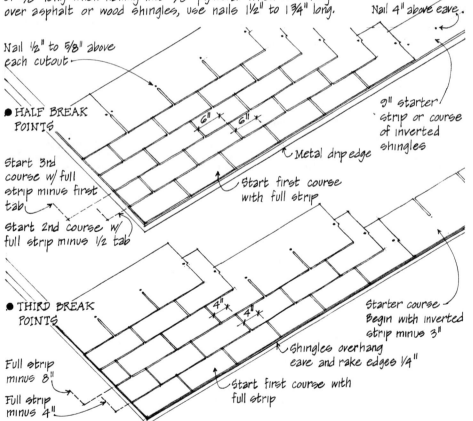

Nail ½" to ⅝" above each cutout

● HALF BREAK POINTS

Start 3rd course w/ full strip minus first tab

Start 2nd course w/ full strip minus ½ tab

● THIRD BREAK POINTS

Full strip minus 8"

Full strip minus 4"

Nail 4" above eave.

9" starter strip or course of inverted shingles

Metal drip edge

Start first course with full strip

Starter course Begin with inverted strip minus 3"

Shingles overhang eave and rake edges ¼"

Start first course with full strip

APPLICATION OF SQUARE BUTT STRIP SHINGLES

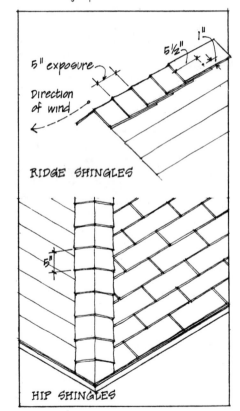

5" exposure

Direction of wind

5½"  1"

RIDGE SHINGLES

5"

HIP SHINGLES

# REROOFING

A new asphalt shingle roof can be laid over an existing wood or asphalt shingle roof if the existing roof structure and sheathing are sound.

The existing roofing should be inspected carefully. To prepare an existing wood shingle roof, remove all loose or protruding nails, and renail the shingles in a new location. Split and nail down shingles that are warped; nail down loose shingles; replace missing ones. Add beveled wood strips along the butts of each course to provide a smoother surface for the new shingles. If the eave and rake shingles are badly weathered, cut back and remove them, and install 1"×6" boards.

To prepare an existing asphalt shingle roof, nail down any loose or curled shingles. Reset any nails that have popped. Replace any missing shingles.

The procedure for applying the new shingles is similar to that described on the previous page. The starter course for an existing asphalt shingle roof, however, is trimmed to a strip that is as wide as the exposure of the existing first course. The first course is then laid in the normal fashion. The second course overlaps the first and leaves a 3" exposure. Succeeding courses then have the normal 5" exposure.

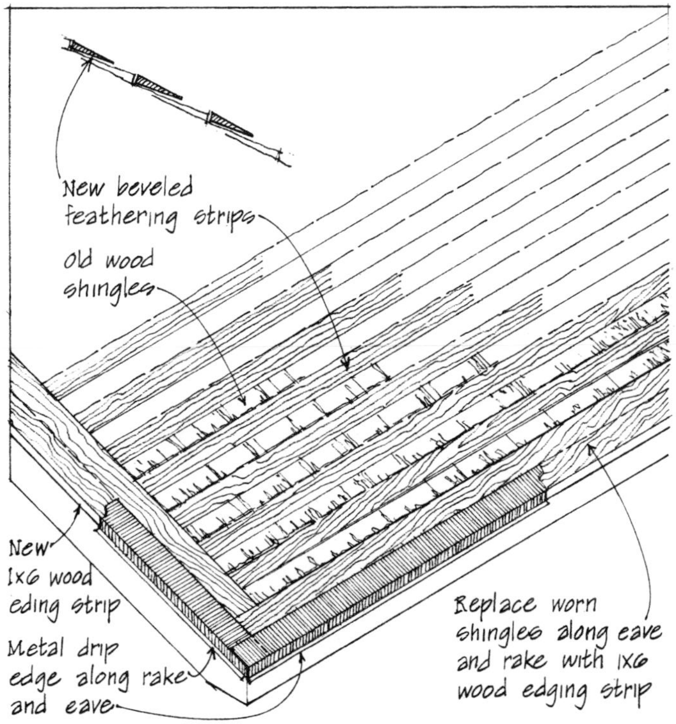

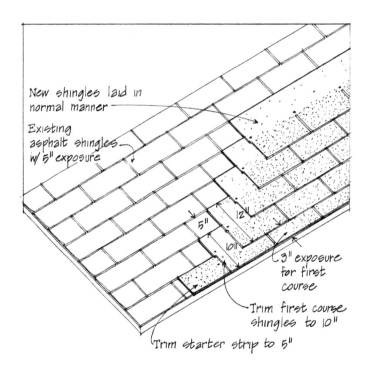

New beveled feathering strips

Old wood shingles

New 1x6 wood edging strip

Metal drip edge along rake and eave

Replace worn shingles along eave and rake with 1x6 wood edging strip

PREPARATION OF EXISTING WOOD SHINGLE ROOF

New shingles laid in normal manner

Existing asphalt shingles w/ 5" exposure

12"

5"

10"

3" exposure for first course

Trim first course shingles to 10"

Trim starter strip to 5"

APPLICATION OVER EXISTING ASPHALT SHINGLES

## WOOD SHINGLES & SHAKES

Wood shingles and wood shakes provide a warm, attractive, textured roof finish. They are normally red cedar, although white cedar, redwood and cypress shingles may be available. They are characterized by fine grain, a low ratio of expansion and contraction with changes in moisture content, and a natural resistance to water and rot.

Wood shingles have an expected life of 15 to 25 years, while wood shakes may last 25 to 50 years. A preservative treatment should be applied every 5 to 7 years to obtain the maximum life of a wood roof. When installed on slopes 4:12 and steeper, the shingles and shakes have good wind resistance.

Wood shingles and shakes are flammable unless chemically treated to receive a UL Type Class C rating. A Class B rating may be possible if Class C shingles or shakes are applied over solid 5/8" plywood (with exterior glue) sheathing, with a layer of plastic-coated steel foil and underlayment of asbestos felt. The interlayment required for wood shakes should also be of asbestos felt.

Wood shingles are available in 16", 18" and 24" lengths and in the following grades:

№ 1 Premium Grade: All edge grain, 100% heartwood, 100% clear, (Blue Label).
№ 2 Good Grade: 10" clear on 16" shingles, 11" clear on 18" shingles, 16" clear on 24" shingles, (Red Label).
№ 3 Utility Grade: 6" clear on 16" and 18" shingles, 10" clear on 24" shingles, (Black Label).

№ 1 grade wood shingles are normally used for roofs, while № 2 grade shingles may be used for sidewall applications.

While wood shingles are sawn, wood shakes are split, resulting in at least one highly-textured side. Shakes are 100% clear, heartwood, and come in 18" and 24" lengths. Tapersplit and straightsplit shakes have 100% edge grain, while handsplit-and-resawn shakes have at least 90% edge grain.

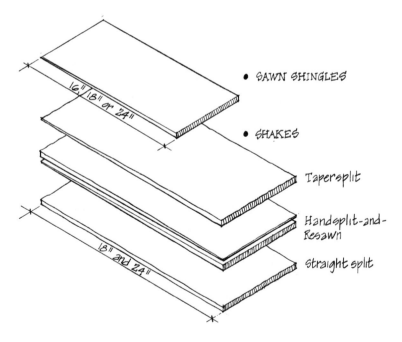

- SAWN SHINGLES — 16", 18" or 24"
- SHAKES — 18" and 24"
  - Tapersplit
  - Handsplit-and-Resawn
  - Straight split

MAXIMUM EXPOSURE FOR WOOD SHINGLES & SHAKES

| Shingle Length/Grade | | Roof Slope | |
|---|---|---|---|
| | | 4:12 & steeper | 3:12 to 4:12 |
| 16" | № 1 | 5" | 3 3/4" |
| | № 2 | 4" | 3 1/2" |
| 18" | № 1 | 5 1/2" | 4 1/4" |
| | № 2 | 4 1/2" | 4" |
| 24" | № 1 | 7 1/2" | 5 3/4" |
| | № 2 | 6 1/2" | 5 1/2" |
| Shakes | | | |
| 18" | | 7 1/2" | Not recommended |
| 24" | | 10" * | " " |

* 7 1/2" for resawn handsplit shakes on slopes 4:12 to 8:12.

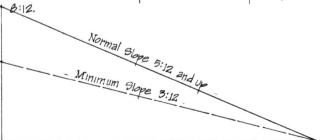

Normal Slope 5:12 and up
Minimum Slope 3:12

## WOOD SHINGLES

Wood shingles are normally laid over open sheathing of 1" x 3" or 1" x 4" boards to provide ventilation for the shingles, particularly in areas of high humidity. These boards are spaced at the same distance on center as the shingles' exposure to weather, but the spaces between the boards should not be greater than the width of the boards. No underlayment is required except for eave flashing requirements.

Solid sheathing with a layer of №15 felt underlayment may be desirable for added insulation and to minimize air infiltration, and in areas subject to blizzard conditions.

Flashing at valleys should consist of minimum 26 gauge corrosion-resistant sheet metal. In cold climates, the flashing should be laid over underlayment. The metal sheet should extend at least 10" to either side of the valley centerline. Where necessary, overlaps should be not less than 4". As a precaution against water splashing down the valley and under the shingles, a center crimp is often used along with edge crimps. The open portion of the valley should be 4" wide.

Valley shingles should be cut from wide pieces and laid first. Shingles are then laid in a direction away from valleys.

The first course of shingles is doubled and extended beyond the eave line about 1½" to form a drip. Similarly, the shingles extend about ¾" beyond rakes. Metal drip edging, therefore, is not necessary.

Allow ¼" to ⅜" between shingles for expansion when wet. Offset joints at least 1½" from joints in adjacent courses. Avoid aligning joints in every other course.

Use corrosion-resistant nails, such as hot-dipped galvanized steel or aluminum, with threaded shanks. Use 3d nails for 16" and 18" shingles and 4d nails for 24" lengths. Each shingle should be fastened with two nails only, ¾" from the edges and about 1" above the butt line of the next course.

Ridges and hips are covered with pre-formed factory-built units or with site-applied shingles. Shingles of uniform width, 4" to 5", are laid with an alternating overlap. Ridges and hips have their first courses doubled, and have the same exposure as the rest of the roof. Use nails 2 sizes larger than the normal nails.

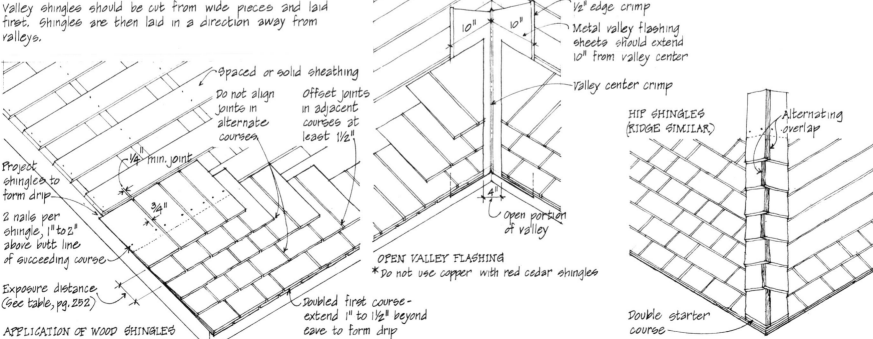

**APPLICATION OF WOOD SHINGLES**

- Spaced or solid sheathing
- Do not align joints in alternate courses
- Offset joints in adjacent courses at least 1½"
- ¼" min. joint
- ¾"
- Project shingles to form drip
- 2 nails per shingle, 1" to 2" above butt line of succeeding course
- Exposure distance (See table, pg. 252)
- Doubled first course - extend 1" to 1½" beyond eave to form drip

- 10" 10"
- ½" edge crimp
- Metal valley flashing sheets should extend 10" from valley center
- Valley center crimp
- 4"
- open portion of valley

**OPEN VALLEY FLASHING**
*Do not use copper with red cedar shingles

HIP SHINGLES (RIDGE SIMILAR)
- Alternating overlap
- Double starter course

## WOOD SHAKES

Wood shakes may be laid over open or closed sheathing. Open sheathing consists of 1" x 4" or 1" x 6" boards spaced the same distance on center as the shakes are exposed to weather, but not more than 10". In areas subject to wind-driven snow, solid sheathing is recommended along with eave flashing.

Valley flashing for wood shake roofs is similar to that required for wood shingle roofs except that the sheet metal, laid over a № 30 asphalt saturated felt underlayment strip, should extend at least 11" to either side of the valley centerline.

Valley shakes are cut to fit and provide a 6" wide gutter. Closed valleys are possible if a 1" x 6" is laid under the valley underlayment, and individual undercourses of sheet metal flashing installed with a 2" headlap and extending 10" under the shakes on each side of the saddle.

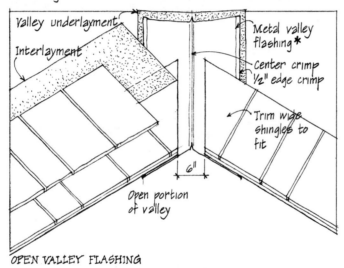

OPEN VALLEY FLASHING

\* Copper flashing should not be used with red cedar. The copper may deteriorate prematurely when in contact with the wood in the presence of moisture.

Because of their rough texture, shakes are laid with interlayment between each course. The interlayment, 18" wide strips of № 30 asphalt saturated felt, serves as a baffle against the infiltration of wind-driven rain or snow.

A 36" wide starter strip of № 30 felt is first laid over the sheathing (except when eave flashing is already required). The first course is doubled and extended beyond the eave line 1½" to form a drip. Shakes along rakes extend about 1".

After each course is laid, an interlayment strip is applied over the top portion of the shakes. The bottom edge of the strip is placed above the butt line a distance equal to twice the shakes' exposure. Allow ¼" to ⅜" space between the shakes for expansion. Offset joints at least 1½" from joints in adjacent courses.

Use corrosion resistant nails, such as hot-dipped galvanized steel, with threaded shanks. Use 5d nails for shakes with ½" to ¾" butts, and 6d nails for ¾" to 1¼" butt thicknesses. Nail each shake with two nails only, about 1" from each edge and 2" above the exposure line. Nails should be driven flush with the surface of the shake without crushing the wood.

Ridge and hip shakes should be applied over a 12" wide strip of № 30 felt, with a doubled first course and the same exposure as the rest of the roof. Uniform 6" widths are laid with an alternating overlap. Use nails two sizes larger than the normal required.

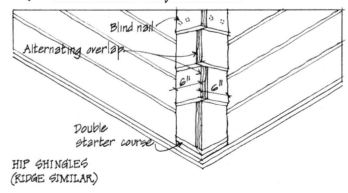

HIP SHINGLES
(RIDGE SIMILAR)

# REROOFING

Wood shingles and shakes can be laid over an existing wood or asphalt shingle roof. To prepare the existing roof, the old shingles are cut back along the eaves and rakes to allow a 1"x 6" strip to be nailed directly to the sheathing. A thinner board may be necessary where application is over an asphalt shingle roof. The new wood strips along the roof perimeter should be cedar, redwood, or wood that is pressure-treated to resist rot and decay.

Old ridge shingles are removed and replaced with bevel siding, with the butt edges overlapping at the peak.

If new flashing is necessary at valleys, use 1"x lumber to separate the new flashing from the old.

Once the existing roof is prepared, the wood shingles or shakes are applied as in new construction. The nails used should be long enough to penetrate into the underlying sheathing.

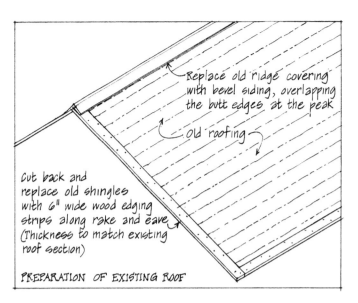

Replace old ridge covering with bevel siding, overlapping the butt edges at the peak

Old roofing

Cut back and replace old shingles with 6" wide wood edging strips along rake and eave (Thickness to match existing roof section)

PREPARATION OF EXISTING ROOF

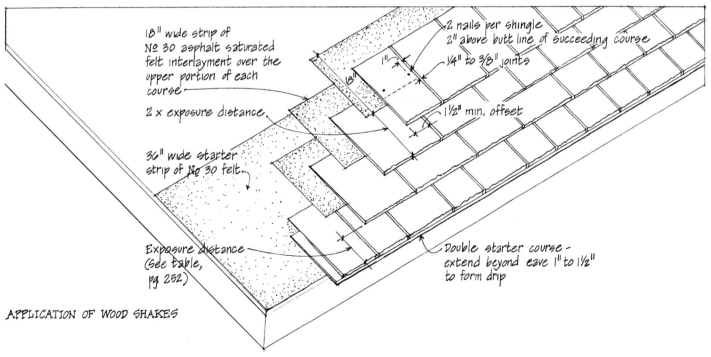

18" wide strip of No 30 asphalt saturated felt interlayment over the upper portion of each course

2 x exposure distance.

36" wide starter strip of No 30 felt.

2 nails per shingle 2" above butt line of succeeding course

¼" to 3/8" joints

1½" min. offset

18"

1"

Exposure distance (See table, pg 252)

Double starter course - extend beyond eave 1" to 1½" to form drip

APPLICATION OF WOOD SHAKES

## OTHER ROOFING TYPES

Less commonly used than asphalt or wood shingles are slate, tile, and various types of metal roofing. They are generally more expensive, but often have greater durability. They all have excellent fire-resistance ratings when properly applied, and on properly sloped roofs, they resist wind forces well.

These roofing materials require special installation techniques. Follow the manufacturer's specifications for sheathing, underlayment, and fastenings.

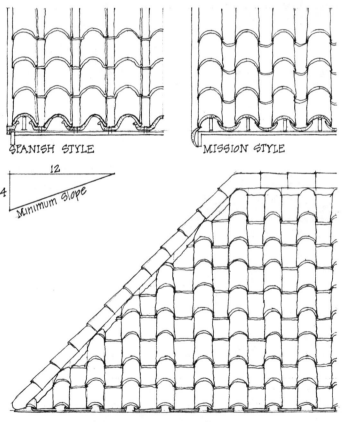

SPANISH STYLE          MISSION STYLE

CLAY TILE ROOFING (ROMAN STYLE)

## SLATE & TILE

Slate is an attractive, extremely durable, fireproof, and low maintenance roofing material. It can last up to a hundred years if good quality materials are used. Individual pieces, however, are susceptible to breakage from falling tree limbs.

Slate is applied similarly to wood shingles, but over solid sheathing and an underlayment of № 30 roofing felt. The individual shingles are usually predrilled for copper nails.

Tile roofing consists of clay or concrete units. These units may be flat shingles, or have barrel mission or Spanish style shapes. Like slate, tile roofing is durable, fire-resistant, and requires little maintenance.

Roofing tiles require careful laying over solid sheathing with a good quality № 30 or № 40 felt underlayment. Special tile units are used at ridges, hips, and gable ends.

Both slate and tile are heavy, weighing from 700 to 1600 lbs. per square (100 s.f.). They therefore require stronger roof framing to support the additional dead load.

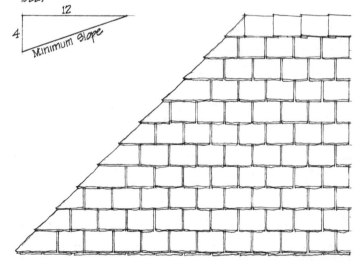

SLATE ROOFING

## MINERAL FIBER SHINGLES

Mineral fiber shingles are made of cement reinforced with asbestos fibers, and are highly fire-resistant. Their texture may resemble that of slate or wood shakes.

In addition to the rectangular shingle shape of slate, other shapes have been developed to decrease the amount of material required to cover a given area. These include diamond, hexagonal, and Dutch lap shingles.

The individual shingles are predrilled for nailing. Because the shingles have only a small overlap, storm anchors or clips are also used to hold the exposed edges of the shingles down. To simplify the application of the shingles, eave starter strips, hip and ridge shingles, and ridge rolls are prefabricated.

A special cutter is available to cut the shingles or to punch holes where extra holes are needed.

## METAL ROOFING

Metal roofing, of aluminum, steel or copper, is available in shingle form, flat sheets or panels, and in corrugated sheets.

Aluminum is the lightest and the least expensive of the metal roofings. They may have pre-painted or porcelain enamel finishes. To avoid the electrolytic action that can deteriorate it, aluminum should not be installed in contact with other metals.

Steel roofing can be galvanized or stainless steel, or be coated with terne (a tin-lead alloy) or copper.

Metal shingles are formed to look like wood shingles or tile roofing units. Seamed metal roofing is distinguished by the pattern of strong vertical lines created by the interlocking seams between the sheets. Both metal shingle and sheet roofing require a solid deck. Corrugated metal roofing, because of its structural cross-sectional shape, can span up to 3' between rafters and purlins.

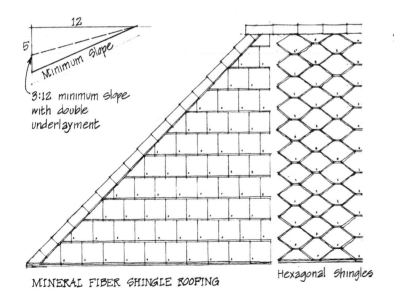

12
5
Minimum Slope

3:12 minimum slope with double underlayment

MINERAL FIBER SHINGLE ROOFING

Hexagonal Shingles

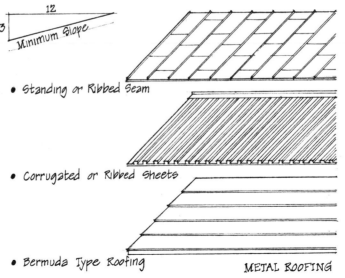

12
3
Minimum Slope

• Standing or Ribbed Seam

• Corrugated or Ribbed Sheets

• Bermuda Type Roofing

METAL ROOFING

Because flat and low-pitched roofs do not shed rain and melting snow easily, they require a continuous, waterproof roofing material. There are newly developed materials that form a virtually continuous, single-ply, flexible membrane, such as polyvinyl-chloride (PVC) or chlorinated polyethylene (CPE). These are laid loosely, seamed into a single piece, and fastened only at the roof edges and at roof interruptions. Another roof coating, neoprene hypalon, is applied in liquid form. It air-cures to form an elastomeric film.

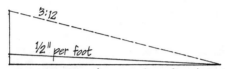

Maximum slope for gravel-surfaced built-up roofing is ½" per foot. With special asphalt, slopes up to 3:12 are possible.

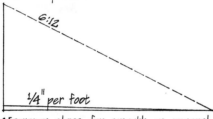

Maximum slope for smooth or mineral-surfaced built-up roofing is 6" per foot. Minimum slope is ¼" per foot.

# BUILT-UP ROOFING

The most common type of membrane roofing is the built-up roof. It consists of alternating layers of roofing felt and bitumen, and a final surface coating of bitumen and gravel embedded in the bitumen. Excellent fire-resistance is possible (UL Type Class A) depending on the type of deck, insulation, slope, number of plies, and surface material used.

The roofing felt provides support for the bitumen that keeps the felt watertight. The first layer of felt is laid dry to prevent the asphalt or tar from entering the roof spaces. Subsequent layers of felt are then laid and mopped with hot bitumen. The final coat of bitumen is covered with roofing gravel.

This type of built-up roofing may have 2, 3, or 4 plies, but for convenience, the roofing is often referred to as 10, 15, or 20 year roofs, depending on the method of application and the warranty period.

A vapor barrier is required in cold or humid climates to prevent condensation from collecting under the built-up roof and blistering the membrane. The roof spaces should also be vented to allow any moisture-laden air to escape to the outside.

The installation and application of a built-up roof is not easily done by the homeowner. This job should be sub-contracted to a licensed, bonded roofer.

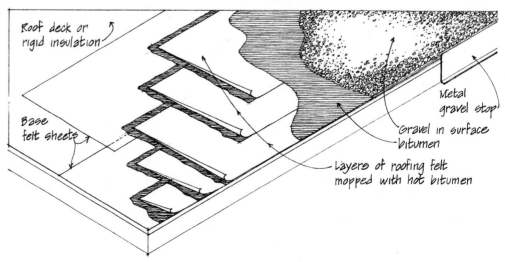

Roof deck or rigid insulation

Base felt sheets

Metal gravel stop

Gravel in surface bitumen

Layers of roofing felt mopped with hot bitumen

## ROLL ROOFING

Roll roofing is an asphalt roofing product that is suitable for application over low-sloping roofs. It is made by adding a coating of weather-resistant asphalt to asphalt-saturated felt. Some types have a smooth black surface, while others are surfaced with mineral granules (similar to asphalt shingles) for color, texture and protection of the roof surface.

The roofing material comes in 36" wide rolls (36' long), and typically carries a UL Type Class C fire-rating. Fiberglass-based roll roofing has a Class-A fire-rating.

Single-coverage applications of roll roofing are not as durable as other roofing materials. For greater durability, double-coverage application of fiberglass-based roll roofing is recommended.

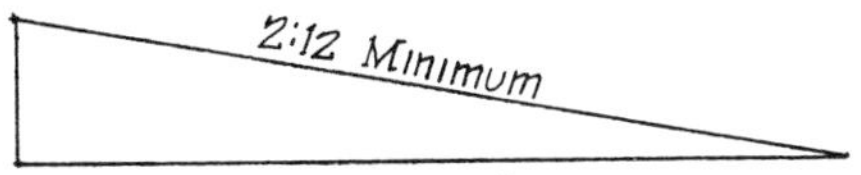

2:12 Minimum

Slope Limit for Single Coverage

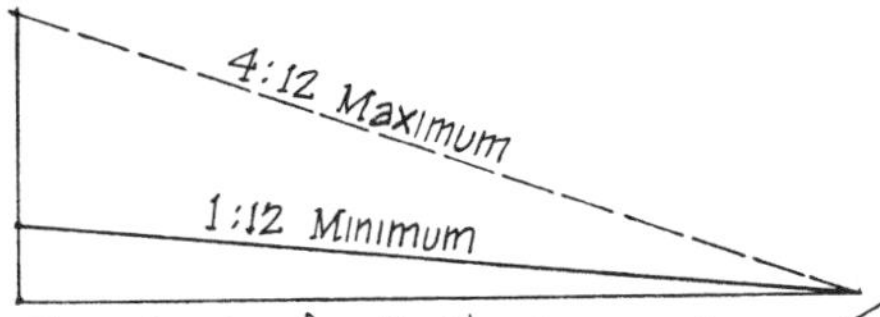

4:12 Maximum

1:12 Minimum

Slope Limits for Double Coverage

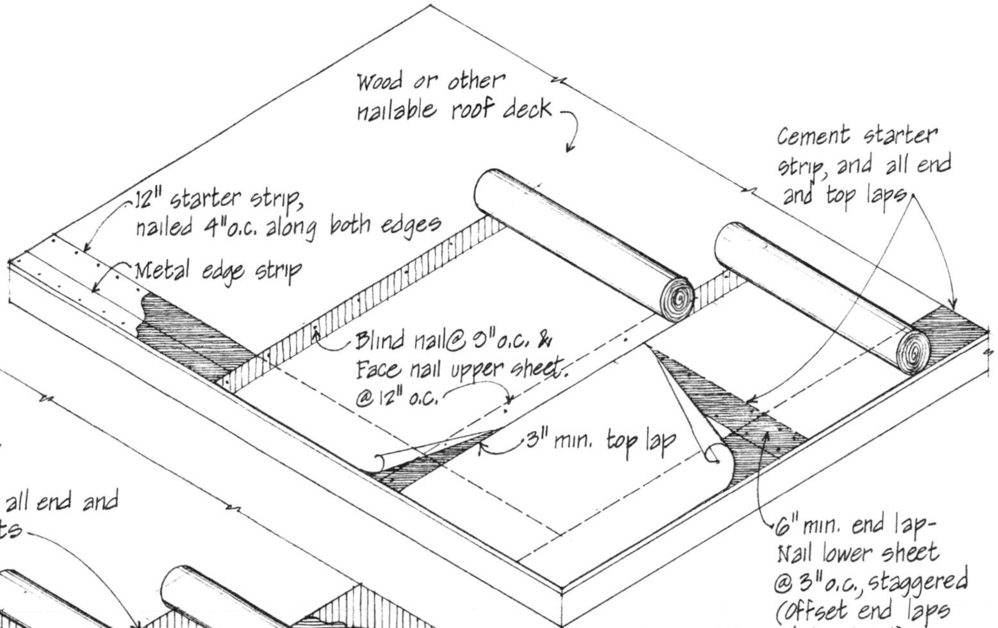

Wood or other nailable roof deck

12" starter strip, nailed 4" o.c. along both edges

Metal edge strip

Cement starter strip, and all end and top laps

Blind nail @ 5" o.c. & Face nail upper sheet. @ 12" o.c.

3" min. top lap

6" min. end lap- Nail lower sheet @ 3" o.c., staggered (offset end laps at least 3')

SINGLE COVERAGE

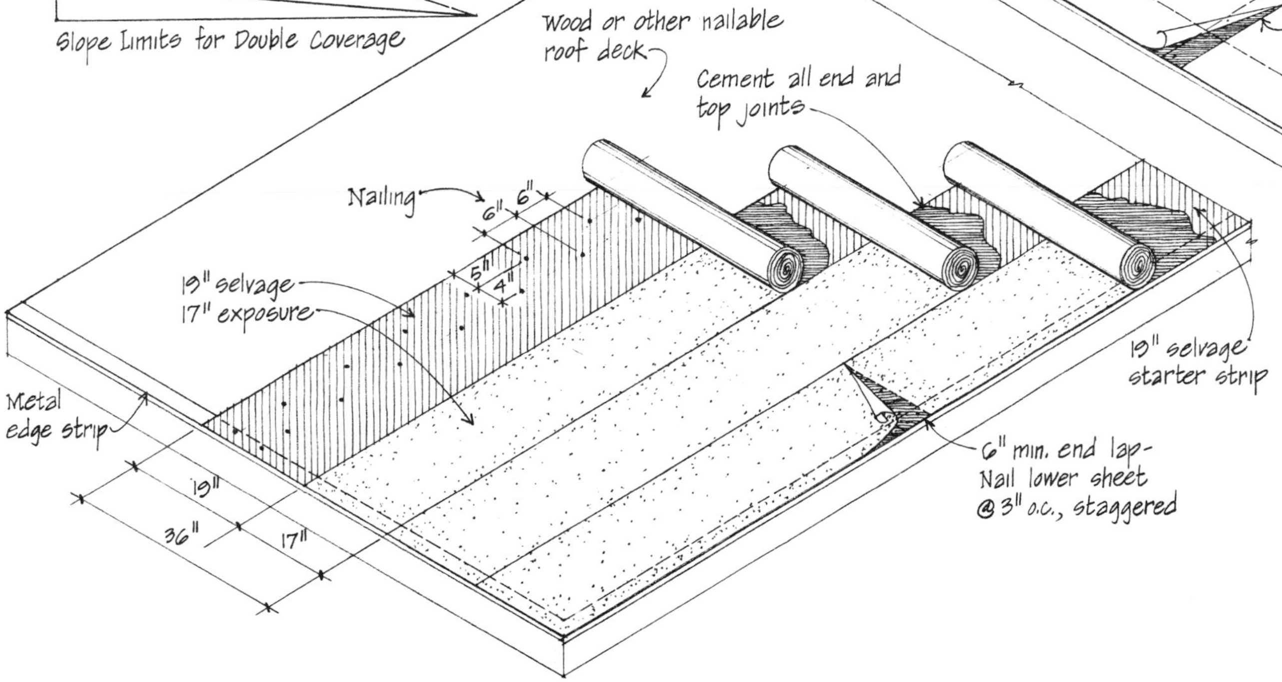

Wood or other nailable roof deck

Cement all end and top joints

Nailing

6" 6"

5" 4"

19" selvage
17" exposure

Metal edge strip

19"

36"   17"

19" selvage starter strip

6" min. end lap- Nail lower sheet @ 3" o.c., staggered

DOUBLE COVERAGE APPLICATION

259

# GUTTERS & DOWNSPOUTS

Rainwater shed from a roof should be caught by gutters at the eaveline and channeled to downspouts that will discharge the water into a drain tile system, drywell, or a storm sewer. This roof drainage system is important in preventing soil erosion around the house, and more importantly, minimizing the chance of water leaking through foundation walls into basement and crawl spaces.

In dry climates, and for small roof areas, gutters and downspouts may be omitted. Rain can fall freely off the roof onto masonry or gravel strips set in the ground under the eaveline.

Older houses may have wood gutters. If in sound condition, they should be sanded down to bare wood, and a coat of linseed oil applied. After this is dry, apply two coats of roofing cement.

To maintain existing metal gutters, first clean them of any debris. Scrape and wire brush any rusted areas, and apply a thin coat of roofing cement or asphalt-aluminum paint. Check for low spots, and re-align as necessary. If missing, install wire-cage strainers at downspouts. To protect the gutters from falling leaves, install a vinyl-coated screen over the gutters.

New gutters may be of aluminum, galvanized steel, or vinyl. Aluminum is the most popular metal gutter. It is lightweight, only moderately expensive, corrosion-resistant, and fairly longlasting. Aluminum gutters may have enamel or plastic-clad finishes. They can be bought in sections or be cold-formed on site to eliminate joints in long runs.

Galvanized steel gutters are less expensive than aluminum, but require periodic maintenance.

Vinyl gutters are sturdy, durable, and will not rust or rot. Although they are more expensive than aluminum gutters, they often carry a lifetime guarantee.

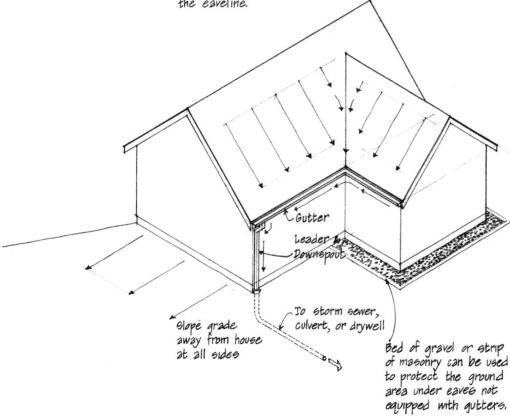

Gutter

Leader & Downspout

Slope grade away from house at all sides

To storm sewer, culvert, or drywell

Bed of gravel or strip of masonry can be used to protect the ground area under eaves not equipped with gutters.

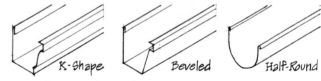

K-Shape — Beveled — Half-Round

TYPICAL GUTTER SHAPES

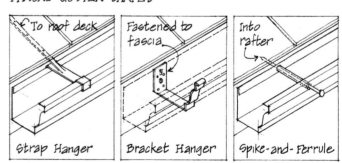

To roof deck — Strap Hanger

Fastened to fascia — Bracket Hanger

Into rafter — Spike-and-Ferrule

TYPES OF GUTTER HANGERS

Metal and vinyl gutters may have half-round or pre-formed shapes, and are available in 4", 5", and 6" widths. They are hung from the roof edge or fascia with strap hangers, brackets, or spike-and-ferrule hangers. Of these, the spike-and-ferrule hangers are the easiest to use, but they are also the weakest, and may not hold up well under ice and snow loads.

The hangers should be spaced 24" to 32" o.c. Where ice and snow loads are heavy, space the hangers 18" apart.

The gutters should be hung away from the fascia so that any water backing up will have a chance to drip over the back edge rather than work into the roof structure. In heavy snow areas, the gutter should also be placed below the slope line so that snow and ice can slide clear.

Gutters should be installed in a straight line and slope toward the downspouts, dropping an 1" in 16'. Expansion joints should be installed on straight runs over 40' long, or on straight runs that have corners at both ends. All other slip or locked joints should be caulked or otherwise sealed.

Downspouts may be circular or rectangular. They are usually corrugated for added stiffness and strength. Elbows and a leader connects the gutter to a downspout. The downspout is fastened with either hooks or straps every 6', and terminates with an elbow and a splash-block. It can also terminate in a terra cotta fitting that leads to an underground drain tile system or a drywell.

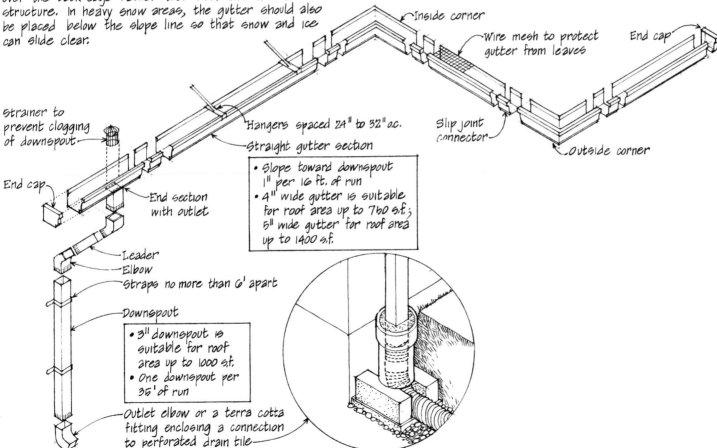

Inside corner

Wire mesh to protect gutter from leaves

End cap

Strainer to prevent clogging of downspout

Hangers spaced 24" to 32" o.c.

Straight gutter section

Slip joint connector

Outside corner

End cap

End section with outlet

• Slope toward downspout 1" per 16 ft. of run
• 4" wide gutter is suitable for roof area up to 760 s.f.; 5" wide gutter for roof area up to 1400 s.f.

Leader
Elbow
Straps no more than 6' apart

Downspout

• 3" downspout is suitable for roof area up to 1000 s.f.
• One downspout per 35' of run

Outlet elbow or a terra cotta fitting enclosing a connection to perforated drain tile

## EXTERIOR TRIM

Exterior trim is required to close off and seal openings in a house exterior not covered by exterior siding or roofing. This trim includes the finish woodwork around windows, exterior doorways, and the cornice and rake construction along the roof edge.

The material used for exterior trim should have good working and painting qualities, and be free of warp. Because these trim pieces are exposed to the weather, they should also have good weathering qualities. For their natural resistance to decay, the heartwood of cedar and redwood are often used. Less durable species can be treated to make them decay resistant.

The exterior trim around windows and exterior doorways is usually applied before exterior siding; cornice construction is usually built before the roofing is laid. As with exterior siding, corrosion-resistant nails should be used.

## CORNICES

The cornice is the roof projection at the eaveline that forms the connection between the roof and the exterior wall of the house. Cornice construction may have the following forms: boxed, open, or closed.

Box cornice construction is the most common method of closing off the roof edge. It can be narrow or wide, depending on the amount of overhang desired. With narrow box cornices, the projecting rafters are cut to provide a nailing surface for the soffit, fascia board and trim. If narrow enough, the soffit can be a single board. The fascia board extends below the soffit about an inch to form a drip edge. A frieze board is often used to terminate the siding at the top of the wall.

A wide box cornice requires additional members to support the wider soffit. These lookout members are toenailed to a wall ledger and facenailed to the projecting rafters. The soffit may be several tongue-and-groove boards or be cut from plywood. A 2"x header ties the rafter ends together and provides a nailing area for the fascia and soffit edge. For a sloping soffit, the lookout members are eliminated and the soffit material nailed directly to the underside of the projecting rafters.

Open cornices leave the projecting rafters exposed. The spaces between the rafters are sealed at the exterior wall line with frieze boards. The ends of the rafters may be exposed or finished with a fascia board. Since the rafter ends and the underside of the roof decking are exposed, they should be clear, exterior-grade materials, of good quality.

Closed cornices have very little, if any, projection beyond the exterior walls. The roof edge is terminated simply with a fascia, crown molding, or frieze board.

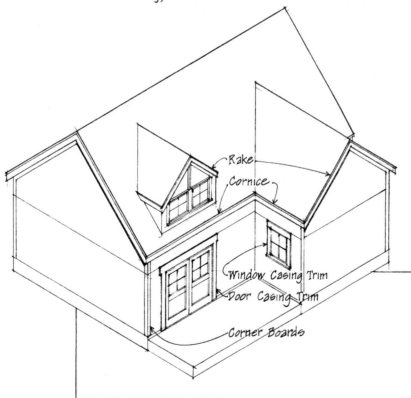

Rake

Cornice

Window Casing Trim

Door Casing Trim

Corner Boards

TYPES OF EXTERIOR TRIM

✱ For window & door trim, see pgs. 76 & 87

The rake section is the projection of a gable roof beyond the end walls of a house. As with cornice construction, a rake section may be closed, or be a boxed or open extension of the roof.

A closed rake section may be used with closed or narrow box cornices. It continues the same detail that occurs along the eave. If a small projection is desired, a continuous 2"x fascia block can be used, to which the fascia trim or crown molding is nailed.

For small projections, short lookout members can be used perpendicular to the last rafter to support the soffit and fascia. For moderate projections, up to 18", the roof sheathing extends from the inner rafters out to a fly rafter, with additional support being provided by the lookout members. For greater projections, lookout rafters should be used that span from an inner, doubled rafter to the fly rafter, over the gable end wall. (See pg. 231)

Box cornices usually have their fascias carried around the corner to form cornice returns. The rake section at a gable end then is brought down to meet the eave cornice at these points. A box cornice with a sloping soffit can simply be carried around to the gable end rake section without a cornice return.

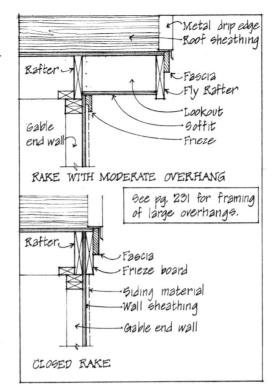

RAKE WITH MODERATE OVERHANG

See pg. 231 for framing of large overhangs.

CLOSED RAKE

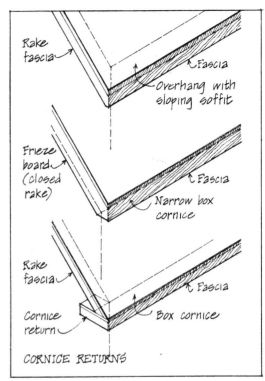

CORNICE RETURNS

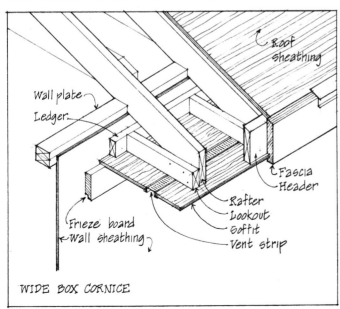

WIDE BOX CORNICE

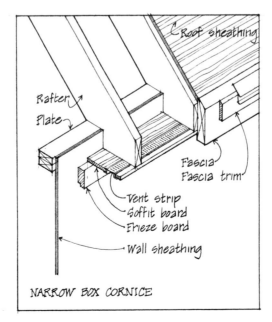

NARROW BOX CORNICE

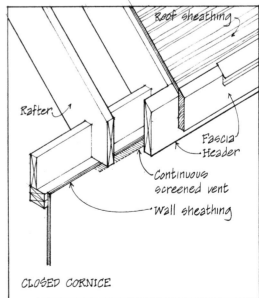

CLOSED CORNICE

## WOOD SIDING & SHINGLES

The materials used to cover and finish exterior walls should be weather-resistant, durable, and as maintenance free as possible. They should be able to withstand the wetting of rain, the drying heat of the sun, and the effects of wind. Together with the exterior wall framing and sheathing, exterior wall coverings should provide a weathertight seal for a house.

Wood remains the most popular material for covering exterior walls, and offers the widest range of styles, textures and finishes. Wood siding may be horizontally lapped, or laid vertically with shiplap joints or batten strips. Wood shingles can be laid over open or closed sheathing. Wood panels of plywood or hardboard can combine the appearance of board siding with faster installation time and a tighter seal.

Qualities to look for in a wood siding material include freedom from warp, easy workability, and a good grain for staining or painting finishes. For natural resistance to moisture, decay and insects, the heartwood of cedar and redwood is often used. These woods can be sealed for a natural appearance, stained, or left unpainted to weather to a natural grey.

Other woods that can be used for exterior siding include white pine, cypress, hemlock, ponderosa pine and spruce. For a painted finish, these woods should be high-grade lumber, free of knots, pitch-pockets, and irregular edges. To minimize movement due to changes in moisture content, vertical or edge grain lumber is preferred.

Some wood siding is available factory-stained or painted. Others may be pre-sealed for a natural appearance. Still others are available already primed for painting.

The color, texture and pattern of exterior siding materials affect to a great extent the form and appearance of a house. The horizontal lines of bevel or lap siding can elongate the length of a house, while vertical board siding can emphasize its height. Shingle siding can have relatively uniform coursing, or a more random, heavily-textured pattern. Whichever pattern you select, its scale should be coordinated with the windows and doors, and the style and size of the exterior trimwork. If adding on to your house, select a pattern that will complement what already exists. If the existing siding is in disrepair, consider re-siding both the house and addition with new material.

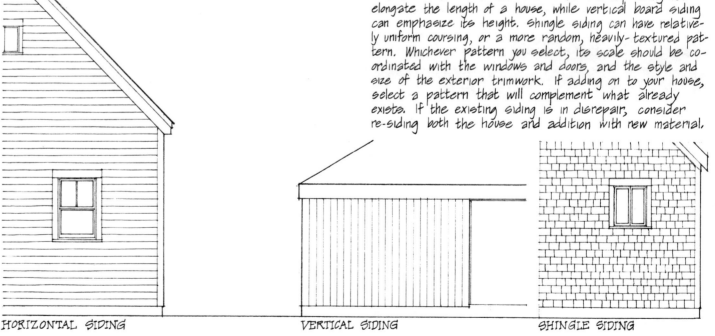

HORIZONTAL SIDING          VERTICAL SIDING          SHINGLE SIDING

## BEVEL SIDING

Bevel siding, also known as lap siding, is a popular form of horizontal siding. The bevel siding is made by cutting a board diagonally across its cross-section so that the siding is narrow along one edge and thick along the other. The thick or butt edge may be rabbeted for a shiplap joint. The rough, resawn side can be exposed for stained finishes, while the planed side can be either stained or painted.

Bevel siding is available in nominal 4" to 12" widths. Their finished widths are about 1/2" less than their nominal widths. Their narrow edges are about 3/16"; their thick butt edges are 1/2" for 4" and 6" widths, and 3/4" for widths 8" to 12". The width of the exposed surfaces has a dramatic affect on the scale of your house. An exposure greater than 7" is generally not compatible with the scale of a residential structure.

The bevel siding should be applied over a smooth surface. In new construction, the base may be plywood or board sheathing. While building paper is used over board sheathing, it is not generally required over plywood sheathing.

While new horizontal siding can be applied over an existing siding that is flat, it is usually better to remove the older siding first, or apply the new siding over furring that is nailed to the underlying studs.

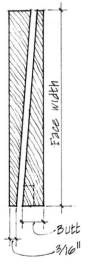

| FACE DIMENSIONS | | BUTT END |
|---|---|---|
| Nominal | Actual | Actual |
| 4" | 3 1/2" | 15/32" |
| 5" | 4 1/2" | 15/32" |
| 6" | 5 1/2" | 9/16" |
| 8" | 7 1/4" | 3/4" |
| 10" | 9 1/4" | 3/4" |

Face width

Butt
3/16"

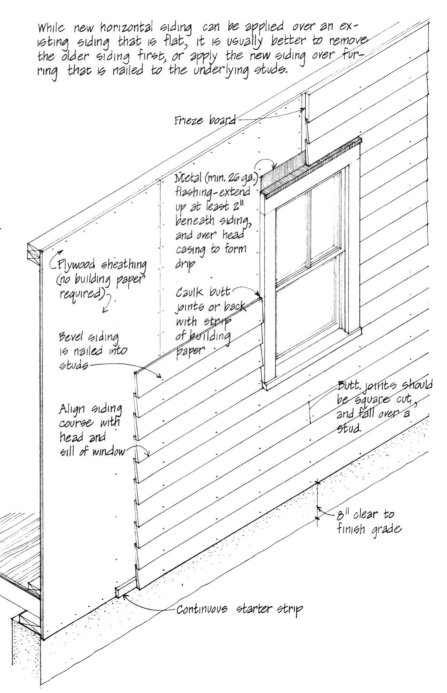

Frieze board

Metal (min. 26 ga.) flashing-extend up at least 2" beneath siding, and over head casing to form drip

Plywood sheathing (no building paper required)

Caulk butt joints or back with strip of building paper

Bevel siding is nailed into studs

Butt joints should be square cut, and fall over a stud.

Align siding course with head and sill of window

8" clear to finish grade

Continuous starter strip

## BEVEL SIDING

The bevel siding boards should lap a minimum of 1". For wider boards, a 1½" or 2" lap is often used. The exact spacing of the bevel siding, however, must be adjusted to the overall height of the wall, and the heights and locations of any windows and doors in the wall.

For weather resistance and appearance, the first course of siding above a window or door opening should coincide with the drip cap over the opening. If possible, the siding should not be notched at these points. Similarly, at the window sill, the bottom of the siding course should line up with the bottom of the sill. To do this, first divide the window height by the exposure distance for the size of the bevel siding being used. Re-divide the window height by the result of the first division, rounded off as necessary, to arrive at the exact spacing of the bevel siding.

eg. For a window height of 44" and 6" bevel siding with an exposure distance of 4½", divide 44 by 4.5 to arrive at 9.77 or 10 courses of siding. Re-dividing 44" by 10, you arrive at 4.4" or 4⅜" for the spacing of the bevel siding.

The spacing from the foundation wall to a first-story window sill may vary from the spacing for the window height. There may be another variation from the first-story window to the sill of a second-story window or the top of the wall. If these variations are slight, however, they will not be noticeable, especially if narrow bevel siding is being used. If the variation is large, use the same exposure distance for the entire height of the wall, and notch the siding, if necessary, around the windows.

The siding is installed starting with the bottom course. Use a starter strip the same thickness as the narrow edge of the siding. Each succeeding course overlaps the upper edge of the one below.

The siding is nailed at each stud, using 6d nails for bevel siding less than ½" thick, and 8d nails for thicker siding. The nails should be corrosion-resistant (galvanized, stainless steel, or aluminum) finishing or siding nails that will not stain, spot or split the material. They should penetrate well into the studs, about 1½". Drive the nails till their heads are flush with the siding surface; do not crush or damage the surface.

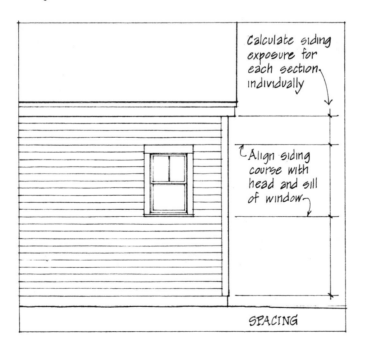

Calculate siding exposure for each section individually

Align siding course with head and sill of window

SPACING

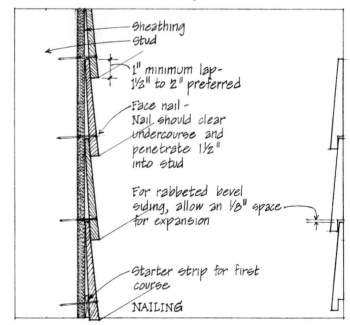

Sheathing
Stud

1" minimum lap- 1½" to 2" preferred

Face nail - Nail should clear undercourse and penetrate 1½" into stud

For rabbeted bevel siding, allow an ⅛" space for expansion

Starter strip for first course

NAILING

The siding nails driven into each stud should be located high enough above the butt end of the siding to clear the top of the siding course below. This is to allow for some movement of the siding with changes in moisture content without splitting.

The top course of siding fits under a frieze board which may be notched or furred out to overlap the siding.

When installing the bevel siding, minimize the number of butt joints. Any joint is a potential spot for water penetration. If a butt joint is necessary, it should be square-cut, centered over a stud, and staggered from any other joints in adjacent courses. Treat any cut ends with a water-repellent preservative.

When bevel siding is installed over an existing wall, the trim around windows and doors may have to be extended with new trim applied over or perpendicular to the existing trim.

Bevel siding can be mitered where the boards meet at external corners. The joints must be carefully fitted to remain tight without opening. More simply, the siding can be square-cut and butt up against corner boards, similar to the way the siding butts up against window and door casing trim. At these points, building paper should be carried across the joints to seal them against water penetration. Caulk the joints.

Internal corners are also fitted with a corner board against which the bevel siding is butted.

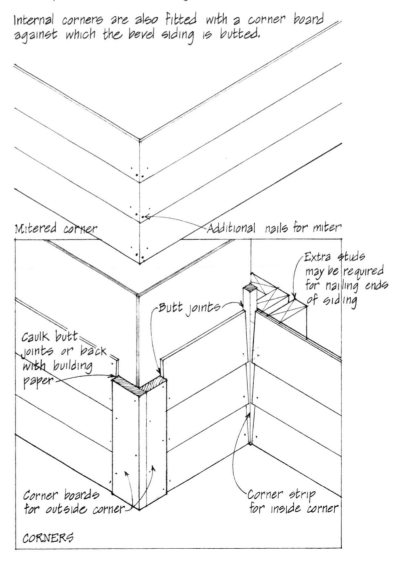

Mitered corner — Additional nails for miter

Extra studs may be required for nailing ends of siding

Butt joints

Caulk butt joints or back with building paper

Corner boards for outside corner

Corner strip for inside corner

CORNERS

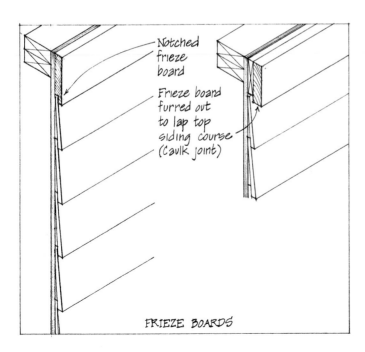

Notched frieze board

Frieze board furred out to lap top siding course (Caulk joint)

FRIEZE BOARDS

# VERTICAL SIDING

Vertical siding can be laid in various patterns. Matched, tongue-and-groove, or shiplap boards that interlock or interlap can have flush, V-groove, or beaded vertical joints. Square-edged boards can be used with other boards or battens to protect their vertical joints, and form board-and-board or board-and-batten patterns.

While horizontal siding is nailed directly to the wall studs, vertical siding materials require solid blocking or plywood sheathing at least 5/8" or 3/4" thick. Over thinner sheathing, 1" x 4" furring must be installed horizontally at 16" or 24" o.c. It is good practice to use a breathing-type building paper under vertical siding.

Vertical siding can also be laid directly over existing siding if it is nailed through the existing material to the underlying sheathing.

As with horizontal bevel siding, corrosion-resistant nails that will not stain or spot the siding material should be used. They should penetrate well into the blocking, furring strips or solid sheathing.

Matched, tongue-and-groove siding is blind nailed with 7d finishing nails through the tongue into each furring strip, or when laid over solid sheathing, at 16" o.c. For boards wider than 6", an additional 8d nail should be face nailed at mid-width, or use two face nails.

Shiplap and channel-groove siding are laid in a similar manner, but face nailed with two 8d or 9d siding nails at each furring strip, or at 16" o.c. These nails should be about an inch in from each edge.

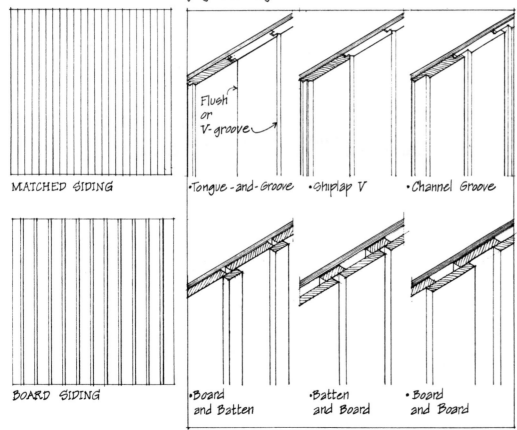

MATCHED SIDING

BOARD SIDING

Flush or V-groove

•Tongue-and-Groove    •Shiplap V    •Channel Groove

•Board and Batten    •Batten and Board    •Board and Board

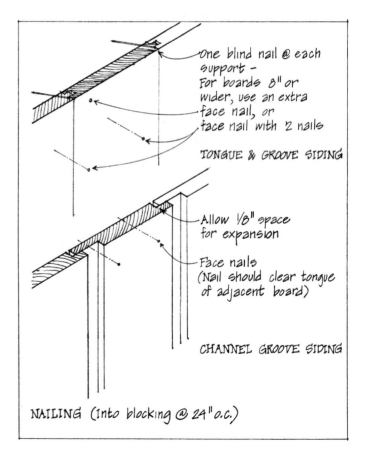

One blind nail @ each support – For boards 8" or wider, use an extra face nail, or face nail with 2 nails

TONGUE & GROOVE SIDING

Allow 1/8" space for expansion

Face nails (Nail should clear tongue of adjacent board)

CHANNEL GROOVE SIDING

NAILING (into blocking @ 24" o.c.)

With board-and-batten and board-and-board siding, the first boards or battens are nailed with 8d nails at 16" o.c. along their centerline. For wide boards, use two nails 2" apart along the centerline. The top boards or battens are then nailed with 12d nails at 16" o.c. These nails should be driven between and not through the first boards or battens.

The external corners of vertical siding can be mitered, lapped, or emphasized with corner boards. Mitered corners should be cut carefully to provide a tight fit through the full depth of the miter. When vertical siding is lapped at corners, the lapping board is nailed to the adjacent corner board as well as to the supporting material underneath.

Treating the ends and edges of vertical siding, and the backs of batten strips, with a water-repellent preservative can help the vertical joints resist the penetration of water and wind-driven rain.

At window and exterior doorways, caulking may be required to seal the joints between the vertical siding and the side casing trim.

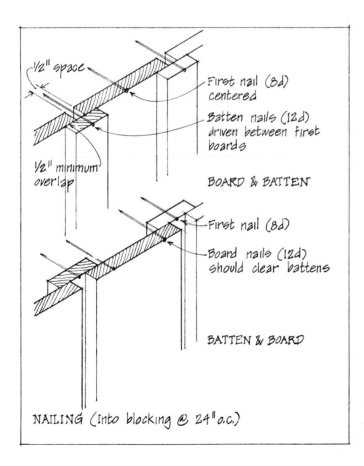

½" space

First nail (8d) centered

Batten nails (12d) driven between first boards

½" minimum overlap

**BOARD & BATTEN**

First nail (8d)

Board nails (12d) should clear battens

**BATTEN & BOARD**

NAILING (into blocking @ 24" o.c.)

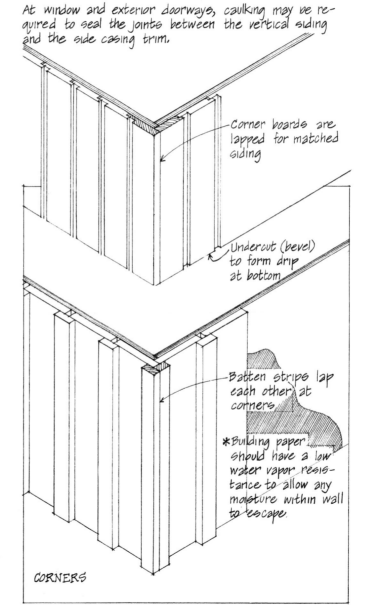

Corner boards are lapped for matched siding

Undercut (bevel) to form drip at bottom

Batten strips lap each other at corners

*Building paper should have a low water vapor resistance to allow any moisture within wall to escape.

CORNERS

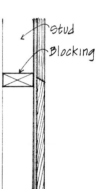

Stud

Blocking

End joints, if they occur, should be beveled and caulked during installation.

# PLYWOOD SIDING

Exterior-grade plywood used for siding is available in a variety of patterns and textures. The most common patterns imitate the board-and-batten or vertical channel groove styles of siding. Their surfaces may have brushed, grooved, or roughsawn textures. The rough textures may be treated with a clear water-repellent finish or be stained. A paper-overlaid plywood is also available that provides a smooth surface for painted finishes (MDO).

Plywood is a popular siding material since it is fairly easy to apply, and can cover a wall rapidly. Another advantage is that it can double-function as both wall sheathing and wall covering, eliminating the need for a separate layer of sheathing.

Plywood siding that is laid directly over stud wall framing should be at least 3/8" thick for 16" stud spacing, and 5/8" thick for 24" stud spacing. Grooved plywood is normally 5/8" thick with 1/4" deep grooves. When plywood is laid over a separate layer of wall sheathing, it can be thinner. Although 1/4" is the minimum thickness, 5/16" and 3/8" thicknesses will provide a more even surface.

Plywood siding comes in 4' widths and lengths of 8', 9', and 10', and is usually applied vertically. If you plan to use plywood or other panel siding on a wall higher than the panel length, plan the layout carefully. The horizontal joints between plywood panels cannot be masked easily and can be very noticeable. Try to coordinate these horizontal lines with the tops of window and door openings or with other horizontal wall elements.

If horizontal joints are necessary, they should be protected by flashing, a shiplap joint, or by overhanging the upper panels slightly over the ones below. Some manufacturers have joining devices designed specifically to protect these joints.

Plywood siding panels should be nailed directly into the underlying studs, with an effective penetration of the nails into wood of 1½". Around each panel perimeter, nailing is at 6" intervals, and into intermediate supports, 12" intervals. Allow 1/16" edge and end spacing between all plywood panels.

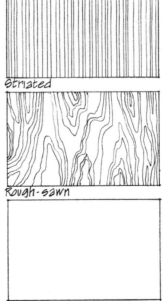

Striated

Rough-sawn

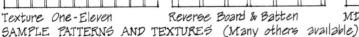

Texture One-Eleven    Reverse Board & Batten    MDO for painted finish
SAMPLE PATTERNS AND TEXTURES (Many others available)

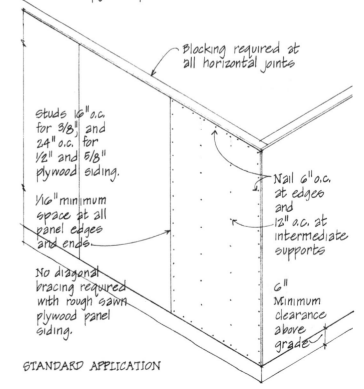

Blocking required at all horizontal joints

Studs 16" o.c. for 3/8" and 24" o.c. for 1/2" and 5/8" plywood siding.

1/16" minimum space at all panel edges and ends.

No diagonal bracing required with rough sawn plywood panel siding.

Nail 6" o.c. at edges and 12" o.c. at intermediate supports

6" Minimum clearance above grade

STANDARD APPLICATION

The side edges of plywood panel siding should have shiplap joints. If the edges are square-cut, either caulk the vertical joints or protect them with 1" x 2" batten strips, nailed with 8d casing nails at 12" o.c. Additional batten strips can be nailed over each stud if desired for a board-and-batten effect.

For additional protection, the edges of plywood siding should be treated with a water-repellent preservative or high-grade exterior primer, and strips of building paper laid under vertical joints.

Caulking is generally required wherever the plywood panels butt against window and door trim, and at external and internal corners.

## HARDBOARD SIDING

Tempered hardboard panel siding is available in 4' widths and lengths up to 10'. The panels, like plywood, imitate vertical or lap siding styles. They are usually factory-primed for painting, or factory-finished with matching batten strips and trim. Some are vinyl-clad for greater weather resistance and easier maintenance.

Hardboard siding panels are installed similarly to plywood siding. They are nailed around their perimeters at 4" intervals, and at intermediate supports at 8" intervals.

Since hardboard and other sheet siding materials are resistant to the passage of water vapor, a vapor barrier should always be installed on the warm side of the exterior walls that they cover.

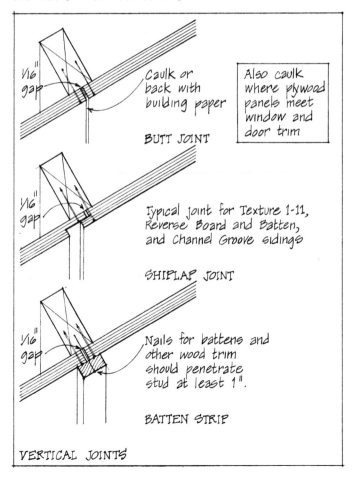

1/16" gap

Caulk or back with building paper

Also caulk where plywood panels meet window and door trim

BUTT JOINT

1/16" gap

Typical joint for Texture 1-11, Reverse Board and Batten, and Channel Groove sidings

SHIPLAP JOINT

1/16" gap

Nails for battens and other wood trim should penetrate stud at least 1".

BATTEN STRIP

VERTICAL JOINTS

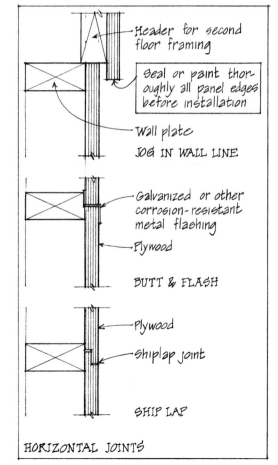

Header for second floor framing

Seal or paint thoroughly all panel edges before installation

Wall plate

JOG IN WALL LINE

Galvanized or other corrosion-resistant metal flashing

Plywood

BUTT & FLASH

Plywood

Shiplap joint

SHIP LAP

HORIZONTAL JOINTS

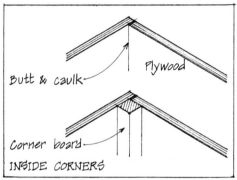

Butt & caulk

Plywood

Corner board

INSIDE CORNERS

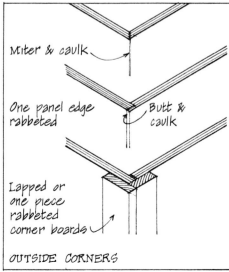

Miter & caulk

One panel edge rabbeted

Butt & caulk

Lapped or one piece rabbeted corner boards

OUTSIDE CORNERS

# 4

# WOOD SHINGLE SIDING

Wood shingle siding provides an appealing and attractive textured finish for exterior walls. The shingles are usually laid in uniform courses that resemble lap siding. As with lap or bevel siding, these courses should be adjusted to meet the sills and tops of windows neatly. Also, since shingles come in standard lengths but varying widths, try not to concentrate narrow shingles in one area and wide ones in another area. Spread the widths out as evenly as possible for an even texture.

Dimension and fancy-butt shingles that are cut to uniform widths and shapes can also be used on exterior walls to create certain effects, such as scalloped and fishscale textures.

The most common species for shingles is western red cedar. White cedar, redwood and cypress shingles are also available. These can be painted or stained. The heartwood of these species can be left unpainted to weather naturally.

While Nº 1, first-grade shingles are used primarily for roofs, they are often used in double-course wall applications. Nº 2, second-grade shingles are most often used in single-course wall applications since only one half or less of the butt portion of the shingles is exposed. Third-grade shingles can be used as the undercourse in double-course wall applications.

The maximum exposure distance for shingles on walls are as follows:

| SHINGLE LENGTH | MAXIMUM EXPOSURE (inches) | |
|---|---|---|
| (inches) | Single-course | Double-course |
| 16 | 7½ | 12 |
| 18 | 8½ | 14 |
| 24 | 11½ | 16 |

Consider the spacing you want for the desired visual or textural effect before selecting a shingle length.

Shingle siding can be applied over any nailable sheathing such as plywood, boards, or high-density fiberboard. Over non-nailable sheathing, or over existing siding that is uneven, use 1"x 3" or 1"x 4" nailing strips applied horizontally, and spaced with centers 2" above the buttline of each course.

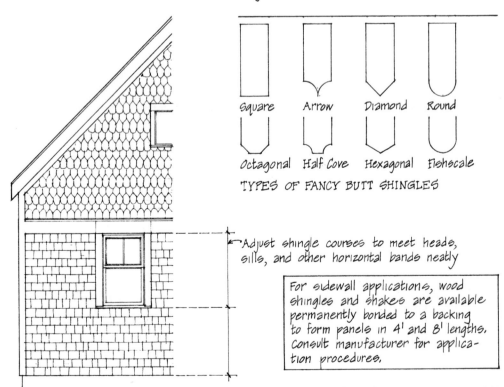

Square   Arrow   Diamond   Round

Octagonal   Half Cove   Hexagonal   Fishscale

TYPES OF FANCY BUTT SHINGLES

Adjust shingle courses to meet heads, sills, and other horizontal bands neatly

For sidewall applications, wood shingles and shakes are available permanently bonded to a backing to form panels in 4' and 8' lengths. Consult manufacturer for application procedures.

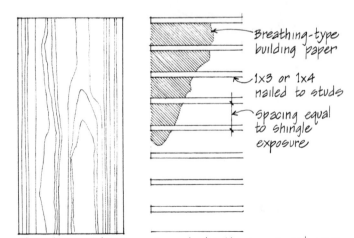

Breathing-type building paper

1x3 or 1x4 nailed to studs

Spacing equal to shingle exposure

Plywood or nail-base fiberboard (Building paper not required.)

Spaced sheathing required over non-nailable sheathing or siding.

TYPES OF SHEATHING

Wood shingles may be applied in single or double courses. In single-course application, the first course is doubled and laps the foundation wall about 1". Each shingle is nailed with two 3d or 4d nails, 3/4" in from each edge and an inch above the buttline of the succeeding course. If the shingle is wider than 8", use a third nail centered between the first two. Use corrosion-resistant nails; when nailing into plywood sheathing, use nails with threaded shanks.

Succeeding courses overlap each preceding one according to the length of the shingles used. See table. Adjust the spacing so that shingle courses fit neatly over and under windows. A straight piece of 1" x 4" or shiplap board can be used as a guide to help align the shingle bottoms.

Allow an 1/8" to 1/4" space between shingles for expansion during rainy weather. If the shingles are fresh and damp, they may be laid tighter. The joints in one course should be spaced at least 1½" away from joints in adjacent courses. Do not align joints in alternate courses.

At corners, lap alternating courses over the adjacent corner shingles on the other side. Trim and plane the ends of the overlapping shingles, and treat or stain the exposed ends. Corner boards may also be used to receive the shingles at both external and internal corners. Color-matched metal corners are available for use with pre-finished shingles.

In double-course application, the first or undercourse can be a lower grade of shingle, and is laid up as in single-course application. The shingle exposures are greater, however, and the shingles are nailed only enough to hold them in place until the top courses are laid.

Because much of their faces is exposed, the top course shingles should be № 1, first-grade. They are laid over the undercourse with their butt ends projecting 1/4" to 1/2" below the buttline of the undercourse. The top course shingles are nailed with two 5d nails, 3/4" in from each edge and 2" above their butt ends.

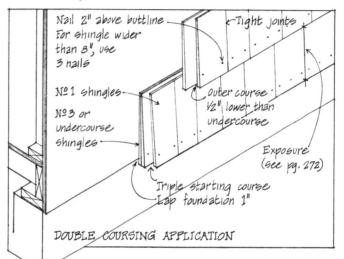

Nail 2" above buttline.
For shingle wider than 8", use 3 nails

Tight joints

№ 1 shingles

№ 3 or undercourse shingles

Outer course ½" lower than undercourse

Exposure (see pg. 272)

Triple starting course Lap foundation 1"

**DOUBLE COURSING APPLICATION**

Nail 2" above buttline of succeeding course.

1/4" joints

3/4"

Breathing type building paper over board sheathing

1½" min. offset between joints

Exposure (see table, pg. 272)

Double starting course Lap foundation 1"

**SINGLE COURSING APPLICATION**

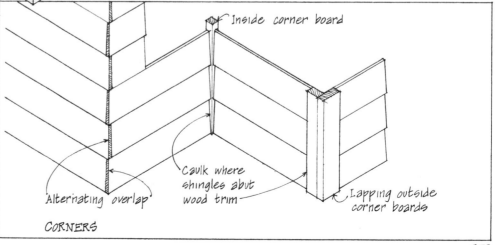

Inside corner board

Alternating overlap

Caulk where shingles abut wood trim

Lapping outside corner boards

**CORNERS**

# MOISTURE & THERMAL PROTECTION

In addition to properly roofing your house and any new spaces added to it, moisture and thermal protection extends to and includes insulation, vapor barriers, weather-stripping, and ventilation systems. Insulation keeps heat inside the home during the winter, and helps keep it out in hot weather. Weatherstripping keeps cold air out. Vapor barriers control the flow of moisture vapor. Ventilation systems exhaust stale and moisture-laden air, and help eliminate excess heat in the summer.

This section discusses each of these elements and systems, the types of materials and equipment used, and where they are needed. Together, they effectively weatherize your house, provide comfortable interior living conditions, and help protect your house structure and finishes.

On the following page is an illustration of a home and addition indicating areas, features and equipment that should be checked to help reduce heating and cooling loads, conserve energy, and provide comfortable interior conditions.

1. Weatherstrip around windows and doors; caulk any air cracks in exterior walls, such as around outside faucets, electrical service entries, and TV cable entries.
2. Check for adequate insulation in the attic. Consider adding insulation during any remodeling.
3. Check for adequate insulation in exterior walls, floors over crawl spaces, and around foundation or basement walls.
4. Use storm windows and doors, or install insulating glass windows.
5. Ventilate unfinished attic spaces and crawl spaces.
6. Shade interior spaces from direct sunlight to protect them from overheating during hot weather; let sunlight in during cold weather.
7. Use landscaping elements to shade during hot weather, and to buffer walls from cold winds in the winter.
8. Heating system: Clean or replace filters when necessary; furnace should be correctly sized and serviced regularly; insulate ducts in unheated spaces.
9. Insulate the hot water heater and any hot water pipes in unheated spaces. Lower thermostat setting to 120°F. (140°F for dishwashers).
10. When replacing appliances, select energy-efficient models.
11. Use energy-efficient light fixtures.
12. Set house thermostat to 65°F. during winter and 78°F. in summer. Infants, the sick, and elderly may require higher settings in the winter.

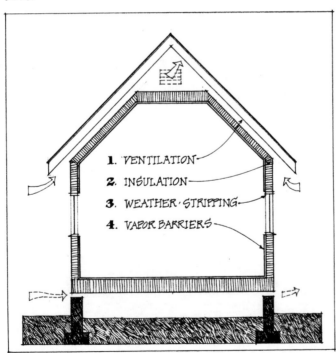

1. VENTILATION
2. INSULATION
3. WEATHER·STRIPPING
4. VAPOR BARRIERS

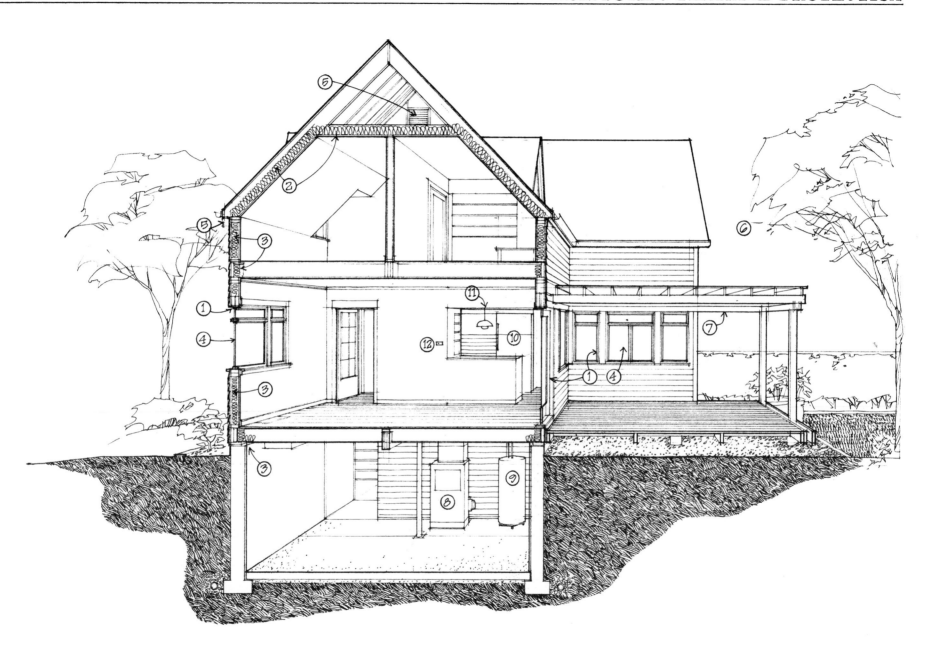

# THERMAL INSULATION

The primary purpose of thermal insulation is to control heat transfer between the interior spaces of your house and the outside, and thereby protect them from excessive heat loss during cold weather and excessive heat gain in hot weather. The right amount of insulation, properly installed, can significantly reduce the amount of energy required to maintain conditions of human comfort.

Heat may be transferred by convection, radiation, or conduction. In convection, air molecules transfer heat from warm surfaces to cooler ones. In large spaces, the warm air will rise and, as it cools, fall, setting up convection currents. Within the cavity of a wall, these currents can cause heat to be lost through the wall. In very small spaces, however, these currents cannot develop. If well-sealed, small air spaces can be effective insulators, as in double-paned insulating glass for windows.

Heat energy can be radiated directly from a hot surface to a cooler one without warming the air in between. If our warm bodies lose heat too quickly to the cool surface of an uninsulated wall, we feel uncomfortable. When the wall is insulated, however, its inner surface will be warmer, we lose less heat by radiation, and we will feel more comfortable, even though the air temperature may only be 65°-68°F.

Heat can also be conducted through the mass of a material. This is the way heat moves through a building's materials and construction. All building materials offer some resistance to heat flow. Generally, the denser a material, the more quickly heat will move through it. Most insulating materials rely on many, tiny trapped pockets of air for their insulation value and to retard the flow of heat.

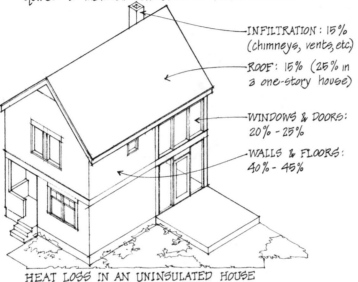

INFILTRATION: 15%
(chimneys, vents, etc.)

ROOF: 15% (25% in a one-story house)

WINDOWS & DOORS: 20% - 25%

WALLS & FLOORS: 40% - 45%

HEAT LOSS IN AN UNINSULATED HOUSE

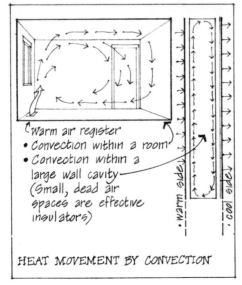

• Warm air register
• Convection within a room
• Convection within a large wall cavity (small, dead air spaces are effective insulators)

• warm side
• cool side

HEAT MOVEMENT BY CONVECTION

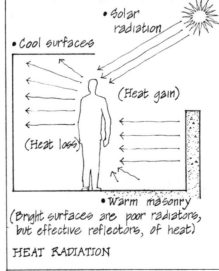

• Solar radiation

• Cool surfaces

(Heat gain)

(Heat loss)

• Warm masonry
(Bright surfaces are poor radiators, but effective reflectors, of heat)

HEAT RADIATION

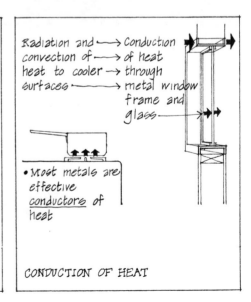

Radiation and convection of heat to cooler surfaces → Conduction of heat through metal window frame and glass

• Most metals are effective conductors of heat

CONDUCTION OF HEAT

The measure of a material's resistance to heat flow is its R-value (°F/BTU/hr.-s.f.) - the temperature difference required to cause heat to flow through a unit area (s.f.) of a material at the rate of one BTU/hr. The higher the number, the greater the resistance to heat flow. The total R-value of a wall, floor or roof construction is the sum of the individual R-values of the composite materials.

The U-value of a material is its heat transfer co-efficient - the rate of heat transfer through a unit area of the material caused by a difference of one degree of air temperature. The U-value is therefore the reciprocal of (R), and the total U-value of a wall, floor or roof is equal to 1/R of the construction assembly. The lower the number, the less the rate of heat transfer.

The rate of heat flow (Q) through a unit area of construction is a product of the assembly's U-value, its area, and the difference between the indoor and outdoor design temperatures. eg. If the coldest temperature in your area is 0°F. and the desired indoor air temperature is 68°F., the value (Q) for a 160 s.f. insulated wall with an R-value of 12.5 is:

$$1/12.5 \times 160 \times (68-0) = 870.4 \ BTU's/hr.$$

In a similar manner, knowing the total R-value of exterior walls, roof, windows and other areas through which your house loses heat in the winter, you can estimate the cumulative heat loss. To this figure can be added the heat loss due to infiltration of cold air around windows, doors and through chimneys. The estimated total heat loss for your house then should be compared to the size of your heating plant.

If you are considering adding insulation, compare the total heat flow with and without the additional insulation, and use the difference to compute possible energy savings.

Other factors that will affect heat loss and gain include the color and reflectivity of your house walls and roof, the orientation of its spaces to the sun and wind, and sources of latent heat such as cooking equipment, lighting fixtures, etc.

APPROXIMATE R-VALUES OF COMMON BUILDING MATERIALS

| MATERIAL | R-value |
|---|---|
| Aluminum | 0.0007/inch |
| Asphalt shingles | 0.44 |
| Brick | 0.1 - 0.2/inch |
| Carpet w/ pad | 2.0 |
| Concrete, 8" | 1.6 |
| Concrete block, 8" | 1.1 - 2.0 |
| Door, 1 3/4" solid core wood | 1.96 |
| Door, steel w/ polystyrene core | 2.13 |
| Glass, single pane | 0.95 |
| Glass, double pane w/ 5/16" airspace | 1.61 |
| Gypsum board, 1/2" | 0.45 |
| Hardwood flooring, 3/4" | 0.68 |
| Plaster, 3/4" | 0.15 |
| Plywood, 3/4" | 0.8 |
| Resilient flooring | 0.05 |
| Softwood | 1.25/inch |
| Wood shingles | 1.2 |
| Wood bevel siding | 0.8 - 1.0 |

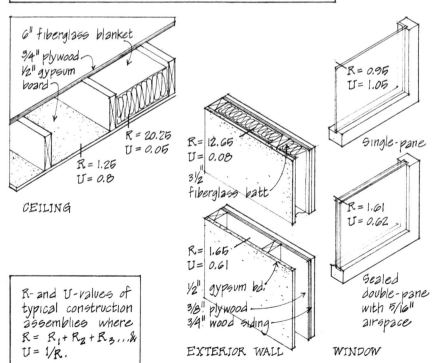

6" fiberglass blanket
3/4" plywood
1/2" gypsum board
R = 20.25
U = 0.05
R = 1.25
U = 0.8

CEILING

R = 12.65
U = 0.08
3 1/2" fiberglass batt

R = 1.65
U = 0.61
1/2" gypsum bd.
3/8" plywood
3/4" wood siding

EXTERIOR WALL

R = 0.95
U = 1.05
Single-pane

R = 1.61
U = 0.62
Sealed double-pane with 5/16" airspace

WINDOW

R- and U-values of typical construction assemblies where
$R = R_1 + R_2 + R_3 \dots \&$
$U = 1/R$.

# INSULATING MATERIALS

A wood stud framed wall with 3/8" plywood sheathing, wood bevel siding, and a 1/2" gypsum board interior finish has an approximate R-value of 1.65 (or U-value of 1/1.65 or 0.61). The addition of a 3½" blanket of fiberglass insulation can increase the R-value of the wall to 12.65 or 4 times its original value. This illustrates how the resistance of a wall, roof or floor construction to heat flow can be enhanced with the installation of insulating material.

Insulating materials differ according to their composition and the form in which they are manufactured. The R-value of an insulating material is usually measured per inch of thickness. The total R-value for an insulation product should be clearly labeled on the package or wrapping. This R-value, of course, assumes that the insulation is properly installed.

Common types of insulation include:

1. Fiberglass and Rock Wool:

   These consist of matted weavings of glass fiber strands or spun slag. They are moisture and fire resistant, and are available in batt or blanket form, shredded for loose fill, or compressed into rigid boards.

   The batts and blankets come in 15" and 23" widths to fit into standard stud, joist, and rafter spacing. The batts have 4' and 8' lengths, while the blankets come in rolls that can be cut to the desired length. They may be friction-fit, or have flanges that are stapled to the framing.

2. Plastics:

   Polystyrene, polyurethane, and polyisocyanurate are common types of plastic insulation. These are foamed, expanded or extruded into rigid panels or boards, 1" and 2" thick, and 2' wide x 4' or 8' long. Though more expensive than other insulating materials, they have greater R-values per inch.

   Because these plastics are highly combustible, they must be protected by a fire-resistant material such as gypsum board. The denser plastics, such as extruded polystyrene, are weather and moisture resistant and can be used for exterior sheathing and below grade around foundation and basement walls. They are compressible and should be protected against denting.

3. Cellulose:

   These recycled paper products come in loose form for filling cavities of walls and ceilings. They should be clearly labeled as being treated for resistance to fire and rodents. They become ineffective when wet.

4. Vermiculite and Perlite:

   These are also loose fill materials made from expanded mica or volcanic rock. They are not moisture resistant, and for their weight, have low R-values. But they are useful in insulating hard-to-reach cavities.

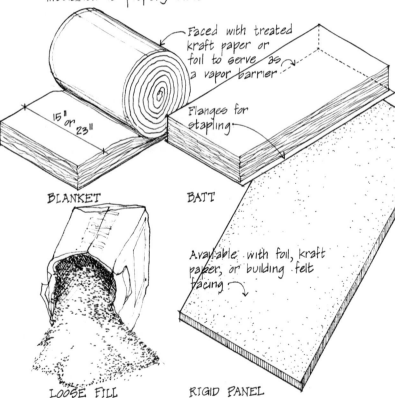

Faced with treated kraft paper or foil to serve as a vapor barrier

15" or 23"

Flanges for stapling

BLANKET          BATT

Available with foil, kraft paper, or building felt facing

LOOSE FILL          RIGID PANEL

TABLE OF INSULATING MATERIALS

| FORM | MATERIAL | R-value/inch | USES |
|---|---|---|---|
| Batt | Fiberglass | 3.0 - 3.3 | Wood-frame construction: roofs; ceilings under unfinished attics; walls; floors over crawl spaces; furred spaces over masonry or concrete walls. |
| | Rock Wool | 3.0 - 3.3 | |
| Blankett | Fiberglass | 3.1 - 3.3 | |
| | Rock Wool | 3.0 - 3.3 | |
| Rigid | Polystyrene | 4.0 - 5.4 | Roof decking; wall sheathing; friction-fit into framing or cemented directly to concrete walls or slabs. |
| | Polyurethane | 6.7 - 8.0 | |
| | Polyisocyanurate | 8.0 | |
| Loose | Fiberglass | 3.1 - 3.3 | Unfinished attic floors or accessible cavities of walls; can be poured or mechanically blown into place; perlite and vermiculite are often used to fill the cores of concrete block walls, and to fill cavities in masonry construction. |
| | Rock Wool | 3.0 - 3.3 | |
| | Cellulose | 3.7 - 4.0 | |
| | Vermiculite | 2.0 - 2.6 | |
| | Perlite | 2.0 - 2.7 | |

| R-value | Thickness Required for Specific R-values | | | |
|---|---|---|---|---|
| | Fiberglass Blanket | Loose Fill Fiberglass | Loose Fill Cellulose | Rigid Polystyrene |
| R-11 | 3½" | 5" | 3" | 2" |
| R-19 | 6" | 8½" | 5" | 3½" |
| R-22 | 6½" | 10" | 6" | 5" |
| R-30 | 9½" | 13½" | 8" | 5½" |
| R-38 | 12½" | 17½" | 10½" | 7½" |

5. Reflective Foil Insulation:

Unlike the other listed porous materials that rely on tiny, trapped pockets of air to retard heat flow, reflective foil re-radiates heat back into a room. It is available packaged in corrugation and backed with kraft paper. Inner divisions reduce convection currents; the enclosed layer of air space gives it some insulation value. Reflective foil is most effective when the heat flow is downward, and can therefore be most useful in a floor construction.

Reflective foil, when used as a backing with batt, blanket or rigid insulation, double-functions as a vapor barrier. When using foil-backed insulation in a floor, leave at least 3/4" air space between the foil and the subfloor to allow the foil to re-radiate the heat properly.

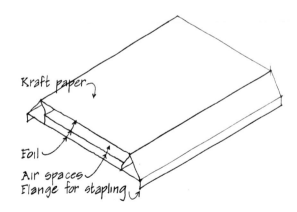

Kraft paper

Foil

Air spaces
Flange for stapling

# INSULATING YOUR HOUSE

The cost of energy decreases as the cost of insulation (the cost of the material and the labor required to install it) increases. Therefore, to measure the effectiveness of installing or adding insulation, compare the annualized cost of the insulation (material and labor) to the annual cost of energy loss (if insulation were not installed).

The type of fuel you use, its cost in your area, and the efficiency of your heating system all have a direct bearing on how much insulation you need in your home. Your energy budget must strike a medium between how much is spent on energy consumption and how much is spent on energy-conservation improvements.

There are heating and cooling zone maps that provide insulation guidelines for various parts of the country. This is an abbreviated table of recommended values for (roofs or ceilings/exterior walls/floors over unheated spaces).

Minimum Recommended:  (R-19 / R-11 / R-11)
Temperate Zones:  (R-26 / R-19 / R-13)
Northern Zones:  (R-38 / R-19 / R-22)
Between Any Heated and Unheated Space: R-11

These are only general recommendations. As the supply and price of heating fuels change, so may these guidelines. Check your local or state energy code for requirements, or with the nearest office of the U.S. Department of Housing and Urban Development.

As you consider adding insulation to your home, keep in mind that at some point, the amount of energy saved will diminish in proportion to the amount of insulation added. The first three inches of insulation are the most effective, and an R-value of 5 reduces the rate of heat transfer about 80%. An R-value of 10 will reduce the rate by 90%; an R-value of 20 will reduce it by 96%. For every increase of 5 points in the R-value over 20, there may only be a reduction of 1% in the heat transfer rate.

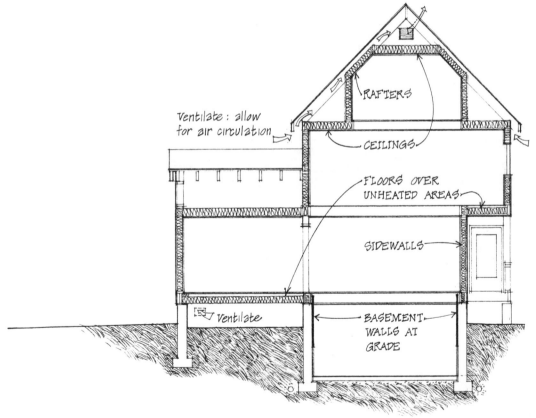

Ventilate: allow for air circulation

RAFTERS

CEILINGS

FLOORS OVER UNHEATED AREAS

SIDEWALLS

Ventilate

BASEMENT WALLS AT GRADE

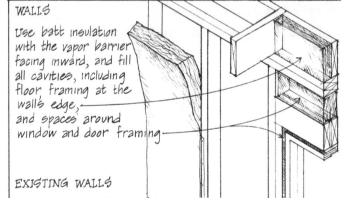

## WALLS

Use batt insulation with the vapor barrier facing inward, and fill all cavities, including floor framing at the wall's edge, and spaces around window and door framing

## EXISTING WALLS

The best choice for insulating an existing wall is to remove the interior finish and install batts with a vapor barrier. A second alternative is to remove the exterior siding, apply rigid insulation to the sheathing, and re-side the wall. A third alternative is to have loose-fill insulation blown in through holes drilled in the wall. Since there is no vapor barrier, any moisture that can render the loose insulation ineffective must be allowed to escape through plug ventilators.

Insulation should form a complete envelope around the living or heated spaces in your home, and separate them from unheated or outdoor spaces. Any windows, doors or other openings that break this envelope should be weatherstripped, caulked, or otherwise sealed.

This envelope may consist of:

1. Floors of unfinished attic spaces, or the rafter spaces, knee walls, and dormers of finished attics.
2. All exterior walls.
3. Floors over unheated spaces.
4. Perimeter of concrete ground slabs. (See pg. 205)
5. Perimeter of foundation or basement walls. (See pg. 136)

Spaces often missed include:

6. Small spaces around window and door frames.
7. Where floor framing meets exterior walls, and floors that cantilever over exterior walls.
8. Where exterior walls meet roof framing, and at sill plates.
9. Behind electrical outlet boxes on exterior walls.
10. Openings that lead to attics.
11. Heating ducts in unheated spaces.

Blanket or loose insulations should not be packed too tightly; rigid insulation panels should not be crushed or dented. Any insulation with an integral vapor barrier should be installed with the barrier facing the warm side of the construction, or into a heated room.

Allow about 3" clear space around heat-producing equipment such as recessed ceiling fans or lighting fixtures.

Finally, it is better to have a little insulation everywhere it is needed, rather than have a lot in only a few places.

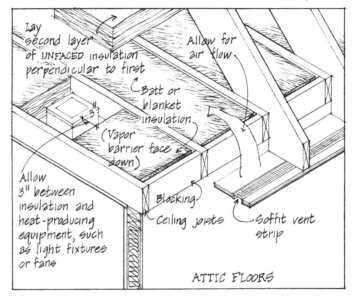

Lay second layer of UNFACED insulation perpendicular to first

Allow for air flow

Batt or blanket insulation

3"

(Vapor barrier face down)

Allow 3" between insulation and heat-producing equipment, such as light fixtures or fans

Blocking

Ceiling joists

Soffit vent strip

ATTIC FLOORS

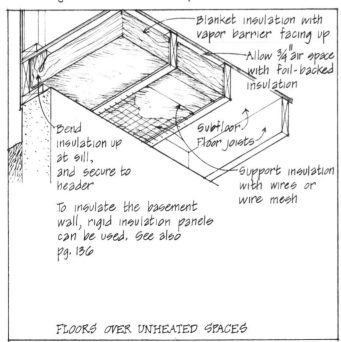

Blanket insulation with vapor barrier facing up

Allow 3/4" air space with foil-backed insulation

Bend insulation up at sill, and secure to header

Subfloor. Floor joists

Support insulation with wires or wire mesh

To insulate the basement wall, rigid insulation panels can be used. See also pg. 136

FLOORS OVER UNHEATED SPACES

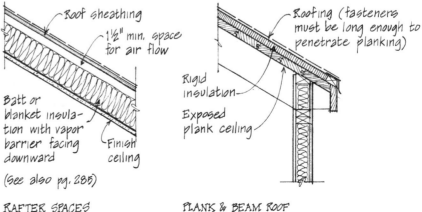

Roof sheathing

1½" min. space for air flow

Batt or blanket insulation with vapor barrier facing downward

Finish ceiling

(See also pg. 285)

RAFTER SPACES

Roofing (fasteners must be long enough to penetrate planking)

Rigid insulation

Exposed plank ceiling

PLANK & BEAM ROOF

# VAPOR BARRIERS

Moisture is naturally present in the air as water vapor. The evaporation from activities such as showering, laundering and cooking can significantly raise this humidity level in a home. As a gas, water vapor migrates from high to low pressure areas, and warm air is capable of holding more water vapor than cooler air. Warm, moist air will therefore tend to move to cooler, drier areas.

Most building materials are permeable to water vapor and offer little resistance to its movement. As warm, moist interior air passes through an exterior wall, ceiling, roof or floor, and meets an exterior cold surface whose temperature is at or below the dew point of the air, the water vapor will condense. This condensation can be absorbed by building materials. In severe cases, condensation can lead to the decay of structural materials, stain interior finishes, blister exterior paint, and saturate insulation materials, lessening their efficiency.

To prevent condensation from forming, vapor barriers are used to block the vapor from penetrating the concealed construction spaces of exterior walls, ceilings or roofs, and floors over unheated spaces. The ventilation of attic and crawl spaces is also important to allow moist air to escape to the outside before being transformed into a liquid state.

The measure of a material's resistance to the transmission of water vapor is its perm-rating. The lower the number, the greater the resistance. For a vapor barrier, use a material with a perm-rating of 0.25 or less. Materials commonly used as vapor barriers include asphalt-laminated building paper, foil, and plastic (polyethylene) film.

Some insulating materials come with a vapor barrier. Batt and blanket insulations may have a foil or treated kraft paper facing. Some rigid insulation panels and gypsum board also have a foil backing.

In new construction or in a remodeling, you can lay large sheets of polyethylene film over a wall or ceiling frame after the insulation and any electrical work has been installed. The sheets are stretched tightly and stapled to the frame. All joints should be lapped 2" and any breaks should be taped or caulked. The new interior finish materials can then be applied.

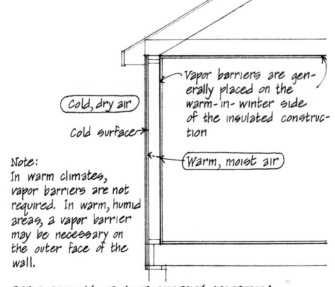

Cold, dry air

Cold surface

Vapor barriers are generally placed on the warm-in-winter side of the insulated construction

Warm, moist air

Note:
In warm climates, vapor barriers are not required. In warm, humid areas, a vapor barrier may be necessary on the outer face of the wall.

PERM RATINGS OF SOME BUILDING MATERIALS

| | | |
|---|---|---|
| Aluminum foil, 1-mil | 0.0 | Perm |
| Polyethylene, 6-mil | 0.08 | " |
| Polyethylene, 4-mil | 0.06 | " |
| Kraft paper, foil-faced | 0.5 | " |
| Exterior oil-base paint | 0.9 | " |
| Extruded polystyrene, 1" | 1.2 | " |

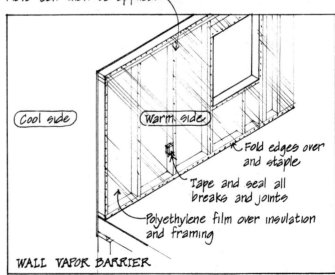

Cool side

Warm side

Fold edges over and staple

Tape and seal all breaks and joints

Polyethylene film over insulation and framing

WALL VAPOR BARRIER

A vapor barrier should always be installed on the warm (in winter) side or face of the construction - facing downward on ceilings or roofs, facing inward when on exterior walls, and facing up when in floor construction.

When an effective vapor barrier is installed, it is not advisable to have a vapor barrier of equal resistance on the cooler side of the exterior wall or roof. Any water vapor that does manage to get through the first barrier should be allowed to vent to the outside and not get trapped within the construction space.

If a new vapor barrier cannot be installed, consider as a last resort using two coats of a paint with a perm-rating of not more than 1.0.

With the increased emphasis on the use of vapor barriers to reduce heat loss due to infiltration, there is some concern for the stale air that can accumulate in a tightly-sealed house. An air-exchanger or other means of ventilating the house air may be necessary to compensate for the normal air changes that would occur in a house that "breathes."

There are other places in your house where condensation may occur. Window and door glass areas are susceptible to surface condensation when their surfaces are cooler than the dew point of nearby air. This situation can be remedied by using double-pane insulating glass and by directing a warm air supply toward these surfaces. Surface condensation can also occur on a concrete ground slab if its perimeter is not properly insulated and it is not laid over a granular base course with a vapor barrier.

The ground in a crawl space contains moisture that can rise and condense on the first floor supports and framing. In addition to laying a polyethylene vapor barrier over the ground, the space should be ventilated to the outside.

When a wall is well-insulated and has an effective vapor barrier, any building paper used over the exterior sheathing should be permeable (ie. have a low resistance to water vapor) to allow any moisture within the wall to escape.

— Full batt insulation

— Continuous vapor barrier

— Exterior sheathing

(Cool side)   (Warm side)

USE OF SHEATHING PAPER WITH VAPOR BARRIERS

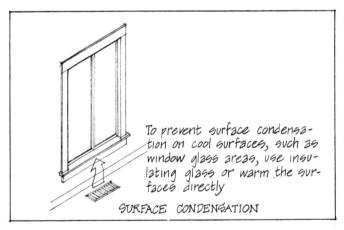

To prevent surface condensation on cool surfaces, such as window glass areas, use insulating glass or warm the surfaces directly

SURFACE CONDENSATION

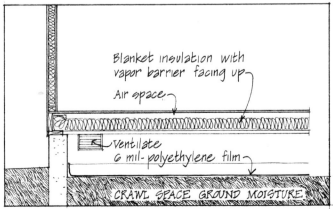

Blanket insulation with vapor barrier facing up

Air space

Ventilate

6 mil- polyethylene film

CRAWL SPACE GROUND MOISTURE

The tighter you make your house with the use of vapor barriers, weatherstripping and caulking, the greater will be the need to ventilate the interior spaces to get rid of unwanted stale air, heat, moisture, fumes and pollutants. Ventilation may be by natural or mechanical means. In either case, fresh air must replace the air that is vented to maintain an even pressure within the house.

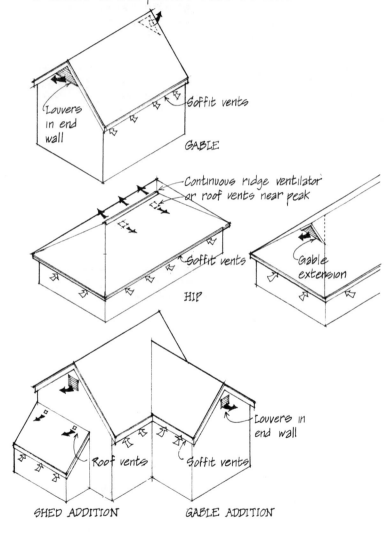

VENTILATING AREAS FOR TYPICAL ROOF FORMS

## ATTIC VENTILATION

Attic ventilation is necessary for a number of reasons. Even when a vapor barrier is installed, some moisture may work itself into the attic space. In the winter, when condensation of this moisture can occur, a steady flow of air through the attic can help carry the moisture to the outside.

Also in cold weather, heat rising from the house interior may melt any snow on the roof. As this water reaches the cold surfaces along the eave, it can refreeze and form an ice dam. This ice dam, in turn, can cause water to back up into the wall or ceiling construction. Ventilating the attic space, along with proper insulation, can lower the attic temperature and reduce the chance of snow melting over the attic space.

In hot weather, heat can build up within an attic space. If not removed, this heat can eventually be conducted or radiated to the living spaces below. Ventilating the attic space is the most effective means to remove any heat build-up and lower the attic temperature.

An attic space should first be ventilated by the natural flow of air through vents. Even if a power roof ventilator is used, vents are still necessary. Although wind can aid in creating air movement, it is the difference in temperature between incoming outside air and the outgoing attic air that induces the air flow through the attic space.

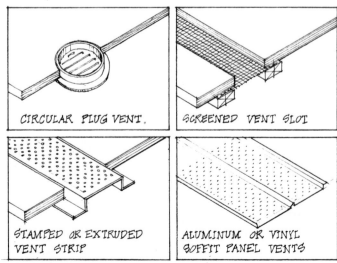

TYPES OF SOFFIT OR EAVE VENTS

Inlet vents are most effective when located in soffits along lower eavelines. They should be located close to the outer edge to minimize the chance of wind-blown snow entering, and be well distributed. A number of small vents is generally better than a few large ones. A continuous screened or peforated vent strip along the length of the soffit works well, especially if individual rafter spaces must be ventilated.

Outlet vents should be located close to the peak at gable ends, or along the ridgeline of hip or shed roofs. The openings at gable ends may consist of wood louvers, or be pre-fabricated and framed metal louvers, ready for installation.

Hip roofs may use small gable end ventilators, wind-activated turbine ventilators, or several roof vents installed within rafter spaces. For a less obstrusive appearance, a continuous ridge vent can be used.

The net clear area for the ventilation openings is based on the area of the attic floor or the building area between the eavelines. If the attic space has a vapor barrier, the vent openings should have a net area equal to 1/300 of the attic floor area, equally distributed between inlets and outlets. If there is no vapor barrier, double the required area.

All ventilation openings should be screened to prevent insects from entering. The actual area of the openings must therefore be increased to allow for the restrictions of screening, mesh or louvers. Use as coarse a screen pattern as possible. For 1/8" screening, multiply the required area of the openings by a factor of 1.25. For 1/16" screening, double the required area.

It is important that the air flow from inlet to outlet not be restricted by any solid framing or bridging, or by a ridge board or beam. Drill 1" diameter holes through the obstructions when they occur. Adequate space (at least 1 1/2") should also be provided above any insulation that is placed within the depth of rafters.

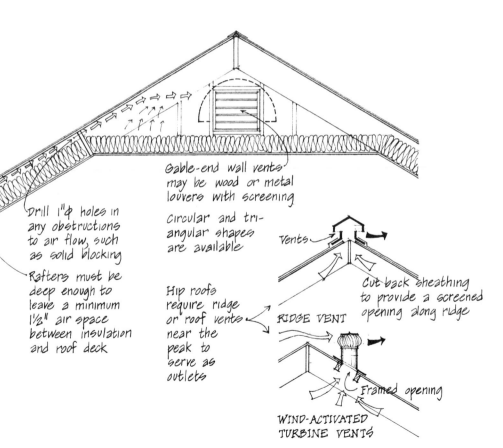

Plug ventilators or breathers in frieze board

Screened soffit vent (continuous strip or one slot for each rafter space)

Blocking, if required

Drill 1"ø holes in any obstructions to air flow, such as solid blocking

Rafters must be deep enough to leave a minimum 1 1/2" air space between insulation and roof deck

Gable-end wall vents may be wood or metal louvers with screening

Circular and triangular shapes are available

Hip roofs require ridge or roof vents near the peak to serve as outlets

Vents

RIDGE VENT

Cut back sheathing to provide a screened opening along ridge

Framed opening

EXPOSED RAFTER ENDS

BOX CORNICE

WIND-ACTIVATED TURBINE VENTS

# 4

# POWER VENTILATORS

Power ventilators are capable of moving large amounts of air in a short period of time, and exhausting this air along with unwanted heat, moisture and fumes to the outside. There are small fan units to ventilate a piece of equipment, such as a cooking range, or a single room. Larger units can ventilate an attic space or even an entire house.

The measurement of a fan unit's ability to move air in a given period of time is specified by its CFM (cubic-feet-per-minute) rating. A fan unit should be selected according to its CFM-rating, the size of the room or space to be ventilated, and the rate at which the air must be changed over.

Other considerations in selecting a fan unit include the noise level of the fan while in operation, the type of mounting required, and how the fan is controlled.

The noise a fan unit generates is related to the horse-power of the motor, the fan RPM, and how the fan housing dampens or isolates the noise. The noise level of a fan unit is usually expressed in sones. The lower the number, the quieter the unit. Most fans are tested by the Home Ventilating Institute and assigned CFM and sone ratings. Check for these before purchasing a fan unit.

Fans may be controlled by a simple hand switch or by a timer. Hand switches are satisfactory for fans used to ventilate a piece of equipment during operation. Timers are more useful in controlling fans that should continue to operate for a specific period of time after you leave a room.

There are also thermostatically controlled switches that activate a fan when the temperature in a space reaches a certain level, as in an attic. Humidistat controls, sensitive to moisture build-up, can also be used.

POWER ATTIC AND ROOF VENTILATORS

A power attic or rooftop ventilator can be used to assist the natural air flow through an attic space. These fan units are pre-wired for easy installation. Most have thermostatically-controlled switches. Some also have humidistats that are sensitive to moisture build-up and will activate the fan unit at a pre-determined setting.

Roof-mounted fan units have lightweight housings with self-flashing flanges that will slip under the roofing material. They are sized to conveniently fit between two rafters. To operate efficiently, roof-mounted fan units should be located close to the ridge line of the roof.

Wall-mounted fans for gable ends have housings with flanges that slip under the exterior siding material. Automatic louvers open when the fan is on, and close when the fan is off. These units should be located as high as possible in a gable-end wall, or near the peak of a shed roof.

To estimate the required CFM-rating of an attic or roof ventilator, multiply the attic floor area by a factor of 0.75. If the roofing material is dark and will absorb heat, increase the required CFM by 15%. (The exhausted air must by replaced by fresh air entering through eave vents.)

Opening for fan housing is cut into sheathing between two rafters.

Roofing felt

Flange is fastened to roof deck. Use roofing cement to seal all joints

Flange is tucked under roofing above and to the sides, and laid over roofing below.

ROOF FAN UNIT

## WHOLE-HOUSE VENTILATORS

Whole-house ventilators pull hot, stale air from the living areas of a house and exhaust it through attic vents. Cooler, fresh air is drawn in through open windows. These large fan units can eliminate the need for air-conditioning in temperate climates. In warm climates, they can reduce the air-conditioning load.

A whole-house ventilator is usually located on the attic floor over a hallway or stairway that leads to the rest of the house. The rooms or areas of the house to be ventilated can be controlled by selectively opening and closing doors and windows. Whole-house fans are powerful units. Closing off a portion of the house will result in greater air velocities; closing all the windows can result in negative pressure.

Whole-house ventilator units come with louvers that open and close automatically with the fan operation. Automatic heat sensors should be used that will shut down the fan when the attic temperature reaches 200°F. for any reason, including fire. Two-speed motors are available to vary the ventilation rate. Control may be by a manual switch, timer, or thermostat.

To control the noise and vibration that a whole-house fan can generate and transmit through the house structure, felt or rubber gaskets should be used to isolate the fan housing from its supporting frame; resilient mountings should help dampen the fan motor noise and vibration; felt seals should help quiet the operation of the metal louvers.

Some whole-house ventilators can be housed to ventilate either the house or the attic space. Automatic shutters can be used to determine the direction from which air is being drawn through the fan.

The required CFM-rating of a whole-house ventilator can be estimated by determining the volume (in cubic feet) of your house living areas. Use half of this figure if you live in a cold, northern climate; use the entire amount if you live in a warm climate and require more cooling. An alternate method is to simply multiply the square-footage of your living areas by a factor of 3.

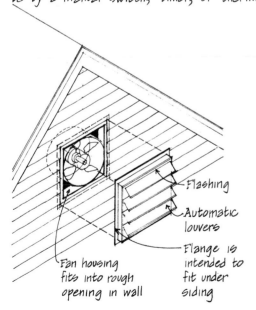

Flashing

Automatic louvers

Flange is intended to fit under siding

Fan housing fits into rough opening in wall

WALL OR GABLE FAN

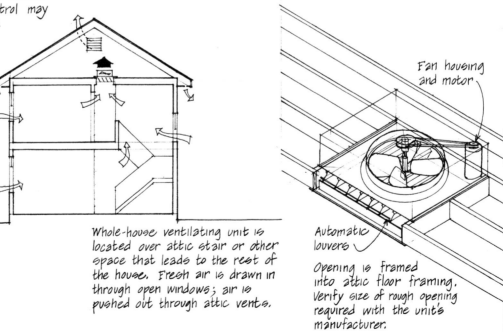

Fan housing and motor

Automatic louvers

Opening is framed into attic floor framing. Verify size of rough opening required with the unit's manufacturer.

Whole-house ventilating unit is located over attic stair or other space that leads to the rest of the house. Fresh air is drawn in through open windows; air is pushed out through attic vents.

WHOLE-HOUSE VENTILATOR

# WEATHER-STRIPPING

The infiltration of cold air through gaps or cracks in the exterior of your house can account for up to 50% of the heating bill, and can negate the effect of any heat saved through insulation. Installing weather-stripping can effectively cut down on infiltration and reduce the heating load significantly. While caulking is used to seal cracks between fixed elements, weather-stripping products are used to seal gaps around doors and the operating sections of windows.

There are several types of weather-stripping, varying according to material, cost, effectiveness of seal, durability, appearance and location of use.

1. Spring metal weather-stripping, of bronze, aluminum, or stainless steel, has a flange that compresses between the frame and the door, or between the operating sections of casement, double-hung, or sliding windows. When the door or window is closed, the spring metal is concealed.

Cushion metal weather stripping has two flanges and operates in a similar manner. Both spring and cushion metal weather stripping can be cut to length and nailed in place. Their flanges can be adjusted to assure a tight seal. Although moderately expensive, they provide an efficient seal and are fairly durable.

Along eave and gable trim

Around window trim

Where wires and pipes penetrate a wall

Where framing meets foundation

Around roof flashing, vents & pipes

Where different materials meet

Where siding abuts corner and door trim,

LOCATIONS FOR CAULKING

The best caulks are the elastomerics, such as silicones and polyurethanes. They are flexible, will adhere to almost any material, and will last up to 15 or 20 years. Before purchasing and using any caulk, read the label carefully. Determine its characteristics, limitations, and appropriate uses. Check for elasticity, paintability, flammability, and possible harmful vapors or adverse effects to skin and finishes.

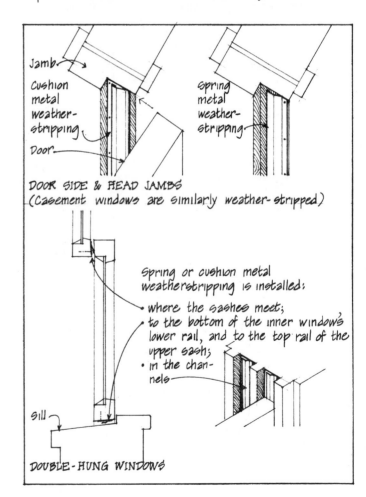

Jamb

Cushion metal weather-stripping

Door

Spring metal weather-stripping

DOOR SIDE & HEAD JAMBS
(Casement windows are similarly weather-stripped)

Spring or cushion metal weatherstripping is installed:
• where the sashes meet;
• to the bottom of the inner window's lower rail, and to the top rail of the upper sash;
• in the channels

Sill

DOUBLE-HUNG WINDOWS

2. Interlocking metal or "J" strips are more expensive than spring metal weather stripping, but they are more durable and provide an excellent seal for doors and casement windows against both wind and rain. One section attaches to the frame, while the other is fastened to the edges of the door or casement window. When the door or window is closed, the two sections interlock.

Interlocking types of weather stripping may be surface-mounted, or be concealed in recesses cut into the door or window. In either case, the two interlocking sections must be carefully aligned to operate properly.

3. Rigid gasket weather stripping consists of felt, vinyl or neoprene gaskets attached to a metal or vinyl strip. These are used primarily to seal door openings. They are screwed to the door frame and are quite visible. Select a type that has elongated screw holes so that the strips can be adjusted periodically.

Pliable gasket weather stripping consists of felt or polyurethane foam strips. The least expensive and the least durable of these is adhesive-backed foam. A more durable type is a rolled vinyl gasket that can be used to weather-strip doors as well as casement, awning, and double-hung windows. These are fastened to door jambs, or to the operating window sections.

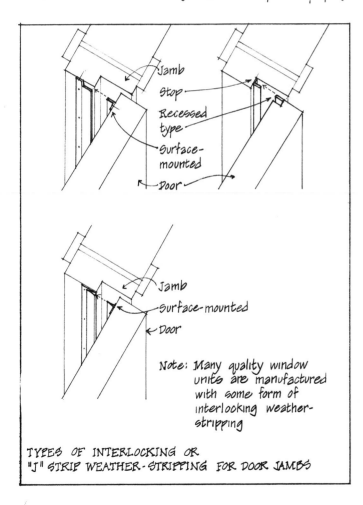

Jamb
Stop
Recessed type
Surface-mounted
Door

Jamb
Surface-mounted
Door

Note: Many quality window units are manufactured with some form of interlocking weather-stripping

TYPES OF INTERLOCKING OR "J" STRIP WEATHER-STRIPPING FOR DOOR JAMBS

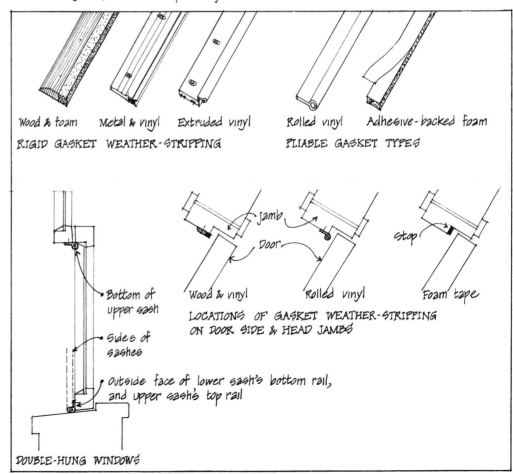

Wood & foam    Metal & vinyl    Extruded vinyl    Rolled vinyl    Adhesive-backed foam

RIGID GASKET WEATHER-STRIPPING          PLIABLE GASKET TYPES

Jamb
Door
Stop

Bottom of upper sash

Sides of sashes

Outside face of lower sash's bottom rail, and upper sash's top rail

Wood & vinyl    Rolled vinyl    Foam tape

LOCATIONS OF GASKET WEATHER-STRIPPING ON DOOR SIDE & HEAD JAMBS

DOUBLE-HUNG WINDOWS

# DOOR BOTTOMS & THRESHOLDS

The bottoms of exterior doors require special types of weather-stripping treatment. The simplest is a door sweep that consists of a vinyl or neoprene flap attached to a metal strip. The sweep is screwed to the inner face of inward swinging doors, or the outer face of outward swinging doors, and remains visible.

An automatic door bottom is a felt or neoprene sweep that is spring-loaded in a metal housing. When the door is closed, the door jamb forces the sweep down to seal the gap. When the door is opened, the sweep is retracted into its housing. The housing may be surface-mounted or recessed into the door bottom.

A door shoe consists of a rounded vinyl gasket in a metal retainer that attaches to the bottom edge of a door. When the door is closed, the vinyl gasket compresses against the threshold.

A rounded vinyl gasket can also be retained in the threshold rather than the door bottom. For the most effective seal, the bottom door edge should be beveled slightly. If it gets worn, the vinyl gasket can be replaced.

In cold climates, an insulated threshold is desirable. It consists of two sections separated by a strip of vinyl or plastic to retard heat flow through the threshold metal.

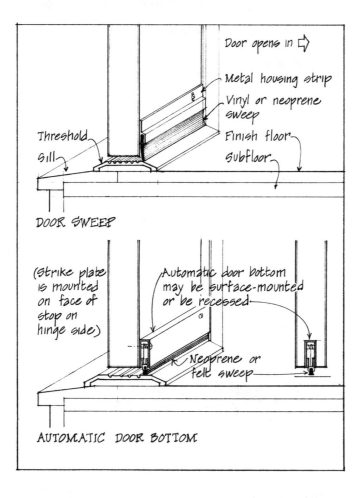

**DOOR SWEEP**

Door opens in ⇨

Metal housing strip

Vinyl or neoprene sweep

Finish floor

Subfloor

Threshold

Sill

**AUTOMATIC DOOR BOTTOM**

(Strike plate is mounted on face of stop on hinge side)

Automatic door bottom may be surface-mounted or be recessed.

Neoprene or felt sweep

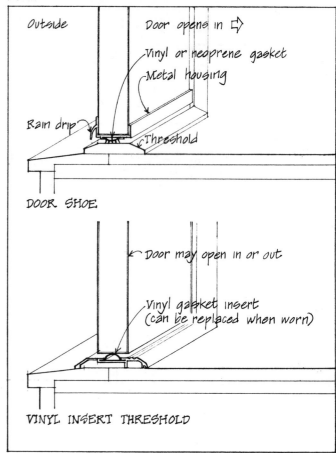

**DOOR SHOE**

Outside

Door opens in ⇨

Vinyl or neoprene gasket

Metal housing

Rain drip

Threshold

**VINYL INSERT THRESHOLD**

Door may open in or out

Vinyl gasket insert (can be replaced when worn)

The most effective seal against wind and rain is provided by an interlocking threshold. The threshold has a lip that interlocks with a hook strip attached to the door bottom. This hook strip may be surface-mounted or recessed. As with other types of interlocking weather stripping, an interlocking threshold must be aligned carefully to operate carefully.

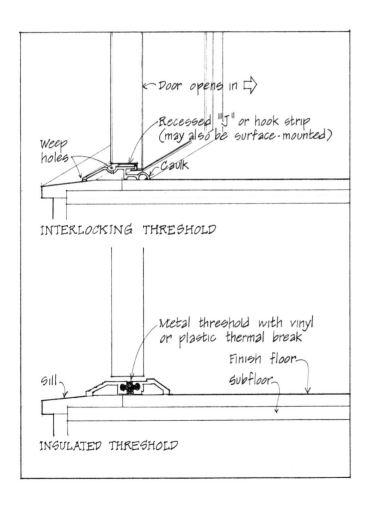

Door opens in ⇨

Recessed "J" or hook strip
(may also be surface-mounted)

Weep holes

Caulk

**INTERLOCKING THRESHOLD**

Metal threshold with vinyl or plastic thermal break

Finish floor

Subfloor

Sill

**INSULATED THRESHOLD**

# EXTENDING HEATING LINES

In addition to fully insulating the new space, weather-stripping doors and windows, and utilizing solar heat gain where feasible, some mechanical or electrical heating will probably be required for a room-size addition. The existing heating system can be extended, or one or more individual space heaters can be added. Extending your present heating system, if it has adequate heating capacity, is usually the least expensive method of getting heat to your addition. The following is a brief outline of what is involved. If you have any questions regarding the ability of your heating system to support an extension, check with a heating specialist or your utility company.

An existing forced air heating system can be extended by adding a new warm air distribution duct and registers. The room will be more comfortable if the registers can be located along an exterior wall and under a window (where the coldest air surfaces can be heated). The typical register is 3" to 4" wide and 10" to 12" long, while the supply duct is usually a 6" round duct. For installation within a stud wall, a 3"x12" rectangular duct is used.

Often the most difficult aspect of extending a forced air heating system is finding the space to run the duct-work to the location where the heat is needed. To extend a heating duct to a second story addition, a closet on the first floor and the space between the floor joists of the addition may provide you with the space you need. Other choices are to build a duct enclosure in the corner of an existing first floor room, or to open up a wall surface to allow the installation of a duct in the stud space. In choosing a route for a new duct run, remember that each turn in the duct run creates resistance to the air flow. Also, warm air tends to flow upward. It is therefore more difficult to force warm air down into lower areas.

Supply register located in the floor at the perimeter under a window

Center end boot

Supply riser

Return air

Main warm air supply duct

Fresh air supply

Top take-off
Side take-off

Flue connection

6" ø supply duct

90° angle boot

Plenum or bonnet

Furnace

WARM AIR SUPPLY SYSTEM

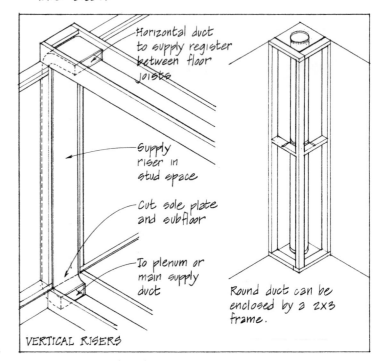

Horizontal duct to supply register between floor joists

Supply riser in stud space

Cut sole plate and subfloor

To plenum or main supply duct

Round duct can be enclosed by a 2x3 frame.

VERTICAL RISERS

The new warm air supply duct must be connected to the warm air plenum or main distribution duct from the furnace. Use a metal chisel and sheet metal shears to cut a hole in the existing sheet metal ductwork. You can also drill starter holes and cut the new opening with a metal saw blade. The duct connection is made with a takeoff collar, which is a standardized part that can be purchased from most sheet metal or heating companies. The collar may have mounting tabs that are folded inside the hole, or have flanges that are caulked and fastened with sheet metal screws.

The boot is also a standardized part that connects a round duct to the register. It must be located between two floor joists and fit into a hole cut in the flooring and subfloor.

6" round duct is generally manufactured in 5' long sections that slide together, straight end over crimped end. The ends are pushed together for a tight fit and fastened with two self-tapping metal screws. The crimped ends of a supply run should always face away from the furnace.

Rectangular duct that is used within a stud wall space uses S-shaped connectors that snap together.

To prevent loss of warm air, wrap all duct joints with duct tape. In addition, any warm air supply duct that goes through an unheated space (eg. a crawl space or attic) should be insulated to avoid a major heat loss.

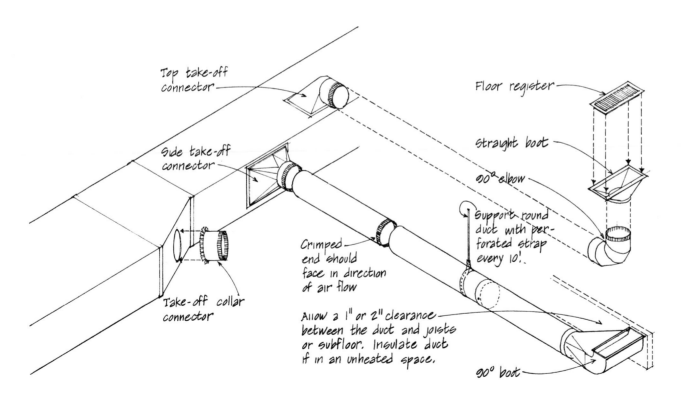

Top take-off connector

Side take-off connector

Take-off collar connector

Crimped end should face in direction of air flow

Allow a 1" or 2" clearance between the duct and joists or subfloor. Insulate duct if in an unheated space.

Floor register

Straight boot

90° elbow

Support round duct with perforated strap every 10'.

90° boot

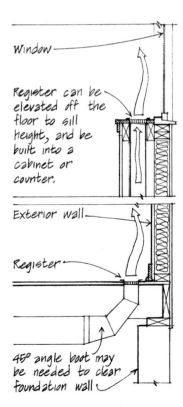

Window

Register can be elevated off the floor to sill height, and be built into a cabinet or counter.

Exterior wall

Register

45° angle boot may be needed to clear foundation wall

# EXTENDING HEATING LINES

Extending a hot water heating system requires basic plumbing work. To figure out where to tap into the existing pipes, you must determine the direction of water flow in the pipes. You must also determine whether you have a one-pipe loop system with a combined supply and return pipe, or a two-pipe system with separate supply and return pipes.

To extend the system, first install the convector in the new room. As with warm air registers, it is preferable to locate the convector along an exterior wall under a window. Next, run the supply and return pipes (copper is usually used) to the supply and return mains. Before cutting the existing main pipes, turn off the heating system and drain the pipes. The main pipes are then cut and tees installed to connect to the new supply and return lines. In a one-pipe system, special venturi tees must be used to ensure warm water flow through the new convector is adequate.

If the new convector is more than 20' away from an existing one, or if you need more than two, have a professional size and lay out the extension.

If installation of a space heater is the desirable solution for heating your addition, the most convenient power/fuel source is electricity. The simplest form of efficient electric heat is the 240-volt baseboard heater. There are, however, other methods of providing electric heat.

1. Radiant heat panels can be surface-mounted or recessed in the ceiling.
2. Forced air electric heaters can be installed in a wall.
3. Individual hot water (hydronic) convectors, heated by electricity, can be installed along the baseboard.

Before deciding to add electric heat, check the capacity of your existing electrical service, and the ability to run a cable from the existing service panel to the new heater and its thermostat. If the present electrical service is adequate and safe, but incapable of handling an additional heating load, the cost of changing the service and adding the heater will be substantial.

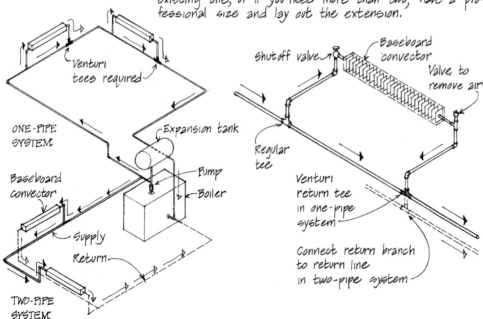

HOT WATER HEATING

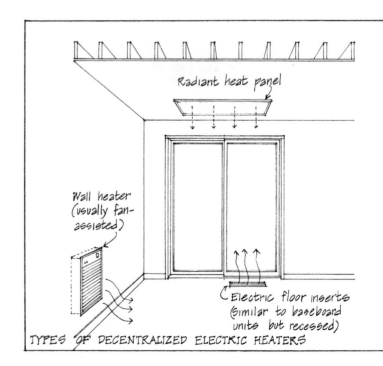

TYPES OF DECENTRALIZED ELECTRIC HEATERS

To install electric heat, first determine the location of the new heater and the thermostat. The heater should generally be on an exterior surface, and the thermostat on an interior wall near the room entrance. Next plan the route of the electrical cable, and install it from the service panel to the thermostat location, and from the thermostat to the heater. The wattage of the heater determines the size of the wires needed. Up to 3000 watts can generally be handled with 12-gauge copper wire. Two conductor wires and a third ground wire (insulated within a moisture-resistant, flame-retardant plastic sheathing) are needed. Carefully follow the manufacturer's instructions in connecting the heater and thermostat to the wires.

Finally, the wires are connected to a new circuit breaker in the service panel box. Be sure the main breaker is off, or the electricity disconnected to the service panel, before removing the face of the service panel box. It is strongly recommended that any connections to the service panel be made by a licensed electrician.

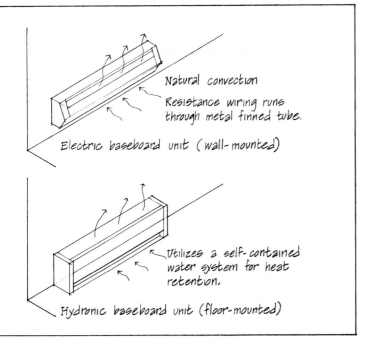

Natural convection

Resistance wiring runs through metal finned tube.

**Electric baseboard unit (wall-mounted)**

Utilizes a self-contained water system for heat retention.

**Hydronic baseboard unit (floor-mounted)**

A woodstove is another popular form of space heater. If a woodstove is installed, carefully follow the manufacturer's instructions and local code requirements for installation. The major hazards with a woodstove are locating it too close to combustible building materials, and incomplete separation and insulation between the flue or chimney and combustible materials. Burning wood at too low of a temperature can also be hazardous, leading to a creosote build-up in the flue and an eventual chimney fire.

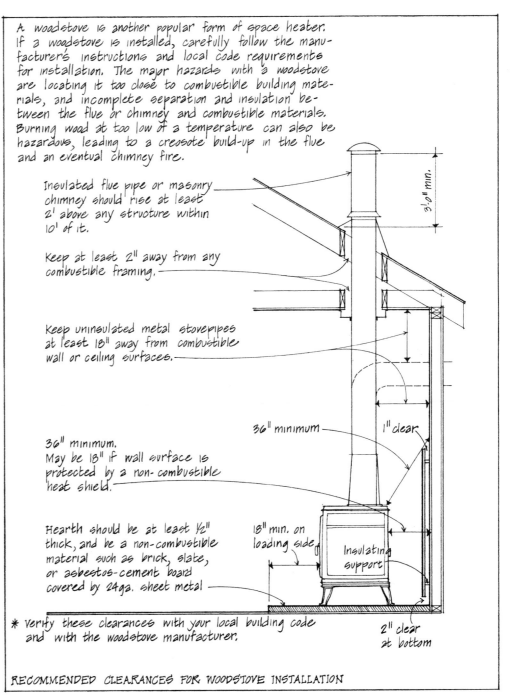

Insulated flue pipe or masonry chimney should rise at least 2' above any structure within 10' of it.

Keep at least 2" away from any combustible framing.

Keep uninsulated metal stovepipes at least 18" away from combustible wall or ceiling surfaces.

3'-0" min.

36" minimum

1" clear

36" minimum.
May be 18" if wall surface is protected by a non-combustible heat shield.

18" min. on loading side

Insulating support

Hearth should be at least ½" thick, and be a non-combustible material such as brick, slate, or asbestos-cement board covered by 24ga. sheet metal

2" clear at bottom

\* Verify these clearances with your local building code and with the woodstove manufacturer.

**RECOMMENDED CLEARANCES FOR WOODSTOVE INSTALLATION**

# 5 KITCHENS & BATHROOMS

Perhaps the two areas of a home that receive the greatest attention during a remodeling are the kitchen and the bathroom. Advances in fixture and equipment design, changes in lifestyle, and the continued emphasis on the efficient use of space, all have had an impact on the planning and design standards for kitchens and bathrooms. In addition, studies of human body dimensions, and the energy we expend in performing certain tasks, have resulted in more efficient layouts, and more comfortable, convenient proportions and dimensions of fixtures, work surfaces, and storage spaces.

To the purely functional requirements of kitchens and bathrooms must be added, of course, the considerations of aesthetics and style. New materials, lighting concepts, and changes in how we use kitchens and bathrooms, have resulted in their becoming more than utilitarian spaces, but rather attractive living areas.

Perhaps no where else in a house is there also a greater need for the careful integration of the house's systems. Electrical requirements for large and small appliances are greater than ever before. Effective lighting in both kitchens and bathrooms is essential in making them functional and attractive. Plumbing for new fixtures, or for those that are moved, must meet strict code requirements for health and sanitation. Ventilation systems are needed to control and exhaust moisture, smoke, fumes, and grease.

This chapter discusses on a broad basis the functional and technical considerations for planning and designing kitchens and bathrooms in a remodeling or addition. It should be emphasized that the complexities of building a new, or remodeling an older kitchen or bathroom, may warrant the assistance of an expert professional - a kitchen planner, contractor, designer or architect. The assistance can help you narrow down the vast array of choices, guide you in developing your design, and most importantly, help you avoid costly mistakes.

## KITCHENS

Begin planning a kitchen remodeling or addition by determining the specific needs the new kitchen must satisfy. The desire for morning sunlight, easy access to the dining area, and proximity to an exterior entry to your house may determine whether an existing kitchen is remodeled, or a new kitchen built in a new location. How much time you or others spend in the kitchen, how many people it must serve, and whether you entertain a little or a lot, will affect the size of the kitchen and its appliances, the amount of work surface and storage space it has, and how it is laid out. Whether your lifestyle is formal or casual, well-organized or spontaneous, will influence the overall design of the kitchen's storage areas, lighting and materials.

Before evaluating your present kitchen and studying the possibilities for its remodeling, there are certain fundamental principles of kitchen design and layout that should be reviewed. These include basic dimensions and required clearances in a kitchen, the planning of work centers, and guidelines for their layout.

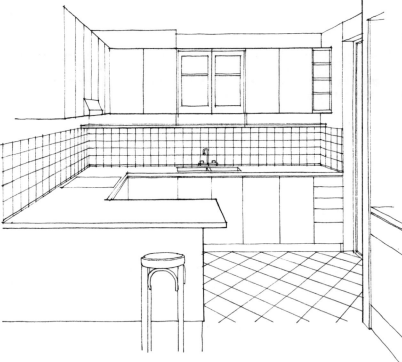

## DIMENSIONS & CLEARANCES

It is always difficult to establish standards for dimensions and clearances that will suit every one of us. Certain standards, however, have been developed from studies of those using kitchens, while others are dictated by the sizes of manufactured products and equipment. These are illustrated here only as guidelines, and you should adapt them to suit your own needs.

The sizes of appliances and other equipment are a matter of choice when you purchase them. Other dimensions you may be able to alter during the construction of your kitchen. For example, you may be able to raise or lower the standard height of base cabinets, or have them custom-made to your specifications.

Important dimensions to consider in the design of your kitchen include:

1. The height of countertops, sink, and cooktop. This is most often 36" although you may prefer a lower height.
2. The clearance between base cabinets, walls, and appliances for circulation and movement. This is a matter of comfort as well as safety, and often depends on the kitchen layout.
3. The accessibility of overhead and below-counter storage. Things should be arranged according to size, and frequency and location of use. Adjustable shelving is always desirable.
4. Proper visibility of work surfaces, especially the cooktop.
5. Clearance of cabinet and appliance door swings, a simple matter of convenience.

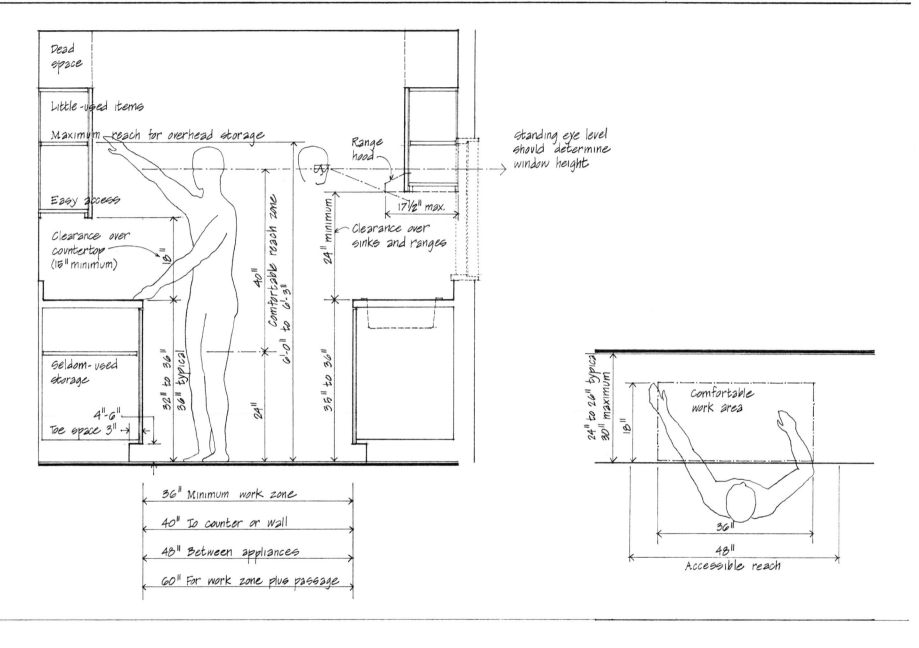

Dead space

Little-used items

Maximum reach for overhead storage

Easy access

Clearance over countertop (15" minimum)

18"

Seldom-used storage

4"-6"
Toe space 3"

40"
Comfortable reach zone 6'-0" to 6'-3"

32" to 36"
36" typical

24"

Range hood

17½" max.

Standing eye level should determine window height

Clearance over sinks and ranges

24" minimum

35" to 36"

36" Minimum work zone

40" To counter or wall

48" Between appliances

60" For work zone plus passage

24" to 26" typical
30" maximum
18"

Comfortable work area

36"

48"
Accessible reach

# WORK CENTERS

There are three major, essential work centers in a kitchen: a preparation and clean-up area, a cooking and serving area, and a storage and mixing area. Each of these has specific functions and specific equipment, work surface, and storage requirements. Of these, the most used is the preparation and clean-up area. And more work is typically done between the preparation and cooking areas than between the others. Keep in mind that the following are only guidelines that should be adapted to your own needs.

There are other areas that you may wish to incorporate into your kitchen design if they are important to you, and there is enough space available. These include:

- An eating area at a counter, or a small dining table.
- A mixing and baking center, with a nice marble top, close to the oven and range.
- A desk and telephone area, away from but accessible to the work areas.
- A laundry area.

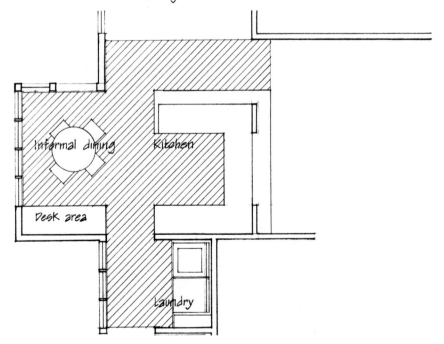

**1.** PREPARATION AND CLEAN-UP CENTER

The preparation and clean-up area centers around the sink. There should be a minimum of 18" of counter space to either side of the sink, although 24" is better for cleaning activities, and 36" is ideal. If you have a dishwasher, it should be immediately adjacent to the sink for easy loading, but should not open perpendicular to it. With a dishwasher, it is better to have a single large sink for oversized pots and pans than a double sink with smaller bowls. If there is no dishwasher, a double or triple bowl sink is useful.

Sinks come in two basic materials: enamel (on cast iron or steel) or stainless steel. Enameled cast iron is more expensive than enameled steel, but it is more chip-resistant and quieter. If the colors available in enamel sinks do not attract you, consider the durability of stainless steel sinks. Stainless steel sinks should be 18 or 20 gauge, and be of the nickel-bearing type for better corrosion resistance. A fine satin finish will also hide use marks better. Of the various mounting types available, self-rimming sinks are preferred.

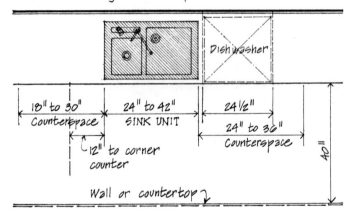

## 2. COOKING AND SERVING CENTER

The cooking and serving area centers around the range or cooktop unit. To either side should be 18" to 24" of counter space, preferably of a heat-resistant material such as stainless steel or glass ceramic, for placing hot pans. Any overhead cabinets should be at least 30" above the cooktop surface. The cooking and serving center should ideally be oriented toward the dining area, with storage for cooking utensils, serving ware, etc.

The range may be a slide-in model with unfinished sides, or a drop-in model that rests on cabinetry or a special floor unit. A built-in cooktop offers the greatest flexibility, especially if you desire the cooking surface to be below the standard 36" countertop height.

If a separate wall-mounted oven or microwave oven is desired to conserve counter space, the opened oven door should be 3" to 4" below your elbow level, and there should be at least 24" of adjacent countertop space.

## 3. STORAGE AND MIXING CENTER

The storage and mixing center is anchored by the refrigerator. The refrigerator should be located at the end of a counter to avoid dividing a countertop into small areas, and it should open onto the kitchen work area. On the latch side of the door should be at least 15" of countertop space, although 36" to 42" of uninterrupted countertop between the refrigerator and the sink is preferred. The door itself should be able to open fully without interference, and not interfere with passing traffic.

The refrigerator should not be located next to a wall-mounted oven, dishwasher, or range. And enough space should be allowed around, behind, or above the refrigerator for heat dissipation from the condenser coils.

The storage center should also be located close to any pantry or mixing area you may have.

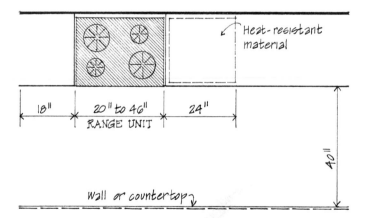

Heat-resistant material

18" | 20" to 46" RANGE UNIT | 24"

40"

Wall or countertop

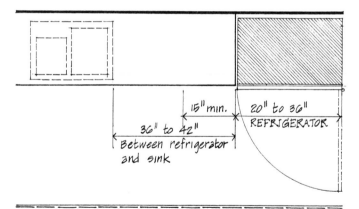

15" min. | 20" to 36" REFRIGERATOR

36" to 42"
Between refrigerator and sink

## PLAN LAYOUTS

The basis for any kitchen layout is a work triangle that connects the three major work centers. The sides of this triangle should add up to no more than 22', nor less than 12'. Under ideal circumstances, the distance from the sink to the cooktop should be 4' to 6'; between the sink and the refrigerator, 4' to 7'; between the cooktop and the refrigerator, 4' to 9'. With these dimensions in mind, there are these basic kitchen plan layouts:

### 1. U-SHAPED KITCHEN

A U-shaped kitchen affords the most workable arrangement for a kitchen. It accommodates an efficient work triangle, and ensures that traffic will not interfere with the work area. The sink usually occupies the base of the U, with the range and refrigerator to either side. For a dishwasher to be placed beside the sink, and to allow at least 5' between the counters, the back wall of the U should be at least 9', but not longer than 13'. A U-shaped kitchen can be elongated if it is organized around an island counter.

A variation of the U-shaped layout involves transforming one of the side counters into a peninsula or pass-through, opening up the kitchen onto an adjacent room.

### 2. L-SHAPED KITCHEN

The L-shaped kitchen layout also accommodates an efficient work triangle if one leg of the L does not get too long. It is a popular layout that fits small, square rooms well. The sink is usually placed in the middle of the continuous counter space to create a refrigerator-to-sink-to-range work flow. If the room is large enough, the space opposite the L can be used as a dining area.

An island can sometimes be used to buffer the work area from traffic, and provide additional countertop and storage space. The island should be at least 4' from any counter and 3' from any wall.

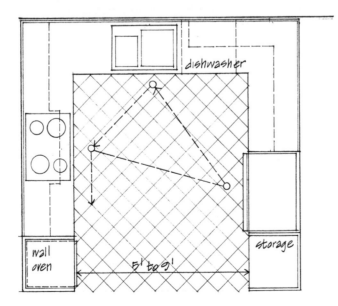

dishwasher

wall oven

storage

5' to 9'

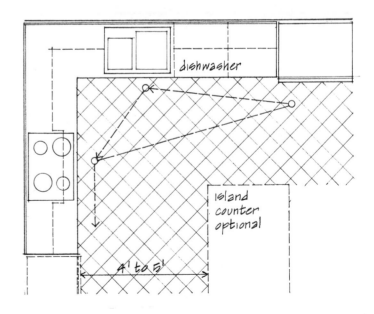

dishwasher

island counter optional

4' to 5'

## 3. CORRIDOR PLAN

The corridor plan can fit into a narrower space than either the U- or L-shaped layouts, and can be very efficient if through-traffic is eliminated by closing off one end of the corridor, or if not more than one or two people use the kitchen at any one time. The aisle should be at least 48" wide to provide clearance for the cabinet and appliance doors. If there is traffic through the kitchen, a 54" or 60" wide aisle is preferred. The sink and range are usually on one side while the refrigerator is on the other. The refrigerator door should not interfere with the oven door.

One side of the corridor or galley kitchen can open onto an adjacent dining or living room with a pass-through or a row of base cabinets serving as a divider.

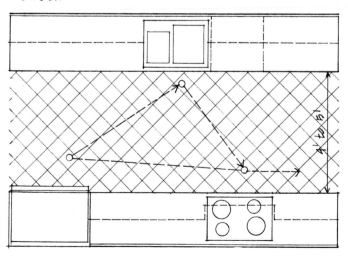

## 4. ONE-WALL LAYOUT

Single-wall layouts are extremely compact but suitable only for studio apartments or where space is extremely limited. The layout should not be more than 12' long, and the use of scaled-down appliances should be considered to maximize the amount of counter space. As with other layouts, the sink is usually located in the middle, with the refrigerator at one end and the range at the other.

A single-wall layout can be located in an alcove or closet space with door panels to screen the kitchen from view. To supplement the counter space, a portable dishwasher or serving cart can be used.

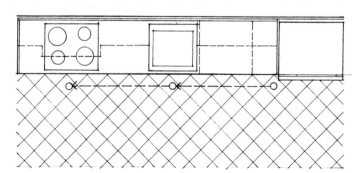

## PLANNING THE LAYOUT

After you have selected a layout that you feel can work in your specific situation, test its efficiency and how it fits into the existing room with its patterns of walls, windows and doorways.

Doorways are often the cause of a kitchen's layout problems. Too many doors leading into a kitchen can create awkward paths through the work area. Doors can occupy valuable wall space, especially at corners, that can better be used for cabinets, countertop space, or appliances. First, eliminate any unnecessary doorways. Second, move doors away from corners, if possible, and locate them so that traffic bypasses the major work centers of the kitchen.

Windows are always desirable for daylighting a kitchen. The existing windows, however, may interfere with the placement of the wall cabinets and shelving you need. First study how storage cabinets and shelving can fit around or in between the windows. If there is not enough wall space, consider running in front of the windows open shelving that will provide storage space but also let daylight in and allow you to see out. As a last resort, you may have to move or consolidate the windows in another location.

If the existing window sill height is less than 36" above the floor, it may restrict the placement and continuity of the base cabinets and countertop. Rather than raising the sill height, consider deepening the counter top so that a small window well for plants can be built in front of the window and allow the countertop to be continuous.

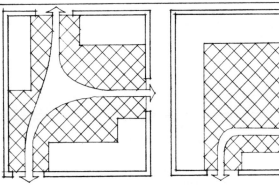

Doorways use up valuable wall space at corners, and generate paths that can interfere with the work area.

Place doorways to define a simple and direct path that by-passes the work area.

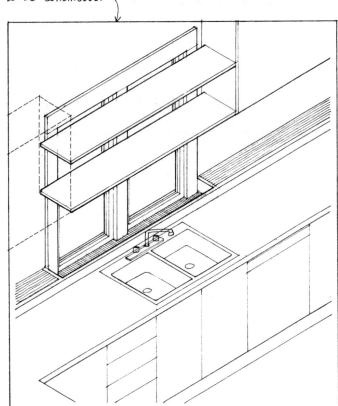

Most remodeling of kitchens that are too small or awkwardly shaped involve the rearranging of its walls and doorways, and the annexing of adjacent closets, utility areas, and even parts of hallways. The consolidation of these small spaces can make the kitchen larger and improve the proportion of its floor area. Before removing any walls, however, determine whether they are load-bearing, or contain any utility lines. (See pgs. 96-101.) Also remember that any enlargement of your kitchen should not adversely affect adjacent living spaces.

If rearranging the walls around your kitchen is not possible, consider extending it outward. A small extension can often be cantilevered over the existing foundation. And even a two or three foot addition can gain you a lot of space, and allow you to design into the remodeling an entirely new wall, with windows and shelving as you want them.

The other possibilities for you to explore involve locating the kitchen in another room, or building a room-sized addition for the kitchen.

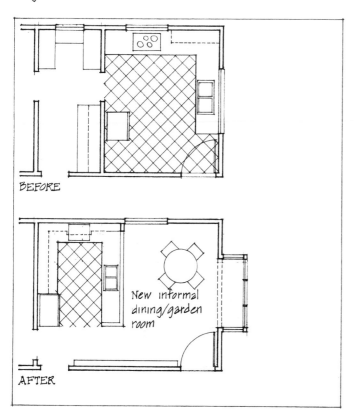

BEFORE

AFTER

New informal dining/garden room

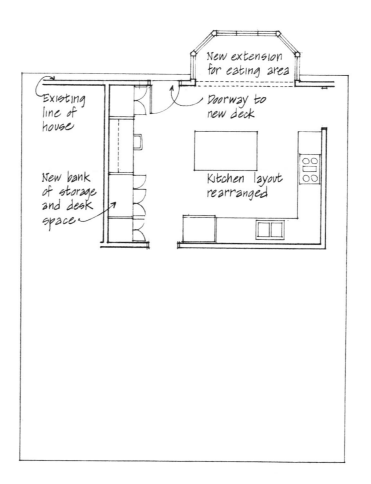

New extension for eating area

Existing line of house

Doorway to new deck

New bank of storage and desk space

Kitchen layout rearranged

## CABINETS

You may want to recycle your existing kitchen cabinets, or have new ones installed. If the space in your existing cabinets and their layout work well, the cabinets can be refinished, or new fronts and countertops installed. Re-surfacing the existing cabinets can give your kitchen a totally new look without the expense of all new cabinets.

New cabinets can be custom-made, tailored and finished to your specifications, and are especially appropriate for odd-shaped kitchens. Before deciding to have your cabinets custom-built, however, investigate the many styles and types of stock cabinets that are available. Most stock cabinets conform to industry standards set by the National Kitchen Cabinet Association (NKCA), and the better grades are generally competitive with custom-built cabinets in quality of construction and finish.

Cabinets are usually made of particle board or plywood with hardwood frames, with lacquer, plastic-laminate or hardwood veneer finishes. The design of the door and drawer fronts sets the style of the cabinets, and often for the entire kitchen as well.

Stock cabinets are manufactured in 3" modules. Their modular dimensions enable them to be laid out and arranged in a number of ways. In addition, there are three basic types of cabinets: base units, wall units, and special units.

Base units are 23" or 24" deep, and usually 34½" high. With the addition of the countertop, their total height will typically be 36", although you can adjust this height either way a few inches. The countertop can be raised with blocking, or the height of the kickplate or base reduced.

Single-door base units vary from 12" to 24" in length. Double-door units range from 27" to 48" in length. Drawer units are 15" to 24" long. Special base units for sinks, ranges, and built-in cooktops may be 30" to 96" in length.

Base units for desktops and buffets are similar but only 28½" high; base units for bathroom vanities are 30" high.

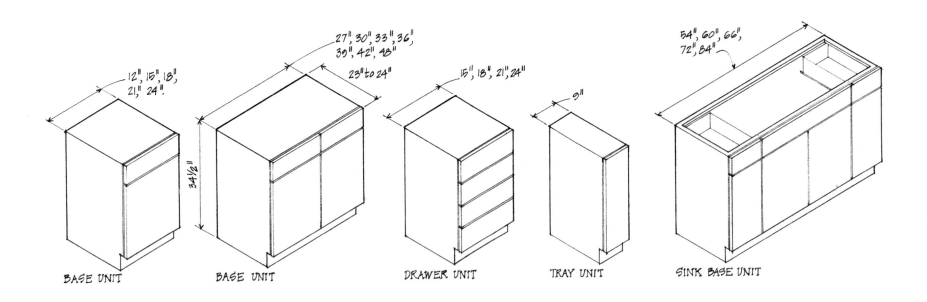

BASE UNIT     BASE UNIT     DRAWER UNIT     TRAY UNIT     SINK BASE UNIT

Wall units are typically 12" or 13" deep, and 12" to 33" high. Their lengths generally correspond to the lengths of base units. Some wall units are made for installation over island counters, and have finished backs.

There are special corner units for both base and wall cabinets. Some have revolving or lazy-susan shelving, while others have a blank or open area where the adjacent base or wall unit can be joined at a right angle.

Other special units include tall (84") cabinets for refrigerators and wall-mounted ovens, or use as pantries or utility closets.

Depending on the manufacturer, there is a host of accessories for these cabinets. There are pop-up trays for small appliances, flour and sugar bins, slide-out cutting boards, door-mounted storage racks, cutlery trays, drawer organizers. Consult the cabinet manufacturer's catalog for a complete listing.

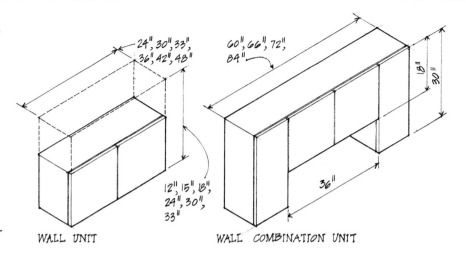

WALL UNIT                    WALL COMBINATION UNIT

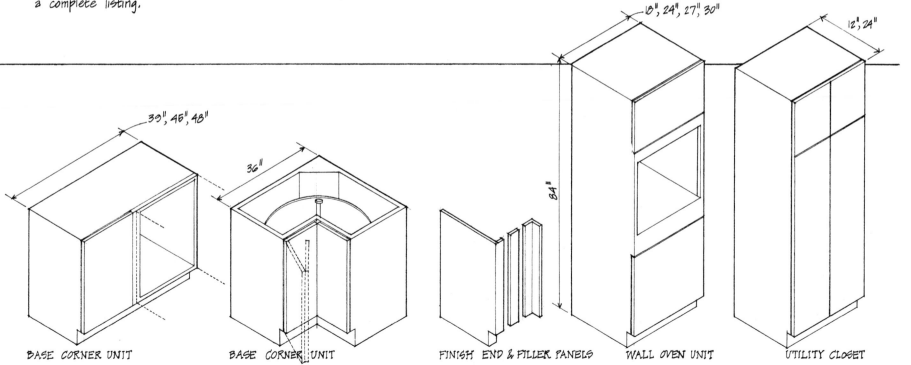

BASE CORNER UNIT        BASE CORNER UNIT        FINISH END & FILLER PANELS        WALL OVEN UNIT        UTILITY CLOSET

## LAYING OUT CABINETWORK

After your preliminary kitchen plan has been adapted to and laid out within the existing space, and the sink and appliances located where you want them, work out the base and wall cabinets you need to tie the kitchen space and its elements together.

Inventory and measure the cooking ware, utensils, serving trays, dishes, etc. that need to be stored. Determine the amount of shelving and pantry space you need for food-stuffs. Allocate space for cleaning equipment, supplies, and the trash can.

Visit a kitchen cabinet showroom, and look at the various styles and finishes of cabinets available. Study their construction. To judge the quality of a cabinet, inspect its door and drawer fronts, how their joints are fitted, the interior back and side finishes, and the quality of the hardware used. The doors should swing freely and latch securely; the drawers should open smoothly. Obtain literature, showing the types and sizes of cabinet units and accessories available, to take home and use as a reference while planning your cabinet layout.

With this information, work out the type, number, and sizes of cabinets you need. Keep in mind the modular dimensions of the cabinets, the type of storage you need – whether they be cabinets, open shelving, or drawers – and where you need the storage.

As you lay out the cabinets, include on your plan the exact dimensions of the appliances, the location and height of windows, door swings, and the location of heating outlets. Also check for potential conflicts between the cabinets and window or door trim.

At corners of base cabinets, clearance must be provided for any projecting knobs or pulls. This clearance is necessary for any drawer at the corner to slide out and not hit the projecting hardware. For this purpose, corner filler panels are available.

There are also filler panels for base and wall cabinets to make adjustments between the fixed, modular dimensions of the cabinets and the specific dimensions of your kitchen space.

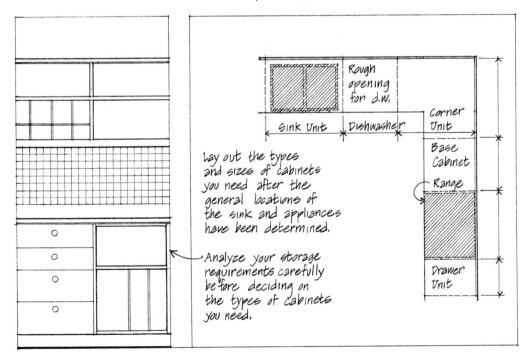

Rough opening for d.w.

Sink Unit    Dishwasher

Corner Unit

Base Cabinet

Range

Drawer Unit

Lay out the types and sizes of cabinets you need after the general locations of the sink and appliances have been determined.

Analyze your storage requirements carefully before deciding on the types of cabinets you need.

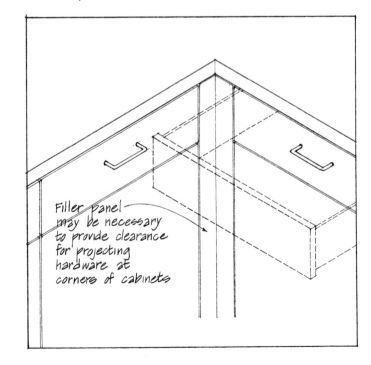

Filler panel may be necessary to provide clearance for projecting hardware at corners of cabinets

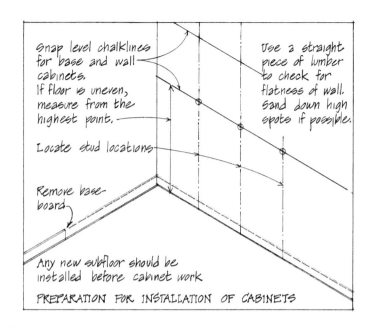

Snap level chalklines for base and wall cabinets.
If floor is uneven, measure from the highest point.

Use a straight piece of lumber to check for flatness of wall. Sand down high spots if possible.

Locate stud locations

Remove base-board

Any new subfloor should be installed before cabinet work

PREPARATION FOR INSTALLATION OF CABINETS

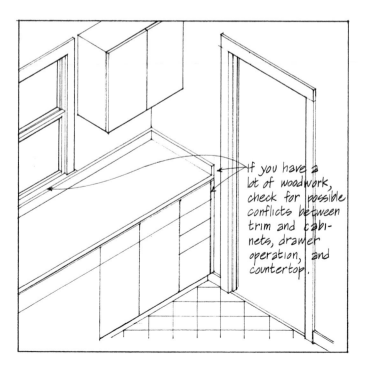

If you have a lot of woodwork, check for possible conflicts between trim and cabinets, drawer operation, and countertop.

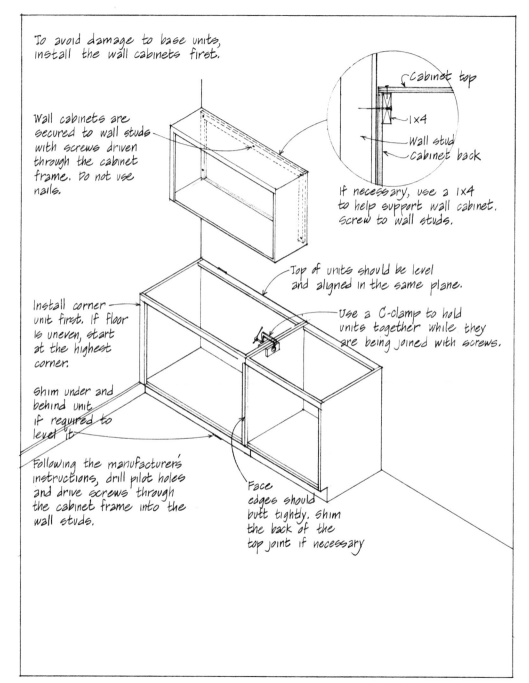

To avoid damage to base units, install the wall cabinets first.

Wall cabinets are secured to wall studs with screws driven through the cabinet frame. Do not use nails.

Cabinet top
1x4
Wall stud
cabinet back

If necessary, use a 1x4 to help support wall cabinet. Screw to wall studs.

Install corner unit first. If floor is uneven, start at the highest corner.

Shim under and behind unit if required to level it.

Following the manufacturer's instructions, drill pilot holes and drive screws through the cabinet frame into the wall studs.

Top of units should be level and aligned in the same plane.

Use a C-clamp to hold units together while they are being joined with screws.

Face edges should butt tightly. Shim the back of the top joint if necessary

## COUNTERTOPS

Countertop surfaces in kitchens must be durable, easy to maintain, and resistant to grease and moisture. In addition, sections of countertops must be able to endure sharp knives and hot pots and pans. The following is an outline of materials which can be used on kitchen countertops. Many of these can be used in bathrooms as well.

Plastic-laminate, available in a wide range of colors and patterns, is the most popular countertop surface. It provides a hard, durable, water-resistant surface. Although it is heat-resistant, it can be scorched or blistered by extreme heat (270°F.), and damaged by some abrasives, knives, and chlorine.

Plastic-laminate is available in sheets 2' to 5' wide and 5' to 12' long, in two thicknesses. The 1/16" thick sheets are used for horizontal applications on countertops and tabletops, while 1/32" thick sheets are used for vertical applications on door fronts and walls. In addition to the various colors and patterns available, the plastic-laminate surface may have a gloss, satin, low-glare, or textured finish.

## PLASTIC-LAMINATE

Plastic-laminate can be bonded with contact adhesive to most flat, dry surfaces, such as plywood, particle board, or hardboard. For countertops, a minimum 3/4" thick particle board is usually used as core stock.

Even though plastic-laminate is a tough material, its edges must be protected from chipping. It can also snap if bent too much during handling.

When laying out the plastic laminate, any seams should be at corners. Stresses at unbroken corners can lead to cracking. Similarly, cutouts for sinks and cooktops should have radius corners.

A sheet of plastic-laminate can be cut in a number of ways. The best is to use a router for the finish cut. For general cuts, a circular saw with a fine-tooth blade, or a backsaw at a low angle can be used, cutting with the good face down. Special laminate scissors can also be used for general cuts. For small pieces, use a carbide-tipped knife blade to score the laminate, then snap it upward against a metal straightedge.

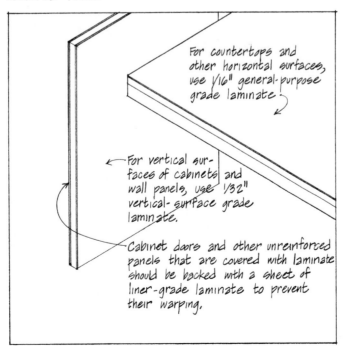

For countertops and other horizontal surfaces, use 1/16" general-purpose grade laminate.

For vertical surfaces of cabinets and wall panels, use 1/32" vertical-surface grade laminate.

Cabinet doors and other unreinforced panels that are covered with laminate should be backed with a sheet of liner-grade laminate to prevent their warping.

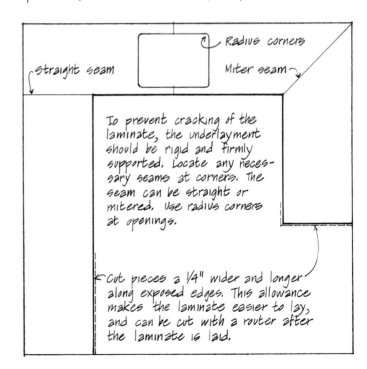

Radius corners

straight seam        Miter seam

To prevent cracking of the laminate, the underlayment should be rigid and firmly supported. Locate any necessary seams at corners. The seam can be straight or mitered. Use radius corners at openings.

Cut pieces a 1/4" wider and longer along exposed edges. This allowance makes the laminate easier to lay, and can be cut with a router after the laminate is laid.

After the laminate is cut to size, apply the contact cement to both the surface of the countertop base material and the back of the laminate sheet. Apply the cement with a brush or roller, and let it set, as per the manufacturer's recommendations. Since the plastic-laminate will adhere to the base surface on contact, the cutting and fitting of the sheet must be done carefully. Once in place, the sheet will be difficult to move or remove.

Lay strips of wood down on the surface after the contact cement is set. Place the plastic-laminate on top, being careful the two surfaces do not touch. Instead of the wood strips, a dry sheet of heavy, brown wrapping paper can be used to keep the laminate from contact with the base surface.

Position the laminate sheet carefully. Working from one end, remove the wood strips or the wrapping paper, and let the laminate come into contact with the base surface. Once the laminate sheet is down, use a small hand roller to press the laminate firmly to the base surface and remove any air pockets that may develop.

With a router or laminate cutter, trim the plastic-laminate sheet along the exposed edges. (The original sheet should be cut slightly larger than needed along any exposed edges.) At this time, also cut out any openings for a sink or cooktop with an electric saber saw.

If you are also edging the countertop with plastic-laminate, pre-cut the strips and apply as described above. Do this before the top surface is covered. Trim where the top overlaps the edge piece with a router and a bevel cutter, or use a smooth mill file to form a bevel.

You can also finish the countertop edge with hardwood trim or ceramic tile.

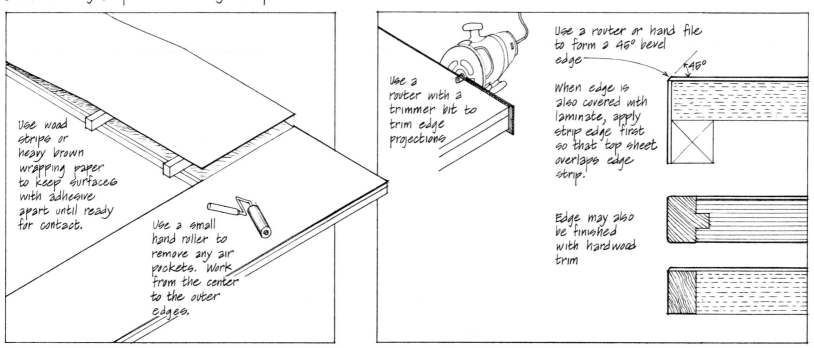

Use wood strips or heavy brown wrapping paper to keep surfaces with adhesive apart until ready for contact.

Use a small hand roller to remove any air pockets. Work from the center to the outer edges.

Use a router with a trimmer bit to trim edge projections

Use a router or hand file to form a 45° bevel edge

When edge is also covered with laminate, apply strip edge first so that top sheet overlaps edge strip.

Edge may also be finished with hardwood trim

## COUNTERTOPS

In addition to plastic-laminate, other materials can be used for part or all of a kitchen counter. For those that do a lot of cutting and chopping and need a lot of working space, a butcher block top can be an attractive working surface. Although more expensive than plastic-laminate tops, butcher block wears and ages well, and can be maintained with light sanding and a periodic coating of mineral oil. Edge grain maple is the best butcher block material. It should be well laminated, and be at least 1½" thick.

If an entire countertop of butcher block is not needed, consider setting it into a section of the counter. There are also ready-made butcher block counters with a built-in backsplash.

Ceramic tile is often used adjacent to the range or cooktop surface since it is heat-resistant and can take hot pots and pans without being damaged. Available in a range of colors and sizes, it can also be used over an entire counter, and continue up the wall behind the counter as well. The ceramic tile must be installed carefully with tight grout joints. The grout should be treated and sealed for mildew-resistance.

Stainless steel makes a good, heatproof insert next to the cooktop surface. It will show nicks and scratches, and, if not supported properly by a solid, firm base, it can be dented.

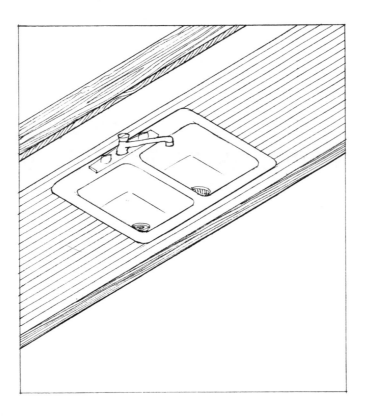

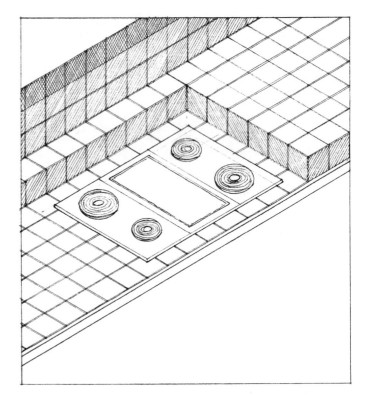

Corian, a registered trademark of the DuPont Corporation, is a mineral-filled acrylic plastic. It is fairly expensive but has a beautiful texture. Unlike other synthetic marbles, its color and pattern runs clear through its thickness. So while it is resistant to heat marks and stains, minor burns and nicks can be removed with a household cleanser or a fine grade of sandpaper. It can also be cut, drilled and shaped with woodworking tools, and requires no special edge treatments.

Corian is available in sheets 30" wide and up to 10' long. For vanity tops and countertops, 1/2" and 3/4" thicknesses are used; for walls, and shower and tub enclosures, 1/4" thick panels can be used. Also available are countertops with integral bowls.

The natural, cool surface of marble makes it attractive for use as a pastry slab. It can be used in the mixing area of your kitchen or over all of the countertop surfaces. Used or remnant pieces may be as reasonably priced as synthetic marbles. There are also 12" square marble tiles that can be laid over the countertop surface. Any marble used should have its porous surface treated with a sealer.

Granite, although quite heavy and expensive, also makes a beautiful and durable countertop that is easy to maintain.

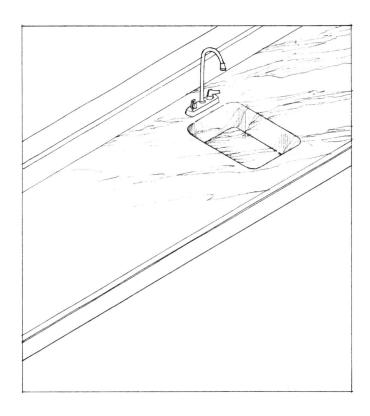

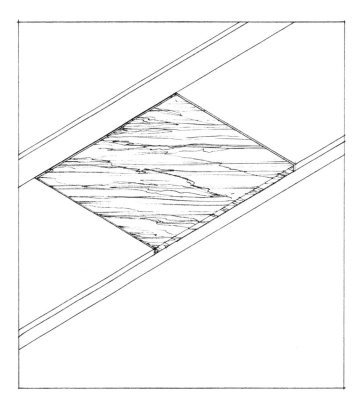

# VENTILATION

The proper ventilation of the kitchen is necessary to rid the air of moisture, unwanted heat, grease, fumes and smoke generated by cooking activities. Moisture vapor and heat can be vented by a wall or ceiling mounted exhaust fan near the range. Grease and smoke must be filtered by a ventilating hood over the cooktop.

There are a variety of room exhaust fans available. They vary in size, type and capacity of fan used, mounting location, and direction of discharge.

1. Wall fans that require no ductwork are the most economical and often the most efficient room fans to use.
2. Exterior fans are similar to wall fans, but are quieter since their fan or blower motors are mounted on the outside of the wall or roof to pull rather than push the air through.
3. Ceiling fans are mounted between the ceiling joists and discharge vertically through a duct and roof cap.
4. Side discharge fans fit within standard stud or joist spacing. They use rectangular ducts, and can be mounted in a wall to discharge vertically, or in a ceiling to discharge horizontally, to the outside.
5. Blowers are interior ventilating units that can be installed in a ceiling or soffit, and discharge through rectangular ducts through the roof or horizontally between ceiling joists. These centrifugal blower units are effective in overcoming duct resistance and can be used with long duct runs.

To estimate the size of a room exhaust fan needed, allow 2 CFM per square foot area of the kitchen. See also pg. 286.

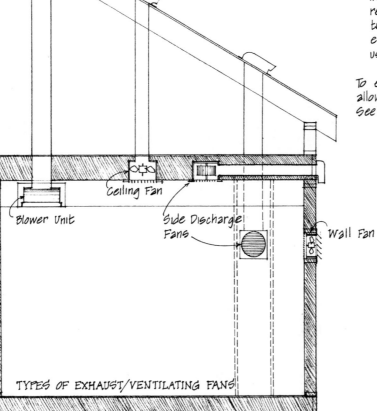

Ceiling Fan

Blower Unit

Side Discharge Fans

Wall Fan

TYPES OF EXHAUST/VENTILATING FANS

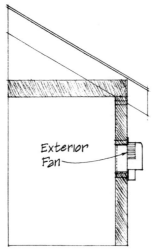

Exterior Fan

Fans with air-to-air heat exchangers are available to save energy.

Ventilating hoods filter out grease, smoke and odors from the air at their source, before the air is vented, either directly or through ductwork, to the outside. The hood assembly should be mounted directly over, and from 21" to 30" above the cooktop surface. Various styles and and sizes are available that can be wall-hung, mounted under cabinets, or suspended from the ceiling. They are usually pre-wired for a fan unit with a variable-speed control switch, as well as a light fixture.

The fans are usually centrifugal blower units. They may be interior-mounted, or be located at the end of a duct run and mounted on an exterior wall or roof. To estimate the size of the fan unit needed, allow 40 CFM per foot of hood length when along a wall, or 50 CFM per foot of hood when it is over an island or peninsula cooktop. For duct runs over 10' long, add 50 to 100 CFM.

When ductwork is not possible, ductless hoods are used. These have fans that draw air in through a filter that eliminates the grease and odors before releasing the air back into the kitchen space. They do not rid the room of unwanted heat and moisture, and are not as effective as ducted ventilating hoods.

Since the grease that collects in a hood's filter can be a fire hazard and also reduce the efficiency of the fan unit, the filter should be cleaned regularly, at intervals specified by the manufacturer.

Some built-in cooktops are self-venting and require no hood. Their enclosed fan units require ducting to the outside, either through an exterior wall, or if the cooktop has an island location, through the floor framing.

Any ductwork required should have as direct and straight a run as possible, with a minimum number of turns. The longer the duct run, and the more turns it has, the more power the fan unit must have to push the air through, and the greater the chance grease will have to collect in it.

Rectangular 3¼" x 10" ducts are used to fit within stud and joist framing, while 6" or 7" diameter round ducts are used elsewhere. The ductwork is terminated at the exterior by a wall or roof cap. These caps usually have a weather or back-draft damper, or louvers, and insect screening.

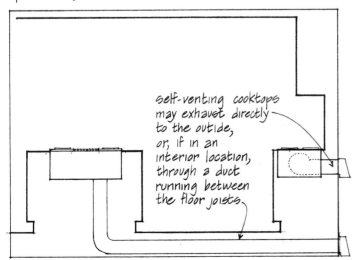

self-venting cooktops may exhaust directly to the outside, or, if in an interior location, through a duct running between the floor joists.

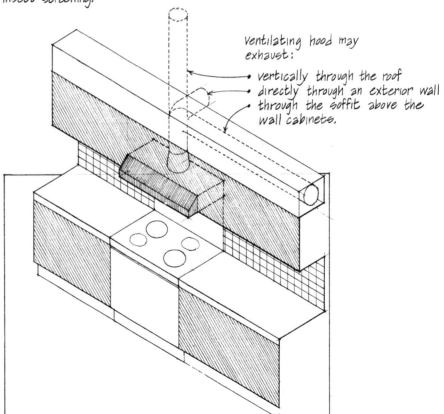

Ventilating hood may exhaust:
- vertically through the roof
- directly through an exterior wall
- through the soffit above the wall cabinets.

## LIGHTING

Natural daylighting in a kitchen is always attractive. Morning sunlight can be especially desirable. Since windows use up wall space, their placement should be coordinated with the layout of the wall cabinets or shelving you require for storage. Whatever daylighting you have, it must, of course, be supplemented by artificial lighting.

Kitchens require both general area lighting and specific task lighting over work surfaces for food preparation, cooking and clean-up activities. This light should be evenly distributed and placed so that you can see the work surfaces, and into cabinets and drawers, without working in your own shadow or in shadows cast by overhead cabinets.

Incandescent lighting is preferred for its warm, flattering light, and more appetizing rendition of food. The point sources of incandescent bulbs also render forms and textures attractively.

Fluorescent lighting uses longer-lasting, more energy-efficient lamps, and creates less glare than incandescent bulbs. Their color rendition, however, varies with the type of lamp used. For kitchens, deluxe warm white lamps that are warmer than other fluorescent tubes are recommended.

As a practical matter, it is generally best to combine both warm incandescent and warm fluorescent lighting in your kitchen. See also pgs. 58-60.

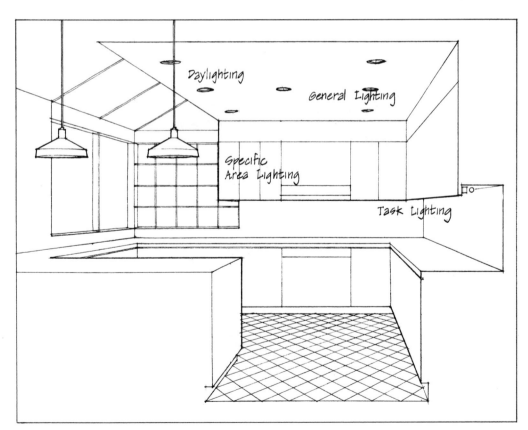

Daylighting

General Lighting

Specific Area Lighting

Task Lighting

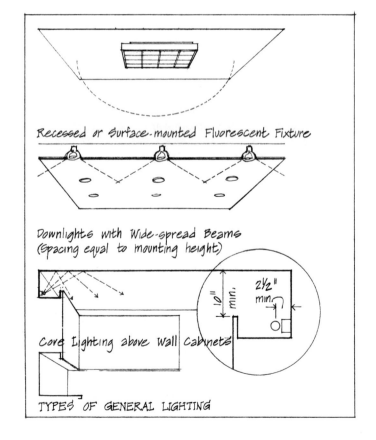

Recessed or Surface-mounted Fluorescent Fixture

Downlights with Wide-spread Beams
(Spacing equal to mounting height)

Core Lighting above Wall Cabinets

10" min.

2½" min.

TYPES OF GENERAL LIGHTING

General lighting in a kitchen can be provided by overhead ceiling fixtures, an illuminated ceiling, or perimeter soffit lighting. For average-sized kitchens up to 75 s.f. in area, use a total of 200W incandescent or 80W fluorescent lighting in surface-mounted ceiling fixtures. For recessed fixtures, use four 100W incandescents. If the kitchen has dark cabinet, wall or floor finishes, the wattage will have to be increased.

For larger kitchens, use 2W of incandescent or 1W of fluorescent surface-mounted lighting per square foot of kitchen area. For recessed lighting, use 100W of incandescent per 30 s.f., or 20W of fluorescent per 60 s.f. of kitchen area.

General area lighting can also be provided by a single row of fluorescent tubes mounted over the wall cabinets or in a soffit.

Over sinks and ranges without ventilating hoods, use two 30W or three 20W fluorescent tubes, or two 75W incandescent floods or soft-white bulbs. These may be surface-mounted behind a shielding faceboard, or be in recessed fixtures.

Over countertop surfaces, lighting is best installed under wall cabinets or shelving, and shielded from direct view by an opaque faceboard. Use the longest fluorescent tube that will fit and cover at least two-thirds of the counter length - a 24", 20W tube for a 36" counter, a 36", 30W tube for a 48" counter, etc. This type of lighting is generally effective up to a height of 22" above the countertop surface.

If you prefer the warmer rendition of incandescent lighting, use double-socket brackets with 60W bulbs for every 3' of counter length.

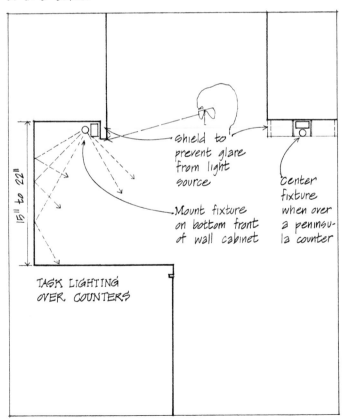

shield to prevent glare from light source

Mount fixture on bottom front of wall cabinet

Center fixture when over a peninsula counter

15" to 22"

TASK LIGHTING OVER COUNTERS

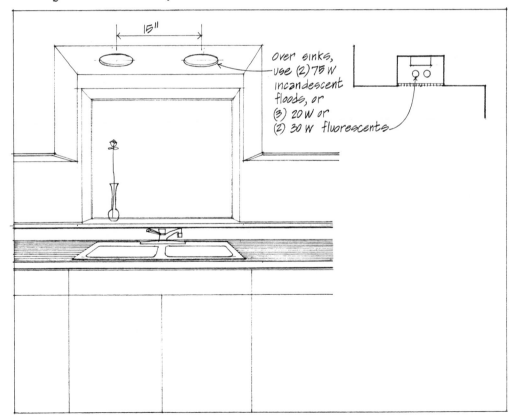

15"

Over sinks, use (2) 75W incandescent floods, or (3) 20W or (2) 30W fluorescents

# BATHROOMS

Bathrooms receive as much attention as kitchens during a house remodeling, and for good reasons. New fixtures, materials and accessories are now available that can transform an existing bathroom into a more attractive, comfortable and functional space. New durable finishes also make bathrooms easier to maintain and care for.

If the existing bathroom works well, and its fixtures are in good condition, a renovation of its wall, floor and ceiling surfaces may be all that's needed. Perhaps new lighting, a heat lamp and a ventilating fan can make it more comfortable as well.

To make more efficient use of the bathroom space, consider replacing the existing fixtures with new, more compact models. These can also add color to and brighten your bathroom.

If space is tight, adding space and rearranging the bathroom layout can provide you with more usable floor area and needed storage for linen, toiletries, etc. This, of course, can lead to a more expensive project that requires careful planning.

While remodeling a bathroom, or building a new one, you must obviously take into account the location of existing plumbing supply and waste lines. Consideration should also be given to the convenience of the bathroom location and the comfort of its users. Determine what part of the house the bathroom must serve, who will be using the bathroom, and what type of access is needed.

Half-baths are typically located on the main house level, close to the main living areas and the entry, for use by the household members and guests. Full bathrooms are located closer to the bedrooms. Except for bathrooms in master bedroom suites, they should be conveniently accessible from a common space.

The planning for a bathroom begins with its floor plan. When laying a bathroom out, too much attention is often given to the location and length of plumbing lines, and not enough to the requirements of those using the bathroom. In laying out the fixtures, any countertop surfaces, and storage spaces, consider the factors on the following page.

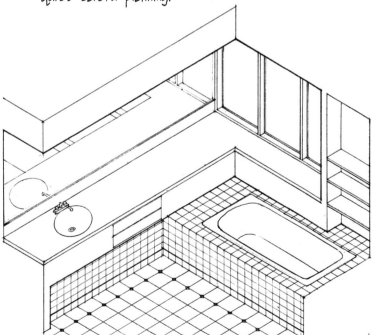

1. How much space is available and its shape:
   More than any other room in the house, a bathroom can efficiently utilize alcove spaces for its fixtures, while leaving a reasonably shaped floor area for its users.

2. The manner in which the fixtures are used:
   The lavatory sink is the most used fixture. The sink, countertop, and storage spaces should be the most accessible, and closest to the bathroom entry. The toilet and bathtub or shower unit are usually further removed for privacy. If desired, they can be compartmentalized as secondary spaces off of the main space.

3. The space requirements for each fixture and its use:
   For the user's convenience, minimum clearances between fixtures, and from a fixture to a wall or other obstruction, are usually specified by code. In addition, there should be sufficient space for toweling off, dressing, grooming, etc.

4. How much storage is needed:
   Sufficient space should be planned and provided for toiletries, towels, linen, cleaning supplies, etc.

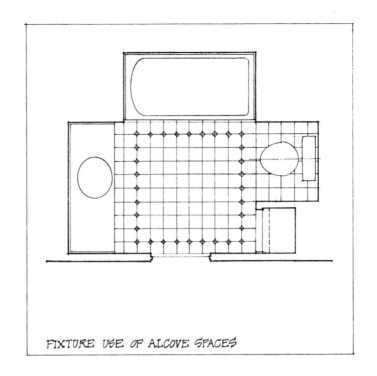

FIXTURE USE OF ALCOVE SPACES

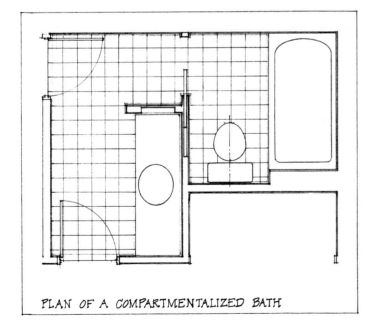

PLAN OF A COMPARTMENTALIZED BATH

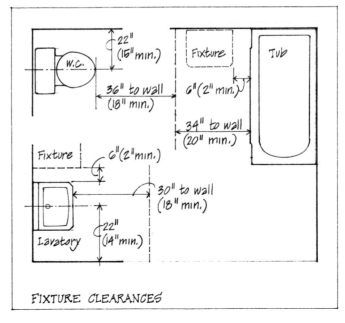

FIXTURE CLEARANCES

# BATHROOM LAYOUTS

Fixtures may be arranged with their plumbing located
on one, two, or three "wet" walls of the bathroom.

### 1. ONE-WALL LAYOUTS

A one-wall layout, with the bathroom fixtures
arranged along a single wall, is the simplest and
requires the fewest fittings. It is often used where
space is limited, but offers few design possibilities,
and may not efficiently use the available floor space.

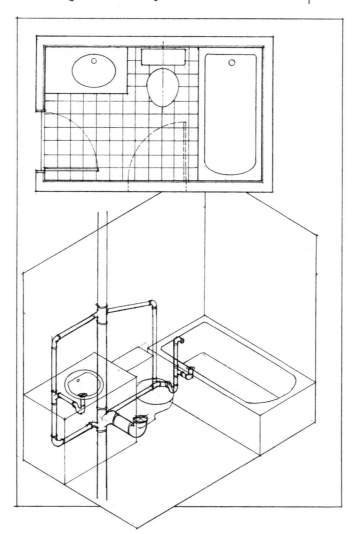

### 2. TWO-WALL LAYOUTS

A two-wall layout requires slightly more plumbing, but
offers more floor area and storage space around the
lavatory where they are needed. Making connections
between the floor joists can minimize the cutting of
walls.

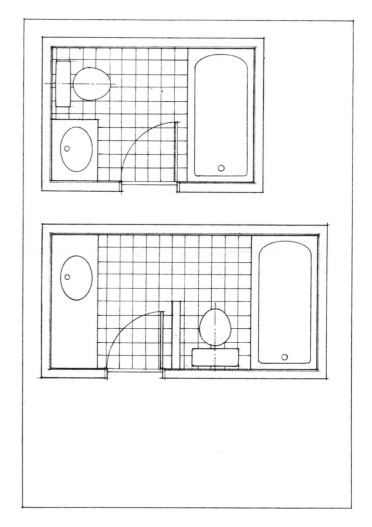

## 3. THREE-WALL LAYOUTS

A three-wall layout requires a larger bathroom space and more complicated plumbing, but offers the most flexibility in laying out the bathroom. The fixtures can usually be arranged to gain more wall, storage, and countertop space.

A compartmentalized bathroom can provide the convenience of two bathrooms in a space slightly larger than that required for one bathroom.

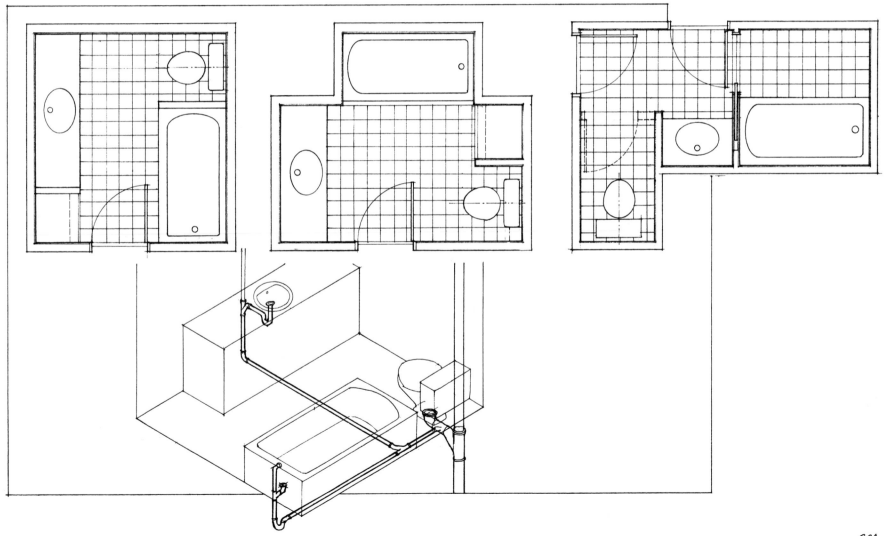

# BATHROOM FIXTURES

In selecting any bathroom fixture, you should consider its convenience of use, durability, ease of cleaning, and water usage.

## TOILETS

Check for efficiency of the flushing action, and quietness of operation. Washdown toilets are inexpensive, inefficient, and prohibited by some codes.

Reverse-trap toilets, quieter and more efficient than washdown toilets, are the least expensive of the siphon-action toilets. Siphon-jet toilets are quieter still, and have larger water surface areas and larger trapways.

The most expensive type of toilet, and the quietest, is the low-profile siphon-action model. Its bowl and tank are of one piece. Another quiet, extremely sanitary toilet is the siphon-vortex model. The vortex action scours the bowl each time it flushes.

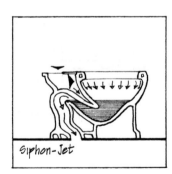

Siphon-Jet

Siphon-Action

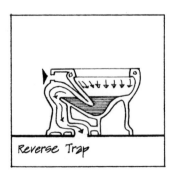

Reverse Trap

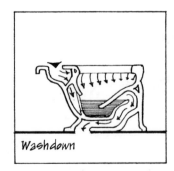

Washdown

## LAVATORIES

A wide range of lavatories is available, varying in material, size, shape and color. They may be of vitreous china, porcelain enamel over steel or cast iron, stainless steel, or plastic. They may be oval, round, or triangular for corner locations.

Wall-hung lavatories are the least expensive and take up the least amount of space, but leave their plumbing exposed and provide no storage. Floor-mounted pedestal models are similar but conceal their plumbing.

Of the types that are made to fit into a countertop, self-rimming models offer the cleanest installation. There are also countertops with integral bowls that are seamless and easy to clean. These are usually of plastic or synthetic marble.

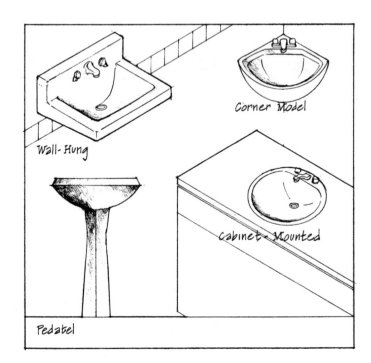

Corner Model

Wall-Hung

Cabinet-Mounted

Pedestal

## BATHTUBS

Bathtubs may be of enamel over steel or cast iron, or of fiberglass. Enameled steel tubs are relatively light-weight and inexpensive; cast iron tubs are much heavier, more expensive, but more durable. Fiberglass tubs are more expensive still, but are both lightweight and durable. Fiberglass, however, can be damaged by abrasive cleaning materials.

Standard tubs are 2'-6" to 3'-0" wide, 4'-6" to 5'-0" long, and 12" to 16" high. For limited spaces, smaller square tubs can be used.

If you plan to replace an existing tub with a new one, you may confront two problems. The first is removing the old tub - either it must be carefully broken into small pieces, or a portion of a wall removed for the tub's removal. The second is bringing the new tub in. For remodelings, lightweight fiberglass or enameled steel tubs are preferred.

If you have the space, and the floor framing can be rein-forced, consider one of the many oversized tubs, whirlpool baths, or soaking tubs now available. They can be sunken over an unused space, or be built into a raised platform. Many are formed with integral backrest, arm supports or seats. These large tubs will, however, increase your hot water costs if used often.

A shower can be installed in place of, or in addition to a bathtub. It can be built in as small as a 32" x 32" space, but a 36" x 36" shower is considered the minimum comfort-able size. It can be purchased in kit form, complete with receptor base, walls, and a folding door, or be built in a custom tiled space.

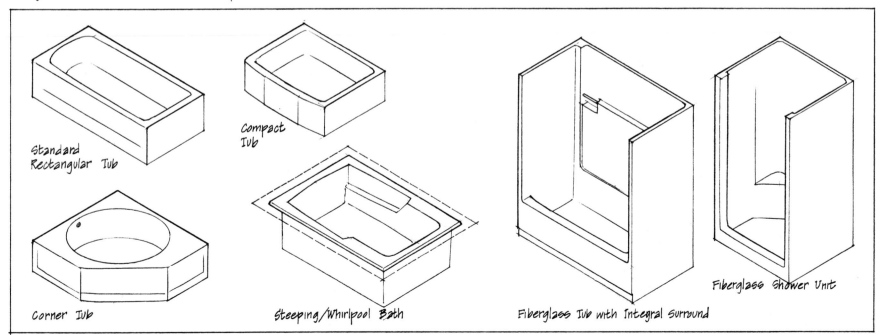

Standard Rectangular Tub

Compact Tub

Corner Tub

Steeping/Whirlpool Bath

Fiberglass Tub with Integral Surround

Fiberglass Shower Unit

## LIGHTING

Windows in bathrooms are always desirable for daylighting as well as ventilation. If wall space is limited and needed for fixtures or storage, consider the use of skylights. They can brighten a bathroom space even on cloudy or overcast days.

Artificial lighting is needed for both general area lighting and for directional lighting over mirrors, lavatory sinks, and compartmentalized bathtubs and toilets. While fluorescent lighting is more efficient, incandescent lighting is preferred for its warmer, more attractive rendition of skin tones and color. If fluorescent lighting is used, install deluxe warm white tubes.

For general area lighting, provide 3 to 4w of incandescent or 1.5 to 2W of fluorescent lighting per square foot of bathroom area. Over separate bathroom compartments, use a 75 or 100W ceiling fixture. Over bathtubs and showers, use a similar size recessed fixture that is vapor-proof. The switch for a bathtub or shower light should be located outside of the tub or shower area.

Over mirrors and lavatory sinks, use an incandescent fixture with two 60W bulbs, and to either side of the mirror, install wall-mounted fixtures with a 75W or two 60W bulbs. If fluorescent lighting is used, run a double row of 30 or 40W tubes in a soffit over the mirror and sink. For a small mirror, use two 20W tubes and a 20W tube on each side of the mirror.

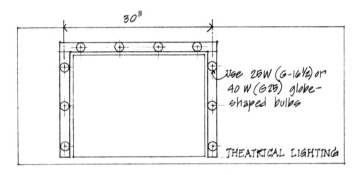

30"

Use 25W (G-16½) or 40 W (G25) globe-shaped bulbs

THEATRICAL LIGHTING

Any electrical convenience outlets should be protected by a ground-fault interrupter (GFI). A GFI device trips (breaks the circuit) almost instantaneously when any leakage of the current occurs. This protection is usually provided by a GFI receptacle, although a GFI breaker can also be provided at the service panel.

Bathroom outlets should be located where they are needed but away from water or wet areas.

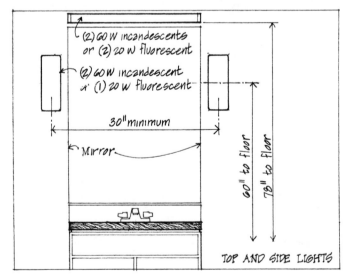

(2) 60 W incandescents or (2) 20 W fluorescent

(2) 60 W incandescent or (1) 20 W fluorescent

30" minimum

Mirror

60" to floor

78" to floor

TOP AND SIDE LIGHTS

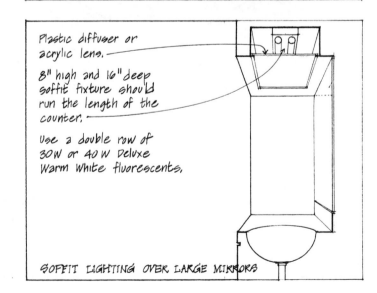

Plastic diffuser or acrylic lens.

8" high and 16" deep soffit fixture should run the length of the counter.

Use a double row of 30W or 40W Deluxe Warm White fluorescents.

SOFFIT LIGHTING OVER LARGE MIRRORS

## VENTILATION

Bathroom spaces must be ventilated to eliminate unpleasant odors, and the moisture generated by bathing and showering. Moisture, particularly, not only mists mirror surfaces and windows, but also can lead to deterioration of the bathroom finishes.

The exhaust fan should be located close to the shower or bathtub, and be switched independently of the light fixtures. A short-duration timer switch is often used to control the fan. If the fan is installed within a tub or shower enclosure, it should be UL Listed for the location and installed on a GFI branch circuit.

Many bathroom fans are combined with a light fixture, or a heat lamp for radiant heating of a bathroom's cold spots.

Most bathroom fans are ceiling mounted, and made to fit within the joist spacing. Since grease is not a problem as with kitchen exhaust fans, 3" or 4" diameter flexible duct that is easier to handle and bend around corners can be used.

To estimate the size of fan needed, divide the volume of the bathroom space in cubic feet by a factor of 7.5. For bathrooms with an 8' ceiling height, simply multiply the bathroom area in square feet by a factor of 1.07. This amount of CFM should result in the 8 air changes per hour recommended for bathroom spaces.

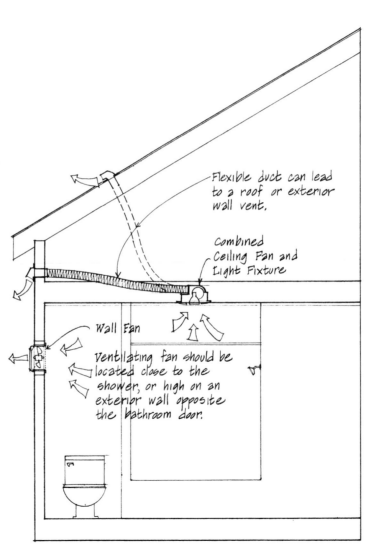

Flexible duct can lead to a roof or exterior wall vent.

Combined Ceiling Fan and Light Fixture

Wall Fan

Ventilating fan should be located close to the shower, or high on an exterior wall opposite the bathroom door.

Fan and Light Combination Fixture

Radiant Heat Lamp and Ventilating Fan Unit

Fixture combines Ceiling Light, Ventilating Fan, and a Fan Forced Heater.

COMBINATION FIXTURES

# THE PLUMBING SYSTEM

When adding or moving fixtures in a kitchen or bathroom remodeling, due consideration must be given, for economy and ease of installation, to the location of the existing plumbing lines in your house. How the new drain and water supply lines are run will also depend on the floor and wall framing, and the requirements of your local plumbing code. Any plumbing work done must meet strict code requirements. A diagram or plan of the proposed work is usually required before a permit is issued.

Since the sanitary drainage system is more complicated, and involves larger pipes, it is usually installed before the water supply lines. It depends solely on gravity flow for its proper functioning and its layout must therefore be as direct and straightforward as possible, with properly sloped horizontal lines and angular connections.

The main vertical house drain line, called the soil stack, is usually 4" in diameter, and runs from the lowest point in the system to 12" or more above the roof. At the point above the highest fixture, the soil stack becomes the stack vent which admits fresh air into the drainage system and permits waste gases to escape.

Each new or moved fixture must connect with the soil stack through a horizontal branch drain line. Since drain lines empty their waste by gravity flow, the branch lines must be sloped a 1/4" per foot. Any drop that requires a slope steeper than a 1/2" per foot should be accommodated by a vertical line. Too steep of a slope will cause the water to run off rapidly while leaving solid waste matter behind.

When an entire group of fixtures is installed away from an existing plumbing core, a new soil stack and vent is required. The new soil stack is connected to the main house drain by a soil branch line in the basement or crawl space. This soil branch, like branch drain lines, should slope 1/4" to 1/2" per foot.

Vent for fixture too distant from stack vent.

Extend 12" or more above the roof.

Stack Vent

Vent stack for kitchen sink

New stack vent for fixtures located too distant from existing stack vent

Expand to 4"ø @ roof

2"ø

Soil Stack

Existing Bathroom

Kitchen Sink

Vent

Clothes Washer

Trap

Cleanout at bottom of soil stack where it turns into house drain

To Sewer Main or Septic System

House Drain
House Trap

NEW BATHROOM

Vent

Lavatory Drain (1 1/2"ø)

Trap

Elbow

1 1/2"ø

Vent Pipe (1 1/2"ø)

Toilet Drain (3" or 4"ø)

Closet Bend

Overflow

Bathtub Drain (1 1/2" or 2"ø)

Trap

Sanitary Tee with side inlets

New Soil Branch Slope 1/4" to 1/2" per foot (3" or 4"ø)

Provide a cleanout at the end of a long soil branch run

SYSTEM OVERVIEW

At each fixture, a trap is required to form a water seal that prevents the back penetration of gases into the room through the fixture. Toilets have these traps built into them. Other fixtures have these traps formed in their drain lines.

Each fixture must also be vented to exhaust waste gases to the outside, allow fresh air to enter the system, and prevent the water seals in traps from being siphoned out. Fixtures may be vented in two ways. Fixtures that handle only liquid wastes, such as lavatories and bathtubs, may be wet-vented (vented through their drain lines) if they are located close enough to the soil stack. Check your local plumbing code.

More commonly, a pipe vent is used to connect the branch drain to a vent stack at a point at least 6" above the overflow rim of the uppermost fixture being served by the branch drain. The vent stack may be an extension of the soil stack or, when venting fixtures at two different floor levels, be a separate stack.

Extending water supply lines generally poses fewer problems than new drain lines. Since the water supply system operates under pressure, the supply pipes are smaller, and can, within reason, bend and turn around obstructions in their path. (If your supply system has low pressure, consult a licensed plumber before adding new fixtures.)

Use the shortest, most direct route to connect each new fixture to existing branch lines. Do not, however, tap into any lines smaller than the new lines. Hot and cold water supply lines generally run parallel to each other, but they should be kept at least 6" apart.

Shutoff valves are required in a pressurized water system to isolate portions of the system for repair. Plan on installing valves at new risers and horizontal branch lines, and at the runouts to individual fixtures.

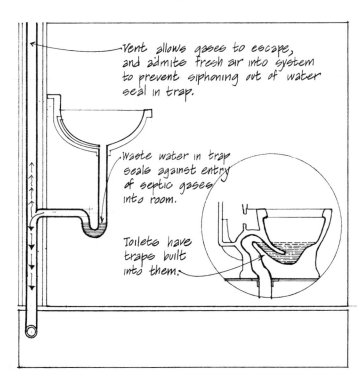

Vent allows gases to escape, and admits fresh air into system to prevent siphoning out of water seal in trap.

Waste water in trap seals against entry of septic gases into room.

Toilets have traps built into them.

3/4" or 1" mains

Shut-off Valves with Drain outlets

3/8"⌀ flexible connections with compression fittings

12" extensions are air chambers to eliminate air hammer noise in pipes

Angle-stop shut-off valves

Tub and Shower Valve

1/2"⌀ fixture branches

1/2" or 3/4"⌀ Hot Water Branch

1/2" or 3/4"⌀ Cold Water Branch

In-line shut-off Valves

Slope slightly toward drain outlets at shutoff valves

To save energy, insulate hot water pipes in unheated passages. If sweating of cold water lines is a problem, insulate those pipes also.

SUPPLY SYSTEM EXTENSION

# 5

# ADDING FIXTURES

When you have your bathroom space laid out (or a new sink located in your kitchen), determine the connections required for the new drain and water supply lines. This should be diagrammed along with the rough-in dimensions for each fixture.

The rough-in dimensions, contrary to the term used, should not be rough. They should be precisely measured for the fixtures to be located properly. Although there is some standardization of rough-in dimensions for each type of fixture, verify them for the specific fixtures you plan to use.

To make the connection between the existing lines and the new fixtures, the existing pipes must be supported and then cut for installation of a new T or Y-fitting. Before cutting into a water supply line, locate the valve that controls that branch. Close the valve, open all the faucets, and flush the toilets on that branch.

A drain line must be installed at the precise location required to obtain proper drainage. A supply line, however, can be tapped into the existing system at the most convenient location for performing the work (as long the existing line is not smaller than the new line).

Cutting into a cast iron drain line requires a special tool which can be rented from a tool rental outlet. Galvanized steel, copper or plastic pipes can be cut with a hacksaw.

Showerhead

Framing support for wall-hung lavatory

6" to 8"

1x4 support framing for pipes

Hot water supply

Cold water supply

4"

Lavatory sink drain

72"

H  C

10"

Faucets Spout

10"

8"

8"

Cold water supply

12" (may be less for compact toilets)

Toilet (Water Closet) drain

Support for tub

14"

12"

Access for tub and overflow drain

8" to wall

Double header

Joist

Closet bend

Cut joist

FRAMING FOR CLOSET BEND

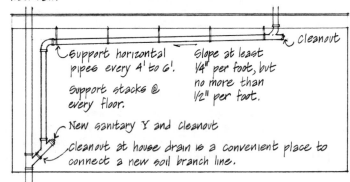

Support horizontal pipes every 4' to 6'.

Support stacks @ every floor.

Slope at least 1/4" per foot, but no more than 1/2" per foot.

Cleanout

New sanitary Y and cleanout

Cleanout at house drain is a convenient place to connect a new soil branch line.

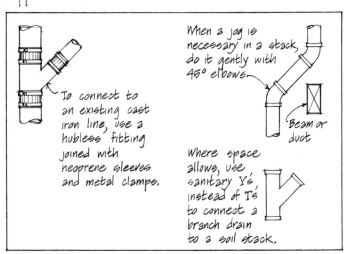

When a jog is necessary in a stack, do it gently with 45° elbows.

Beam or duct

To connect to an existing cast iron line, use a hubless fitting joined with neoprene sleeves and metal clamps.

Where space allows, use sanitary Y's instead of T's to connect a branch drain to a soil stack.

For installations over a basement, horizontal lines can be run between or below the first floor joists. For second story installations, the first floor ceiling or the floor in the room must be removed. If the ceiling height will allow, an alternative is to build a new raised floor in the room in which the fixtures are being installed.

Vertical plumbing lines can most easily be installed within a furred out space along an existing wall. Other alternatives include using closet space behind the new fixtures, or building a new wall.

Whenever possible, install new plumbing lines within existing stud or joist spaces. Avoid notching studs and joists. If necessary, a notch should be limited to 1/6 of the joist depth and be cut only in the end quarter of the span. Reinforce the notch with a well-nailed plywood scab or two 2"x s. Limit any notches in a stud to 2½" square and reinforce with a 1/8" steel strap.

A small hole can be drilled through the center of a stud or joist without significantly reducing the structural member's strength. A hole drilled through a joist should be no larger than 2" in diameter and be no closer than 2½" from the top or bottom edge of the joist. A hole cut in a 2x4 stud should be centered and be no larger than 1½" in diameter.

A brief note on pipe materials: Copper is the most popular material for water supply lines. It is lightweight and non-corrosive. Installing copper piping requires care and some skill with a pipe cutter, propane torch and solder.

If your plumbing code permits their use, plastic pipes are easier to install. They can be cut to length easily with a hacksaw, and glued together with manufactured fittings and special solvent cement.

For both hot and cold water supply lines, the only rigid plastic pipe that can be used is CPVC (Chlorinated Polyvinyl Chloride). Polybutylene plastic pipe can also be used for hot and cold water supply lines. Unlike CPVC, it is partially flexible and is joined together with clamps instead of a solvent cement.

Cast iron pipe, traditionally used for drain lines, is both heavy and difficult to install. Again, rigid plastic pipe, if permitted by the plumbing code, is an easier-to-install alternative. Two types can be used - ABS (Acrylonitrile Butadiene Styrene) or PVC (Polyvinyl Chloride). Don't mix the use of different plastics together. They require different cements and expand at different rates.

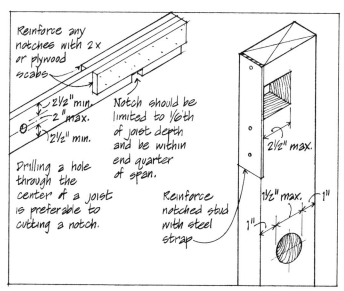

Reinforce any notches with 2x or plywood scabs

2½" min.
2" max.
12½" min.

Drilling a hole through the center of a joist is preferable to cutting a notch.

Notch should be limited to 1/6th of joist depth and be within end quarter of span.

Reinforce notched stud with steel strap

2½" max.

1½" max.
1"
1"

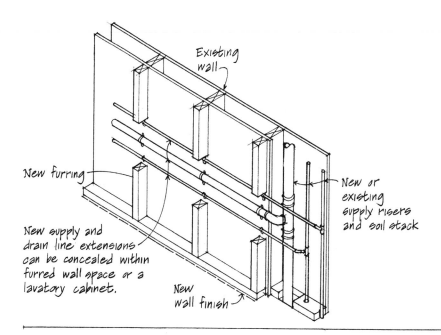

Existing wall

New furring

New supply and drain line extensions can be concealed within furred wall space or a lavatory cabinet.

New or existing supply risers and soil stack

New wall finish

# THE ELECTRICAL SYSTEM

Your electrical system begins with the service connection from your public utility company. The power from the service connection flows through a meter supplied by the power company. From the meter, the electrical power line, consisting of three cables, is brought through rigid conduit into the main service panel. To minimize voltage drop along the run, and because the cables have no over-current protection, the service panel should be located as close as possible to the service entrance head. The service panel and its main disconnect switch should also be easily accessible in case of an emergency or fire.

The main service panel distributes the incoming power into branch circuits. Each circuit is provided with a safety device that limits the amperage (the flow of electrical energy) through the circuit. Without this protection, accidental overloading of a circuit (i.e. connecting too many appliances or fixtures to it) could occur, causing the wiring to overheat and start a fire.

Two types of safety devices are used to protect circuits from being overloaded. The first is the fuse, a screw-in device with a short length of wire that has a low resistance to heat. If the predetermined amount of amperage. (the rating of the fuse) is exceeded, the metal wire melts because of the heat generated, and the circuit is broken.

The second type of safety device is the circuit breaker. It operates like a switch. When more current flows than the circuit breaker is designed to handle, it automatically opens up, thus breaking the circuit. Unlike fuses which must be replaced when blown, circuit breakers can be reset.

Branch circuits from the main service panel distribute electrical power to the various rooms in your house. A branch circuit operates in a manner similar to your water supply system. The flow of electrons (current) is delivered by a system of wires (conductors) to light fixtures, convenience receptacles, appliances, and equipment. While a water supply system operates under pressure, electrical energy flows through a circuit because of a difference in electrical charge between two points in the circuit. This potential energy is measured in volts ($V$). The actual amount of electrical energy flow is measured in amperes ($A$). The power required to keep an electric current flowing is measured in watts ($W$). The relationship among these three elements can be described by the formulas: $W = A \times V$, or $A = W/V$.

A 3-wire system is commonly used in residences. With this system, a low voltage (120 V) for light fixtures, outlets and small appliances, as well as a higher voltage (240 V) for high-wattage appliances, can be made available. Two of the three wires (color-coded red and black) are "hot", while the third (white) is the neutral. When the wires in a circuit are connected to a "hot" wire and a neutral, it will supply a voltage of 120 V. If the circuit is connected to two "hot wires", it will supply 240 V (120 + 120).

Each branch circuit is sized according to the amount of load it must carry. About 20% of its capacity should be reserved for flexibility, expansion and safety. For residences, there are three types of circuits: the general purpose or lighting circuit, the small-appliance circuit, and the special, single-outlet circuit.

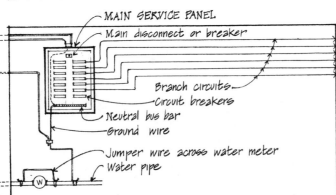

Entrance head
Power lines
Insulators
Drip loops
Conduit
Meter
Conduit
Grounding rod
Underground water line

MAIN SERVICE PANEL
Main disconnect or breaker
Branch circuits
Circuit breakers
Neutral bus bar
Ground wire
Jumper wire across water meter
Water pipe

| RATED CIRCUIT AMPERAGE | COPPER WIRE SIZE (Ga.) | FOR GENERAL PURPOSE CIRCUITS | | |
|---|---|---|---|---|
| | | Maximum Circuit Length | 80% Max. Wattage | Nº of Receptacles |
| 15 A. | Nº 14 | 40 Feet | 1440 W | 8 @ 1.5 A |
| 20 A. | 12 | 50 Feet | 1920 W | 10 @ 1.5 A |
| 30 A. | 10 | | | |
| 40 A. | 8 | | | |
| 55 A. | 6 | | | |

CIRCUIT LOAD TABLE
Verify requirements with your local Electrical Code.

General circuits supply power for lighting and receptacles for portable lamps and minor appliances. The continuous loading of a circuit should generally not exceed 80% of its rating. For example, a 15-Amp. circuit can have a continuous load of 12 Amps. This is enough to handle 8 convenience outlets (@ 1.5 A per outlet), or 1440 watts (12A x 120V). To determine the load on an existing circuit, you can simply add up the wattage ratings of the appliances and light fixtures hooked up to it. When adding a new general circuit, provide a convenience outlet at least every 12' along walls in living areas, and have at least 2 GFI (ground-fault interrupter) receptacles in the bathroom.

In the kitchen, the electrical code generally requires a minimum of two separate 20A.-120V circuits for small appliances, such as toasters and blenders. Each counter area longer than 2', and the areas on either side of the sink and cooktop, should have at least one outlet, mounted about 6" above the counter.

Special, single-outlet circuits are required for permanently installed appliances with heavy power loads. The range and oven require a separate 50A, 120/240V circuit. If the cooktop and oven are separate, each may require a 30A, 120/240V circuit. These appliances may be wired directly to a junction box, or they may require a heavy-duty plug and receptacle.

Separate 20A, 120V circuits are also needed for appliances such as the refrigerator, dishwasher, garbage disposal, microwave oven, and clothes washer. An electric clothes dryer will require up to a 30A, 120/240V circuit.

While a circuit breaker protects a circuit from too much current flowing through a conductor, grounding of your electrical system is required to protect it (and its users) from a surge of excess electric power. Circuit breakers protect against too much amperage, while grounding protects against too many volts.

Grounding simply provides an alternate route by which excess electricity can be discharged. It is accomplished by connecting the neutral wire in the system to the earth by means of a wire leading to a water pipe or a metal rod driven into the ground. Some codes require both be done. Check your local code for specifics. The ground wires of a system should form a continuous path to the earth and are never broken by a switch, fuse, or circuit breaker.

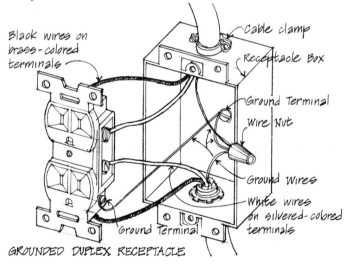

Black wires on brass-colored terminals

Cable clamp

Receptacle Box

Ground Terminal

Wire Nut

Ground Wires

White wires on silvered-colored terminals

Ground Terminal

GROUNDED DUPLEX RECEPTACLE

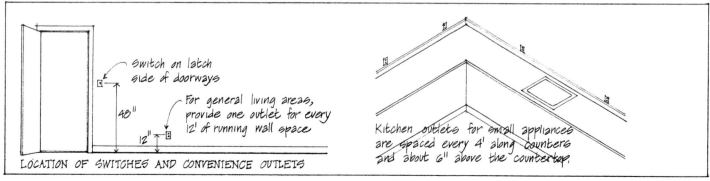

Switch on latch side of doorways

For general living areas, provide one outlet for every 12' of running wall space

48"

12"

LOCATION OF SWITCHES AND CONVENIENCE OUTLETS

Kitchen outlets for small appliances are spaced every 4' along counters and about 6" above the countertop.

# ADDING OR EXTENDING A CIRCUIT

If only adding a light fixture or a couple of convenience outlets, the new wiring can usually be extended from an existing general purpose circuit. First check the circuit's current load by adding up the wattage-ratings of the lighting fixtures, appliances and equipment. Dividing the total wattage by the voltage in the circuit (120V) will give you the total amperage. Any additional loads should not cause the total amperage to exceed the carrying capacity of the wire or the size of the circuit's breaker or fuse. See table, pg. 330.

Before adding any new circuits for an addition or a kitchen or bath remodeling, be sure to check the capacity of your present electrical service. The local electric utility company will often assist you in completing this review.

The electrical code will specify the type of cable you may install. The cable commonly consists of two or three insulated wires and a ground wire housed in a moisture resistant, plastic sheathing. The cable markings will identify the number and size of the conductors and the permitted area of use. Copper wire is preferred. If you have aluminum wiring in your home, have a professional inspect your system. Do not use copper and aluminum wire together.

Before starting any wiring or electrical work, draw a map of the new electrical system and carefully plan on how to get the cable from the service panel to the new receptacles, light fixtures or switches. If extending an existing circuit, first disconnect all power to the circuit at the service panel.

Plastic-sheathed cable must always be installed in protected locations such as within a wall between studs, or between floor or ceiling joists. Whenever possible, route new cable through the basement or attic, and then up or down the wall where the new or existing boxes are located. This will minimize the cutting of existing ceilings.

If at all possible, do not notch studs, joists and beams. When running a cable through a structural member becomes necessary, use a hole drilled through the center of the member. If the cable is within 1½" of the edge of the member, a metal protector must be installed to protect the cable from potential damage by nails or screws.

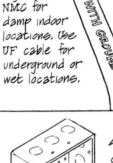

(2) 12 ga. insulated wires

Ground Wire

NM for indoor use only. Use NMC for damp indoor locations. Use UF cable for underground or wet locations.

NM 12/2 WITH GROUND 600V

4" x 4" x 1½" box can hold 10 Nº 14 or 9 Nº 12 wires.

Used for fixtures and as a junction box.

Square Box

4" x 1½" box can hold 7 Nº 14 or 6 Nº 12 wires.

Used for fixtures and as a junction box.

Octagonal Box

2" x 3" x 1½" box can hold 3 Nº 14 or 3 Nº 12 wires. If 2½" deep, it can hold 6 Nº 14 or 5 Nº 12 wires.

Switch or Receptacle Box

Note: Boxes are available with various types of attachment devices. The type of tab, clamp or bracket used depends on whether the box is being attached to an exposed structural member or a finish surface.

ELECTRICAL BOXES

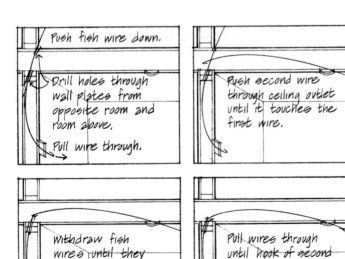

Push fish wire down.

Drill holes through wall plates from opposite room and room above.

Pull wire through.

Push second wire through ceiling outlet until it touches the first wire.

Withdraw fish wires until they hook together.

Pull wires through until hook of second wire appears. Attach cable and pull back up through wall & ceil'g.

Installing new wiring in existing houses often requires the cable to be "fished" through enclosed spaces. Special fish tapes can be rented from a tool rental shop to help in this process.

Where appearance is not a major factor, new wiring can also be installed within special metal moldings on a wall or ceiling surface. These surface metal raceways are least obtrusive when run along the baseboard of a room. Special fittings - elbows, T-connectors, junction boxes, switches and outlets - are available. Some raceways have regularly-spaced outlets built into their wiring and face plates.

When installing a new circuit, run the cable from the main service panel to the first box location. Do not, however, connect the conductors to the power source until all of the wiring, fixtures, switches, and outlets are installed. The cable is flexible and must be supported every 3' or 4' with cable staples. In addition, the cable must be installed without any splices or breaks between junction boxes.

All splices, switches, outlets and light fixture (except fluorescents) must be protected by boxes. There are several types. Your choice will depend on their use (ie. is it for a ceiling fixture or a wall switch?), how they are secured to the wall or ceiling, and how many wires will be in the box.

After a box has been installed and you have the cable to the box, the cable must be clamped to the box. The cable sheathing is then stripped and removed back to the point where the cable enters the box.

After all boxes and cable runs have been installed, the fixtures, outlets and switches are connected to the wiring by following the instructions of the manufacturer of each fixture. Throughout all wiring, consistently use the black and red wires as the live or hot wire, the white or yellow wires as the neutral, and the green or bare wire for the ground. (See exception below.)

Before making the final connection to the power source, be sure to disconnect the electricity to the main service panel or the junction box from which a circuit is being extended. If you are not an expert, any connections to the main service panel should be done by a licensed electrician.

If unable to extend a circuit from a junction box in the basement, extend it from an existing outlet. To minimize cutting of the wall surface, pry off the baseboard and run the wiring behind it.

When using a surface metal raceway, run it along the baseboard for the least obtrusive appearance.

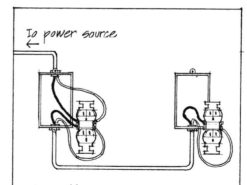

To power source ←

When adding a new convenience outlet beyond an existing one, connect the white (neutral) wires to the silver-colored terminals, and black (hot) wires to the brass-colored terminals. See pg. 331 for attaching of ground wires.

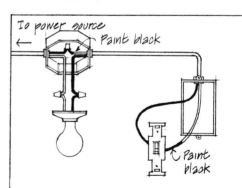

To power source ←   Paint black

Paint black

When adding a wall switch to control a light fixture at the end of a run, the white wire leading to the switch must be "hot" to complete the loop. Its ends must therefore be painted black to indicate this condition.

This book has intended to give you a broad overview of the design, planning and construction principles involved in the renovation and improvement of your home. To help provide you with more detailed information in specific areas of construction, the following bibliography is recommended.

# BIBLIOGRAPHY

Becker, Norman. PE. The Complete Book of Home Inspection. New York: McGraw-Hill, 1980.

Better Homes and Gardens Book Editors. Complete Guide to Home Repair, Maintenance and Improvement. Des Moines, Iowa: Meredith Corp., 1980.

Engelsman, Coert. Residential Cost Manual. New York: Van Nostrand Reinhold Company, 1983.

Hutchins, Nigel. Restoring Old Houses. New York: Van Nostrand Reinhold Company, 1982.

Love, T.W. Construction Manual: Rough Carpentry. Los Angeles: Craftman Book Company of America, 1976.

Mazria, Edward. The Passive Solar Energy Book. Emmaus, Pennsylvania: Rodale Press, 1979.

Mullin, Ray. Electrical Wiring Residential. New York: Van Nostrand Reinhold Company, 1981.

Sunset Books and Magazine Editors. Series on Building, Remodeling and Home Design:
    Basic Carpentry Illustrated
    Basic Home Wiring Illustrated
    Basic Plumbing Illustrated
Menlo Park, California: Lane Publishing, 1975-.

Time-Life Books Editors. Series on Home Repair and Improvement. Alexandria, Virginia: Time-Life Books, 1976-.

Time-Life Books Editors. How Things Work in Your Home. New York: Time-Life Books, 1975.

# INDEX

# INDEX